Klaus Scherer brings together leading scholars from the social sciences to discuss recent theoretical and empirical studies of justice. They examine the nature of justice from the current perspectives of philosophy, economics, law, sociology and psychology, and explore possible lines of convergence. A critical examination of theories of justice from Plato and Aristotle, through Marx, to Rawls and Habermas heads a collection which addresses the role of justice in economics and the law and which evaluates contemporary sociological and psychological stances in relation to justice, distributive and procedural. All the material is of clear cross-disciplinary interest; and it provides a framework with which administrators and researchers in social institutions can inform their practice.

Justice: interdisciplinary perspectives

The **European Science Foundation** is an association of its 59 member research councils and academies in 21 countries. The ESF brings European scientists together to work on topics of common concern, to co-ordinate the use of expensive facilities, and to discover and define new endeavours that will benefit from a co-operative approach.

The scientific work sponsored by ESF includes basic research in the natural sciences, the medical and biosciences, the humanities and the social sciences.

The ESF links scholarship and research supported by its members and adds value by co-operation across national frontiers. Through its function as a co-ordinator, and also by holding workshops and conferences and by enabling researchers to visit and study in laboratories throughout Europe, the ESF works for the advancement of European science.

This volume arises from exploratory discussions and reviews on justice research initiated by the ESF Standing Committee for the Social Sciences.

Further information on ESF activities can be obtained from:

European Science Foundation
1 quai Lezay-Marnésia
67080 Strasbourg Cedex

Justice: interdisciplinary perspectives

Edited by

KLAUS R. SCHERER

Professor of Psychology, University of Geneva

Published by the Press Syndicate of the University of Cambridge
The Pitt Building, Trumpington Street, Cambridge CB2 1RP
40 West 20th Street, New York, NY 10011-4211, USA
10 Stamford Road, Oakleigh, Victoria 3166, Australia

First published 1992

Printed in Great Britain at the University Press, Cambridge

*A catalogue record for this book is available
from the British Library*

Library of Congress cataloguing in publication data

Justice: interdisciplinary perspectives/edited by Klaus R. Scherer.
     p.   cm.
Includes bibliographical references and index.
ISBN 0 521 41503 9.
   1. Justice. 2. Sociological jurisprudence. 3. Distributive
justice. I. Scherer, Klaus R.
K246.J82 1992   340'.115–dc20   91-20389CIP

ISBN 0 521 41503 9 hardback

Contents

Contributors

Wil Arts
Department of Economic Sociology
and Psychology
Erasmus University Rotterdam
Postbox 1738
NL-3000 DR Rotterdam
The Netherlands

John Bell
Faculty of Law
University of Leeds
Leeds LS2 9JT
England

Bernard Cullen
Department of Scholastic Philosophy
The Queen's University of Belfast
Belfast BT7 1NN
Northern Ireland

Klaus R. Scherer
Department of Psychology
University of Geneva
CH-1211 Geneva
Switzerland

Erik Schokkaert
Katholieke Universiteit
Leuven
Center for Economic Studies
B-3000 Leuven
Belgium

Kjell Törnblom
Department of
Anthropology and
Sociology
University of Colorado at
Denver
Campus Box 105
P.O. Box 173364
Denver
Colorado 80217-3364
USA

Romke van der Veen
Institute for Law and Public
Policy
Leyden University
NL-Leyden
The Netherlands

Preface

The study of justice may be one of the prime examples of the negative consequences of the increasing specialization and professionalization of modern academic writing, particularly in the humanities and the social and behavioural sciences. Concern with justice in society dates back to the very beginning of principled reasoning about human social association. Ancient philosophers approached the problem in an integral fashion dealing both with the sense of and the need for justice as a basic aspect of human psychology and with justice as a normative political and legal concept with important implications for the exercise of government. A first fragmentation of the academic study of justice occurred around the thirteenth century when the thriving universities were divided into different faculties, thereby recognizing the growing importance of subjects such as philosophy, medicine, grammar and rhetoric. The study of justice as an ideal for law making and as a legal procedure became separated from philosophical and ethical concerns about justice in society based on reflections concerning the nature of man and of the state. A further fragmentation arose when British political philosophers, in particular Locke, Smith and Bentham, treated distributive justice as a fundamental concept for economic policy. The rift widened with the development of modern economics in the nineteenth century. At the same time, owing in large part to the influence of early French sociologists such as Comte and Durkheim, sociology started to become established as a separate and largely empirical discipline, concentrating on the observation of the effects of justice and injustice on society and social movements. Finally, the emancipation of social psychology from both psychology and sociology as an independent discipline dealing with individual motivation and subjective experience in a social context gave rise to yet another approach, descriptive and experimental, to the study of justice.

While not at all an expert in the area of justice research, I was struck by the discrepancy between the importance of justice as a general social and political problem and the fragmentation of scholarship and research across the various disciplines concerned with it. It seemed that, with a few exceptions such as the work of Rawls, there was little overlap between the relevant work in the different disciplines and, even more worrying, generally little awareness of the scholarship in other areas.

Since I happened to be serving as a representative of social psychology on the Standing Committee of the Social Sciences of the European Science Foundation at the time, I suggested to the ESF that they envisage an interdisciplinary workshop series to remedy that situation. I proposed the commissioning of a series of state-of-the-art reports on the work in the various disciplines concerned with justice to serve as a basis for the discussion at such workshops. The ESF approved the proposal, a coordinating committee was set up, expert authors were identified with the help of the committee and the ESF member organizations, and the reports were commissioned. The draft manuscripts were discussed during a workshop at the University of Edinburgh and, on a basis of multiple inputs, the authors proceeded to establish the final manuscripts which form the bulk of this book.

Owing to the outstanding efforts of the contributors and the general enthusiasm for an attempt to break through the disciplinary boundaries, this volume has become much more than a collection of isolated state-of-the-art reports. Given the possibilities for repeated discussion of the manuscripts among the authors and because of the commentaries from a number of experts in different areas, a multi-authored interdisciplinary monograph emerged. In an introductory chapter, I attempt to identify some of the major questions on justice as they seem to present themselves in the different disciplines. Furthermore, two of the contributors, John Bell and Erik Schokkaert, have written a concluding chapter in which they tie together some of the different strands of thought and empirical evidence emerging in the different chapters and highlight the importance and the potential of future interdisciplinary research.

Some limitations should be mentioned. In an effort to keep this volume to a manageable size some sacrifices had to be made. First, and most regrettably, several authors had to cut their manuscripts quite drastically, eliminating the discussion of some topics, detail on some issues, and copious notes. However, appropriate references have been provided and the interested reader may consult these works. In addition, from the outset priority has been given to issues of distributive justice, assuming that this issue would be of greatest interest for interdisciplinary work. While there is some discussion of procedural justice, large parts of the copious literature could only be referred to. Retributive justice, i.e. punishment for wrongdoing, had to be virtually excluded from the discussion in this volume. As far as completeness of coverage of the relevant disciplines is concerned we have tried to include most of the major approaches. There is a deplorable absence of ethological and anthropological work dealing with the comparative approach to justice. In addition, within some of the larger disciplines represented in the volume, such as law and economics, not all of the different schools or traditions could be given equal weight or even represented. Finally, given the enormous amount of relevant literature of justice in scholarly publications from many countries of the world, some selection had to be made and some preference was given to European publications. Because of the limited linguistic expertise of both authors and editor, there is also some bias, as usual, towards publications in English (and, to a more limited extent, in French and German).

We hope that this volume will prove useful as a text for all those eager to embark on the study of justice by learning about the fundamental contributions in the different disciplines concerned with this topic and as a manual of reference for all those established scholars of justice who feel the need for stronger interdisciplinary efforts in this area. Greater familiarity with the concepts and approaches used in the various fields may help to encourage more constructive discussions and to launch new interdisciplinary research. Finally, we hope that the 'practitioners of justice', dealing daily with problems of distributive and procedural justice in the context of the administration of law, of social politics or of private enterprise, to name but a few domains, will benefit from this volume by encountering some of the major facets of theory and research on justice in philosophy and the social and behavioural sciences.

Klaus R. Scherer

Acknowledgements

The authors and the editor of this volume would like to express their sincere gratitude to the following institutions and persons whose contributions have been invaluable in producing the book:

the European Science Foundation, its Standing Committee on the Social Sciences, and in particular John Smith, without whose unswerving loyalty to the project and remarkable skills in the politics of science this volume would not have been possible;

the members of the coordinating committee who have generously contributed their expert advice at all stages of the project: Wil Arts, Anthony Bradley, Göran Hermeren, Serge-Christophe Kolm and Carlo Rossetti;

the Centre for Criminology and the Social and Philosophical Study of Law, and in particular Neil MacCormick, its director, and Zenon Bankowski for the organization of the Edinburgh workshop on the Nature and Administration of Justice, which, because of its scientific stimulation and atmosphere of relaxed interdisciplinary interchange, greatly contributed to the enthusiasm which carried this volume through many of the difficulties en route;

the following colleagues from many disciplines who have spent many hours reading and commenting on various parts of the manuscript and whose input has been the single most important factor in ensuring the scientific quality of the enterprise (with the authors obviously accepting complete responsibility for any shortcomings and oversights persisting despite such excellent advice): Z. Bankowski, B. Barry, L. Bouckaert, A. Decoster, P. De Grauwe, U. Foa, W. Griffiths, S.-C. Kolm, M. Lerner, G. Mikula, D. Raphael, H. Treiber, W. van Trier, P. van Parijs;

last but not least, Marion Smith, our editor at Cambridge University Press, who has seen this volume through the production process with an unusual sense of commitment and with great efficacy.

1 Issues in the study of justice

Klaus R. Scherer

Man, the social animal! For all its triteness, the statement somehow does not lose its appeal – reminding us both of our animal heritage and of the fact that we could not survive without the protective cocoon of the social fabric which surrounds us. Yet this figure of speech is patently wrong, at least judging from its surface meaning: man is not *the* social animal, in fact many animals, particularly among the mammals, are social, living in pairs, troupes, herds, swarms, or even in complex caste societies. What the trope conveys, then, at a deeper level of meaning, is that human sociality is special and that it marks out human nature. Just as man's repertoire of behaviour and modes of adaptation to the environment are vastly more extensive and complex than the species-specific and partly instinct-based behaviour of all animal species, so is human social organization much less constrained by genetic determination of forms of association and aggregation than animal social systems.

The very freedom from biological constraints on human social life has produced a plenitude of forms of social organization during the evolution of mankind, particularly as a consequence of a large part of the human race abandoning hunting and gathering as a way of life. It seems that, as a consequence of this malleability of social arrangements, and ever since acquiring the capacity for consciously evaluating factual and imagined forms of association, humans have been questing for the optimal, or at least the most desirable form of human coexistence and social interaction, for the ideal type of society and government.

The quest is still going on, unabated. The political developments in what used to be called the 'Eastern bloc' provide a dramatic example. Entrenched communist regimes have been toppled by massive protest movements in the population, the Berlin wall has come down, ethnic groups are struggling for self-determination, and mass demonstrations for a new social order are taking place even in the heart of the former Soviet Union. If one is to believe the political analysts, these events mark the pitiful end of a major experiment with a particular form of social organization, conceived by Marx and Engels, once heralded as the end of the quest for the ideal form of society and state: a social order that, among other things, was to be more *just*.

Ever since the beginning of human concern with desirable forms of social organization, justice has been one of the essential postulates for Utopia, the ideal state. But it is by no means the only one. In fact, it is conspicuously absent from the banner lines of some of the most treasured visionary postulates outlining the nature of such an ideal social order, as found for example in the manifestos of the French Revolution, or in the American Declaration of Independence. Freedom, equality and fraternity have often taken precedence in the various catalogues of demands for a new order. One might argue that the call for equality implies that for justice. However, acceptance of this argument is likely to be limited to proponents of a strictly egalitarian ideal of justice.

The reason for the relatively infrequent appearance of justice in revolutionary slogans may be due to its role as a fundamental and indispensable organizing principle for any kind of human association. The notion that every human being should be free and capable of self-determination is a very modern and very recent claim, slavery and caste systems with varying degrees of constraints of civil liberty having been an organic part of many societies over the past millennia. Similarly, the abstract notion of unconditional equality of human beings, irrespective of their station in life and their prior investments, as the major principle for the distribution of resources, treatment and esteem is a revolutionary conception and one that would have been considered as quite ludicrous by many social philosophers across the ages. Fraternity, finally, even today carries a somewhat visionary, romantic connotation which seems to embarrass *realpolitik*, even of the revolutionary kind; the ancient belief of *homo homini lupus* or Hobbes' pessimistic views of human social nature have probably been considered as a more adequate assumption for the construction of sociopolitical arrangements throughout history.

In consequence, societies openly based on slavery, inequality and cut-throat competition have thrived in many parts of the world and, with the likely exception of slavery, still find proponents today. However, no system of government, no matter how despotic or tyrannical, could have survived very long by openly admitting injustice as a principle of treating its subjects or for regulating relations and interactions between the members of the society. Tyrants seem to have dug their own graves precisely at the moment when they neglected to *justify* their political action within the context of the prevailing social beliefs, provoking feelings of injustice.

The relationship between 'justice' and 'justification' is revelatory (see also Kelsen 1953/75, pp. 15–18). A system of social distribution of rights and resources is considered just if it is justified by a particular principle of justice, based on entitlement, deserts, equality or needs. This principle must find a minimal consensus in a society, by accrediting the existence and legitimacy of any such entitlements, deserts, or needs or modes of equal distribution, and by rectifying any situation of injustice.

This is a social psychological definition of justice, of course. It focuses on the perception of injustice by individuals and groups and attempts to predict social and political behaviour on the basis of beliefs and judgements concerning the justness of the prevailing system of distribution and retribution. According to this view, judgements concerning justice and the behavioural choices which ensue are based on social representations, i.e. culturally shared systems of values and beliefs concerning the appropriate principles or criteria of justice, the legitimacy of government (which certifies the criteria and administers justice enforcement), and of the relative entitlements of significant others in the society.

As we know only too well, the social representations underlying justice perception are extraordinarily variable and changeable and highly subject to manipulation and manifold pressures for conformity. This is why despotic ruling elites have been able to 'justify' systems of social order and distribution that seem totally unreasonable and unjust to us, for considerable periods of time. Given the resulting fickleness of actual definitions and systems of administration of justice, it is understandable that social philosophers sought to discover principles of ethics that forcibly prescribe the ideal or at least optimal principles of justice and procedures for its administration, and find the social psychological approach, based on underlying social representations and consequent justice perceptions, of little appeal. We will return to the opposition between empirical and normative approaches below and at various points in the chapters in this book (see in particular Bell and Schokkaert, this volume).

To return to the arguments. The assertion is that no sociopolitical system regulating human social association and interaction can afford to neglect the maintenance of perceived justice and the need for corrective action in situations of perceived injustice, at least for any length of time. In consequence, justice is seen as such a basic component of any human society that it does not have to appear as an explicit postulate for an ideal social order. This implies that perceived injustice will readily provoke strong protest and demands for the reestablishment of justice. How can we explain the existence of such a powerful need for perceived justice in human social life? Some social psychologists have postulated a basic 'justice motive' which is seen as determining the perception of justice and the choice of behavioural alternatives with respect to justice considerations (Lerner 1977; Lerner and Lerner 1981). Since many social psychologists are hesitant to accept innate motives or 'instincts', the notion of a specific justice motive is not universally accepted (see Folger 1984; Törnblom, this volume). However, since so far no culture has been identified in which the concern with justice is totally absent, we may assume that a very primitive sense of justice is part of human nature as it has developed during biological and cultural co-evolution (Cavalli-Sforza and Feldman 1981; Chagnon and Irons 1979; Gruter and Bohannan

1983; Hof 1983; see also B. Moore 1978; Weinberger 1985). Obviously, this assumption is quite compatible with theories highlighting the instrumental nature of justice, since co-evolution would obviously favour the development of this type of social-binding mechanism.

This claim may remind the initiated of the nativist position within the natural law tradition and of the famous speech (apparently to one of the most select audiences a jurist has ever confronted) in which Rudolf von Jhering ridiculed the nativist postulate of an innate and universally valid *Rechtsgefühl*, and argued that the acquisition of this human character-istic, the existence of which seems undisputed, is due to being socialized into a moral atmosphere shaped by historical development (using the simile of an inhalation of millions of moral spores) (Jhering 1884/1986). Unfortunately, the German *Rechtsgefühl* is generally translated as 'sense of justice' rather than 'sense of law'. Sense of justice is closer in meaning to *Gerechtigkeitsgefühl* in German and it is doubtful whether Jhering would have objected to the notion of the universal existence of a fundamental feeling of what is just or unjust and which is experienced by all members of a society. Obviously, the 'sense of justice' in the natural law tradition is something much more elaborate (more like a 'sense of what the law should be like') than the primitive 'feel for justice' which is postulated here as one of the psychological pillars of the organization of society. *Rechtsgefühl* (sense of law) implies notions concerning the func-tions of law, particular legal principles, and even specific prescriptions. Comparative legal studies and anthropological fieldwork have in fact produced little evidence for the universality of such elaborate social representations of law which could be used as evidence for the existence of an equally elaborate system of natural law (Pospisil 1974). While anthropological studies may reveal a number of general values which many societies use in their construction of justice systems, it has proved difficult to develop a consensual prescriptive theory, with specific shape and content, on the basis of a set of abstract principles distilled out of the actual practices in different societies (see also Finnis 1980).

It would seem that such elaborate systems are too far removed from the level of phenomena directly shaped by bio-sociocultural co-evolution to expect any degree of universality. The large number of different con-cepts of natural law which have been proposed across the centuries is in itself evidence for the difficulty of finding the one 'natural' basis for a sense of justice that prescribes a particular system of law (see Mayer-Maly 1984). More recent attempts to anchor the development of a com-prehensive 'sense of justice' in mechanisms such as Freudian identifica-tion (see Rehbinder 1983) are interesting attempts at combining insights from different disciplines. However, in the final analysis, these may be more relevant for the understanding of the social representations of justice consequent upon rather than antecedent to or independent of the system of existing moral and legal values in a society (but see Würtenberger 1988, for an interesting discussion of how *Zeitgeist* can change *Rechtsbewusstsein* and in consequence affect adjudication).

The primitive 'feel for justice' postulated here, which is closer to socio-psychobiological thinking than to legal philosophy, has not so far been subject to serious intercultural and historically comparative investigation, simply because notions such as the 'justice motive' have appeared only recently in social psychology and have not yet been well conceptualized. Similarly, recent attempts to exploit ethological and sociobiological concepts and data for the comparative study of law and legal institutions (see Gruter and Bohannan 1983) have suggested a large number of interesting leads for investigating the evolutionary origin of a 'sense of justice' but have not yet yielded a clearly defined concept. While it cannot be the task of this introduction to attempt such a conceptualization, it might be useful to examine some of the likely features of such a concept in trying to understand the need for future interdisciplinary study of justice in the social sciences.

It may be useful to ask what would be the most fundamental, abstract way of evaluating outcomes of human behaviour and social exchange in interpersonal and group interaction without presupposing any content in the sense of particular moral or legal norms. The notion of 'feeling of entitlement' which one already finds in Hume's treatise on human values is an interesting candidate for such a mechanism (see also van der Veen and Van Parijs 1985; Lerner 1986). It is possible to derive a basic feeling of entitlement from very modest assumptions about fundamental characteristics of human behaviour, mostly linked to notions about the perception of causality. Modern psychology has been able to show quite convincingly that the perception of causality is a powerful determinant of human experience and human behaviour. Heider's (1944) and Michotte's (1946) early experimental demonstrations of the overpowering tendency humans have to interpret even movements of inanimate objects, by attributing causality and intention have laid the ground for one of the most lively areas of psychological research. The results of theorizing and research on the perception and attribution of causality and its powerful influence on impression formation, judgement and decision, and behaviour now fill volumes (Fiske and Taylor 1984; Harvey, Ickes and Kidd 1976, 1978, 1981; Hewstone 1983). It seems quite reasonable to assume that this powerful human propensity toward causal analysis, which has the function of making the world more predictable and thus confers a sense of control, plays a major role in the perception of the justness of behavioural or interactional outcomes.

The argument could be construed as follows. Whether there is an innate propensity or not, the young infant quickly learns that virtually all of its behaviours have immediate effects. Similarly, children very quickly

learn to perceive the patterns of causality that underlie effects that have
been produced by other people or inanimate forces (Piaget 1927). In
consequence, very early on there is a strongly developed and quite
sophisticated representation of the cause–effect link, including the notion
that a certain input behaviour will reliably produce a particular output
effect. While there is little formal work on this (even though one finds the
idea in Aristotle's *Nicomachean Ethics*), it seems reasonable to assume
that this perceived cause–effect link is subject to an equivalence or proportionality rule, i.e. type and magnitude of input should be matched by
type and magnitude of output effect, albeit transformed (in a sense, an
extension of the conservation of energy principle into the perceptual
domain). If I hit my doll with heavy blows I should see more and deeper
dents than if I tap it lightly (if only ever so briefly, as with a rubber doll).
In other words, I feel entitled to an outcome that is equivalent to my
input – as a direct consequence of a proportionality rule in the perception
of causality. This, one could argue, is the most primitive form of a 'feel
for entitlement' – the right to expect proportional effect to behavioural
input – which could be the precursor of a 'feel for justice' (see Cohen
1979 for a discussion of the relationship between these concepts). Inter-
estingly, even at that very rudimentary level we find an emotion that
antedates the powerful emotional reactions to perceived interpersonal
injustice (see Mikula 1986, 1987; Mikula, Petri and Tanzer 1990),
namely frustration and disappointment. For animals and humans alike,
the non-occurrence of expected effects, particularly if a strong
behavioural investment has been made, reliably produces disgruntlement
and even aggression (see Baron 1977).

The extension of this mechanism to interpersonal interaction is
obvious. Any action intended to have an effect on another person can be
considered a causal investment for which proportional effect (in type and
magnitude) can be expected. If I hit my brother hard I expect strong
blows in return, if I give many of my sweets to him I expect him to give
me many of his marbles. We are on familiar ground here since anthropo-
logists and sociologists have long since postulated fundamental norms of
reciprocity (Mauss 1965; Gouldner 1960) in human interaction (a recur-
ring idea in writings about the dealings between members of the human
race, see the Latin *do ut des*). Similarly, exchange theory (Homans 1961)
and equity theory (Adams 1965; Walster, Walster and Berscheid 1978;
see detailed discussion of these two theories in Arts and van der Veen and
in Törnblom, this volume) have attempted to specify the psychological
dynamics underlying expectations of proportionality of investment and
outcome and of reciprocity in human exchange. These theories make
assumptions about underlying motivational factors, like learning-theory
notions of incentive in the case of Homans, or affectively toned reactions
to the lack of equity in the case of Adams. It would seem, though, that the

constant experience of a proportionality rule in cause–effect links may be sufficient to set up the exchange/equity expectations. Strong expectations coupled with the feeling of having invested in making the expectations come true obviously produce feelings of entitlement. Violations of such entitlements can then be defined as perceived injustice and will reliably provoke strong negative emotional reactions.

While the mechanism itself seems reasonably straightforward, its actual use in scientific prediction presents almost insurmountable problems, mainly because of two factors: one, the extreme variability of inputs (e.g., the perceived origin of the entitlement), and, two, the subjectivity of the evaluation of inputs and outcomes. The criticism levelled against exchange and equity theories exemplifies these problems very well: almost any situation of interpersonal exchange can be readily and elegantly analysed with the conceptual instrumentarium of these theories, identifying investments and outcomes and explaining the protagonists' reactions on the basis of the adequation between input and output. However, it is extremely difficult to conduct this analysis other than in a *post hoc* manner and other than by using the protagonists' evaluations of the respective worth of investments and outcomes.

Unfortunately, the predictive weakness of such models is a direct consequence of the nature of the phenomenon: perceived entitlement is in fact an expectation, and thus of necessity highly personal and subjective, based on differential perception and evaluation. Obviously, people can construe entitlements in very different ways and one of the strengths of such subjective models of investment–outcome adequation is that any of the principles of justice proposed in the literature can be derived from specific types of construals of entitlement. Desert is the most obvious, given a direct adequation between investment and pay-off. Merit, often couched in terms of status or position, in some sense is accumulated desert, or desert passed down the generations (it would be interesting to analyse transferability of merit and desert across time and family lineages). Need as a principle of distribution can be justified by entitlement to a minimum by the fact of one's very existence, or in terms of prior investments of some higher principle, such as a deity, on behalf of a person. Similarly, equality can be treated as perceived entitlement, owing to all human beings having been created equal and in consequence having equal rights.

The feature which is at the same time the strength and the weakness of a psychologically orientated subjective perception of entitlement approach, then, is to allow very plausible *post hoc* explanations of individual construals of entitlement, taking into account the individual's background, motivations and experience as well as the social context, the cultural ideology and other particularistic factors, at the expense of generalizability of the determinants or the principles used for a reckoning and compensation of the different factors. In addition, this approach is highly dependent on the protagonists' ability and willingness to verbalize the respective motives and beliefs, if indeed they are represented in consciousness to begin with.

But access to consciousness, verbalizability or subjectivity are not the most significant hindrances to the utilization of a subjective entitlement approach in theories of justice. The subjectivity and relativity of value judgements underlying entitlement perceptions are, according to Kelsen (1953/75), among the major reasons why there could never be, according to this view, consensus on justice criteria which could help to settle conflicts of interest concerning distribution.

But Kelsen goes further than this. Very much in the spirit of legal positivism, of which he is one of the leading proponents, he firmly asserts that *Sein*, i.e. that which is, existing fact, can or should never be used to derive *Sollen*, that which ought to be, the prescribed state. In consequence, even if one were able to identify a consensus about a priority of values determining entitlement, this should not in any way inform the quest for a normative, and presumably ideal, solution to the problem.

This, in fact, is one of the key problems in the social sciences' concern with justice – to what extent should one attempt to distinguish the strictly separate empirical, often psychologically or sociologically orientated, approaches (which are mainly concerned with subjective factors likely to intervene in judgements of injustice), and normative, ethical approaches, generally originating from social philosophy, law, or economics (which are concerned with issues of moral desirability and/or socio-economic functionality)? While it is too early to answer this question in the introduction to this volume, it seems that a hermetic separation between the two approaches may be detrimental if not downright dangerous to both. Normative philosophy which attempts to be practical philosophy should guide ordinary individuals in everyday life – it must therefore reflect the psychological, social and economic conditions in which these individuals live. The empirical sciences, on the other hand, must be aware that they are unlikely to find universal truths for many areas of social life by merely observing regularities. They will scarcely affect normative and political action by the blind accumulation of ever greater mountains of data without a concern for ethical and normative perspectives towards which present-day society should evolve. It would seem, then, that healthy debate between the two approaches might be more profitable for both than strict separation.

A corollary of the position that justice is a basic and indispensable principle for any kind of human social association is that it will be very difficult to find examples of societies that are to be considered unjust, based on the empirical perception rather than an ideal normative definition, since such societies should be unable to survive for very long, even using severe repression. In consequence, there is little empirical evidence on which forms of distribution and retribution need to be actively avoided. In other words, an *empirically* guided quest for an ideal normative definition of justice cannot proceed by default, i.e. identifying which justice-related social arrangements need to be avoided. The ideal system of justice needs to be positively described. Given the many different models of justice definitions and modes of administration that have survived, it is difficult to find obvious models for normative prescription, based on past experience.

Given the multitude of possible entitlements, the manifold contradictions between them, the large variety of possible alternative justice principles for distribution, and the apparent lack of clear-cut empirical evidence for the relative superiority of one model over another, a plethora of proposed justice norms has resulted. This has led many scholars in the area to conclude that we will never be able to find consensus for an ideal justice norm, binding for all. The suggestions on how to deal with this unsatisfactory situation are abundant. Among these suggestions one finds calls for tolerance (Kelsen 1953/75) or attempts to define rules for discourse or negotiation procedures that at least allow a rational debate about the principles to be used in a particular case (e.g. Rawls' (1971) reflective equilibrium or Habermas' (1983) and Alexy's (1989) discourse proposals; see Cullen, this volume).

In view of the complexity of the issues and the important role of value relativity this may in fact be the only solution, modest but realistic: defining a *procedure* to adopt in the discussion of justice questions and relinquishing the dream of being able to agree on universal principles of justice. However, before going that far, we might want to explore whether all of the different approaches that our disciplines offer have been used to good effect in the quest for understanding and defining justice. Obviously, this does not obviate the need to develop appropriate procedures for discussing justice issues – on the contrary, this might be one of the preconditions for interdisciplinary dialogue. Looking at the state of the art in the different disciplines relevant to this enterprise, as represented by the chapters in this volume, one would think that much remains to be done. So far, each discipline seems to have contented itself with a detailed investigation of the phenomena and concepts within its proper domain, generally neglecting issues studied in other areas. Because of the basic importance of the justice principle for all forms of human association, social interaction, social institutions, economic exchange, political-legal organization, with an important interdependence between these domains with respect to justice norms, it is obvious that any attempt at a definition of an ideal justice norm has to take into account the specific demands as well as the constraints identified by the discipline specialized for a particular domain. For example, economists have attempted to determine empirically the effect of specific forms of income distribution on the economic system, e.g. on productivity, labour supply, investment and overall effect on GNP. Clearly, such data and the models built upon them constitute important constraints for any normative theory of justice.

Similarly, no normative-ethical theory of the *Sollen* of justice can afford to overlook the *Sein* in the sense of the givens, such as the 'nature' of man, as a product of biocultural co-evolution or of fundamental facts related to the environment or to historical development. Any attempt to do so, following Kelsen for example, must necessarily lead to disaster since it would seem unthinkable to devise a social organization that is not at least minimally adapted to the characteristics of its members or to its environmental and historical niche. No engineer would ever think of designing a blueprint for a machine without taking into consideration the nature of the parts to be used and the fundamental laws of physics. It is no wonder, then, that the idealistic approaches toward a definition of justice have had so little effect on politics and legislation – the idea that the ideal systems are to be constructed in the head of a social philosopher, unconstrained by the constraints of reality, will seem like starry-eyed *naïveté* to the practitioners of justice politics – including members of the legal profession, called upon to safeguard the daily administration of justice (see Bell, this volume).

One of the most important constraints for any normative justice principle is the fact that the people whose affairs are governed by the said principle are, on the whole and in the long run, willing to accept and be satisfied by the outcomes of its rulings. If the assumption about the fundamental role of perceived justice in human association outlined above is correct, no principle will survive that leads to perception of injustice and consequent political action. Many liberal social scientists see the incipient decline of communism as empirical evidence of the failure of Marxian justice principles (however implicitly they may have been defined; see Cullen, this volume) which tried to satisfy the need for perceived justice but neglected some fundamental characteristics of human motivation (with others arguing, of course, that the true Marxist socialist ideas have never been put to the test in the Eastern Leninist/Stalinist-inspired socialist states).

Obviously, it is patently true that the contradictions and conflicts in entitlement perception will never allow a situation where all members of a society will feel justly treated, and so most normative theories argue in terms of majorities or minorities (e.g. the greatest happiness for the greatest number, or the most tolerable situation for the worst-off minority; see chapters by Cullen and Schokkaert, this volume). It seems that both the need to avoid the perception of injustice by large parts of a population and the need to balance the demands of different groups require subjective and empirical approaches, in other words social psychological and sociological work must be taken into consideration in constructing normative edifices.

The empirical sciences, on the other hand, particularly social psychology, are in danger of removing themselves ever further from the focus of the sociopolitical discussion of justice by often indulging in experimental *l'art pour l'art* or in mindlessly repetitive questionnaire studies. Subtle and methodologically fancy manipulations of minor variables in relatively artificial settings or pretty path analyses of large but superficial data sets may delight colleagues and rigorous journal editors but will find little attention elsewhere. Researchers in these areas stand to benefit from the normative approaches in directing their attention at major, salient issues which might be elucidated by empirical findings and from outside assessment of the methodology and the findings.

Economic, legal-procedural and social-structural constraints on justice norms, as well as the need to consider relevant aspects of human nature, as determined by scientific investigation rather than philosophical decree, and empirical facts and laws, require the study of justice to proceed in a strongly interdisciplinary fashion. Unfortunately, this has been the exception rather than the rule in the past.

This volume attempts to lay the groundwork for increased interdisciplinary work in this area by identifying some of the major strands of thought as well as empirical findings in the major disciplines dealing with justice – philosophy, law, economics, sociology and social psychology. One could visualize the relationships between the topics dealt with in these disciplines as shown in Fig. 1.1 (some disciplines addressing themselves to several topic areas). The drawing is meant to illustrate that any realistic attempt at an ethically satisfactory normative theory of justice (which would be exemplified by the aesthetically pleasing Gestalt of a circle) corresponds to the squaring of the circle (given the constraints operating in the different domains that are inextricably linked to justice administration).

Social philosophy seems squarely to occupy the central structure in the figure, trying to develop theoretically homogeneous prescriptions for a universal justice principle that corresponds to commonly held moral ideals. The task would seem to be to work out a coherent set of ideal demands concerning the nature of entitlements, their respective priorities, and ways to establish claims relative to entitlements and the settlement or arbitration of conflicts. This task is one that requires bold and idealistic normative thinking in the endeavour to maximize the potential for the pursuit of dignity and happiness in human social association given the many degrees of freedom provided from the release of human behaviour and forms of social association from biological constraints. This task also implies an effort towards the establishment of logical consistency of the norms and corollaries as well as a stringent operation-alization of concepts and ideals in terms of behaviour, law and institutions. Social philosophers have the worst lot of all the scientists working on justice. Given their position in the central circle they have to take into account all the constraints demonstrated by the disciplines pulling from all four directions.

Economists are mainly concerned with distributive justice, in particular income distribution and welfare considerations. While normative-ethical considerations also play an important role in this tradition, it would seem that the central task for economics in an interdisciplinary approach to justice would consist in highlighting the consequences of alternative forms of distributive justice principles for the economy. This work will have to proceed on the level of modelling, assuming particular economic models, as well as on an empirical basis, using data from comparative economic research. The emphasis here should be on the demonstration of the effects of alternative models, given the value relativity of some of the major parameters, e.g. productivity vs. satisfac-

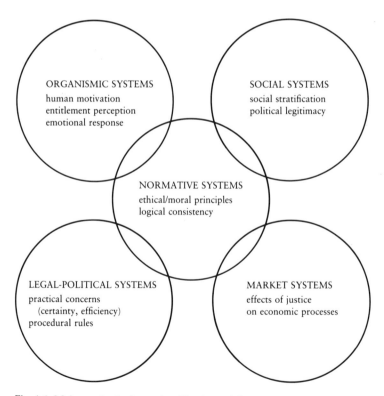

Fig. 1.1 Major topics in the study of justice and their interrelationships

tion, risk vs. stability, etc. Evidence concerning the role of economic laws, both on a micro and a macro level, is of major significance for any attempt to develop a logically consistent blueprint for the development of a normative theory, spelling out the choices and their implications.

Legal scholars, and particularly practising lawyers, across the centuries have pointed out that real law is often quite different from ideal law (which may be closer, emotionally, to the *ius gentium*, i.e. the folk representation of justice). One of the reasons is that, for law, justice is only one, albeit the major, concern. In addition there are other considerations such as unequivocal and efficient administration of the law (*Rechtssicherheit, Zweckmässigkeit*; see also Bell, this volume) which, because of their importance for the administration of justice as a system in the long-term perspective, may take precedence over justice in an individual case. Because of these considerations, lawyers are more concerned with procedural justice than with distributive justice. Furthermore, because of the central role of the courts in enforcing the norms of society, retributive justice (i.e. sanctioning norm violations) is another major concern in this discipline. For written law, the major considerations are need for stability (citizens need to be able to base long-term decisions on legal stipulations), simplicity (anybody should be able to understand the terms of law), universality (the validity of law should be independent of social context and situation), and efficiency (law should be enforceable within the resources of society within a reasonable period of time and without stifling other social activities). Obviously, all these considerations imply constraints for a normative theory (unless one would want to differentiate between the ideal normative theory and its watered-down realistic version for everyday use, a solution which will produce considerable problems of its own).

Sociologists will remind us of yet another set of powerful constraints that limit idealistic normative definitions. Distribution is very strongly linked to social stratification which is a very sensitive issue with respect to social representations of entitlement and, consequently, of social satisfaction and preceived legitimacy of government (see Arts and van der Veen, this volume). Much of the classic work in sociology has been concerned with the relative importance of achievement vs. ascription in relation to status and stratification, an issue which bears directly on entitlement, and one that is closely linked to the role of elites in a society. Similarly, sociological work on power is directly relevant to problems of justice. Obviously, then, a normative theory of justice will have to take into account the incidence of the justice principles invoked on the social structure of the society concerned.

As we have seen above, social psychological approaches are highly subjective and dependent upon the preferences or priorities of the perceived entitlements (which may be strongly biased by cultural ideology or personal partiality). In addition, the empirical findings in this area may be beset by experimental artifacts or by powerful situational influences (see Törnblom, this volume). Does this relegate social psychological approaches to the status of a discipline mainly concerned with epiphenomena such as the subjective consequences of objective sociolegal conditions or irrelevant psychological biases? Obviously not. Psychosociobiological work, using both interspecies and intercultural comparison, can help to provide a sounder basis for the speculations on human nature which have permeated the social philosophy of justice for centuries. This is particularly relevant in relation to the motivational underpinnings of human behaviour, the nature of social affiliation, and the perception of causality and proportionality of exchange. In addition, social psychological work can help to evaluate better the criteria at work in entitlement perception and justice criteria. For example, many welfarist theories have developed very elaborate ideas on how to deal with differences in ability. However, social psychological attribution theory and massive experimental evidence show that causal attribution and entitlement judgements are based on both ability and motivation inferences (something everybody who has had to listen to popular diatribes about the laziness of the chronically unemployed or of welfare recipients can testify to). Thus, social psychological work can be very useful better to understand the inner workings of the entitlement calculating machine which seems to be at the basis of subjective perceptions of justice. The basis for these calculations seems to be a very complex, interdependent set of variables with elaborate rules for reckoning and compensation. Empirical social psychological work, together with sociological approaches, can help to determine preferences and priorities for different groups of the population and for different cultures, and it can keep track of changes in such social values (e.g. those related to the *Zeitgeist*, see Würtenberger 1986). Much neglected so far is the psychological study of the powerful emotions, and the impulsive actions unleashed by them, that are provoked by the perception of injustice (see Kleist's novella *Michael Kohlhaas* for a dramatic illustration).

In conclusion, one could state that serious integrative work on justice has barely begun. It seems evident that isolated empirical studies on justice perceptions are of little consequence for a universal theory of justice with practical normative implications. It is equally obvious that armchair philosophizing in a vacuum, uninformed by social-system and human-nature constraints, will produce little else but philosophical debate. The very nature of the phenomenon as well as the constraints limiting normative approaches to justice urgently require an interdisciplinary and intercultural social science approach to the study of justice in all its different forms.

2 Philosophical theories of justice

Bernard Cullen

1 Introduction

The concept of justice has been a topic of philosophical analysis and dispute since ancient times. As Alasdair MacIntyre has recently underlined, our contemporary discussions of justice are themselves an extension and continuation of conflicts within the Athenian social and cultural order during the fifth and fourth centuries BC (MacIntyre 1988, p. 13).[1] Thus, the various positions on the nature of justice articulated by Plato in Book I of his *Republic* reflect conceptions of justice then current, to which Plato counterposed his own view that justice (*dikaiosúné*) consists in performing the function within the city (the *polis*) for which one is by nature best suited (433a–434c) (cf. Raphael 1987, p. 11). Aristotle in turn introduced distinctions among different kinds of justice which have had a decisive influence on almost all subsequent Western discussions. Thus, in the fifth book of his *Nicomachean Ethics*, justice (*dikaiosúné*) characterized as 'the sum of the virtues' is distinguished from *tò díkaion*. The English language is, unfortunately, relatively impoverished at this point: '*tò díkaion*' is 'justice' in the sense of the Latin *justum*, the French *le droit*, the German *das Recht*; terms which are, in turn, conceptually quite distinct from *leges*, *lois*, and *Gesetze*, respectively. 'Justice', in this sense, designates for Aristotle not merely a set of positive 'laws', but a system of 'right'.[2] This way of thinking about justice – which retains the essential interpenetration of legality and morality – lays the foundations for the tradition of 'natural law', the subject of subsection 5.1 below. (For a brief survey, see Raphael 1987, pp. 11–13.)

Aristotle distinguishes between *general* justice and *particular* justice. Particular justice consists in acting so that each will have his own, treating equals equally and unequals unequally but *in proportion* to their relevant differences. Under the heading of particular justice, he further distinguishes between, on the one hand, *rectificatory* justice, which aims at the impartial preservation of social order and the general welfare, for example by the regulation of dealings between individuals (1130b30–1131a1), and, on the other, *distributive* justice, that is, justice in the distribution or allocation of wealth, rights, honours and other benefits, and also duties. The most important quality of rectificatory justice is impartiality: the law and those who administer it must be 'no respecter of persons', and those subject to the law must be treated alike unless *relevant* differences have been proved. With respect to distribution, the most important quality is equity or fairness, but what Aristotle calls 'geometrical' equity or equity in the sense of the proportional: 'the just is the proportional, the unjust is what violates the proportional' (1131b18–19). Again, like cases must be treated alike and unlike cases differently, and 'benefits should be awarded according to merit' (1131a10–29). In Aristotle's view, flutes, for example, should be distributed only to those who have a capacity for flute-playing; and similarly, a share in political rule should be given only to those capable of ruling. Subsequent philosophers, however, have had to wrestle with the problem of deciding which likenesses and which merits are relevant in the distribution of benefits and duties and which are not.

Aristotle's distinctions foreshadow the widely accepted modern distinction between (a) what is variously called formal or abstract or procedural justice and (b) justice as a substantive moral category, commonly referred to in recent literature as social or distributive justice (and sometimes as material or economic justice). To caricature ever so slightly, jurists (including philosophically inclined jurists, such as Hans Kelsen and H.L.A. Hart) have tended to claim that 'moral' justice is one thing (on which, incidentally, no two philosophers can agree!) and the law (or 'procedural' justice) is another; that the two are quite distinct; and that lawyers are concerned exclusively with the latter and not at all with the former. This is the theory of law commonly known as 'legal positivism'.

The *locus classicus* of the application of legal positivism to matters of justice is Alf Ross's claim that 'to invoke justice is the same thing as banging on the table: an emotional expression which turns one's demand into an absolute postulate' (Ross 1974, pp. 274–5; cf. Callicles the sophist, in Plato's *Gorgias*, 482e–484c). According to this view, the only justice worth talking about (and *a fortiori* worth having) is procedural justice, that is, absolute judicial impartiality in the following of rules laid down and generally agreed for the proper conduct of legal business (what the fifth and fourteenth amendments to the US Constitution call 'due process of law'). This is the conception of justice traditionally symbolized by the figure of Justice holding the balanced scales, and wearing a blindfold. Although undiluted positivism appears to have loosened its former grip on the community of legal scholars, this is the restricted conception of justice with which most legal theorists probably still feel most comfortable. In this chapter, I shall have little more to say about formal or procedural justice, or (owing to limitations of space) about retributive justice and the theory of punishment; on these issues I happily defer to chapter 4 on 'Justice and the law' by John Bell. We shall see, however, how principles of formal justice are often used by philosophers to ground their theories of social or distributive justice: for example, the wide-spread use of the formal principle 'give to each his or her due' as a basis for substantive principles of social justice, Rawls' crucial use of 'pure procedural justice', and Barry's theory of 'justice as impartiality'.

When the moral and social philosophers reawoke to normative issues again in the 1960s, after a generation of paralysis induced by their fixation with meta-ethics, they turned their attention in increasing numbers to the issues and problems associated with social or distributive justice. This period of germination culminated in the publication of John Rawls' *A Theory of Justice* in 1971. Since then there has been an exponentially increasing outpouring of philosophical writing dealing with the manifold problems posed by any attempt to ground rationally a judgement as to the justice of social and economic arrangements and institutions. The philosophical challenge has been to state and establish criteria for such a judgement, and to be able to answer the charge that the choice of criterion is either arbitrary or merely a reflection of one's own prejudices.

In the literature reviewed in this survey and listed in the Bibliography,[3] four such suggested criteria are 'justice as fairness' (Rawls 1971), 'justice as entitlement' (Nozick 1974), 'justice as equality' (Nielsen 1979 and others), and 'justice as impartiality' (Barry 1989b). Other suggested criteria include need, respect for rights, and some form of desert or merit. Some writers have suggested that there is a plurality of relevant criteria, with some of them claiming that we can distinguish priorities among them and some insisting that we cannot. While the discussion has mostly been in terms of criteria of social justice at a particular time and within a specific political jurisdiction (usually a modern state), there has been growing concern for the issues of justice between generations (especially our obligations of justice towards future generations) and 'global justice' or obligations of justice between and among states.

A large body of literature has been devoted to the views of Karl Marx on justice and specifically his attitude to distributive justice. In section 4, I chart the course of this bitterly debated controversy in Marxist scholarship, which has obvious implications for contemporary Marx-inspired analyses of social justice. Finally, constantly present in this literature is an ongoing debate in the field of moral epistemology: that is, the search, in an increasingly pluralistic and sceptical world, for rationally convincing foundations for our knowledge of moral categories such as justice. This concern motivates theorists as diverse as Ackerman and MacIntyre, Finnis and Habermas, Walzer and the neo-Heideggerian Werner Marx.

2   Modern social contract theories

2.1   *Justice as fairness – Rawls*

A Theory of Justice, by John Rawls, has dominated the philosophical discussion of justice since it was first published in 1971. Rawls tells us that his aim was to work out a theory of justice that represents an alternative to utilitarianism, which had, in its various guises, dominated English-language moral philosophy for several generations. The most glaring deficiency of utilitarianism is that it would tolerate the situation in which the benefit attained by some could compensate for the misery suffered by others, even taken to extremes. According to Rawls, however, 'each person possesses an inviolability founded on justice that even the welfare of society as a whole cannot override' (p. 3; all page numbers in brackets in this subsection refer to Rawls 1971). This follows from his conviction of 'the primacy of justice': 'justice is the first virtue of social institutions ... Laws and institutions no matter how efficient and well-arranged must be reformed or abolished if they are unjust ... The rights secured by justice are not subject to political bargaining or to the calculus of social interests ... An injustice is tolerable only when it is necessary to avoid an even greater injustice' (pp. 3–4).

The topic of the book, he states, is social justice, since the primary subject of justice is 'the basic structure of society', or the way in which the major social institutions (namely, 'the political constitution and the principal economic and social arrangements') distribute fundamental rights and duties and determine the division of advantages from social cooperation (p. 7). These fundamental rights and duties and 'the appropriate distribution of the benefits and burdens of social coopera-tion' (p. 4) are to be assigned in accordance with what Rawls terms 'the principles of justice'. The 'Main Idea' of his theory (presented as a theory which 'generalizes and carries to a higher level of abstraction the familiar theory of the social contract' (p. 11)) is the claim that the principles of justice rest neither on mere intuition nor utilitarian principles nor any other kind of teleological theory that holds that there is some form of good to be sought and maximized. Instead, the principles of justice are to be conceived as

those that free and rational persons concerned to further their own interests would accept in an initial position of equality as defining the fundamental terms of their association. These principles are to regulate all further agreements; they specify the kinds of social cooperation that can be entered into and the forms of government that can be established. This way of regarding the principles of justice I shall call justice as fairness. (p. 11)

Thus we are to imagine a 'hypothetical situation of equal liberty' (which he dubs 'the original position'), in which people choose together, in one joint act, the binding principles which are to regulate their social life. The resulting principles of justice are 'the result of a fair agreement or bargain. For given the circumstances of the original position, the symmetry of everyone's relations to each other, this initial situation is fair between individuals as moral persons' (p. 12). Rawls quite consciously uses the old and relatively uncontroversial Aristotelian notion of treating equals equally, in strict accordance with the rules, to ground a theory of justice which allows considerable discrepancies in equality. 'The aim is to use the notion of pure procedural justice as a basis of theory' (p. 136).

The essential point about the original position is that, in order to nullify the effects of specific contingencies that leave people open to the powerful temptation of self-interest, we are to assume that the initial choice was made behind a 'veil of ignorance'. In this original position,

no one knows his place in society, his class position or social status; nor does he know his fortune in the distribution of natural assets and abilities, his intelligence and strength, and the like. Nor, again, does anyone know his conception of the good, the particulars of his rational plan of life, or even the special features of his psychology such as his aversion to risk or liability to optimism or pessimism. More than this, I assume that the parties do not know the particular circumstances of their own society ... It is taken for granted, however, that they know the general facts about human society. They understand political affairs and the principles of economic theory; they know the basis of social organization and the laws of human psychology. Indeed, the parties are presumed to know whatever general facts affect the choice of the principles of justice. (p. 137)

The answer to the question 'who chooses?' is quite straightforward. I simply have to ask how *I* would choose in the original position, since each of us can assume, according to Rawls, that others (being 'equally rational and similarly situated') would vote similarly: 'The veil of ignorance makes possible a unanimous choice of a particular conception of justice. Without these limitations on knowledge the bargaining problem of the original position would be hopelessly complicated' (pp. 139–40). (For Brian Barry's remarks on this point, see subsection 2.3 below.)

The next question is: what general strategy would I, as a rational person in the original position, use in choosing a binding charter of justice? Generally speaking, there are thought to be three possible strategies of choice available under conditions of uncertainty such as those obtaining in the original position: (1) the strategy of the optimist is known as the *maximax* one, since it means encouraging and striving for the maximum among the maxima, the best outcome among the best outcomes; (2) the strategy of the pessimist is known as the *maximin* one, since it means pursuing the maximum of the minima, or maximizing the welfare of those with the minimum advantages in society; (3) the strategy of *the gambler* is to try to take into account all the outcomes for each option before one, putting a probability figure on the chance of each coming about if that option is chosen and using these figures as a base for maximizing expected utility.

It is generally accepted in the relevant literature that it would not be rational for me to adopt the maximax strategy, for this foolishly optimistic approach, while *hoping* that I will hit the jackpot, leaves wide open the possibility that I will get the worst outcome of all in whatever society I find myself in. Of the two remaining strategies, Rawls argues (a psychological claim on which he has been widely thought to be at his most vulnerable) that the rational course for each person in the original position is not to gamble but to maximin: in other words, to go for the safe option. He argues that the original position, by its very definition, implies that the maximin rule will apply. The parties behind the veil of ignorance have no basis for determining the probable nature of their society, or their place in it; and thus they have strong reasons for being wary of probability calculations if any other course is open to them. They must also take into account the fact that 'their choice of principles should seem reasonable to others, in particular their descendants, whose rights will be deeply affected by it' (p. 155). Much of the subsequent criticism of Rawls, as we shall see, has focused precisely on his adherence to the maximin principle.

The 'general conception of justice', from which the parties in the original position would in turn derive the agreed principles of justice, is stated as follows: 'All social values – liberty and opportunity, income and wealth, and the bases of self-respect – are to be distributed equally unless an unequal distribution of any, or all, of these values is to everyone's advantage' (p. 62). Much of the rest of the book is devoted to the justification and implications of this 'general conception of justice' and of the two 'principles of justice' that are held to follow from it. In their final formulations, the principles of justice are stated as follows:

> *First Principle*
> Each person is to have an equal right to the most extensive total system of equal basic liberties compatible with a similar system of liberty for all.
> *Second Principle*
> Social and economic inequalities are to be arranged so that they are both:
> (a) to the greatest benefit of the least advantaged, consistent with the just savings principle [what he now calls 'the difference principle'], and
> (b) attached to offices and positions open to all under conditions of fair equality of opportunity. (p. 302)

These two principles are supplemented by rules of priority as between the two principles and between the two parts of the second principle; and these, as Barry puts it, 'radically affect the whole thrust of the theory' (Barry 1973, p. 9). According to the first priority rule ('the priority of liberty'), 'liberty can be restricted only for the sake of liberty'. According to the second priority rule ('the priority of justice over efficiency and welfare'), the second principle of justice is prior to the principle of efficiency and to that of maximizing the sum of advantages; and fair opportunity is prior to the difference principle: that is, 'an inequality of opportunity must enhance the opportunities of those with the lesser opportunity' (pp. 302–3).

Rawls does not explicate the 'system of equal basic liberties' with any precision. He does indicate that it includes political liberties (the right to vote and to be eligible for public office, freedom of speech and of assembly, liberty of conscience and freedom of thought); freedom of the person; the right to hold personal property; and freedom from arbitrary arrest and seizure, as defined by the concept of the rule of law. In choosing their first principle of justice, therefore, the people in the original position choose equality in these liberties. Some less than kind commentators have pointed out that it is an amazing coincidence that they end up choosing (in their own rational self-interest behind the veil of ignorance) an inventory of those very liberties dear to North American mainstream liberal democracy. Furthermore, they give this 'basic liberties' principle priority over the second principle: that is to say, they choose an institutional structure that will guarantee that the equal liberties of all will not be sacrificed for any gain in respect of income, wealth or power. They do so because they do not know what position they will hold in society, nor what things will be valued by the persons they turn out to be. They do know that there are 'social primary goods' (the 'social values' of the 'general conception of justice') that *every* rational person wants. These include liberty and opportunity, income and wealth, and the bases of self-respect. The rational person will realize that by choosing to guarantee the basic liberties (s)he will be in the best position to obtain the other social primary goods and whatever other ends (s)he will turn out wishing to pursue; whatever about any other goods, Rawls insists that it would be irrational of people in the original position to take any chances with their liberty.

On first glance, this series of principles might be thought to lead directly to an insistence on the equal distribution of wealth and other benefits in a society, but Rawls points out that if we accept certain plausible assumptions about the positive effect of incentives and the benefits that may flow to all from the productive labours of the most talented members of society, the maximin principle could allow considerable inequality: 'If there are inequalities in the basic structure that work to make everyone better off in comparison with the benchmark of initial equality, why not permit them?' (p. 151). As we saw above, the second principle of justice assumes the existence of such inequalities; but it is interesting and illuminating to see the way in which Rawls came round to accept inequalities, from the provisional egalitarian position of his 'general conception of justice': 'All social values – liberty and opportunity, income and wealth, and the bases of self-respect – are to be distributed *equally* unless an unequal distribution of any, or all, of these values is to *everyone's* advantage' (p. 62, my emphasis).

2.2   Some responses to Rawls

Rawls' commitment to maximinning and his related 'difference principle' is the aspect of his theory that has probably excited the greatest volume of hostile comment. Of the many critical assessments of *A Theory of Justice*, among the earliest and most sustained (and most pungent) is the book-length critique by Brian Barry. When discussing Rawls' second principle of justice, Barry focuses on his toleration (indeed advocacy) of inequality and asks: 'how do we define the "worst off" whose position is to be improved as much as possible?' Rawls acknowledges this 'serious difficulty', according to Barry, but his attempts to solve it are merely perfunctory. Furthermore, 'his "solutions" such as they are rob the principle of whatever egalitarian content it might appear on first sight to have. . . . Surely not since Locke's theory of property have such potentially radical premises been used as the foundation for something so little disturbing to the *status quo*' (Barry 1973, pp. 49–50). The chief causes of poverty in the advanced industrial societies 'could remain untackled while either of Rawls's indices for the "worst-off representative man" were maximized' (Barry 1973, pp. 50–1).[4]

Barry then focuses on the second part of the second principle, the 'fair equality of opportunity' stipulation, which Rawls proceeds to qualify with his 'family' proviso: after emphasizing the vital importance of maintaining equal opportunities of education for all, Rawls admits that 'the principle of fair opportunity can be only imperfectly carried out, at least as long as the institution of the family exists' (Rawls 1971, p. 74). Barry pounces: 'It need hardly be said that we know enough now about the effects of different family backgrounds to be aware that Rawls's proviso is virtually a nullifying condition!' (Barry 1973, p. 51). (This line of criticism is taken up and developed in Fishkin 1983, especially at pp. 152–8.)

Barry challenges Rawls' claim to derive the maximin criterion from the original position without falling back on a specific (and highly debatable) attitude to risk. The key question is whether it is possible to decide whether or not it is rational for self-interested people to maximize their minimum or their average expectations without attributing to the choosers a specific attitude to risk, a move which Rawls explicitly rejects. Barry's point is that there is no other way of deciding the issue: 'Since it is not *a priori* irrational to accept risks of catastrophe in this way [e.g., by flying across the Atlantic rather than going by boat] it cannot be said to be *a priori* irrational for those in the "original position" to be prepared to accept catastrophic outcomes. Nor can it be said to be rational: it really does depend on attitude to risk' (Barry 1973, pp. 106–7). Rawls' derivation of the maximin criterion therefore, according to Barry, rests on very shaky foundations.

J.R. Lucas (1980), in the course of his book-length deliberations on the concept of justice, also assails Rawls' maximin strategy and his use of the difference principle, because 'it seems to be a rational reconstruction not of justice but of prudence. . . . Prudence may suggest, but justice has not been shown to demand, a maximin strategy' (Lucas 1980, p. 186). He admits, however, that the difference principle is 'a powerful dissuasive to extreme egalitarian measures, and should go some way to reconciling the victims of modern industrial society to their lot' (Lucas 1980, p. 187).[5] Although the poor have come off worst, they have done better than they would have done in a pre-industrial society, and the consolation prizes are quite substantial. But this is not an argument for justice: 'Justice is more exact. It is concerned with particular individuals and their particular wrongs, and seeks to remedy these' (Lucas 1980, pp. 186–7).

David Gauthier (1974) is another who argues against Rawls' derivation of the difference principle. John Harsanyi (1975) also rejects the maximin principle, this time on utilitarian grounds. (For Gauthier's version of bargaining theory and the social contract, together with his criticism of fellow bargaining theorist Harsanyi, see subsection 2.3 below. For the sketch of a reply to both of them, see Rawls 1978). Holly Goldman (1980) also defends utilitarianism against Rawls, claiming that he has failed to implement his stated intention of demonstrating the inadequacy of a utilitarian theory of justice.[6]

On a more general level of criticism, the core of Barry's critique of Rawls' derivation of the two principles of justice is in chapter 11 of his book, where he uses the principle that 'even if it is accepted that primary goods [such as liberty or wealth] are things each person would (other things being equal) sooner have more of than less of, it does not follow that it is rational to choose, in the original position, principles of general application for the distribution of as much as possible of these primary goods' (Barry 1973, p. 116). The Rawlsian fallacy moves illicitly, he claims, from 'I would prefer more of X than less of X, all else remaining the same' to 'I should like society to be arranged so that I get as much as possible of X'. It is quite rational for an individual to want the greatest liberty or wealth available to him or her in circumstances in which the aggregate level of wealth remains relatively low and *still* not want the greatest wealth or liberty available to him or her in circumstances in which everyone else has a similar abundance. It does not follow, as Barry puts it succinctly, from the fact that everyone would like to win the pools that everyone would like everyone to win the pools: 'It is quite rational to say that if you could specify your position you'd like to be a rich man in a fairly poor society, but if you're not allowed to make exceptions for yourself you'd sooner be poor in a poor society than rich in a rich one' (Barry 1973, p. 119). It is simply a matter of individual judgement and preference; there is no obviously rational choice of one option rather than another. And the same point could be made with reference to each of Rawls' primary goods. It follows from this that in maximinning, the person in the original position will not necessarily choose the system whose worst-off position gives maximal satisfaction of the primary goods on Rawls' list. It all depends on certain social developments, which in turn produce essentially individual responses. This underlines Barry's general criticism that Rawls has not adequately explicated his primary goods; and in general, an adequate case for the derivation of his principles of justice in the original position has not been made.

On the question of Rawls' primary social goods, H.L.A. Hart (1973) examines Rawls' argument for the priority of liberty over wealth, again derived on the basis of rational self-interest behind the veil of ignorance. Hart acknowledges that Rawls has a deeply held ideal of 'the public-spirited citizen who prizes political activity and service to others as among the chief goods of life and could not contemplate as tolerable an exchange of the opportunities for such activity for mere material goods or contentment' (Hart 1973, p. 252). However, Rawls' argument for the priority of liberty purports to rest on interests, not on ideals; fur-thermore, it claims to *demonstrate* that 'the general priority of liberty reflects a preference for liberty over other goods which every self-inter-ested person who is rational would have' (ibid.). Rawls ultimately fails, claims Hart, to demonstrate this priority.[7]

Of course, Rawls has not been lacking in admirers. Neil MacCormick (1982), while acknowledging the real difficulties involved in applying Rawls' second principle of justice, accepts it in principle and argues for a more radical reading of it than Rawls himself gives. He agrees with Rawls that we should adjust our legal, economic and social systems so that 'they allow for no inequalities save those which advance best the lot of those who enjoy the lower positions on the existing scales of inequality. If in the end that should lead us to discover their total elimin-ability, I should be none the sadder for that' (MacCormick 1982, p. 102). (On the 'radical egalitarianism' proposed by Kai Nielsen as an alternative to Rawls' second principle, see Nielsen 1979 and subsection 3.2 below.) Harri Wettstein (1979) also agrees that Rawls' theory is basically sound; the task now is to correct some lingering problems with the theory (for example, he argues that Rawls' defence of the priority of liberty is circular); and to augment and supplement it, principally by probing the relations between liberty and power and between liberty and responsi-bility.

One of the most interesting analyses of Rawls' theory, and of its effectiveness in the devising of social policy, is that offered by Percy Lehning (1986). Lehning begins by considering the fact that in modern welfare states 'the political order suffers from a legitimacy crisis': in practical policy terms, there is no agreement on what a just political order should look like. His central thesis, however, is that normative political theories can, in fact, make an effective contribution to the debate among citizens, and between citizens and authorities, over what the tasks of the state ought to be. According to Lehning, the one normative political theory that fulfils the conditions necessary for such an effective role, and that provides a normative foundation for a political order that can be labelled a 'welfare state', is Rawls' theory of 'justice as fairness'. The theory is subjected to close analysis, especially Rawls' methods of justification, his principles of justice, and the institutional design of the basic structure of a political order in conformity with those principles of justice. This is not an uncritical analysis: in the course of it, Lehning claims to show, for example, that serious doubts can be raised as to whether the primary good 'self-respect' can indeed be realized by dealing with it in the way Rawls does.

In a confrontation with three rival theories, Lehning concludes (a) that Rawls' theory is compatible with some forms of utilitarianism; (b) that it is incommensurable with and rationally superior to libertarianism (as represented by Nozick; see subsection 3.1 below); and (c) that 'democratic socialists should be Rawlsians'. At the very least, he claims, the Rawlsian theory of justice is not incompatible with democratic socialist principles. (Cf. Nielsen 1979, 1982, and 1985; DeMarco 1980, who urges a synthesis of Marxian and Rawlsian theories of justice. But see also Wolff 1977, who rejects this possibility utterly.) Finally, Lehning examines what he (like many another commentator) considers to be the most important aspect of Rawls' theory, viz. the difference principle; and uses it to identify which social inequalities can be rationally labelled 'just' and which social inequalities should be labelled 'unjust' and, as a consequence, removed.

Finally in this brief review of some responses to Rawls, Joseph Raz (1982) analyses the method Rawls has developed for moral philosophizing, the method of 'reflective equilibrium'. According to Rawls, 'reflective equilibrium' between our moral principles and our 'considered judgements' is what we aim to achieve by doing moral philosophy. We work towards this goal by going back and forth, modifying our principles and/or revising our judgements: 'From the standpoint of moral philosophy, the best account of a person's sense of justice is not the one which fits his judgements prior to his examining any conception of justice, but rather the one which matches his judgements in reflective equilibrium' (Rawls 1971, p. 48). Raz, however, is far from impressed by

'reflective equilibrium', and concludes that 'it fails in the basic requirement of a method of moral argument, i.e. the ability to guide the agent's
choice of moral views' (Raz 1982, p. 329).[8]

2.3 Liberal social contract, bargaining, and impartiality – Kolm, Gauthier, and Barry

We saw above that Rawls' theory is explicitly a social contract theory of
justice. Attention must now be devoted, however briefly, to three competing contractarian theories: Serge-Christophe Kolm's theory of 'the
liberal social contract'; David Gauthier's theory of 'morals by agreement', within which 'liberal individuals' bargain their way to an understanding of justice; and Brian Barry's theory of justice as impartiality.

Kolm (1985) begins with his definition of liberalism as 'the conception
of the good in a society that bases justice on freedom'. This definition
produces the concept of 'liberal social justice' (Kolm 1985, pp. 14–15).
This is a theory of the good and the just. The liberal social contract is 'the
permanent latent unanimous agreement among real people, with their
freely legitimate rights' (ibid., p. 21). According to Kolm, Locke was
right to posit a hypothetical social contract to bestow legitimacy on a
public authority that would protect individual rights; his mistake was to
assume that the social contract was merely hypothetical, since 'the social
contract is a permanent feature of human society' (ibid., p. 19). Kolm
proceeds to examine the full implications for public action and the state
of a liberal social contract that respects and actualizes individual liberties
to the full.

He contends that only a slight shift in attitude is required to tip the
balance in human affairs dramatically from a tendency towards fear and
suspicion to altruism and positive reciprocity. Within the community
organized in accordance with the liberal social contract, envy and
jealousy are replaced by altruism, compassion, charity, voluntary
solidarity and fraternity (ibid., p. 49). The figure of Justice retains her
scales but discards her sword (ibid., p. 48). As the problem of having to
justify and protect the legitimacy of rights loses its immediacy, justice
becomes less a matter of protecting those rights and more a question of
satisfying needs in the society. The highest possible degree of altruism,
and to begin with, of mutual understanding, 'must be the first principle of
a society, with priority over all others, simply because it is a human
society and not a basket full of crabs' (ibid., p. 49). By definition,
however, and by nature, altruism cannot be promoted by force or by
coercion, first because it is a sentiment, and second because the use of
force is contrary to altruism: 'Altruism can only grow by a process of the
unfolding of the desire to practise it, by reflection, education, cultural
diffusion, and the collective awareness that it is the solution preferred by
everyone so long as everyone else practises it as well' (ibid., p. 49).

Kolm considers the common assertion that social justice is incompatible with social and economic efficiency. The key point of his critique is that the transfers associated with redistribution are usually thought of as forcible appropriations, impersonal with respect to both donor and recipient. This kind of arrangement has the added defect that it is detrimental to efficiency. Kolm posits in its place an alternative arrangement, one involving voluntary direct agreements and exchanges between citizens. This arrangement would be efficient and would, therefore, win the unanimous assent of the citizens. He recognizes, however, that there are potent factors hindering this kind of desirable altruistic transfer – factors such as lack of information – which are quite independent of the will of the citizens affected by them. He suggests, therefore, that government intervene, in accordance with the criterion of liberal social justice, to implement the potential free agreements and exchanges, which will, in turn, bring about greater efficiency and greater justice in the society.[9]

A very different contractarian theory of justice is offered by David Gauthier. Gauthier claims that only 'a bargaining model of morality captures ... Rawls's essential, but too often ignored, requirement that moral theory "take seriously the distinction between persons"' (Gauthier 1985, pp. 29–30). Ironically, although his aim is to refute the attack on Rawls' maximin principles by the utilitarian bargaining theorist John Harsanyi (see Harsanyi 1975), he has no wish to support what he calls the 'aberrant Kantianism' of Rawls' book (see especially Rawls 1971, pp. 251–7); rather he wishes to defend 'the contractarian theory that might have been developed from insights in [Rawls'] early papers' (Gauthier 1985, p. 30). Harsanyi was right, according to Gauthier, to demonstrate the irrationality of the maximin principle as a criterion for *individual* decision-making. What Rawls lacks is 'the idea of bargaining, as the procedure by which principles of justice are selected' (ibid., p. 41). Maximation is indeed the rational choice of individuals in isolation. But *bargaining* free individuals are not maximizers, they are maximinners: that is, 'in requiring that slices of the pie be determined by a maximin principle, in which each person is assured that the smallest proportionate gain is as large as possible, each is assured that his concerns are not being sacrificed to those of any other person. No maximizing procedure can do this' (ibid., p. 41). Gauthier agrees with Rawls that society is 'a cooperative venture for mutual advantage' (Rawls 1971, p. 4). But he insists that there would be no cooperation at all if individuals did not agree on acceptable social principles that determine the institutions and practices of the society, and those principles would only become objects of agreement through a process of rational bargaining.[10]

The impressive first volume of Brian Barry's three-volume *Treatise of Social Justice* is devoted to an exposition and critical analysis of the two theories of justice that he identifies as the leading contenders: 'justice as mutual advantage' and 'justice as impartiality'.[11] A theory of justice, he says, 'is a theory about what kinds of social arrangements can be defended' (p. 3; unless otherwise indicated, all page numbers in brackets in the rest of this subsection refer to Barry 1989b). More precisely, the central issue is the defensibility of the 'huge inequalities in political power, in social standing, and in the command over economic resources' (p. 3).

Part I of the book is a critical survey of the work of the game theorists of the past forty years or so, 'more sophisticated technically than philosophically' (p. 139). He is particularly scathing in his rejection of the version of game-theory-based moral philosophy put forward by David Gauthier. As for Rawls ('the most original and interesting political philosopher of this century'), Barry shows how, on the one hand, he wants to retain rational bargaining between egoistic individuals eager to maximize their advantage as an essential element of choosing a just practice; while on the other hand, he recognizes that initial inequalities of power will lead to practices that favour those who go into the bargaining process with the initial advantages, and that the only way to prevent this is to *impose* conditions of *impartiality* on the choosing participants. These conditions are, indeed, 'the constraints of having a morality', formalized in Rawls (1971) as the 'original position'. Barry applauds this recognition by Rawls that bargaining between rational egoists (whatever else it might produce) will not produce fair or just divisions of goods.

He concludes this first volume by addressing three questions about justice. In answer to the first one, he insists that social or distributive justice is an attribute primarily of institutions. We can say that an existing institution is just or unjust, that some alternative to what exists would be more just, and 'that it would be just for a kind of institution that does not now exist (for example, a scheme providing for systematic and nondiscretionary transfers of income from rich countries to poor ones) to be created' (p. 355).

The second question concerns justice and motivation: what is the claim that justice has upon us? *Why* should we be just? Otherwise put, is it possible to show that the demands of justice are rational? Barry rejects utterly the view that justice is the rational pursuit of mutual advantage: 'It is not really possible to prove that it is advantageous to be disposed to be just on all occasions' (p. 164). This is strongly reminiscent of C.B. Macpherson's contention that the concept of what he calls 'economic justice' presupposes the 'social nature of man': 'For a theory which, like Hobbes's or the social Darwinists', starts from a postulate of an essentially unsocial nature of man, is left without any ethical principle that could override the economic behaviour logically required of unsocial man, i.e. pure individual maximizing behaviour, either in the market or by open force' (Macpherson 1985, p. 3). This is where the notion of *impartiality* exercises its full force: 'the desire to be able to justify our conduct in an impartial [that is, unselfish] way is an original principle in human nature and one that develops under the normal conditions of human life' (p. 364). This natural desire to be impartial has clear and far-reaching implications for the structure of social institutions. 'Self-interest cannot be expected to bring about just institutions in general, so it is crucial that the sense of justice should operate there' (p. 366).

But how (and this is his third and last question) do we determine what justice requires? Barry considers three 'constructions', three different decision processes. The first construction (the Sophists/Hobbes/Gauthier approach) creates a game: we ask what rational self-interested players would finish up with. In the second construction (essentially Rawls' veil of ignorance in the 'original position'), the parties are also pursuing their own interests as effectively as possible, except that now they do not know what these interests are, so that, with no conflict of interest in the original position, we no longer have the characteristics of a competitive game, but a problem of individual choice-making. The third construction (the tradition that can be traced from the Stoics through Kant to Rawls and Barry himself) is not a game (in which it is natural and rational for each of the players to do everything in their power to *win*), but a *debate*, in which the objective is to *convince* your opponent. But the parties in this decision mechanism must debate in good faith, 'which means that they must be prepared to be convinced as well as to try to convince others. They must be willing to acknowledge a good argument *even if it runs against their interests to do so*' (p. 371, my emphasis). The parties to the agreement are aware of 'a wide range of cultural and historical experiences' (p. 372). But their main concern is to reach agreement on principles that it would be *unreasonable* of any of the parties to reject; and the criterion of reasonableness here is 'the requirement that everybody's point of view must be taken into account . . . To say that a principle could not reasonably be rejected by anyone covered by it is, I suggest, a way of saying that it meets the test of impartiality' (p. 372).

3   Justice, rights, equality and desert

3.1   *Justice and rights – Nozick and Dworkin*

Injustice is often associated in the public mind with the violation of rights. And so it is not to be wondered at that some philosophers have developed theories which claim justice is essentially a matter of respecting individual rights, irrespective of the effect on the level of overall utility in the society. According to this view, justice dictates that my rights be respected, because (as Ronald Dworkin has put it) 'rights are trumps'. Jerry Cohen (atypically for a Marxist) expresses the point even more forcefully: 'The language of natural (or moral) rights is the language of justice, and whoever takes justice seriously must accept that there are natural rights' (Cohen 1981, p. 12). But even if we agree that justice primarily (or even exclusively) involves the respecting of individual rights, we have only got to first base. The task remains of establishing to what exactly we are entitled to claim rights. In this subsection, I shall consider two prominent rights-based theorists of justice, of very different political complexions: Robert Nozick and Ronald Dworkin.[12]

According to Nozick (1974), the justice of social arrangements has nothing whatsoever to do with the way in which the aggregate wealth and power of society is distributed (what he calls 'the end result'), but is exclusively concerned with protecting the individual's right (or 'entitlement') to his or her property. Nozick's theory of justice is a theory of 'entitlement' to possessions or 'holdings', couched in terms of three principles. (a) 'The principle of justice in acquisition' concerns 'the original acquisition of holdings', 'the appropriation of unheld things'; that is, the way in which things that were hitherto unowned become owned by someone. (b) 'The principle of justice in transfer' deals with the transfer of holdings from one person to another. Nozick puts these two principles together to produce the first version of the 'entitlement' theory of justice:

1. A person who acquires a holding in accordance with the principle of justice in acquisition is entitled to that holding.
2. A person who acquires a holding in accordance with the principle of justice in transfer, from someone else entitled to the holding, is entitled to the holding.
3. No one is entitled to a holding except by (repeated) applications of 1 and 2. (Nozick 1974, p. 151)

(c) 'The principle of rectification', which becomes operative only when either of the first two principles has been violated, stipulates that if 'the actual description of holdings' following one or more past injustices does not correspond to any of the descriptions produced by attempts to describe how the present situation *might* have turned out if the past injustices had *not* occurred, 'then one of the [hypothetical] descriptions yielded must be realized' (ibid., pp. 152–3). Put the three principles together, and you have the second version of the 'entitlement' theory of justice: 'the holdings of a person are just if he is entitled to them by the principles of justice in acquisition and transfer, or by the principle of rectification of injustice (as specified by the first two principles)' (ibid., p. 153). This all remains a bit vague and elusive, because, although the logic of the connections *between* the principles is clear enough, and Nozick does spell out what kind of a social system we would have *if* we were to adopt his principles, the actual content of the principles themselves is much less clear: on several occasions, Nozick declines to spell out 'the complicated truth' of his principles, so that we do not learn much more about them or why we should subscribe to them.

As it is understood by Nozick himself, the entitlement theory of justice in property holdings and transactions is a 'hands-off' theory of individual possessions, which proclaims, 'what I have justly earned or otherwise accumulated, I'm *entitled* to keep'. This interpretation has extremely conservative implications for social and fiscal policy: taxation will be permitted only in order to uphold a 'minimal' or 'night-watchman' state, one which has the sole duty of protecting each individual's dominion over his or her person and property holdings; and it is easy to see its superficial attraction for the many people (most of us?) who hate to see so much of our income (however much that might actually be!) siphoned off in taxes. This is a long way from Rawls' 'difference principle', which would promote progressive taxation for redistribution towards the needy, up to the point at which further taxation of the more well-off, by removing incentives to work and generate more tax revenue, would no longer improve the lot of the least advantaged.

But Nozick's theory of the original acquisition of property has been widely criticized. As Alasdair MacIntyre, for example, has pointed out, if all present-day *legitimate* entitlements can be traced back to legitimate acts of original acquisition, there are in fact very few legitimate entitlements. The property owners of the modern world are not, by and large, the legitimate heirs of Lockean individuals who at one time performed legitimate acts of original acquisition; 'they are the inheritors of those who, for example, stole, and used violence to steal the common lands of England from the common people, vast tracts of North America from the American Indian, much of Ireland from the Irish, and Prussia from the original non-German Prussians. This is the historical reality ideologically concealed behind any Lockean thesis' (MacIntyre 1984, p. 251). If this interpretation were accepted, and if the principle of rectification is to be taken at all seriously, then Nozick's entitlement theory of justice would result in the most dramatic and widespread redistribution of all.[13]

Ronald Dworkin, in the course of his essay entitled 'Justice and Rights', argues that Rawls' 'device' of an 'original position' involving a hypothetical contract is not (as Rawls often seems to suggest) the foundation upon which his theory of justice is based; it is rather 'an intermediate conclusion, a halfway point in a deeper theory that provides philosophical arguments for its conditions' (p. 158; subsequent page numbers in this subsection refer to Dworkin 1977a). Dworkin pursues his argument by distinguishing three kinds of political theory. The first group consists of teleological theories, such as utilitarianism, which are ultimately based on goals. The other two groups of theories are both deontological;[14] that is, they rest on convictions about the rightness or wrongness of acts themselves, without regard to the consequences of those acts. The first group of deontological theories, according to Dworkin, are based on rights, and the second group are based on duties (pp. 169–70).

While theories of justice may involve all three justificatory concepts, Dworkin contends that any particular theory 'will give ultimate pride of place to just one of these concepts' (p. 171). Thus, any 'well-formed theory' will be either fundamentally goal-based (for example, utilitarianism), or fundamentally duty-based (for example, Kant's categorical imperative theory), or fundamentally rights-based (for example, Tom Paine's theory of revolution). Although each of these *types* of theory may produce wildly divergent political positions and policies, what is more important philosophically is the *character* of any particular theory, that is, to which one of his three types it corresponds. And this is precisely why the social contract is so important a feature of Rawls' moral methodology: 'it signals that his deep theory is a rights-based theory, rather than a theory of either of the other two types' (p. 173).

The most remarkable aspect of Rawls' social contract theory, according to Dworkin, is the fact that each party to the contract has a veto. This is the case even though the significance of the veto is obscured in the version of the contract that constitutes 'the original position'. The very existence of the veto of each individual contracting party, however, leads to the conclusion that the deep theory underlying Rawls' conception of justice could itself be neither goal-based nor duty-based. In fact, any deep theory that uses the feature of a contract (including 'the deep theory behind the original position') must be a rights-based deep theory of some sort. Furthermore, it must be 'a theory that is based on the concepts of rights that are *natural*, in the sense that they are not the product of any legislation, or convention, or hypothetical contract' (p. 176). Dworkin underlines this point somewhat reluctantly, because the notion of 'natural rights' has, in the minds of some, what he calls 'disqualifying metaphysical associations' (p. 176). But he insists that the 'constructive' model used by Rawls, and favoured by himself, requires nothing more 'metaphysically ambitious' than the hypothesis that the best political programme is one 'that takes the protection of certain individual choices as fundamental, and not properly subordinated to any goal or duty or combination of these' (p. 177). (For Rawls' own later insistence that his theory of justice as fairness is 'political not metaphysical', see Rawls 1985.)

Dworkin now attempts to identify the particular natural right upon which Rawls' theory of justice is fundamentally based. Since the parties to the contract in Rawls' original position are ignorant of all their interests, their judgements must be very abstract, so that the basic right upon which Rawls' deep theory is grounded 'cannot be a right to any particular individual goal, like a right to security of life, or a right to lead a life according to a particular conception of the good' (p. 178). Their basic natural right must, therefore, be an abstract right. There are two traditional candidates for the role of basic abstract right: the right to liberty and the right to equality. Dworkin offers reasons why a right to liberty may not be taken to be fundamental, even though liberty assumes a dominant position in Rawls' two principles of justice: he argues that the basic liberties identified by Rawls are seen by him 'as the product of the contract rather than as a condition of it' (p. 179). The parties to the contract, in the original position of ignorance, would indeed choose these basic liberties; not for their own sake, but as a means to the end of protecting the even more basic goods they value, such as self-respect. (This, incidentally, is precisely what distinguishes Dworkin's rights-based theory of justice from Nozick's rights-based theory.)

The other candidate for the role of fundamental natural right is equality; and Dworkin shows that equality is built into the very design of the social contract and specifically the ignorance of the parties to it. Drawing attention to Rawls' own distinction between 'equality as it is invoked in connection with the distribution of certain goods' and 'equality as it applies to the respect which is owed to persons irrespective of their social position' (see Rawls 1971, p. 511), he concludes that the basis of the social contract is the conviction that all men and women have a natural right to equal concern and respect in the design and administration of the political institutions that govern them, 'a right they possess not by virtue of birth or characteristic or merit or excellence but simply as human beings with the capacity to make plans and give justice' (p. 182). This very abstract right leaves much in the way of political arrangements still open to negotiation among the contracting parties. But the important point is that the right to equality of respect is not a product of the contract, but 'a condition of admission to the original position' (p. 181).[15]

3.2   Justice and equality

The notion of justice is almost always related, in some way or another, to the notion of equality. The previous subsection illustrated the extent to which Dworkin's theory of justice rests upon a natural right to equality of concern and respect. We have also seen (in subsection 2.1) how the parties to Rawls' social contract are in 'an initial position of equality as defining the fundamental terms of their association' (Rawls 1971, p. 11). The 'original position' is, by definition, a 'hypothetical situation of equal liberty' (Rawls 1971, p. 12.) If 'justice as fairness' is meant to convey the idea that 'the principles of justice are agreed to in an initial situation that is fair' (Rawls 1971, p. 12), the initial situation *is* fair precisely because the parties in the original position are equal. The notion of equality is, furthermore, central to the second part of Rawls' second principle of justice, namely 'the liberal principle of fair equality of opportunity' (Rawls 1971, p. 83). To offer just one more example, a similar notion of 'undominated equality' is central to Bruce Ackerman's articulation of a theory of social justice based on 'Neutral dialogue', according to which '*all* power is distributed so that each person might defend his share in a conversation that begins (but does not end) with the move: "because I'm at least as good as you are" ' (Ackerman 1980, pp. 18–19).

The above notions of equality are, however, all very abstract. While they stress the importance of *initial* equality in the *procedures* for determining just social structures for the distribution of benefits and burdens, their theories would seem to permit gross inequalities in the *outcomes* of those procedures. If it could be said that these theorists have emphasized that a theory of justice must be based on the individual's right to *treatment as an equal*, many other theorists have insisted that justice must, in some way, enshrine a right to *equal treatment*. In the remainder of this subsection, I shall examine some of the theories of justice that insist, to varying degrees, on the importance of this latter right, which is often referred to as equality of satisfaction.

Alan Gewirth uses a 'principle of categorial consistency' – viz., 'apply to your recipient the same categorial features of action that you apply to yourself' – to ground his justification of 'egalitarian justice'. According to this principle, agents must be impartial as between themselves and those affected by their actions, 'so that the agent must respect his recipients' freedom and welfare as well as his own ... According to the *PCC*, all men have an equal right to freedom and welfare' (Gewirth 1971, pp. 339, 340). Although Gewirth brings welfare into his conception of 'egalitarian justice', this is not a full-blown egalitarian theory, since an equal right to welfare is clearly not the same as a right to equal welfare.

Many other theorists begin their consideration of the requirements of justice with a presumption of equality in the *distribution* of benefits and burdens, only to modify the demands of equality in the light of other considerations. The notion of equality is central, for example, to the conception of justice of D.D. Raphael, both in the sense of equality of opportunity and in the sense of the equal provision of material means to the satisfaction of needs. It is only when he comes to tease out what are the needs that ought thus to be satisfied that he limits egalitarian distribution to the satisfaction of what he designates as 'basic needs'. (For more on Raphael's conception of justice, see subsection 3.4 below.)

Neil MacCormick is another who regards 'equal well-being of individuals' as basic to social justice, but he is conscious that many theorists (on both the right and the left) consider equality to be incompatible with individual liberty and legal right. His preferred conception of justice is one which reconciles the two: 'What I understand as the "social democratic" view is that there must be a middle way. Despite the admitted tensions between liberty and (material) equality, the good society is one which aims to hold them in balance' (MacCormick 1982, p. v). While he insists on the fundamental importance of legal right and civil liberty, 'for they are indeed essential conditions of respect for persons', he simultaneously recognizes 'a debt of justice owed by the haves to the have-nots, a debt payable by redistribution of assets to the latter to secure to them adequate worth for their legal liberties' (MacCormick 1982, p. 15). He is quick to point out, however, that his argument is 'an argument for diminishing inequalities of fortune, not for abolishing them' (Mac-Cormick 1982, p.14), since there is always a threshold beyond which 'schemes for redistribution become self-defeating' (p. 15).

One social philosopher who insists that social justice requires the *abolition* of material inequalities is Kai Nielsen. Nielsen's response to the many who have condemned Rawls' theory of justice because of its egalitarianism is to defend 'an egalitarian conception of justice both in production and in distribution that is even more egalitarian than John Rawls's' (p. 209; all subsequent page numbers in this subsection will refer to Nielsen 1979). Nielsen's 'radical egalitarian' conception of justice will require, 'if it is to be anything other than an ideal which turns no machinery, a socialist organization of society' (p. 209). His 'principles of egalitarian justice' are presented in a form deliberately reminiscent of Rawls'. The first principle asserts the equal right of each person 'to the most extensive total system of equal basic liberties and opportunities (including equal opportunities for meaningful work, for self-determination and political participation) compatible with a similar treatment of all' (p. 211). This principle gives expression to a commitment 'to attain and/or sustain equal moral autonomy and equal self-respect' (p. 211). The second principle of egalitarian justice stipulates that, once provision has been set aside to satisfy necessary communal needs, 'the income and wealth (the common stock of means) is to be so divided that each person will have a right to an equal share. The necessary burdens requisite to enhance well-being are also to be equally shared, subject, of course, to limitations by differing abilities and differing situations (natural environment, not class position)' (p. 211).

Nielsen's strategy is to compare his principles with Rawls' and show why someone committed to Dworkin's underlying belief about the moral equality of persons, as both he and Rawls are, should opt for something closer to his principles than to Rawls'. While acknowledging his debt to Rawls in the formulation of his first principle, the 'equal liberty principle', he claims that his principle makes more explicit than does Rawls' principle what is involved in such a commitment to equal liberty: 'There can be no popes or dictators, no bosses and bossed; any authority that obtains must be rooted in at least some form of hypothetical consent ... We must in our collective decisions have the right to an equal say' (pp. 212–13). The really significant differences between Rawls and Nielsen emerge with respect to their respective second principle. Nielsen's claim is that 'given our mutual commitment to equal self-respect and equal moral autonomy, in conditions of moderate scarcity (conditions similar to those in most of North America, Japan and much of Europe) equal self-respect and equal moral autonomy require something like my second principle for their attainability' (p. 213). Rawls' theory is defective because, as he interprets his own second theory, he allows inequalities which in practice undermine any effective application of the equal liberty principle.

Rawls would probably respond to this criticism by referring to his difference principle and would claim that 'an equal division of all primary goods is irrational in view of the possibility of bettering everyone's circumstances by accepting certain inequalities' (Rawls 1971, p. 546). Nielsen counters with the charge that Rawls here unjustifiably assumes that people will always give first priority to 'bettering their circumstances', understood in purely monetary terms. But what about the priority that Rawls gives to equal self-respect? Nielsen claims that the disparities in power, authority, and autonomy that commonly obtain, even in welfare state capitalism, and are not only allowed but justified by Rawls' difference principle, effectively undermine the self-respect of many less well-off citizens: 'these disparities attack their self-respect through undermining their moral autonomy; in such social conditions, men do not have effective control over their own lives' (p. 215). Since Rawls' difference principle is in conflict with his own first principle of justice (his 'equal liberties' principle), it should be abandoned.

Should Rawls try to square his two principles of justice and provide moral and conceptual space for both equal liberty and extensive socio-economic inequalities by distinguishing between liberty and the *worth* of liberty, Nielsen responds that a liberty that cannot be exercised is of no value. 'To will the end is to will the necessary means to the end. It is hardly reasonable to opt for equal liberty and then opt for a difference principle which accepts an unequal worth of liberty which, in turn, makes the equal liberty principle inoperable, that is, which makes it impossible for people actually to achieve equal liberty' (p. 216). (See also the similar and more detailed argument, acknowledged by Nielsen, against this distinction between liberty and the worth of liberty in Daniels 1975a.)

Nielsen proceeds to defend his own second principle against some common objections to this brand of egalitarianism. He stresses that this principle does not argue that every individual should have exactly the same amount of income and wealth. It does, however, argue for the reduction and progressive elimination of 'inequalities in primary or basic social goods and goods that are the source of or ground for distinctions that give one person power or control over another' (p. 217). The principle advocates the distribution of benefits and burdens so that they are equally shared, but this is not like equally dividing up a pie, since part of the social product must be used to provide amenities that are of collective value, 'for example, hospitals, schools, roads, clean air, recreation facilities, and the like. And part of it must be used to protect future generations. Another part must be used to preserve the society's productive capacity so that there will be a continuous and adequate supply of goods to be divided' (p. 218). Neither does the second principle of radical egalitarianism advocate a grey uniformity; everyone would not be treated the same. Nielsen insists, however, that a determination to bring about a society in which there is an equal moral concern and respect for all human beings should begin from the presumption of equality in the overall distribution of benefits and burdens. The 'underlying rationale' of his second principle is to satisfy the needs of all the people, as fully as possible, as equally as possible, while allowing for different genuine needs and different abilities.[16]

3.3   Justice and desert

Perhaps the most enduring conviction about justice, already clearly articulated by Aristotle, is that justice is a matter of people getting what they deserve. This principle of justice – which would appear to be applicable to both procedural and social justice – received its classical formulation in the *Institutes* of Justinian: *suum cuique tribuere*, 'give to each his or her own'. The problem remains, of course, of determining what 'one's own' consists of. To what is one entitled? What is to count as a person's due deserts? In the words of a recent commentator: 'while everyone agrees that justice, almost by definition, is giving people what they deserve, there appears to be little agreement concerning what it is that people deserve' (Sterba 1986, p. 1).

Although many accounts of justice have glanced in passing at the notion of desert, only to shy away from it because of its seeming intractability, few have focused on it as an object of detailed investigation. (This is less so in the case of theories of punishment, but it certainly is the case in discussions of social justice.) Feinberg (1970) is a pioneering study (in recent years) of the question of what it is to deserve something and the relation of personal desert to justice. As an aid in clarifying the issues at stake, he lists five classes of treatment in which we get 'what we deserve': awards of prizes; assignments of grades; rewards and punishments; praise, blame and other informal responses; and reparation, liability and other modes of compensation. He also offers the helpful distinction between two kinds of treatment: those in which desert is a 'polar' concept and those in which it is not. In the former case (central to what has traditionally been called retributive justice), one can be said to deserve either good or ill, reward or punishment, praise or blame, and so on. Non-polar justice, which is central to the practice of distributive justice, does not divide people into those who deserve good and those who deserve ill, but into those who deserve a prize, a reward, grades, and so on, and those who do not; and, in some cases, into those who deserve much and those who deserve less, and so on. Feinberg argues that desert is a 'natural' notion (that is, 'one which is not logically tied to institutions, practices, and rules'); that it represents only a part, and not necessarily the most important part, of the domain of justice; and that reward and punishment are only two among the several irreducibly distinct modes of treatment persons are said to deserve (Feinberg 1970, p. 56).

Michael Slote (1973) examines the distinction between rewarding workers (a) in accordance with their actual *success* in contributing to society (what he calls a 'democratic capitalist' social organization) and (b) in accordance with their (conscientious) *efforts* to contribute to society (which he labels a '(utopian) socialist' social organization). He then expresses this distinction in terms of desert and social justice, that is, in terms of 'determining what people deserve from society' (Slote 1973, p. 333). But the criterion of desert, which does not exhaust the idea of justice, must be supplemented by the notion of free consent: 'it is true by definition that a society is ideally or perfectly just if and only if all the equalities and inequalities it provides for are deserved "at its hands" (i.e., from it) or freely consented to by all its members' (ibid., p. 335). Slote then proceeds to use his theory to criticize Rawls' rejection of the principle of distribution in proportion to moral desert. (See Rawls 1971, pp. 310-15; Slote 1973, pp. 336–47.)

Rawls claimed that people never deserve things for reasons prior to or independent of social conventions. The 'defensive' aim of George Sher (1979) is 'to secure the moral import of personal desert against the Rawlsian attack, and so indirectly to cast doubt upon those theories of justice which are insensitive to it' (Sher 1979, p. 362). Robert Goodin (1985), however, sides with Rawls on this issue, and argues that considerations of personal desert should have only a very limited role, if any at all, in social policy-making: 'where causal relationships are complex or considerations of needs are in play, considerations of deserts are simply out of place' (Goodin 1985, p. 590).

A major statement of a largely desert-based theory of justice has been presented by Wojciech Sadurski (1985a). His 'equilibrium' theory, while not a pure desert theory, makes desert central to the idea of a hypothetical balance of benefits and burdens which justice in all its forms (legal as well as social) should seek to establish. The theory depends essentially on a notion of compensation, to restore an ideal of proportionality of desert, either positive or negative: 'whenever an ideal, hypothetical balance of social benefits and burdens is upset, social justice calls for restoring it'

(Sadurski 1985a, p. 101). Sadurski also seeks to demonstrate that, in general, where other commonly championed criteria, such as need or choice, have to do with justice, they are crucially related to and can be understood in terms of desert; and secondly, that where they are not related to desert they are not criteria of justice.[17]

3.4   Multi-criterion theories of justice – Lucas, Raphael and Miller

So far, we have examined theories of justice that privilege one particular criterion: namely, justice *as* fairness, justice *as* rights, justice *as* equality, and so on. But many theorists of justice recognize that justice necessarily involves several such criteria, weighted in different ways, depending on the context. In this subsection, I shall examine three such highly differentiated theories: those of J.R. Lucas, David Raphael and David Miller.

In his wide-ranging reflections on justice, in the course of which he distinguishes among retributive, distributive and contributive justice (his term for fiscal justice), Lucas urges that we follow Aristotle's example and adopt a negative approach, 'discovering what justice is by considering on what occasions we protest at injustice or unfairness' (Lucas 1980, p. 4). He emphasizes the importance of justice as 'the bond of society', which enables the individual to identify with the actions of society: 'I can be happy to be one of We, if We are just, because then We will treat Me as well as reasonably possible; and We will be happy to have Me as one of Us, because We know that I, being just, will see things from Our point of view' (ibid., p. 18).

Justice is to be distinguished from other political ideals, such as liberty, equality or fraternity. Justice is not liberty or freedom, 'because liberty and freedom are concerned with the question who shall take the decisions, whereas justice is concerned with how decisions shall be taken, in what frame of mind and with what result' (ibid., p. 4).[18] Justice is not equality, because equality is concerned only that people should be treated the same, 'whereas justice is concerned to consider each individual case on its own merits, treating, if necessary, different people differently, as when we punish the guilty and let the innocent go free' (ibid.).[19] Justice is not fraternity, because fraternity is a warm virtue, concerned with fellow-feeling, 'whereas justice is a cold virtue which can be manifested without feeling, and is concerned to emphasize that the other chap is not merely a human being like myself, but a separate individual, with his own point of view and own interests that are distinct from mine' (ibid.).

Justice is also to be distinguished from 'what the law lays down': 'We cannot merely identify law and justice: yet we cannot, if we are honest, simply divorce them as the positivists sought to do' (ibid., p. 99). Although an unjust law should, in principle, be obeyed, there can be exceptions: 'grave and gross injustice strikes at the *raison d'être* of law, and hence *lex injustissima non est lex*' (ibid., p. 123). (On the relation between justice and the law, see ibid., chapter 5, pp. 99–123; see also subsection 5.1 below.) In the sphere of distributive justice, benefits may justly be distributed according to several different criteria: although 'reasons based on the individual's deeds and agreements are in some ways pre-eminent, reasons based on individual need, status, merit, entitlement or right are all, in appropriate circumstances, the proper basis of apportionment' (ibid., p. 164). Finally, although justice is a virtue, it does not exhaust morality:

> I can be just, and yet lack many moral virtues. I might be fair-minded and yet lack love. Justice by itself is not enough. It does not make a man happy or fulfilled … Nevertheless, it is not to be despised. It may not be everything, but it is something. It is a virtue, an important virtue, one of the cardinal virtues; for it is the bond of peace, which enables the individual to identify with society, and brethren to dwell together in unity. (ibid., p. 263)

Like Lucas, David Raphael has obvious sympathy for something like natural law when it comes to assessing the justice of situations or laws, while insisting that he is an *empiricist* and referring approvingly to Adam Smith's development of a 'natural law with a difference, a genuinely empiricist natural law' (Raphael 1980, p. 158). Raphael's commitment to equality (which he distinguishes clearly from uniformity) as the basic criterion in determining just action and just social institutions depends in large measure on a conception of human nature: 'the equalitarian does sometimes want to go against nature, for instance when he tries to compensate for natural disabilities. And because these disabilities are departures from the norm of human nature, he may be led to say that his aim is to restore what is truly natural' (ibid., p. 71). What he calls 'extreme equalitarianism' would dictate the simple principle of justice commonly associated with Marx and the French socialists: 'from each according to his capacity, to each according to his needs' (ibid., p. 54). But this leaves unsolved the problem of how we are to identify genuine 'needs', since it is clear that desires or wants are, in practice, limitless. Some more fundamental desires – viz. 'those regarded as essential for tolerable living' (ibid., p. 56) – are identified as basic to a decent life, and these are the needs the satisfaction of which is demanded by justice. These basic needs should be satisfied for all *equally* before further desires are satisfied for any: 'justice is thought to require a basic minimum of equal satisfactions, unrelated to utility or to capacity. Above that line, room is left for individuals to do as they think fit. The position of the line is different in different societies and at different periods of history, depending both on economic circumstances and on the level of social morality' (ibid., pp. 54–5; cf. Miller 1976).

While Raphael emphasizes the interpenetration of justice, equality, merit and utility, foremost among these is 'a right to equality' derived from a Kantian 'respect for persons'. Distributive justice makes two claims of equality: 'first, equality of opportunity, that is, the greatest possible degree of opportunity for all impartially; and second, the provision of material means to satisfaction for all impartially, such provision in practice being limited, for utilitarian reasons, to a standard of basic needs' (Raphael 1980, p. 55). These principles share a fundamental regard for individuals as individuals and are primarily concerned with the good accruing to them as 'ends-in-themselves', irrespective of the collective advantage or common good advocated by utilitarian policies. Their implementation, furthermore, serves to reconcile any tension between justice and liberty.[20]

An analogously differentiated theory of justice is offered by David Miller. Miller claims that what is commonly called 'social justice' is really made up of three widely held but conflicting principles, which relate social justice respectively to rights, deserts and needs; and that the relative weights attached to each principle 'vary systematically from one social context to another' (Miller 1976, p. 253). The most valuable general definition of justice is the traditional one: 'justice is *suum cuique*, to each his due' (ibid., p. 20); the age-old problem remains, however, of determining according to what principle a person's 'due' is to be given. Miller proceeds to analyse what he sees as the three basic ways in which the concept of social justice is used, reflecting three mutually irreconcilable principles of justice: (a) to each according to his or her rights; (b) to each according to his or her deserts; and (c) to each according to his or her needs. He shows how these three principles of justice are represented in the theories of Hume, Spencer and Kropotkin, respectively, with the emphasis on rights corresponding to Hume's underlying pessimism about the 'destructive possibilities' of human nature, the emphasis on deserts corresponding to Spencer's vision of society as a 'competitive market', and the emphasis on needs reflecting Kropotkin's conception of society as a 'solidaristic community' (ibid., pp. 245-6).

In the most interesting part of his book, 'Social justice in sociological perspective', Miller illustrates the social diversity of substantive conceptions of social justice by examining sociologically three types of society – primitive societies, hierarchical societies (particularly medieval feudal society) and market societies – and showing that the values assigned to the three principles of justice identified earlier are significantly different in each type of society. He then argues that our modern concept of social justice (that is, the dominant one within the 'organized capitalism' of Western European and North American society) has 'grown out of' the specific arrangements of market society, but within which various groups suffering from social dislocation have responded by advocating and establishing egalitarian communities embodying a 'deviant' conception of justice as distribution according to need. Our modern concept, therefore, includes both the conflicting principles of desert and need. Rights are still part of the debate; but the issue of the institution or continued possession of rights, he argues, is now typically decided by reference to the main modern criteria of social justice, viz. desert and need; and if a given distribution of rights is considered to be sufficiently unjust (according to the two modern criteria), it may be decided that it ought to be altered. (For the view that the concept of justice is essentially historically determined, see Llompart 1981.)

4   Marx, Marxism and justice – equality and needs

A feature of the past twenty years or so has been the readiness of some social and political philosophers in the analytic tradition to engage in an analysis of the perspectives on social and political issues thrown up by the writings of Karl Marx and subsequent Marxist thinkers. More specifically, there has been a lively debate on how to interpret and assess Marx's attitude towards morality in general, and in particular towards the use of the concept of justice in the evaluation of societies and social institutions. Allen Wood (1972) initiated this debate, with the provocative claim that Marx does not condemn capitalism for being unjust or for failing to exhibit or promote any other moral or social ideal or principle. According to Wood's version of Marx (well documented by telling quotations from the canon), justice is not a standard by which reason measures human actions, practices or institutions in the abstract; rather is it a standard by which each particular mode of production – whether feudal, capitalist or socialist – measures *itself* and only itself. 'There *are* rational assessments of the justice or injustice of specific acts and institutions, based on their concrete function within a specific mode of production. But these assessments are not founded on abstract or formal principles of justice, good for all times and places' (Wood 1972, p. 16).

The concept of justice 'is in the Marxian account the highest expression of the rationality of social facts from the *juridical* point of view', a point of view which is essentially one-sided (ibid., pp. 13–14). In particular, the appropriation of surplus value, widely considered since Marx's own time to be the characteristic injustice of capitalism, involves no unequal or unjust exchange, and the new, revolutionary mode of production will be no more just than the old one. Although 'disguised exploitation, unnecessary servitude, economic instability, and declining productivity' – all characteristics of capitalism – offer excellent reasons for condemning it, in Wood's view, these reasons are not based on any *moral* theory, and 'Marx never tried to give any philosophical account of why these features would constitute good reasons for condemning a system that possesses them' (ibid., p. 41).

While acknowledging that Marx's direct and explicit statements on the subject of justice are 'few and far between', Ziyad Husami (1978) insists that 'in numerous passages throughout his works, Marx employs the sort of language typically used in philosophical discourse on justice and seems to be condemning capitalism for its injustice' (Husami 1978, p. 43). He goes on to illustrate his claim with a series of quotations no less telling than Wood's, in which Marx clearly does characterize exploitation as 'robbery', 'usurpation', 'embezzlement', 'plunder', 'booty', 'theft', 'snatching' and 'swindling' (ibid., p. 45). If the capitalist is said by Marx to 'rob' the worker, it is implied that he takes what is not rightfully his own or what rightfully belongs to the worker: therefore, 'there is no meaningful sense in which the capitalist can simultaneously rob the worker and treat him justly' (ibid.). Husami contends that Wood ascribes to Marx a variant of moral positivism by confusing Marx's moral theory with his *sociology* of morals; but Marx used the latter to show how capitalist exploitation of labour could come to be seen as just, from the point of view of the capitalist class itself. He claims it is clear from the passages he quotes, however, that 'Marx evaluates pre-communist systems from the standpoint of communist society' (ibid., p. 50). From this standpoint, 'exploitation is incompatible with justice. Communist justice is conducive to self-realization; capitalist injustice makes it impossible' (ibid., p. 73). Marx's evaluation of capitalist distributive arrangements is, therefore, 'overwhelmingly *moral*, not legal' (ibid., p. 78).

George Brenkert (1979) tries to offer an interpretation that would mediate between these two conflicting ones. Confining his analysis to Marx's well-known opposition to the institution of private property, he argues, on the one hand, that 'Marx does indeed have an underlying moral reason for opposing private property . . . On the other hand, it is implausible that this underlying opposition is based on a principle of justice because Marx's views on ideology do seem to prohibit such a stance' (Brenkert 1979, p. 81). While agreeing with Wood that 'Marx does not and cannot have a universal or absolute principle of justice that applies to all societies and by which he can criticize capitalist private property' (ibid., pp. 90–1), he argues that Marx's criticism of the private property that underpins the capitalist system is based on 'a principle of freedom and on the effects of private property on individuality and personality' (ibid., p. 81). Freedom is, like justice, related to the particular mode of production, but in a significantly different way. And because of these differences, 'freedom can be used, whereas justice cannot be used, for transcultural appraisals' (ibid., p. 102).

When he comes to reply to the previous two articles, Wood (1979) reiterates his view that Marx does not offer a *moral* critique of capitalist society. In fact, Marx is, 'like Nietzsche, a critic of morality. Like Nietzsche, he seeks to understand the actual function in human life of moral values and standards, and to make an assessment of them on the basis of non-moral goods' (Wood 1979, p. 125). While Wood agrees with Brenkert that Marx condemns capitalism because it limits people's freedom and upsets their security and comfort, he takes issue with Brenkert by denying that freedom is a *moral* good. 'Juridical or moral notions' such as right and justice must be distinguished from *non-moral* goods such as self-actualization, community, freedom, pleasure and happiness, 'things which we would regard as desirable and good for people to have even if no moral credit accrued from pursuing or attaining them' (ibid., p. 122). According to Wood, the value of these non-moral goods is sufficient, without any recourse to moralizing appeals, to convince any reasonable person to favour the overthrow of any social order that frustrates them unnecessarily. (For an interpretation of Marx and justice that takes, as a general orientation, the Wood line in this debate, cf. Buchanan 1982.)

Jerry Cohen begins his examination of the issue of Marxism and justice (together with its implications for contemporary political analysis and political practice in Western liberal democracies) by affirming that 'justice occupies a central place in revolutionary Marxist belief', even if many Marxists strenuously deny as much, 'because of ill-conceived philosophical commitments' (Cohen 1981, pp. 12–13). He cites this as a particular instance of a regrettably widespread intellectual failure: 'revolutionary Marxist belief often misdescribes itself, out of lack of clear awareness of its own nature, and Marxist disparagement of the idea of justice is a good example of that deficient self-understanding' (ibid., p. 12). He then confronts his predominantly revolutionary Marxist audience (the occasion was the 1980 Isaac Deutscher Memorial Lecture) with the 'justice' critique of capitalism he insists they believe 'in their hearts': 'the socialist objection of justice to the market economy is that it allows private ownership of means of existence which no one has the right to own privately, and therefore rests upon an unjust foundation' (ibid., p. 13).

Cohen claims that the widespread Marxist disdain for the notion of justice rests upon a misreading of some key passages of Marx's *Critique of the Gotha Programme* (which figure prominently in the debate between Wood and Husami). Cohen emphasizes that, in these passages, Marx is not saying to his followers, 'Give up your obsession with just distribution'; he is, however, saying, 'Prosecute your concern about distribution at the appropriately fundamental level', that is, at the level of the distribution, or ownership, of the elements of production (ibid., pp. 13–14, n. 7). Applying this analysis to contemporary political debates, Cohen insists that capitalism can be claimed to be just 'if and only if capitalists have the right to own the means of production they do, for it is their ownership of means of production which enables them to make profit out of labour, and if that ownership is legitimate, then so too is making profit out of labour' (ibid., p. 15). However, if every actual piece of private property either is or is made of something that was once the private property of no one, then someone who claims a right to hold a certain piece of productive property must be challenged to defend not so much how he in particular came to own it, but the transformation whereby 'the thing came to be (anyone's) private property in the first place . . . I believe we shall find that the original transformation is unjust, that . . . property is theft, theft of what morally speaking belongs to us all in common' (ibid.). This is, of course, the essence of Cohen's telling critique of Nozick's entitlement theory of justice. (See Cohen 1985, and subsection 3.1 above.) Cohen ends his examination of the injustice of capitalism with a quotation from *The Communist Manifesto*: 'The theory of the Communists may be summed up in a single phrase: Abolition of private property' (Cohen 1981, p. 16).[21]

Steven Lukes (1982; 1985) sets out to make sense of the paradoxical fact that 'with some notable exceptions – notably Gramsci, Walter Benjamin, and Ernst Bloch, and critical and humanist marxists of the postwar period, especially in Yugoslavia – marxism has remained, in its distinctive and curious way, both anti-moral and moral' (Lukes 1985, p. 25). He begins by accepting that at least four distinct interpretations, all supported by textual evidence, can plausibly be made out to represent Marx's own views. To the extent that Marx 'did offer a functional account of the norms by which capitalist exploitation is judged just', the interpretation of Wood and Brenkert is correct. To the extent that Marx also offered 'an "external" critique of capitalist exploitation and of the norms and perspective from which it appears just', the interpretation favoured by Husami and Cohen is also correct (ibid., p. 58). But in so far as Marx maintained a range of positions and brought several perspectives to bear at once, Lukes rejects the Husami/Cohen view that Marx had some non-relativist conception of justice, since for Marx there was no such conception: 'all such judgements are perspective-relative. Objectivity, in the sense of perspective-neutrality, was, for him, an illusion, indeed an ideological illusion' (ibid., p. 59).

The best survey of this whole debate is by Norman Geras (1985). His article is in three parts: first, he reviews the texts and arguments put forward by eight authors who deny that Marx condemned capitalism as unjust (including Brenkert, Buchanan, Lukes and Wood); second, he reviews the texts and arguments put forward by sixteen authors who claim he did so condemn it (including Cohen, Elster and Husami), or who at least express reservations about the interpretation of the first group; finally, he argues for his own conclusions, to the effect that 'a real and deep-seated inconsistency on Marx's part and one with not very happy effects' should be recognized, and the absence of 'a properly elaborated Marxist conception of justice' should urgently be rectified.

But he suggests a probable reason for 'Marx's disavowal of all commitment to ethical principle', while acknowledging that Marx's great
strength does not excuse this particular deficiency. With a bitter side-
swipe at the 'moral rhetoric, *mere* moralizing' of most of the contemporary academic discussion of justice (by implication, of most of the material
surveyed in the present chapter), by theorists who typically offer nothing
on how just social arrangements might be achieved, he concludes by
referring to the most striking paradox of all: 'that Marx, despite everything, displayed a greater commitment to the creation of a just society
than many more overtly interested in analysis of what justice is' (Geras
1985, p. 85).[22]

5   Justice and the problem of moral epistemology

While many philosophers have been offering various criteria for the
rational grounding of claims about justice, a growing number of philosophers have been concerned about the difficulty – in an increasingly
pluralistic and sceptical world – of giving any kind of reasons that would
win rational assent for holding substantive moral views. These are issues
of moral epistemology: can we really *know* anything about moral or
other kinds of values, as distinct from holding opinions about them; and
if we can have knowledge about values, how do we know we know?

According, for example, to Hans Kelsen's widely influential 'pure
theory of law', analytical or descriptive jurisprudence must be sharply
demarcated from any moral, political or sociological inquiries or claims
(see Kelsen 1967; cf. Kelsen 1957). The leading anglophone legal positivist, H.L.A. Hart, insists on a similarly sharp demarcation between what
the law is and what the law ought to be. According to this view, the
notion of 'natural justice' refers only to certain technical (non-moral)
rules of legal procedure, which have no significant connection with the
(moral) justice or injustice of the rules' content (see Hart 1961, pp. 202–
4); the core of legal positivism is 'the simple contention that it is in no
sense a necessary truth that laws reproduce or satisfy certain demands of
morality' (ibid., p. 181). Law, therefore, may be valid law although
iniquitous. This kind of moral scepticism (cf. Ross 1974) has been a
perennial problem in the history of philosophy; but it has taken on a new
urgency in recent years, particularly among philosophers who wish to
talk rationally about justice and are disturbed at (and impressed by) the
babel of voices on the subject. Some philosophers offer epistemological
or methodological underpinnings for their theories of justice in any case,
especially if they are aiming to present a fairly complete theory: Rawls'
conception and exemplification of 'reflective equilibrium' is an excellent
example of this. Many, however, do not. In this final section, I shall

examine briefly some recent articulations and responses to the problem
of grounding value claims rationally.

5.1   Natural law theories of justice

One distinctive approach to the problem of justice is represented by the
philosophy of natural law. Natural law does, of course, offer substantive
theories of justice, which typically articulate specific implications of this
approach for individual action and public policy. A discussion of the
natural law approach to justice is not, however, out of place in this
section devoted to meta-ethical issues, because natural law, apart altogether from the implications for action, suggests a quite distinctive
approach to addressing questions of morality.

Natural law theory has a long tradition. Originating in the
philosophies of Plato, Aristotle and the Greek Stoics, it received its first
concise formulation in Cicero: 'True law is right reason in agreement
with nature; it is of universal application, unchanging and everlasting'
(*De Republica* xxii, 33). These Stoic ideas were taken up and adapted by
Church Fathers and early medieval canonists, until they were anthologized in the twelfth-century *Decretum* of Gratian: 'The *ius naturale* is
common to all nations; it is what is received everywhere by natural
instinct, and not by any convention.' Natural law theory received its
fullest and most coherent formulation in the thirteenth-century writings
of Thomas Aquinas, who, as John Finnis has put it, 'occupies a uniquely
strategic place in the history of natural law theorizing' (Finnis 1980, p.
vi). Aquinas adopted the by then familiar distinction between human law
(*ius gentium*) and natural law (*ius naturale*): 'all humanly enacted laws
are in accord with reason to the extent that they derive from the natural
law. And if a human law is at variance in any particular with the natural
law, it is no longer legal, but rather a corruption of law.'[23]

This tradition clearly runs directly counter to the claim of the legal
positivists that the law is logically independent of morals. And it is
largely as an umbrella for opponents of legal positivism that natural law
theory has survived in anglophone moral and political philosophy. It has,
however, never ceased to thrive on the Continent. Jean Dabin's 'general
theory of law' is essentially a very detailed and somewhat updated
account of Aquinas' theory of natural law. For Dabin, the 'rule' of
human conduct known as natural law 'is deduced from the nature of man
as it is revealed in the basic inclinations of that nature under the control
of reason'. While positive law may add to natural law or even restrict it,
'it is prohibited from contradicting it'. We come to know the dictates of
natural law through 'the mechanism of the anguish of conscience' (Dabin
1969, § 203). Dabin sums up the respective roles of natural law and
justice in the elaboration of the positive law as follows: 'Natural law

represents the category of the moral rule . . . As to justice, it represents one of the principal rules of morals, that which regards the right of another to be respected and satisfied, either that of particular private persons (particular justice: commutative and distributive) or that of the public community (legal justice)' (ibid., § 244).

Some of the key elements of traditional natural law theory, as presented by Dabin, are used by Cornelius Murphy (1972) as the basis for a Thomistic critique of Rawls (1971). A central point is the Thomistic premise that in matters of social justice the individual does not have separate, inherent rights: 'whatever rights a person possesses are those which belong to him as a member of the group' (Murphy 1972, p. 154). While Rawls insists that society is composed of free discrete individuals who agree to join in a social venture for mutual advantage. Thomism, on the other hand, views the individual person both as a whole *and* as a part of a greater whole. Rawls' theory has no role for 'temporal perceptions of objective good which transcend desire', that is, 'the operations of moral conscience, by which we become gradually aware of the values inherent in demands of liberty and social justice' (ibid., p. 165).

John Finnis, in his impressive restatement of natural law ethics, claims to be incorporating the valuable insights of legal positivism into a properly elaborated theory of natural law. He defines the task of natural law as exclusively normative: 'a theory of natural law claims to be able to identify conditions and principles of practical right mindedness, of good and proper order among men and in individual conduct' (p. 18; all subsequent page numbers in this subsection, unless otherwise indicated, refer to Finnis 1980). He lists seven basic goods for human beings, 'basic forms of human flourishing': life, knowledge ('considered as desirable for its own sake, not merely instrumentally'), play, aesthetic experience, sociability or friendship, practical reasonableness and religion. He supports the claim of each one of these values to be basic to every human being (pp. 86–9). To these 'basic aspects of human well-being' are added a set of 'basic methodological requirements' of practical reasonableness that enable us, when taken together, to identify the criteria for distinguishing morally right and wrong ways of acting. These include 'a coherent plan of life',[24] 'no arbitrary preferences among values', 'no arbitrary preferences among persons', 'detachment and commitment', 'efficiency, within reason', 'respect for every basic value in every act', 'the requirement of favouring and fostering the common good of one's communities', and 'following one's conscience' (pp. 100–26). This 'complex' of basic goods and basic requirements of practical reasonableness together constitute the unchanging principles of natural law.

It could be objected (and indeed has been objected, by MacCormick 1981) that even assuming that most of us do have drives or inclinations towards the basic goods identified by Finnis, how do we *know* they are good? Finnis replies that they are self-evidently so. In the same way as the basic rules of logic, for example, and other principles of theoretical reasoning are self-evident, in the sense that they are *presupposed* in anything that could count as a proof, so, for example, the proposition that knowledge is a basic good is not open to strict proof. But neither is one demanded – at least, it would be silly and self-defeating to do so.

Crucial to the discovery of what is morally right action is the existence of the 'common good', which is quite different from the utilitarian 'greatest good of the greatest number'. In fact, each of the seven 'basic forms of human flourishing' is a common good, on a different explanatory level. Justice consists in the concrete implications of the requirement to foster the 'common good' in one's community (pp. 161–97). Justice has three elements. First, '*other-directedness*: justice has to do with one's relations and dealings with other persons; it is "inter-subjective" or interpersonal' (p. 161). The second element is '*duty*: of what is owed (*debitum*) or due to another, and correspondingly of what that other person has a right to' (p. 162). The third element of justice he first calls equality, but taken in what he calls an 'analogical' sense. Upon reflection, he thinks better of using the potentially misleading (or at least, disputed) term 'equality': 'To avoid misunderstandings and over-simplifications, therefore, it may be better to think of *proportionality*, or even of *equilibrium* or balance' (p. 163).

He than proceeds to spell out the requirements of justice under three headings: general justice, distributive justice and commutative justice. The requirements of practical reasoning produce, for Finnis, a wide range of substantive policy conclusions. These include: the justice of private property ownership (because of the good of 'personal autonomy in the community' and the finding of experience that resources are more productively exploited by private than by public enterprise); and 'public morality' limitations on the exercise of a wide range of rights (most of which, it must be said, just happen to coincide with the official teachings of the Roman Catholic Church).

Neil MacCormick, one of Finnis' most sympathetic critics, although holding to 'a general moral position according to which the law of the land ought to be aimed at realizing justice and a conception of the common good not very far removed from Finnis's', remains resistant to his 'claims as to the objectivity and self-evidence of basic goods . . . and to his proposal to accept his characterization of the focal meaning of law as requiring an orientation to the common good' (MacCormick 1981, pp. 108–9). Finnis, for his part, is not claiming (unlike some earlier natural law theorists) that 'unjust laws are not law' (p. 351). (Cf. J.R. Lucas' affirmation that '*lex injustissima non est lex*' (Lucas 1980, p. 123).) Nor is he claiming that natural law theorizing will minimize the range or determination of positive law. His main point is that:

the act of 'positing' law (whether judicially or legislatively or otherwise) is an act which can and should be guided by 'moral' principles and rules; that those moral norms are a matter of objective reasonableness, not of whim, convention, or mere 'decision'; and that those same moral norms justify (a) the very institution of positive law, (b) the main institutions, techniques, and modalities within that tradition (e.g. separation of powers), and (c) the main institutions regulated and sustained by law (e.g., government, contract, property, marriage, and criminal liability). (p. 290)

Finnis explicitly claims to be basing his whole theory on a faithful reinterpretation of Aquinas. But Lloyd Weinreb (1987), in the course of an extended discussion of Finnis' book (pp. 108–26), takes grave exception to Finnis' ontological neutrality: 'to extract Aquinas' doctrine of natural law from its context and treat it as separable from the idea of a universal order according to the Eternal Law of God not only radically distorts Aquinas' philosophy as a whole but misconceives the doctrine of natural law itself' (Weinreb 1987, p. 109n). Without the metaphysics, says Weinreb, natural law theory just will not make sense: 'it is because the universe is ordered by divine Providence that there is natural law, and because we know that it is so ordered that we know that there is natural law' (ibid.).

5.2   Epistemological communitarianism – MacIntyre, Sandel and Walzer

Some recent writers on the subject of justice have been particularly alarmed at the plethora of competing theories currently on offer and have concluded that it is rationally impossible to give any one correct or 'true' analysis or theory of justice that would be applicable to all times or even to all societies at the present time. Reminiscent of Hegel's criticism of Kant, these 'communitarian' critics of modern liberalism (as Michael Sandel refers to them) question specifically the liberal assertion of the priority of the right over the good and the related liberal conception of the freely choosing 'unencumbered' individual. Following Aristotle, they tend to argue that we cannot justify political arrangements without reference to common purposes and ends, and that we can neither conceive our personhood nor *know* the good without reference to our role as citizens and as participants in a common life. In this subsection, I shall look briefly at three theorists who specifically address this issue: Alasdair MacIntyre, Michael Sandel and Michael Walzer.

The thesis of MacIntyre (1984) is the product of his deep-seated dissatisfaction with the conception of 'moral philosophy' as 'an independent and isolable area of enquiry', together with his conviction that what unites Marxism, individualistic liberalism and conservatism in their failure to provide rationally and morally defensible standpoints from which to judge and act is their embodiment of the *ethos* of the distinctively modern world. According to this modern *ethos*, moral debate is 'a confrontation between incompatible and incommensurable moral premises'; and moral commitment is 'the expression of a criterionless choice between such premises, a type of choice for which no rational justification can be given' (MacIntyre 1984, p. 39).

This prevailing *ethos* in moral discourse is characterized by MacIntyre as 'emotivism', since the debates (not just among moral philosophers, but also among political figures and ordinary citizens) in which moral disagreements are typically expressed offer no *rational* way of securing moral agreement. The rival positions in moral debates (especially the debate about the concept of justice) suffer from 'conceptual incommensurability', in the sense that 'from our rival conclusions we can argue back to our rival premises; but when we do arrive at our premises argument ceases and the invocation of one premise against another becomes a matter of pure assertion and counter-assertion' (ibid., p. 8). And this is the case not only in interpersonal debate but also within ourselves: if I cannot invoke a good reason against you in support of my basic premise or premises, he argues, it must be because I lack the requisite good reasons. Most participants in such an argument, however, seem reluctant to acknowledge this aspect of their participation, since the response, in a debate, to the question 'Why *should* I do so-and-so?' is usually dressed up *as if* it were framed in the shape of a reason: that is, the response is not usually a variation on 'Because I want you to' (which, according to MacIntyre, would be the most honest response, since the speaker does not really have a good *reason* to underpin his or her moral recommendation or condemnation); instead the response is usually something like 'Because it is your duty' or 'Because it would give pleasure to a number of people.' This paradoxical fact, however, suggests to MacIntyre that 'the practice of moral argument in our culture expresses at least an aspiration to be or to become rational in this area of our lives' (ibid., pp. 9–10).

Emotivism is defined as 'the doctrine that all evaluative judgements and more specifically all moral judgements are *nothing but* expressions of preference, expressions of attitude or feeling, insofar as they are moral or evaluative in character' (ibid., pp. 11–12). What is wrong, he suggests, with our modern culture and with our manner of discourse on topics of morality is that 'to a large degree people now think, talk and act *as if* emotivism were true, no matter what their avowed theoretical standpoint may be. Emotivism has become embodied in our culture' (ibid., p. 22). And this, he contends, marks a degeneration, 'a grave cultural loss' (ibid.). The rest of the book is devoted to his substantiation of this diagnosis and to the task of identifying and describing the lost morality of the past and of evaluating its claims to objectivity and authority. The lost morality of the past is in fact the morality of the virtues or the Aristotelian tradition in moral philosophy, and MacIntyre narrates the history of the virtues, carried forward from the time of Homer's *Iliad* by Sophocles, Aristotle, and the New Testament and medieval thinkers. From this history he disentangles 'the complex, historical, multilayered character of the core concept of virtue' (ibid., p. 186). He identifies three stages in the logical development of this core concept, each of which presupposes the earlier stage or stages: 'The first stage requires a background account of what I shall call a practice, the second an account of what I have already characterized as the narrative order of a single human life and the third an account ... of what constitutes a moral tradition' (ibid., pp. 186–7).

MacIntyre grounds his basically Aristotelian moral theory on the conception of a practice:

> By a 'practice' I am going to mean any coherent and complex form of socially established cooperative human activity through which goods internal to that form of activity are realized in the course of trying to achieve those standards of excellence which are appropriate to, and partially definitive of, that form of activity, with the result that human powers to achieve excellence, and human conceptions of the ends and goods involved, are systematically extended. (ibid., p. 187)

Examples he gives of practices are games, arts, sciences, and the creating and sustaining of human communities, such as households, cities or nations. He then defines virtues (partially and tentatively) in terms of practices. A virtue, such as courage, honesty or justice, is 'an acquired human quality the possession and exercise of which tends to enable us to achieve those goods which are internal to practices and the lack of which effectively prevents us from achieving any such goods' (ibid., p. 191). He goes on to supplement his account of a practice with elaborations on the importance of the notion of a *telos* or the good of a whole human life conceived as a unity; and on the concept of a shared tradition, within which the quest for the good life is always undertaken (ibid., pp. 204–25): 'the story of my life is always embedded in the story of those communities from which I derive my identity. I am born with a past; and to try to cut myself off from that past, in the individualist mode, is to deform my present relationships. The possession of a historical identity and the possession of a social identity coincide' (ibid., p. 221).

After analysing the breakdown of the tradition of the virtues, especially at the time of the eighteenth-century Enlightenment, MacIntyre reminds us that when Aristotle praised justice as the first virtue of political life, he did so because a community which lacks practical agreement on a conception of justice must also lack the necessary basis for political community in the first place. But what does that say for our own society, in which any such shared basis is conspicuously lacking? In chapter 17, MacIntyre analyses the competing theories of justice proposed by Rawls and Nozick, theories which capture roughly the deeply held convictions concerning justice espoused respectively by two 'ideal-typical' non-philosophical citizens of the United States named 'A' and 'B', whose arguments faithfully reproduce a good deal of what is actually said in debates about fiscal policy (whether in the United States or any place in Europe). A will vote for the candidates for political office who will defend his justly acquired property, his plans for himself and his family, and *his* conception of justice; while B will vote for the candidates for political office who will defend redistributive taxation, as a means of reducing inequalities in society, and *his* conception of justice. MacIntyre argues not only that the incompatibility of Rawls' and Nozick's accounts genuinely mirrors the incompatibility of A's position with B's, but also that Rawls and Nozick 'reproduce the very same type of incompatibility and incommensurability at the level of philosophical argument that made A's and B's debate unsettlable at the level of social conflict' (ibid., p. 248).

But much more significant than the conflicting conceptions of justice that separate Rawls and Nozick is the fact that they share the social presupposition of individualism: 'It is, from both standpoints, as though we had been shipwrecked on an uninhabited island with a group of other individuals, each of whom is a stranger to me and to all the others. What have to be worked out are rules which will safeguard each one of us maximally in such a situation' (ibid., p. 250). It is precisely this obsessive individualism of the modern *Zeitgeist*, with its concomitant lack of human community, which is the main reason for the political bankruptcy of contemporary ideologies (whether liberalism, conservatism or socialism), and for the failure of any of them to offer a rationally compelling account of social justice; and this is so because 'we still, in spite of the efforts of three centuries of moral philosophy and one of sociology, lack any coherent rationally defensible statement of a liberal individualist point of view' (ibid., p. 259). (Cf. the emphasis on the 'social nature of man' in Macpherson 1985.)

There is, however, one element in the position of both citizen A and citizen B which neither Rawls' nor Nozick's account captures, an element which survives from the older classical tradition in which the virtues were central. Although neither Rawls nor Nozick makes any reference to *desert* in his account of justice, both A and B do make such a reference. Furthermore, 'it seems clear that in the case of the real-life counterparts of A and B it is the reference to desert which makes them feel strongly that what they are complaining about is injustice, rather than some other kind of wrong or harm' (MacIntyre 1984, p. 249). The philosophical deficiency of the theories of Rawls and Nozick is not surprising, since 'their views exclude any account of human community in which the notion of desert in relation to contributions to the common tasks of that community in pursuing shared goods could provide the basis for judgments about virtue and injustice' (ibid., p. 251). And this is precisely why 'modern politics is civil war carried on by other means' (ibid., p. 253). This deficiency can be remedied, however, and its calamitous social consequences mitigated, since 'the Aristotelian tradition can be restated in a way that restores intelligibility and rationality to our moral and social attitudes and commitments' (ibid., p. 259).

The project of providing a systematic account of rationality and of filling out his narrative theory of the virtues (especially the virtue of justice) has been carried forward by MacIntyre (1988). This investigation (devoted in large part to accounts of the theories of practical rationality and justice of Aristotle, Augustine, Aquinas and Hume) shows that there are 'rationalities rather than rationality', and that there are 'justices rather than justice' (MacIntyre 1988, p. 9). (Cf. the 'sociological' theory of justice in Miller 1976, considered in subsection 3.4 above.) But this does not lead MacIntyre to the pessimistic conclusion that our debates about justice are doomed to intellectual chaos: 'from the standpoint of traditions of rational enquiry the problem of diversity is not abolished, but it is transformed in a way that renders it amenable of solution' (MacIntyre 1988, p. 10).[25]

Michael Sandel (1982) argues, along similar lines, that 'the unencumbered self' presupposed by rights-based liberalism cannot adequately account for such indispensable aspects of our moral experience as character, self-knowledge and friendship. The citizens of Rawls' 'deontological republic', for example, are not just egoists but strangers to each other, who are benevolent only on occasion. Whereas, for Rawls, we need justice because we have only 'direct self-knowledge' and cannot *know* each other well enough for even benevolence or love to be effective in human interaction, Sandel insists that we are subjects who are constituted in part by our central aspirations and attachments, always open to growth and transformation in the light of revised self-understandings. Furthermore, our 'constitutive self-understandings' comprehend a wider subject than the individual alone, whether a family or a tribe, a city or a class or a nation. In effect, these constitutive self-understandings define a community. And what marks such a community is not merely a spirit of benevolence, or the prevalence of communitarian values, or even certain 'shared final ends', but a common vocabulary of discourse and a background of implicit practices and understandings within which the opacity of the participants is reduced, if never finally dissolved. Justice depends for its pre-eminence on the cognitive separateness of persons (as is the case with Rawls, for example), but the priority of justice would diminish as that opacity faded and as the sense of community deepened. Justice will be necessary only so long as we cannot know each other, and our ends, well enough to govern by the common good alone.

Michael Walzer (1983) shares with MacIntyre and Sandel the view that meaningful political discourse can only proceed within the common meanings and traditions of a political community and that the participants in that discourse are situated selves rather than unencumbered individuals. The members of the community are in a situation of 'complex equality' with respect to each other. According to Walzer, there are different 'spheres of justice' which ought to be kept distinct in our deliberations about justice. Justice has to do with the distribution of goods which we in a certain significant sense produce or provide in common, and different considerations apply according to the type of social good in question. It is misguided, therefore, to look for one criterion (or even a single set of criteria) which would cover the just distribution of such diverse goods as social security and welfare, money and commodities, offices, work, leisure, education, love, religion and political power. In each of these cases, Walzer reasons from the nature of the good provided and the character of the agents who have combined to effect its provision.

Thus, he argues that the character of universal citizen self-rule which has become central to modern Western democracies renders illegitimate the exercise of the essentially political power which is derived from the ownership of property (Walzer 1983, pp. 281–311). This leads him to condemn the famous Pullman experiment in Illinois in the last twenty years of the nineteenth century, in which everyone who lived in Pullman (Illinois) was an employee, tenant and banking customer of Pullman (George) (ibid., pp. 295–303). It also leads him to favour workers' control of the workplace (ibid., pp. 301–3).

He also argues for certain principles governing the provision of welfare on the basis of the nature of the goods to be distributed and our common understanding of *membership* of a democratic society. 'Membership is important because of what the members of a political community owe to one another and to no one else, or to no one else in the same degree. And the first thing they owe is the communal provision of security and welfare ... Membership (like kinship) is a special relationship' (ibid., p. 64). Welfare is to be provided to the needy in a society not because the needy have some kind of individual rights to welfare but out of recognition of their membership of a particular political community (ibid., p. 78). The principles to be applied to the distribution of welfare are: 'that every political community must attend to the needs of its members as they collectively understand those needs; that the goods that are distributed must be distributed in proportion to need; and that the distribution must recognize and uphold the underlying equality of membership' (ibid., p. 84).

Analogous arguments are advanced for a radical redistribution of hard and dirty work, supported by analyses of a republican version of the *corvée*, the Israeli kibbutz, and the Sunset Scavenger Company, a San Francisco garbage collection cooperative owned by its workers. Again, workers' control of their working practices and their workplace plays an important role. 'We can conscript, rotate, cooperate, and compensate; we can reorganize the work and rectify its names ... The measures that I have proposed are at best partial and incomplete. They have an end appropriate to a negative good: a distribution of hard work that doesn't corrupt the distributive spheres with which it overlaps' (ibid., pp. 173, 183).

Walzer argues that the tendency in contemporary social philosophy to erect a comprehensive and unitary set of principles of justice only serves to reinforce the politically and morally unfortunate practice of increasing cumulatively the inequalities which may arise legitimately in the distribution of particular kinds of good. For example, through the encouragement of the assumption that the good reasons for inequalities in one sphere are also good reasons for inequalities in all spheres, the resultant distributions of wealth, educational opportunity, political power and so on, tend to coalesce around the same individuals, families and groups. This produces the phenomenon of 'dominance', in which some people are at the beck and call of others in all significant areas of life. This dominance is an evil which can be avoided by making the different spheres autonomous so that there will be in each society a variety of distinct inequalities in different spheres; and this state of affairs is what Walzer calls 'complex equality'.

What a larger conception of justice requires is not that citizens rule and are ruled in turn, but that they rule in one sphere and are ruled in another – where 'rule' means not that they exercise power but that they enjoy a greater share than other people of whatever good is being distributed ... But the autonomy of spheres will make for a greater sharing of social goods than will any other conceivable arrangement ... For rule without domination is no affront to our dignity, no denial of our moral or political capacity. Mutual respect and a shared self-respect are the deep strengths of complex equality, and together they are the source of its possible endurance. (ibid., p. 321).[26]

5.3   Strategies of moral epistemology – discourse and neutral conversation

While all the theorizing about principles of justice with which we have thus far been concerned was proceeding, for the most part within the narrow confines of anglophone philosophy, a different kind of debate about the status of moral claims in general, and justice claims in particular, has been going on in Continental philosophy. This particular debate goes back at least to the moral iconoclasm of Nietzsche[27] and the insistence of Dilthey, in the late nineteenth century, that there is an inescapable 'hermeneutical' component in the human sciences, including philosophy: that is, that all our knowledge of human behaviour is a matter of interpretation and historical context rather than universally true 'scientific' knowledge. Carried forward by the work of Martin Heidegger and especially Hans-Georg Gadamer, the influence of this tradition of inquiry can clearly be seen in the 'contextualism' of MacIntyre, Sandel and Walzer presented in the previous subsection and is the background to the present subsection.

The works of MacIntyre, Sandel and Walzer are but recent manifestations of the growing challenge to universalism in moral and political philosophy. While in general this development could be seen as a healthy sign of declining Western ethnocentrism, in the one area of moral philosophy centrally related to politics – the theory of justice – this conceptual shift has been particularly unsettling, because ever since the time of Plato, 'claims of justice have always been the preferred examples of moral claims that are to be recognized by reason, and as founded in the nature of things, as not essentially diverse, and as not contingent upon any specific type of social order' (Hampshire 1982, p. 148). But even Rawls has had to back away from the strong universalist claims of his famous book, more recently conceding that his theory of justice is directly valid only 'within a democratic society under modern conditions' (Rawls 1980, p. 518). The philosophical attempt to overcome this contextualism and develop an adequate framework within which to defend the link between reason and moral judgements has become known in German-language philosophy as the search for a *Letztbegründung* or ultimate foundation of moral discourse. The most sustained example of this enterprise is the work of Jürgen Habermas.

Habermas proposes a universalist position on the rationality of moral claims which tries to accommodate the insights of contextualist critics. He argues that minimal criteria of justice are derivable from his conceptions of 'communicative action' and 'communicative rationality'. According to this view, knowledge of how to test different claims to validity is intuitively available to communicatively competent speakers. In other words, they have an intuitive sense of what the proper guidelines would be for testing claims and coming to a consensus on whether particular claims are warranted or not, guidelines which can themselves be reconstructed in the form of an explicative representation of the propositional contents of the 'unavoidable presuppositions' of argumentation (Habermas 1983, pp. 100–3). For the truthfulness or authenticity claim, the proper test consists of comparing a speaker's expressed intentions with his or her ensuing actions. For *normative* legitimacy, however, the test requires a suspension of normal constraints of action and the initiation of a mode of communication which Habermas calls 'discourse': 'theoretical discourse' for truth claims and 'practical discourse' for legitimacy claims. In discourse, the actors orientate their communication to the sole purpose of coming to a 'rational consensus' on whether or not a specific claim is supportable. This consensus or 'rationally motivated agreement' is arrived at in an 'ideal speech situation', in which the rules of discourse ensure that all other motives of the participants give way when they clash with the motive of cooperatively reaching a consensus (Habermas 1973, pp. 252–60; 1983, pp. 98–9).

The rules of discourse express what Habermas takes to be the normative core of the modern idea of argumentation: viz. the notion of mutual recognition by each participant in the discourse of the other as an autonomous source of (a) claims that have equal initial plausibility and (b) demands for justification that must be addressed. The rules, which are constitutive of the ideal speech situation, are as follows:

1. Each subject who is capable of speech and action is allowed to participate in discourses.
2. (a) Each is allowed to call into question any proposal.
   (b) Each is allowed to introduce any proposal into the discourse.
   (c) Each is allowed to express his attitudes, wishes, needs.
3. No speaker ought to be hindered by compulsion – whether arising from inside the discourse or outside of it – from making use of the rights secure under 1 and 2 (Habermas 1983, p. 99).

The first two rules of discourse are straightforward criteria of fair argumentation. The third rule, however, implies further rules for eliminating the effects of power, deception and ideology. They are intended to prevent barriers to the initiation of discourse and to its being carried through in a manner that allows no subject matter to remain immune from questioning (Habermas 1973, p. 257).

Habermas further proposes two rules that define 'pure communicative action'. The first prevents actors from taking up a discourse with hidden intentions or motives, or in a manner in which the true attitudes, feelings and needs of some would be unlikely to find expression. It requires both a reciprocal openness of actors about their true intentions and motives and an equal chance to express their attitudes, feelings and needs. The latter part of this requirement is designed to ensure especially that 'traditional interpretations of needs' can be called into question (ibid., pp. 251–6). The second rule defining pure communicative action ensures that any theoretical or practical validity claim can be effectively called into question; in other words, that there will be free access to the test of argumentation. This rule requires that there be an equal distribution of opportunities 'to order and resist orders, to permit and forbid, to make and extract promises, and to be responsible for one's conduct and demand that others are as well' (ibid., p. 256). According to Habermas, the application of all these rules of discourse, in an ideal speech situation, provides the only adequate and generally acceptable form of moral enquiry, in which the content of justice will eventually be arrived at.[28]

Bruce Ackerman has produced an analogous (and entertaining) attempt within analytic philosophy to ground a liberal account of social justice on the practice of 'Neutral dialogue'. Neutral dialogue is the basis of a method by which all justice-related disputes can be legitimately settled, so that 'a particular procedure of dispute resolution – here, the process of constrained conversation – can be transformed into a commitment to particular substantive outcomes' (Ackerman 1980, p. 14). (The best discussion of Ackerman's novel approach is to be found in a symposium, Barry *et al.* (eds.) 1983; see also the helpful discussion in Campbell 1988, pp. 99–122.)

5.4 A phenomenological theory of moral discourse – Werner Marx

Finally, in the tradition of post-Heideggerian phenomenology, Werner Marx (1983) conducts a search for an ethics rooted in human experience. Marx offers a sympathetic but critical reading and a 'further development [*Weiterdenken*]' of Heidegger's work on death, language and poetry, in quest of a 'measure' or a standard for distinguishing good from evil and a reason for preferring the former. Marx (1986) continues the quest for what he calls 'a non-metaphysical ethics of human relations' – *eine Nächstenethik*. He shows how the phenomenological interpretation of basic existential experiences offers a way of experiencing the origin of *ethos* in the shared nature of everyday life (*die Lebenswelt*) and of deriving from that experience a measure or a standard of good and evil, justice and injustice. This measure does not make it possible, as in traditional moral philosophy, to postulate an ethic; rather does it testify to the immediate 'givenness' (*Gegebenheit*) of the ethical. We are not called upon, therefore, to adopt or seize hold of this measure; instead we are seized by it and changed by it. The force of this 'given' measure is immediately apparent in our capacity for shared suffering, which can arise out of our shared experience of mortality. The capacity for shared suffering can train the ethos of a person in the virtues of recognition, compassion and charity. But it does not itself work as a traditional virtue, with adherence to it carrying forward the traditional ideal of realization of the highest good. On the contrary, in the capacity for shared suffering itself we have, so long as this shared experience maintains its hold on us, a reliable measure that prompts us to see the furtherance of the good not as the binding goal of all human action but as one of the possible forms of ethical action.

6 Conclusion

Having surveyed this wide range of philosophical material, can any general conclusions be drawn? The dominant impression is of something approaching philosophical pandemonium. When researchers in other disciplines (social psychologists, sociologists, jurists, economists and so on) concerned with issues of justice and injustice approach the philosophers in search of a generally accepted definition and analysis of the object of their study, they are faced with a cacophony of discordant philosophical voices. Probably the most apt term to characterize the dozens of theories here surveyed, when taken together, is 'incommensurability'.[29] My own view is that philosophical theorists of justice must take account of the trenchant critique of their efforts by Alasdair MacIntyre (1984), as a prelude to the elaboration of reasoned principles of social justice which would win the assent of all (or even most) intelligent interlocutors. That process itself presupposes something like the Habermasian project of developing universally accepted rules of 'rational practical discourse'. Ackerman (1980), MacIntyre (1988) and Barry (1989b) have all, from different philosophical perspectives, made contributions to this kind of work. Only through philosophical work along these lines can a minimal level of agreement be reached on the most general principles of social justice. The quest for agreement on the details is probably doomed to everlasting futility.

Notes

1 Cf. Havelock 1978, a detailed and fascinating study of the concept of justice (*diké*) as developed and transmitted in the 'purely oral and poetic' instruction of Greek poets such as Homer, Hesiod and Aeschylus, and culminating in the philosophical analysis of justice (*dikaiosúné*) in the *Republic* of Plato.
2 The common German equivalent of the word 'justice' is, of course, *Gerechtigkeit*, which retains close kinship to *Recht*.
3 The *Philosopher's Index* contains references (at the last count) to almost 3,000 books or articles published in the last twenty years or so that deal with 'justice'. The overwhelming impression left after wading through much of this vast body of work is that a great deal of it is appallingly derivative and repetitive. This chapter is a very selective review of some of the more interesting and/or more influential contributions to the philosophical discussion of justice in that period. The fact that most of the works here reviewed are in the English language is partly due to the limitations of my own familiarity with the material; but it is largely a reflection of the fact that most of the recent philosophical literature on justice has been written and published in the United States of America. Although the very organization of the chapter and the decision to include an item in the review already constitutes, of course, an evaluative intervention by the author, the review will be almost entirely expository rather than critical. For the most part, I have allowed the authors to speak for themselves, although, in the nature of the exercise, I have been unable to do justice to any of them. Before graduating to Rawls 1971, the reader might be better advised to begin with a survey such as Brown 1986, Campbell 1988 or Pettit 1980. For other helpful introductions to the field, see Kamenka and Tay 1979, Miller 1976, Raphael 1990, Sterba 1986, Walzer 1983 and Williams 1985. This is a good point at which to express my general indebtedness to the authors of the texts here cited.

4 Cf. Robert Paul Wolff 1977, a robust book-length critique of Rawls from a Marxist perspective. According to Wolff, Rawls fails to provide an adequate account of social justice because of his ideological conformism with respect to the capitalist economic structure: 'Rawls' failure grows naturally and inevitably out of his uncritical acceptance of the socio-political presuppositions and associated modes of analysis of classical and neo-classical liberal political economy' (Wolff 1977, p. 210). Cf. Miller 1974, another critique of Rawls from a Marxist standpoint. DeMarco 1980, on the other hand, argues for a synthesis of Rawls and Marx. On Marx, Marxists and justice, see section 4.

5 This, of course, is precisely what commentators such as Barry and Wolff have found unacceptable about the difference principle. See Barry 1973, p. 50; and Wolff 1977, pp. 196–201.

6 These defiant words notwithstanding, utilitarian accounts of justice have not fared well post-Rawls; indeed, they have been few and far between. One of the exceptions is the re-examination of J.S. Mill's account of justice by David Lyons (1978) – an attempt, perhaps, to gain inspiration from one of the founding fathers of utilitarianism.

7 For Rawls' reply, see Rawls 1982b. Wojciech Sadurski (1985b) also examines critically Rawls' commitment to the primacy of liberty over utility.

8 For a sympathetic assessment of the method of reflective equilibrium in moral reasoning, see Nielsen 1985, pp. 24-38. For further consideration of the question of methodology in moral reasoning, see section 5 below. Rawls, meanwhile, has continued indefatigably, since the publication of *A Theory of Justice*, to develop and sharpen its arguments, often in the context of replying to his critics. See, for example, Rawls 1978; 1980; 1982a; 1982b; 1985; 1987. Many hundreds of articles have been written on Rawls: the standard bibliography (Wellbank *et al.* 1982) lists (already by late 1981) 2,512 secondary sources! Some of the better articles are anthologized in Daniels 1975b and Blocker and Smith 1980. Rawls' theory of distributive justice has also attracted the attention of many economic theorists. For a review of this literature, see chapter 3 on 'The economics of justice, welfare and freedom' by Erik Schokkaert, in this volume.

9 Kolm's depiction of his theory of justice in accordance with the liberal social contract is partly philosophical, partly visionary, and partly a matter of economic theory. For a fuller account and assessment, see the discussion of Kolm's theories in chapter 3 of this volume, by Erik Schokkaert. For a fuller exposition of his theory of a 'general reciprocity' within 'a good society', see Kolm 1984. See also Kolm 1972; 1987. On 'justice as reciprocity', cf. Barry 1979.

10 Cf. Gauthier 1986. For a survey of recent work on bargaining and compromise, see Luban 1985, in which he draws attention to what he calls 'the paradox of compromise': 'we see intrinsic moral value in agreement with our fellows: thus the contractarian insight that moral principles are the product of bargaining. On the other hand, we think that moral principles should be justified – and it is an odd theory of moral justification that admits propositions no one will ever be prepared to believe' (Luban 1985, p. 416).

11 The second volume will consist of an even more detailed account and a defence of justice as impartiality, with a look at some of its implications for the distribution of benefits and burdens in a given society. The final volume

62   *Bernard Cullen*

will focus on the implications of the theory for economic institutions, both within states and between them. Since the appearance of his first book-length critique of Rawls (Barry 1973), Barry has been producing a steady stream of articles on justice. On our obligations of justice towards future generations (for example, with respect to the physical environment), see Barry 1977; 1978. On justice in the global economy, see Barry 1982, which concludes that 'the need for humanitarian aid would be reduced in a world that had a basically just international distribution' (p. 250). Most of these articles have now been collected in Barry 1989a. On the application of a *global* difference principle, according to which income should be redistributed internationally so that the worst-off individual in the world is as well off as possible, cf. Beitz 1975.

12 The notion of rights that must be respected plays an important role in many theories of justice (often implicitly), not just the two theories on which I focus here. See also, for example, Finnis 1980 (and subsection 5.1) and Gauthier 1986 (and subsection 2.3 above). Even this small sample of 'rights' theorists demonstrates that 'rights-based' theories of justice can produce amazingly different political principles and social policies.

13 For a collection of articles on Nozick 1974, see Paul 1981: Part IV contains six articles under the heading 'Social justice: entitlement theory versus distributivism'. See also Barry 1975; and Cohen 1985, who, like MacIntyre, focuses his effective critical attentions on Nozick's theory of the original appropriation of private property; and O'Neill 1976, who shows that even if we begin (as Nozick does) with a Lockean-type account of natural rights, it by no means follows that we are then committed to *laissez-faire* capitalism, full capitalist property rights and Nozick's entitlement theory of justice. For an extended critical examination of what he terms the 'arch anti-egalitarian social philosophy' of Nozick, see Nielsen 1985, Part IV, pp. 191–277.

14 For Rawls' discussion of the distinction between teleological and deontological theories, see Rawls 1971, pp. 24–5, 30, 565–6.

15 For a critical assessment of Dworkin's theory, see Campbell 1988, pp. 45–65. Dworkin insists that justice also demands reverse discrimination or affirmative action (in employment, and so on) to rectify past injustices. A sizeable literature has grown up on this subject, which is often referred to as 'compensatory justice'. See Dworkin 1977a, pp. 223–39; and, for a British view, Raphael 1980, pp. 130–56. Alan Goldman, using a contractarian 'moral framework', argues that 'strong reverse discrimination' is justified for *individuals* who have been unjustly denied positions in the past (Goldman 1979, p. 230). The latter contains a good bibliography on the topic.

16 Nielsen 1985 further elaborates and defends his conception of 'radical egalitarian justice'. For other egalitarian conceptions of justice, see Ake 1975 and Richards 1982. For the view that it is utterly wrong-headed to use the principle of equality in assessing justice, see Stone 1979.

17 For a similar conception of justice as equilibrium, see Broekman 1986. For a sympathetic account of Sadurski 1985a, see Campbell 1988, pp. 150–78. Campbell, incidentally, has managed to write an excellent introduction to several of the more prominent theories of justice, without making any great attempt to hide (a) his own preference for what he calls a 'meritorian' theory

of justice, and (b) his conviction that in the order of human or social goods justice must often be considered less important than other goods, such as 'common humanity, or even generous beneficence' (Campbell 1988, p. 35; cf. Lucas 1980, p. 263). For an Aristotelian account of justice, in which the notion of desert is central, see MacIntyre 1984; 1988. On justice and desert, see also Kleinig 1971; Sterba 1976; Garcia 1986. Finally, the issue of just remuneration (that is, how much do people 'deserve' to be paid?) has continued to be hotly debated. An excellent recent analysis is in Barry 1989b, pp. 393–400 ('Economic motivation in a Rawlsian society'), which also presents a defence of Rawls' difference principle, 'if one accepts the premise that inequality is at best a necessary evil' (ibid., p. 234).

18 Cf. Raphael 1980, pp. 33–56 for a persuasive account of the tension between justice and liberty, and how they might fruitfully be reconciled. See also the equally persuasive account in MacCormick 1982.

19 See also Lucas' chapter 9, on justice and equality, pp. 171–84. Cf. subsection 3.2. For a description of a just society embodying a 'complex' egalitarianism consistent with liberty, see Walzer 1983.

20 For more on the importance for Raphael's conception of justice of the Kantian principle that we should treat all human beings as ends-in-themselves, see Raphael 1980, pp. 85–6, 97–8. For his *obiter dictum* that Rawls' self-proclaimed 'highly Kantian' theory of justice 'would indeed be a *sounder* theory, in my opinion, if it deviated less from Kant', see ibid., p. 104. For a defence of the legitimacy of Rawls' 'attempt to claim a Kantian pedigree' for his theory of justice as fairness, see Darwall 1980. On Kant's categorical imperative as a criterion for the justice of actions, see Schnoor 1989. For a critical discussion of Kant, respect for persons and injustice, see Seidler 1986.

21 Jon Elster (1985) shares Cohen's view that in both the theory of exploitation in *Capital* and in the theory of distribution in the *Critique of the Gotha Programme* Marx was using principles of justice but went out of his way to deny it. Elster suggests that the best way of making sense of this is by imputing to Marx a hierarchical theory of justice, in which the desert or contribution principle ('to each according to his contribution') provides a second-best criterion when the needs principle ('from each according to his ability, to each according to his needs') is 'not yet historically ripe for application'.

22 The challenge of developing a 'socialist' theory of the just society (although he rarely mentions Marx by name) has been vigorously taken up by Kai Nielsen: for him, the just socialist society would be one which enshrines his 'radical egalitarian' theory of justice. See Nielsen 1979; 1982; 1985 and section 3.2. Cf. James Daly (1988), who counterposes to 'the undialectical thought (and practice) of ancient Sophism and modern Enlightenment' not only the natural law tradition of classical and medieval dialectics, but also the thought of Marx, 'whose dialectic has close affinities with theirs' (Daly 1988, p. 73). Daly argues that the culmination of Marx's dialectics is community and love, and that justice is compatible only with a genuine communism. For a survey of some recent defences of 'socialist justice', see Sterba 1986, pp. 10–15. Cf. Wolff 1977 for a Marxist critique of Rawls 1971 that owes more to the interpretation of Wood than that of Husami and Cohen. Cf. DeMarco 1980,

who argues for a synthesis of the basic insights of Rawls and of Marx. See also the concluding chapter of Campbell 1988, 'Marx and the socialist critique of justice', pp. 179–204.

23 For the development of natural law theory from Cicero to Aquinas, see Weinreb 1987, pp. 43–66. It has often been noted that natural law theory seems to correspond quite closely to the everyday conceptions of the law held by non-theorizing members of the public, especially in their tendency not to obey 'bad' laws, if they can get away with it. In the United States, for example, the Supreme Court is widely seen as (and often acts as if it were) the natural law incarnate. As Raphael has put it, 'in our own generation at least, the Supreme Court may justly be called the conscience of the nation . . . the mouthpiece of Natural Justice' (Raphael 1980, p. 130).

24 Cf. Rawls' discussion of 'a rational plan of life' (Rawls 1971, pp. 407–24).

25 For an account of distributive justice similarly inspired by 'the Aristotelian meta-view' that the principles of distributive justice are 'related to some notion of the good which is sustained or realized or sought in the association concerned', an account which similarly rejects what he calls 'the atomism of Locke', see Taylor 1985. Justice, for Taylor, consists in 'giving appropriate weight' to 'the principle of equal sharing' and 'the contribution principle' (p. 313).

26 For critiques of Walzer's concepts of 'complex equality' and 'spheres of justice', see Steiner 1985 and Dworkin 1985a, who dismisses the idea of complex equality as incoherent and concludes that 'we cannot leave justice to convention and anecdote'.

27 For his account of Nietzsche's 'historic achievement' of understanding 'more clearly than any other philosopher' that 'what purported to be appeals to objectivity were in fact expressions of subjective will', see MacIntyre 1984, pp. 113–20.

28 This outline barely scratches the surface of a complex and finely elaborated theory. For a sympathetic account of Habermas' consensus theory of truth and justice, see Alexy 1989, pp. 101–37. For a critical assessment of Habermas, see Pettit 1982. Habermas' theory of rational discourse is reminiscent of Chaïm Perelman's influential 'theory of argumentation'. On the many parallels between them, see Haarscher (1986), in an issue of the journal *Law and Philosophy* (pp. 279–391) devoted to the work of Perelman. For Perelman's approach to justice, see Perelman 1978; on Perelman, see also Raphael 1980, pp. 90–101; and Alexy 1989, pp. 155–73. Robert Alexy builds on the accounts of Habermas and Perelman to develop his own theory of 'general rational practical discourse' (ibid., pp. 177–208). For an 'analytico-dialectical' account of the character of deliberations about justice – an alternative but comparable project to that of Habermas – see Weinberger 1981; 1985.

29 It should further be noted, in this regard, that the present survey has considered theories of justice almost exclusively within a fairly narrow Western democratic tradition. There has been no mention at all of justice claims from outside that tradition, such as the claim, according to a recent version of Islamic justice, that it is right and just to execute Salman Rushdie for having written and published a text disrespectful of Muhammad.

3   The economics of distributive justice, welfare and freedom

Erik Schokkaert

1   Introduction

Economics and justice seem to have a somewhat ambiguous relationship. A majority of economists (according to official doctrine at least) consider the problem of justice to be outside their discipline: in their view, economics is about efficiency and solely about efficiency. But at the same time the number of economic writings about justice is so large and their content so disparate that it is quite impossible to give a complete overview within one paper. The paradox reflects the lack of consensus among economists and, also, the ambiguity of the discipline with respect to the problem. For an outsider, this ambiguity must be very puzzling. Sometimes it is even difficult to explain the rationale behind the economic jargon: e.g., why the theory of 'social choice' is normative and mostly attracts people who care about a just distribution of welfare, while 'public choice' is about the actual working of government and often (but not always) has a 'conservative' flavour. This chapter undoubtedly will reflect this ambiguity.

'Justice' also is an important topic for other social science disciplines and for philosophy. It is fair to say that there has been very little contact concerning this problem between economists and other (empirical) social scientists.[1] The economic tradition being rather deductive and theoretical, there has been more cross-fertilization between economics and social philosophy. The books of Rawls (1971) and Nozick (1974), for example, are clearly influenced by economic thinking, and at the same time have had a strong impact on economic work. I will not develop these links but mainly restrict myself to the *economic* approaches *sensu stricto*. Moreover I will concentrate on mainstream academic economics, and neglect, for example, Marxist and Austrian theories (for a classical example of the latter, see Hayek 1976). This restricted focus can be explained by limitations of space and knowledge and should not be interpreted as the reflection of a negative judgement about the importance of these theories. At least, there is an ideological equilibrium in the omissions.

The concept of justice has many aspects. In line with the economic tradition, this paper will focus on *distributive* justice: it is obvious that other (e.g., corrective) justice concepts are less relevant for economists.

The distribution problem is important at different social levels: the family, the firm, the nation. Economists have mostly been interested in *macrosocial* problems and this will also be the line of approach in this paper. It is worth mentioning, however, that game theory has recently yielded some valuable insights into problems of microsocial distributive justice, such as the division of a surplus in a cooperative firm (see Moulin 1987).

Even restricted to concepts of distributive justice at the macrosocial level and discussed within the mainstream of economic science, the field is very broad and disparate. Distributive justice is often interpreted in terms of equality. In this review, we will work within a broader framework: the basic tensions between equality, efficiency and freedom. In section 1.1 we bring together some introductory remarks on the notion of equality. In section 1.2 we will argue that the idea of the market permeates economic science and that the economic approach to equality, efficiency and freedom can only be understood when projected against this historical background. Finally, section 1.3 gives a general overview of the structure of the chapter.

1.1   *The notion of equality*

The notion of equality can be useful for the construction of a theory of justice only if one specifies exactly *what* is to be equalized. The most common 'practical' interpretation of the concept refers to economic justice as equality with respect to the distribution of income. It is obvious, however, that in a broader philosophical perspective the degree of 'equality' of the income distribution is not an adequate criterion of economic justice: one cannot disregard interindividual differences in needs and in effort as ethically acceptable reasons for income differences. Welfare economic theories of justice usually are not concerned with the distribution of monetary incomes. The economic tradition focuses on the utility (or welfare) levels of the individuals. Traditionally, economics is about the market, and in the economic theory of the market individual choice and utility play a dominant role. As we will see, it can be argued that the economic concentration on utility also leads to an inadequate interpretation of justice. Many other interpretations of justice in terms of equality are possible: 'equality' as such is an empty concept.

Moreover, it is difficult to maintain that 'more equality' (however defined) can be the only social objective. Surely, most people will easily accept some inequality if this could lead to a smaller number of people starving to death. Economists have devoted much attention to the incentive problems which arise if society does not respect the 'free' decisions of individuals. To give a well-known example: the imposition of a progressive income tax may lead to a lower labour supply and, hence, a lower output level. *If* there are in economic reality such trade-offs between

Table **3.1.**

Division	A	B	C	Individuals D	E	F	G
I	4	4	4	4	4	4	4
II	1	2	3	4	5	6	7
III	1	2	3.5	4.5	4.5	5.5	7
IV	1.5	2.5	3	4	5	5.5	6.5
V	1	3	3	3	5	5	5
VI	1	1	1	1	1	1	22

different objectives, these trade-offs also become relevant from an ethical point of view. Indeed, a complete theory of justice will have to give some indication about the ethical trade-off between 'equality' and other objectives. (Positive) economic theory tries to estimate how large the 'efficiency' loss will be, when society aims at more equality. Economic theories of justice will have to specify how much efficiency one *wants* to give up for more equality (from an ethical point of view). Most of the theories sketched in this review will indeed formulate a social objective function, with a broader concern than for equality alone.

Finally, there are some problems with the measurement of 'equality'. What is an 'equal' distribution usually is clear enough: but how to rank 'unequal' distributions with respect to their 'degree of inequality'? Table 3.1 shows some possible divisions of a fixed sum of 28 over 7 individuals (A to G). The first division is 'equal'. But it is far from obvious what is the most 'unequal' distribution and, in general, how to determine the 'degree of equality' of the other distributions. Any ranking in terms of equality obviously will imply normative considerations with respect to the weights attached to different income levels.

We cannot go deeply into the huge theoretical literature which has been produced on this subject by economists (e.g., Atkinson 1970; Kolm 1969; Sen 1973). This is not a purely theoretical discussion, however, because some of the confusion in the political debate on income distribution may be caused by the (mostly implicit) use of different inequality measures by different participants. In this respect, Kolm (1976) notes that the best-known measures imply that an equiproportional increase in all incomes leaves inequality unchanged. He calls this a 'rightist' assumption and he presents an alternative 'leftist' measure, in which equal absolute increases in incomes leave inequality unchanged. This distinction seems to be particularly relevant to understanding everyday political and economic discussions.

1.2   The market paradigm: welfare, efficiency and freedom

The elements of 'maximal welfare' (efficiency) and 'maximal freedom' are both present in the traditional economic eulogy of the market. In the first place, there is the well-known idea of the invisible hand, through which the market system coordinates the individual decisions. This coordination mechanism then leads to a maximum amount of social welfare. Social welfare and individual utility by themselves are difficult concepts, to which we will have to return later on. The main point to be made now is that in this view the market is supported because its *results* in terms of *welfare* are good. The second aspect of the market refers to the value of freedom. In the process of exchange, all participants are free and nobody is forced by others to perform certain actions. Many people tend to argue that such a freedom in itself is a basic value and that the respect for property rights and the freedom to exchange are essential features of any morally acceptable economic system.

In popular discussions of the market mechanism the aspects of efficiency, welfare and freedom all come to the fore, often without any explanation of their interrelationship. However, problems and conflicts appear as soon as one wants to give a more concrete content to the concept of social welfare.

The early economic treatment of social welfare was dominated by utilitarianism. In this approach individual utility is assumed to be cardinally measurable[2] and interpersonally comparable: social welfare can then be defined as the sum of the different individual utilities. It soon became clear that applying the utilitarian criterion in some cases could lead to strongly egalitarian conclusions. If individual utility functions are the same (and characterized by diminishing marginal utility of income), the utilitarian will have to divide equally a fixed amount of money.[3] When applied to income taxation, this leads to a very progressive system and, hence, to a sharp conflict with the idea of freedom and property rights.

The conflict remains with the modern interpretations of social welfare, which have become dominant since the beginning of this century: these interpretations can be characterized as 'ordinal' and 'Paretian'.[4] The first adjective points to the rejection of cardinalism. At the end of the nineteenth century it was realized that the cardinal measurement of consumer utility was not realistic and, moreover, not necessary to explain consumer choice. It is sufficient for the consumer that he can *rank* the consumption bundles according to his preferences. This assumption has been called 'ordinalism' in economic jargon. Later on (the best known advocate being Robbins (1938)) it became almost universally accepted that the comparison of individual utility levels between individuals cannot be a purely descriptive exercise, but necessarily involves normative presuppositions. Such normative concepts were deemed to be outside the scope of economic science.

But what content could be given to the concept of 'social welfare' after the rejection of utilitarianism? A first answer was the introduction of the concept of Pareto-efficiency.[5] A social state x is said to be Pareto-superior to a social state *y* if no individual is worse off in *x* and at least one individual is better off in *x* than in *y*. A move from *y* to *x* is then called a Pareto-improvement. Of course, technological and natural constraints limit the number of social states that can be reached. Social states that can be reached are called *feasible* in the economic jargon. A social state *x* in the feasible set is called *Pareto-optimal* if there is no other state in the feasible set, which is Pareto-superior to *x*. This means that a social state is Pareto-optimal if no change can be made which makes someone better off without at the same time making someone else worse off.

Using these definitions, the traditional economic eulogy of the market then takes the particularly simple and transparent form of the *first basic theorem of welfare economics*: under certain conditions (including perfect competition and perfect information), every competitive (market) equilibrium is a Pareto-optimum. The social relevancy of this theorem is extremely limited by the restrictiveness of the conditions under which it holds, but a complete treatment of this topic is far beyond the scope of this paper. However, for our purposes it is important to comment on the limitations of the concept of Pareto-optimality.

At first sight, this criterion is most attractive, because it rests on such easily acceptable ethical foundations. It is difficult to see how anybody could object to Pareto-improvements, since no one is made worse off by the change. One could therefore expect such Pareto-improvements to be unanimously accepted. Once we take Pareto-optimality to be the definition of maximal social welfare, the possible conflict between welfare maximization and freedom therefore seems to disappear. The congruency between the concepts of welfare and freedom also seems to hold at the individual level. In this traditional welfare economic approach the standards to measure someone's individual welfare are his own preferences, i.e. the preferences which guide his own behaviour. The concept of consumer sovereignty is fully accepted and each economic agent is considered to be the best judge of his own interest.

And yet there are problems when we want to identify a Pareto-optimal situation with a maximum of social welfare. Unlike utilitarianism, the concept of Pareto-efficiency does not contain any reference to equality. This implies that not all Pareto-optimal states are desirable from the point of view of almost any definition of economic justice: some Pareto-'optima' may really be horrible. The Pareto-criterion is completely unconcerned about the *distribution* of utility and it is impossible to justify on its basis any redistribution of utility. Indeed, even a redistribution from A, who is very wealthy, to B, who is starving, will make A worse off,[6] and therefore cannot be a Pareto-improvement. Exclusive application of the Pareto-criterion therefore necessarily will lead to the defence of the status quo.

Welfare economics has proved a *second basic theorem*, however. This theorem states that *every* Pareto-optimal point can be attained by means of a decentralized market mechanism if lump sum transfers and taxes may be carried out costlessly. Again, there are problems with the conditions under which the theorem holds. But for our purposes, three ethical questions are more important.

The first is fairly obvious: how to choose between the different Pareto-optimal points? For this purpose, the welfare economic approach introduced the concept of a Bergson-Samuelson[7] social welfare function. In its most general form, this function represents an (ethical or social) *ordering* of the social states and, therefore, it allows us to choose the 'most preferred' point among all Pareto-optimal points. Some economists have claimed that thinking about the form and content of this function was not part of their discipline. During the last decades, however, and mainly as a reaction to Arrow's famous impossibility theorem (1951), one has witnessed the growth of a huge literature discussing the specification and the informational content of various social welfare functions. This has even led to a remarkable revival of utilitarianism. We will return to these discussions in section 2.

There is a second problem, however, and this refers to the 'if' in our formulation of the second basic theorem. We do not dispose of lump sum taxes which could bring us to the 'just' social state. We will therefore have to face the incentive problem, mentioned in section 1.1. Redistributive taxation will lead us away from the (so-called first best) Pareto-frontier and there will be a conflict between equality and efficiency. Moreover, using taxes to redistribute utility is in flagrant contradiction with the value of freedom and the inviolability of property rights. Libertarian[8] thinkers, therefore, will not accept that instrument. As Sen (1985b) argues: 'If the real case for the market mechanism is dependent on a major revolution in the distribution of resource ownership, then the case for laissez-faire and for using the allegedly "non-political" route of the market mechanism is thoroughly undermined. The "converse (second) theorem" belongs to the "revolutionist's handbook".'

The third question points to an even more basic conflict between the traditional welfare economic approaches and the value of freedom. Until now, we have reasoned within a framework that accepted the Pareto-criterion as a necessary, albeit not sufficient, condition of economic justice. In a rightly famous paper, Sen (1970a) has shown that even on a purely abstract level, this ('unanimity') condition can come in conflict with almost generally accepted libertarian values. He denominates this paradox 'the impossibility of a Paretian libertarian'.[9] This paradox has been one of the starting points for the discussion on the limitations of a concept of justice, that relies solely on the distribution of *welfare*.

1.3   Structure of the chapter

The structure of this review follows from the preceding sketch of the market paradigm and of its problems. In section 2 we will give an overview of the economic literature on social welfare functions. After a (concise) treatment of Arrow's impossibility theorem (section 2.1), we will first discuss the so-called 'equity' – or 'fairness' – theories, that try to find an interpretation of justice in welfare terms without accepting interpersonal comparability of welfare levels (section 2.2). We then turn to the specification of social welfare functions in terms of interpersonally comparable individual welfare levels (section 2.3). Basically, this section 2 gives an overview of the mainstream economic literature on justice.

In recent years, the limitations of this mainstream approach have been discussed extensively. In section 3.1 we argue that a welfaristic approach, i.e., the specification of justice in terms of individual welfare levels, indeed is inadequate. It is not easy to interpret the concept of individual welfare and this concept does not sufficiently capture the idea of human rights. In section 3.2 it is shown how biased has been the (welfaristic) economic interpretation of the work of Rawls: this influential work is then used as a starting point for an overview of some alternative theories.

Traditional welfare economics has concentrated on the trade-off between efficiency and equality. There have always been economists, however, who emphasized freedom and the basic autonomy of the individual in their ethical theory. The criticism on welfarism leads us immediately to some recent examples of this libertarian point of view (section 4). These theories of course will have to face the problem that the 'free' market mechanism may lead to a very unequal distribution of welfare. Another problem is the legitimacy of the initial appropriation of natural resources, which is a necessary presupposition to accept the legitimacy of the existing set of property rights.

In a certain sense, libertarianism can be seen as an extreme alternative to mainstream welfarism, because it concentrates exclusively on rights and on the unacceptability of coercion. Some coercion is accepted by social contract theories. In section 5 we present the ideas of two economic proponents of such a social contract approach: James Buchanan and Serge-Christophe Kolm. In section 5.1 we introduce public choice theory in relation to Buchanan; in section 5.2 we combine our discussion of Kolm's work with an overview of the theory of voluntary redistribution.

The basic idea of social contract theories is the need for unanimous consent by all participants. It can be argued that a conception of justice, based on unanimity, does not go far enough into the direction of equality. In recent years, economic theories have been formulated that are *not* welfaristic. They take into account human rights, but do not go as far as libertarianism. Nor do the authors of these theories necessarily subject their scheme to a test of unanimous approval. In section 6 we discuss two examples of this point of view. Dworkin's idea of 'equality of resources' is summarized in section 6.1 and Sen's proposal to treat 'rights as goals' in section 6.2.

Some concluding remarks are presented in section 7. Of course, any review of such a broad field must necessarily be subjective and incomplete. Given the thematic structure of the chapter, it may be difficult for the non-economist to follow the chronological development of economic thinking. Another basic problem is the degree of (mathematical) sophistication of many economic theories. In this review we have avoided mathematical derivations completely. Yet it is not always easy to summarize a theorem in plain language. It therefore is possible that this review will be messy and unrigorous for the mathematically trained reader, and at the same time difficult and abstract for the mathematical (and economic) layman.

2   Welfaristic theories

Given the historical background sketched in the previous section, it is understandable why economic theories of justice have mainly focused on the question of choosing the 'just' social state among all Pareto-efficient states. During the thirties and forties this problem was 'solved' by assuming the existence of a so-called Bergson-Samuelson social welfare function, based on non-comparable ordinal utilities. In section 2.1 we will briefly comment on this approach and indicate how Arrow's impossibility theorem has shown that it cannot work. In section 2.2 we will introduce a 'recent' alternative: the theory of equity or fairness. This theory has some limitations from an ethical point of view. We therefore turn in section 2.3 to richer theories: theories such as utilitarianism and maximin can be integrated into the economic framework by broadening the informational base of the social welfare functions.

2.1   *Bergson-Samuelson social welfare functions and Arrow's impossibility theorem*[10]

The basic idea of a Bergson-Samuelson social welfare function is simple enough. It represents an *ethical* ordering of all social states, indicating what social state is preferable from a moral point of view. As such, of course, it is a quite general concept. From the very beginning, however, 'New Welfare Economists' worked with a restricted version of this general function. The restrictions imposed followed immediately from the market paradigm, as sketched in section 1.2. Social states were judged on the basis of their evaluation by consumers. Accepting consumer sovereignty, these evaluations were represented by the utility functions of these consumers, i.e., by the representation of their own personal preferences, as revealed in their choice behaviour. These utility functions were ordinal (representing a ranking only, without the possibility to attach a meaning to the concrete utility numbers) and the utility numbers could not be compared among individuals. Finally, the social welfare function also satisfied the Pareto-criterion, in that it was an increasing function of the individual utilities. Many welfare economists considered these assumptions as non-controversial and as sufficient to solve the main problem of their discipline, which was the formulation of the necessary conditions to reach the Pareto-frontier. It then would be the task of moral philosophers or of politicians to give a more concrete content, i.e., a more detailed specification to these welfare functions. This, however, was not the province of the economist *as* economist.[11]

This happy world of welfare economics has been brutally destroyed by the famous impossibility theorem of Arrow (1951, revised 1963). This theorem states that, given a condition of universal domain (which requires the social welfare function to be defined for *all* possible individual utility functions), a social welfare function, based on the information described earlier (ordinal utility functions, which are not comparable between individuals), would not satisfy some mild 'rationality' (transitivity) and non-dictatorship conditions.[12] The latter condition basically excludes the situation where the social welfare function would coincide with the utility function of one individual (the 'dictator'). The impossibility theorem certainly has been one of the most influential discoveries in economic science, and in fact lies at the origin of a new economic discipline: the theory of 'social choice'. It cannot be our intention to review critically this huge literature, but we will indicate how it has opened up the field of welfare economics for influences from moral philosophy.[13]

There are many possible ways to escape from the Arrow problem. The first is to relax the rationality conditions imposed on the social welfare function. Obvious possibilities are the relaxation of the transitivity condition or of the condition of universal domain. The former solution seems not very attractive from an ethical point of view (e.g., Sen 1982b). Relaxation of universal domain is more defensible (e.g., Kolm 1969): at any moment of time there is only *one* set of individual preference orderings and it can be argued that it is only necessary to rank the alternatives for this given set of individual preference orderings. Moreover, it is perhaps sufficient for an ethical theory to define the best alternative only, without caring about the ranking of the other social states. In section 2.2 we will comment on theories of 'equity' or 'fairness', which basically follow that route.

A second (and more promising) way to escape from Arrow's impossibility theorem is the broadening of the informational base of the social welfare function. As described earlier this informational base is restricted in two respects: social welfare is derived from individual preferences (and only from such preferences), and these individual preferences are considered to be ordinal and not interpersonally comparable. The first restriction has been christened 'welfarism' and implies that all non-utility characteristics of social states are irrelevant for the ethical ranking of these states. We return to the limitations of welfarism in section 3. The second restriction moreover implies that the information on individual utilities themselves also is extremely limited. In section 2.3 we will argue that the removal of this restriction considerably broadens the scope of welfare economics and opens up the field for moral philosophical argumentation.

2.2   Theories of equity or fairness[14]

In section 1.2, we tried to show that the original intuition of an ideal market system, characterized by free exchange and leading at the same time to a maximum of social welfare, is too optimistic. Yet much of economic theory starts from this original intuition, mainly because of the market's appeal as a form of economic organization. This certainly is the case for the most economic of all economic theories of justice: the theory of equity or fairness. This theory keeps to Pareto-efficiency as a necessary characteristic of optimal social states, but it wants to offer a criterion to choose between the different Pareto-efficient states. However, it does not aim at a complete ordering of all social states, and therefore is less ambitious than the traditional social welfare function approach. This makes it possible to avoid the Arrow impossibility theorem, without enlarging the informational basis. Equity theory does not require cardinality and/or interpersonal comparability of utility and starts from the preferences of economic agents, as these are revealed in their choice behaviour.

The approach chosen to define the desired point was already proposed by Tinbergen in 1953, in a book written in Dutch. It has been made well known in the economic literature by Foley (1967), and since then there has been a rapidly growing number of publications investigating the possibilities and limitations of the concept (see the overview of this literature by Thomson and Varian 1985). The basic idea is to define a *fair* situation as a situation *without envy*, where envy is defined as follows: individual 1 envies individual 2 at a given allocation if he prefers the bundle of *commodities* received by 2 under this allocation over his own bundle. Note that in this definition people envy each other's consumption bundle, and *not* each other's utility level. This latter form of envy is considered to be ethically unacceptable. The no-envy criterion therefore does not involve interpersonal comparisons of utility. Every individual compares the different consumption bundles according to his *own* preferences. In fact, there is no room for envy when everybody gets an identical bundle of commodities, but at the same time there may be huge differences in utility levels (provided one accepts that such differences can sensibly be defined). As we will argue at the end of this section, this is both a strong and a weak point of the criterion.

Another important feature immediately follows from the previous one. In the case of pure distribution,[15] 'fair' allocations always exist: simply give everybody the same bundle of commodities. However, economists want to find a social state which is not only fair, but at the same time also Pareto-optimal. The point of equal distribution probably is not Pareto-optimal if the tastes of the different consumers are different. And here the market procedure enters the picture. One can prove (always still for the problem of pure distribution) that we reach an allocation which is both fair and Pareto-efficient by, first, making an equal division of the total bundle of commodities and next, letting the economic agents exchange parts of their bundle, i.e., trade to a market equilibrium using a perfect price system. This is an attractive result: we can keep to the market procedure (with all its efficiency and 'freedom' advantages), and at the same time we define clearly the starting position, which will lead us to the point of no-envy on the Pareto-frontier.

The problem of pure distribution is only a special case, however. The real problem of distributive justice appears as soon as different economic agents make different contributions to production, because their innate abilities and efforts differ. The consumption bundle of an individual then not only contains goods, but also his labour contribution. It has been shown that fair and at the same time Pareto-efficient allocations in that case do not always exist. Other 'fairness'-concepts have therefore been proposed.

Varian (1974) suggested the concept of 'wealth-fairness': this is the situation where no economic agent prefers the consumption–output bundle of any other agent over his own consumption–output bundle. He can only 'envy' another agent if he is willing to produce the same output: of course, if he is less able, this will cost him more time and/or effort. Wealth-fair and efficient allocations exist and one can follow a procedure which is analogous to the one sketched before: divide equally the initial total of goods (excluding labour) and let individuals trade to a market equilibrium. It is intuitively clear that this concept of fairness does not correct at all for the initial (unequal) distribution of abilities. One might therefore have doubts about its ethical appeal.

Varian (1974) also discusses another fairness concept, which was originally proposed by Pazner and Schmeidler (1978, but circulated earlier as a discussion paper): he calls it 'income-fairness'. The easiest way to explain the content of this concept is by sketching immediately the procedure, which will lead to an income-fair allocation. Varian (1975, p.

152) does this as follows: 'We give each agent an equal division of all goods and an equal share of *each* other agent's labour. This could be done by giving everyone a ticket that would give him complete control over, say, one hour of every other person's time during some period. Given this intial endowment, the agents trade to a market equilibrium.' This solution therefore fully corrects for differences in innate abilities and, in a certain sense, leads to the enslavement of the able by the unable.

It is obvious that the concepts of wealth-fairness and income-fairness both are rather extreme solutions to the problem of differences in innate abilities. There have been other proposals, which lie somewhere between these two extremes, but none of them is entirely satisfactory. An innovative approach to the problem has recently been formulated by the philosopher Dworkin: we will discuss this approach in section 6.1.

The theory of fairness and no-envy is a rather technical one, and largely unknown to non-economists. It must be situated firmly in the welfare economic tradition, as sketched in the previous section. That probably is the reason for its popularity among economists.[16] As a theory of justice, however, this approach has considerable weaknesses. When the market process does not work perfectly (and in reality, it never does) the proposed procedures will not lead to the desired allocation. This is especially discomforting here, because the theory of fairness does not show us how to rank the non-ideal situations. Equity theory therefore is not a practical approach to the global problem of distributive justice, although interesting partial applications have been suggested by Baumol (1986).

From an ethical point of view, there are other (and more basic) problems. One has to infringe on the existing property rights, if one wants to attain the 'right' distribution of original endowments, and a libertarian will hardly be cheered up by the knowledge that, once this starting position has been reached, the market mechanism can work freely. Theories of equity or fairness themselves give no answer to this criticism.

Moreover, the ethical objective of no-envy, for which citizens have to give up a large part of their freedom, is not always attractive. Indeed, it does not always coincide with our moral intuitions about fairness. To quote an example from Boadway and Bruce (1984, p. 175): 'I might envy a friend's "lucky find" in an antique store yet perceive no "unfairness" in the fact that he, not I, owns it.'

As emphasized, the no-envy criterion is mildly egalitarian: it uses only ordinal information and does not require interpersonal comparisons of utility. This can be considered as an advantage, of course. At the same time, it is also a limitation for some relevant distributional problems. Consider the division of a homogeneous and positively valued commodity (say, bread) among two selfish individuals. One is a giant, requiring much food to survive; the other is a dwarf with a much smaller need for food. The only 'equitable' (in the no-envy sense) division of the bread is an equal one. Yet, many observers might feel that this is not a 'just' division, because their moral intuitions suggest that the giant should get a larger share. Interpersonal comparisons of utility seem indispensable for an adequate theory of distributive justice.

2.3   Interpersonal comparability and moral philosophy

We now turn to the second escape route from Arrow's impossibility theorem: the broadening of the informational base of the social welfare functions. This really is the present 'mainstream' in welfare economics: it remains firmly within the welfaristic tradition, but claims that the utility of different individuals is interpersonally comparable. In fact, it has been shown that the lack of interpersonal comparability is the crucial restriction within the Arrow framework: accepting cardinal measurement of utility without interpersonal comparability does not solve the impossibility.

A welfaristic approach therefore has to face the problem of finding an adequate interpretation of these interpersonal comparisons of utility. The closely related ideas of 'extended sympathy' (Arrow) and 'préférences fondamentales' (Kolm 1969, 1972) seem to offer the most attractive starting point.[17] They more or less follow the economic tradition by deriving utility from choice. Of course, some important determinants of personal utility cannot be objects of choice in the usual sense: these include characteristics of the person, which cannot be changed by conscious action (e.g., his tastes, his physical needs). Therefore, the relevant choices here are 'extended and hypothetical' choices. People not only have to compare the economic situation of person i with the economic situation of person j: they compare the complete situations of both persons, i.e., they answer the question whether they would prefer to be person i, in his situation, with the tastes, the personality, the intelligence of person i, or to be person j, in his situation, with the tastes, the personality, the intelligence of person j.

It has been strongly argued by Kolm (1972) and Tinbergen (1975) that these 'fundamental preferences' will be the same for everybody. Indeed, if two people have a different ranking for such broadly defined situations, this difference must be due to one of their personal characteristics. The difference can then be removed by adding this characteristic to the specification of the choice situation. Obviously, some problems remain with this interpretation. For one thing, it can be argued that 'reducing an individual to a specified list of qualities is denying his individuality in a deep sense' (Arrow 1977, p. 225). Yet the construction offers sufficient support to proceed with the formulation of ethical theories, for which interpersonal comparability of welfare is needed.

One can define interpersonal comparability at different levels of measurement. This suggests a new (informational) perspective on welfaristic ethical theories. The best known of these theories is utilitarianism. Another welfaristic criterion is the so-called maximin criterion. This can be formulated as follows: 'The distribution of valuable goods should be equal, unless an inequality increases the utility level of the least-well-off household.' This criterion does not allow us to choose between two situations yielding the same (utility!) result for the worst-off household, even if the results for the others are quite different. Welfare economic theory has therefore proposed the 'leximin' criterion: this proposes to look at the welfare implications for the second-worst-off individuals, if the implications for the worst-off are identical (and go further upwards in the ranking, if the implications for the second-worst-off also are the same).

The maximin criterion obviously is related to Rawls' (1971) difference principle.[18] Yet some people could wonder about the economic tradition of interpreting the criterion in a 'welfaristic' fashion. Indeed, this interpretation severely reduces the content of Rawls' (1971) criterion. We will further discuss this point in section 3.2.

Once we have reduced the difference principle to its welfarist form, we can discuss it within the welfare economic framework. To apply maximin we only have to identify the worst-off individual: what is needed, therefore, is a comparison of the utility *levels* of the different individuals. Such level comparability clearly is not sufficient to apply utilitarianism, because there we have to add the different utilities. This implies that the unit of measurement becomes important. One could call this *unit* comparability.[19] Of course, one can reverse the reasoning: if utility functions are level (but not unit) comparable, then utilitarianism simply is not applicable. On the other hand, when unit (but not level) comparability holds, one cannot apply the maximin criterion. Economists have rigorously explored the consequences of such different informational assumptions and combined them with ethical axioms. This (rather technical) literature undoubtedly has yielded some valuable insights into the ethical structure and the informational requirements of different welfaristic approaches.[20]

Of course, when we are willing to assume that interpersonal comparisons make sense, we can apply different social welfare functions: ethical considerations then become crucial for the choice between them. Following their tradition, many applied economists feel that such choice is beyond their competence and work with the following general specification:[21]

$$\sum_{h=1}^{H} \frac{(u^h)^{(1-\varrho)}}{(1-\varrho)} \tag{1}$$

Different values of ϱ correspond to different social welfare functions. If $\varrho = 0$, formula (1) reduces to the utilitarian function, i.e. the sum of the individual utility levels. It can also be proven that (1) approaches maximin for ϱ going to infinity, i.e., (1) then becomes equivalent to the lowest utility level. For values of ϱ between 0 and infinity, we have a whole spectrum of social welfare functions. The larger ϱ, the larger the relative weights attached to the lower utility levels. The parameter ϱ is often called 'the degree of inequality aversion'. The 'socially optimal' solution to any concrete policy problem, e.g., the determination of an income tax scheme, of course will depend on value judgements concerning the distribution of utilities. When working with equation (1) these value judgements are operationalized via the parameter ϱ; applied workers, who do not want to choose a specific social welfare function, then will compute the optimal solution for different values of ϱ, i.e., will perform a 'sensitivity analysis' with respect to ϱ.[22] This procedure reflects a rather agnostic attitude. The approach is interesting even for the analysis of justice, however, because the results clearly indicate the *practical* implications of different justice conceptions.

Not all economists have adopted the same agnostic attitude. Economic theory has also contributed to the discussion about the basic ethical foundation of the different welfaristic theories. The most influential[23] modern treatment of utilitarianism has been proposed by Harsanyi in a number of papers.[24] He draws a distinction between the 'personal' preferences of individuals and their 'ethical' preferences. The former reflect a ranking of social states on the basis of the self-interest of the individual, the latter a ranking of these states on the basis of moral considerations. This ethical ranking is found when the individual adopts an impartial view. He then chooses between the different social states 'under the assumption that . . . he would have the same probability of occupying any one of the available social positions' (Harsanyi 1982, p. 45). Harsanyi claims that this can be seen as a decision problem under uncertainty, where an equal probability is attached to all 'states of nature' (the social positions). Since he also believes in the interpersonal comparability of welfare, he accepts that the ethical observer can form a reasonable idea about the utility levels attached to the different social positions. He will therefore rank social states on the basis of these individual utility levels: a *rational* economic agent will then maximize expected utility. Under the equiprobability assumption, and taking the size of the population (i.e., the number of social positions) as given, maximizing expected utility is equivalent to maximizing the sum of utilities. In this way we have recovered utilitarianism.

Harsanyi (1976), and other economists such as Arrow 1973 and Kolm 1985, have used the same framework to discuss (the 'economic' version of) the maximin criterion. They then argue that the equiprobability assumption is an attractive operationalization of Rawls' 'veil of ignorance'.[25] If we accept this interpretation, the maximin criterion implies that the ethical decision-maker judges each social state on the basis of the utility level of the worst-off individual only: this can only be rational if he has an infinite risk aversion. This does not seem particularly realistic. Basically the same criticism can also be formulated in a completely diffent way. The maximin criterion does not allow for any trade off between the utility level of the poorest member of society and the other individuals. This means that an increase in the utility level of the worst off (no matter how small) always outweighs a loss in the utility levels of others (no matter how large). It could be argued that this goes too far.

This does not mean that utilitarianism is without its problems, however. As it maximizes the *sum* of the utilities, it is unconcerned about the distribution of these utilities. The 'revolutionary' consequences (that the optimum situation is one of equal income distribution), sketched in section 1.2, only follow when all utility functions are the same (and subject to diminishing marginal utility of income). As soon as utility functions differ, utilitarianism will distribute the resources in favour of the most efficient pleasure machines. This certainly is not attractive from an ethical point of view.

The problem becomes clear when we consider the following axiom, formulated by Sen (1973, p. 18):

> *Weak Equity Axiom.* Let person *i* have a lower level of welfare than person *j* for each level of individual income. Then in distributing a given total of income among *n* individuals including *i* and *j*, the optimal solution must give *i* a higher level of income than *j*.

Many people will accept that this is a minimal requirement for distributive justice. A striking example would be the case where person *i* is handicapped. It can easily be shown that utilitarianism will not always satisfy the 'Weak Equity Axiom'. Indeed, it is possible that the axiom is not satisfied by a general social welfare function (1), even when ϱ is larger than 0.

The economic framework makes it possible to discuss the informational requirements and the ethical consequences of different welfaristic social welfare functions. In this section, I have given only a cursory overview of the literature. In section 3 we will turn to a criticism of the basic starting point of all these theories: that the crucial factors in judgements about distributive justice are the welfare levels of the individuals. It will be argued that this starting point is not optimal to incorporate dominant ethical intuitions. The mathematical tractability of these theories, the economic tradition of analysing the market results in terms of welfare (itself influenced by traditional utilitarianism) and the beauty and elegance of Arrow's impossibility theorem have led economists to an excessive emphasis on these welfaristic theories.

3   Welfarism and rights

The literature reviewed in the previous section follows the economic tradition in ranking all social states on the basis of the individual utilities in these states. Freedom does not play a crucial role. In applied economic work, this tradition almost has a monopoly position. However, in recent theoretical work on justice there is a growing tendency to criticize the limitations of this approach.[26] This criticism will be worked out in section 3.1. The differences between Rawls' own approach and what economists have made of it further illustrate the problems with welfarism. This will be shown in section 3.2. I will then use Rawls' theory as a starting point for a review of economic theories of justice, which try to give 'rights' the place they deserve.

3.1   The limitations of welfarism

The criticism of welfarism can be more or less summarized under two headings. First, it is not easy to find an (ethically) adequate interpretation of the concept of utility and, second, a welfarist approach cannot capture all considerations which are relevant for justice judgements.

The first criticism can start from the traditional economic interpretation of utility. Economic practice relates preferences to choice: it argues that choice is based on utility maximization and, hence, that preferences are 'revealed' by choice behaviour. As long as choices are consistent, the idea that choice reflects the maximization of utility can always be defended by interpreting utility in an (almost?) tautological way: utility then simply is *defined* as the 'representation' of these consistent 'preferences'. It can be doubted, however, whether these 'revealed' preferences have much meaning from a psychological or welfare point of view. Once we start from a substantial concept of individual welfare, then it is an empirical problem whether people choose so as to maximize this a priori defined concept. Indeed, this is highly questionable. The preferences guiding behaviour are moulded by social and historical influences: think of deceptive advertising and addiction to drugs. Surely, many people may doubt that mothers in developing countries, persuaded by advertising to substitute milk powder for breast-feeding, are 'better off' after this substitution. Moreover, actual decisions are also influenced by other than preference considerations: social pressure and ethical norms are straightforward examples.

Of course, the link between utility and behaviour, although crucial for applied economic work, is not necessary to adopt a welfaristic conception of justice. More philosophically inclined welfarists (see, e.g., Broome 1978 and the contributions by Harsanyi, Hammond and Mirrlees in Sen and Williams 1982) indeed propose to work with a 'corrected' notion of utility. But how far must this correction go? The question can be made more concrete by two examples. Consider first the case where wants and desires are adjusted to possibilities, a quite common situation. Would we then accept utility differences as an important determinant of a 'just' distribution? To quote one of the leading critics of welfarism (Sen 1984a, pp. 308–9):

> The most blatant forms of inequalities and exploitations survive in the world through making allies out of the deprived and the exploited. The underdog learns to bear the burden so well that he or she overlooks the burden itself. Discontent is replaced by acceptance, hopeless rebellion by conformist quiet, and – most relevantly in the present context – suffering and anger by cheerful endurance. As people learn to adjust to the existing horrors by the sheer necessity of uneventful survival, the horrors look less terrible in the metric of utilities.

The second example refers to the case of expensive tastes. Consider an individual who is satisfied only if he can consume plovers' eggs:[27] should the 'just' distribution of resources take into account the craving of this unhappy individual? Is it not implausible that the 'just' share of other people should depend on the development of expensive tastes within an individual? Both examples illustrate how difficult it is to find an interpretation of the utility concept, which is satisfactory for a treatment of justice. It has even been argued that 'utility' is necessarily more dimensional and that therefore the economist's 'utility function' is not well defined.[28]

Even if we could find a satisfactory definition of utility, there still remains a second criticism: that utility cannot summarize all information which is needed for equity judgements. A strong example is given by Sen (1979a).[29] Consider three social states (x, y and z), with the following utility numbers for persons 1 and 2:

	x	y	z
Person 1	4	7	7
Person 2	10	8	8

In x person 1 is hungry, while person 2 has an abundant amount of food. In y the second person has a somewhat smaller food amount, and person 1 is no longer starving. Clearly, both utilitarianism and maximin will prefer situation y over situation x.

Let us now consider situation z. Here person 1 is still starving and person 2 has the same amount of food as he has in x. 'However, person 1, who is a sadist, is now permitted to torture 2, who – alas – is not a masochist. So 2 does suffer, but resilient as he is, his suffering is less than the utility gain of the wild-eyed 1' (Sen 1979a, p. 339). The welfarist has to judge both situations z and y alike, since there is no difference in the utility numbers. But certainly, most people will feel a strong moral disapproval of torture, even if the utility numbers are as they are in z:[30] this moral feeling refers to the inviolability of individual rights and cannot be captured by any welfaristic approach. One could try to solve the problem by redefining the concept of utility so as to disregard the feeling of 'happiness' as a consequence of sadistic torture. But that 'solution' would confront us immediately again with the first problem: what is the 'exact' definition of utility? And, if we define utility so broadly as to include all kinds of individual rights, do we then still have a 'welfaristic' theory?[31] Or, what is the relationship between the 'ideal' preferences, the 'actual' preferences and the 'revealed' preferences (the preferences as they show up in behaviour)?

In fact, there are important feelings or intuitions about justice, which are not formulated in utility terms at all. A striking example is the basic libertarian tenet, formulated by Kolm (1987) as follows: 'This is mine, because I bought it with legitimately earned money from my work or because it was given to me.' The example suggests that the conflict between welfarism and the importance of individual rights really is a basic one, in that the two approaches already diverge at the level of the starting principles. This problem was also treated in a huge literature, following a short but influential paper of Sen (1970a), in which he stated 'the impossibility of the Paretian libertarian'.

The theorem is nicely illustrated by his famous *Lady Chatterley's Lover* example, which deserves a long citation[32] (Sen 1979a, p. 342):

Two persons, namely, the prude and the lewd, are considering three states of affairs, namely, p (the prude reading *Lady Chatterley's Lover*), l (lewd reading the book) and o (nobody reading it). The prude's personal utility ranking, in decreasing order, is: o, p, l, while the lewd ranks them p, l, o. The prude likes o (nobody reading the book) best; the lewd likes it least. But both prefer p to l, i.e., the prude reading the book rather than the lewd. It is postulated that in p the lewd is overjoyed at the prude's discomfiture in having to read a naughty book, and the prude is less unhappy, having avoided the dire outcome of that lascivious lewd actually reading and enjoying 'such muck'. This leads to the Pareto-libertarian cycle. On libertarian grounds, it is better that the lewd reads the book rather than nobody, since what the lewd reads is his own business and the lewd does want to read the book; hence l is socially better than o. On libertarian grounds again, it is better that nobody reads the book rather than the prude, since whether the prude should read a book or not is his own business, and he does not wish to read the book; hence o is better than p. On the other hand, both get more utility from the prude reading the book rather than the lewd. The Pareto-preference for p over l, completes the cycle with the libertarian rankings of l over o, and o over p.

The formal theorem, which is illustrated by the previous example, states that it is impossible to have a consistent social ordering, satisfying three conditions: the Pareto-criterion (unanimously preferred social states are also preferred according to the social ordering), minimal liberty (at least two individuals have a personal sphere, in which their own preferences determine the socially preferred state) and unrestricted domain (the social ordering is defined for all possible configurations of individual orderings). There is a basic conflict between freedom (defined as minimal liberty) and the (Paretian) criterion of unanimity, defined in welfare terms. And the conflict already appears at the level of the objectives, the principles, and is not dependent on the instruments used to realize a more 'equal' welfare distribution. The most obvious conclusion of the theorem therefore is that a welfaristic approach is inadequate to treat problems of individual rights: application of the Paretian criterion may lead to a violation of the personal sphere of individuals (e.g., the choice of what they want to read).

The theorem of the impossibility of a Paretian libertarian has been widely discussed in specialized journals.[33] Economists have soon noticed that the *Lady Chatterley's Lover* case is an example of missing markets or externalities and that the conflict with the Pareto-principle would disappear if individuals A and B could engage in mutually beneficial trades. The prudish individual could then agree to read the book under the condition that the lewd does not read it. Such a contract would be based on the (eminently libertarian) principle of the freedom of each individual to trade and to give up some of his rights. But what if they are both attached to libertarian values and therefore refuse to enter the contract?

In the latter case one could claim that the paradox is still solved if only we are willing to accept that these libertarian values should be considered as part of their preferences. Basically, we are then back in the traditional approach of trying to find an interpretation of the concept of preferences which would make welfarism acceptable. An alternative proposal in the same line would be the argument that 'meddlesome' preferences should not count when deriving a social ordering. This also solves the problem in the *Lady Chatterley's Lover* example. But it is difficult to claim that such approaches save welfarism, because we then again complicate the basic problem of defining the 'ethically adequate' preferences. And does it make sense to define a criterion of justice as 'welfaristic', when non-welfaristic considerations are crucial to specify the exact content of the 'welfare' concept to be used?

Another important stream in the literature challenges the relevancy of the 'minimal liberty' condition and argues that the 'social choice' framework is completely inadequate to discuss the problem of freedom. Sugden (1981) argues that freedom essentially means being free to make certain choices and that this is a procedural interpretation, which cannot be translated into the framework of 'social orderings' of outcomes.[34] Nozick (1974) makes a closely related point. In his opinion, the degree of rights fulfilment is not a characteristic of social states which is to be 'chosen' by the social decision process: rights define the *constraints* within which choice can be exerted. 'The exercise of these rights fixes some features of the world. Within the constraints of these fixed features, a choice may be made by a social choice mechanism based upon a social ordering; if there are any choices left to make!' (Nozick 1974, p. 166). The exact interpretation of 'freedom' is of course a basic problem for any theory of justice. We will have to return to it in this review. With respect to the theorem of the Paretian libertarian, however, it must be emphasized that the 'minimal liberty' condition does not aim at a complete characterization of freedom. Surely, most people will accept that it indeed captures a *minimal* condition of freedom.

3.2   *Economics and Rawls' theory of primary goods*

While it is not the intention of this review to discuss thoroughly the theory of Rawls (see therefore Cullen, this volume), it is useful at this stage to describe his position with respect to economics. It has been noted already in section 2.3 that the 'economic' maximin (or leximin) criterion is formulated in terms of welfare levels, while Rawls works with a notion of primary goods. Rawls (1982) quite explicitly differentiates his own approach from the economic idea of 'fundamental preferences'.

He starts from the observation that, in a free democratic culture, a plurality of conceptions of the good is pursued by the citizens. The problem then becomes: how to reach between these different conceptions a social agreement about 'just' institutions? It is well known (see Cullen, this volume) that in Rawls' conception of justice, such an agreement about the basic structure of society takes the form of a social contract, formulated behind a 'veil of ignorance'. The parties in the contract are the citizens, as free and equal moral persons, moved by their desire to realize and exercise their capacity to decide upon and to pursue a conception of the good. Given the incommensurability of different conceptions of the good, there will be no consensus behind the veil of ignorance: at best, there will be a partial agreement.

According to Rawls, free and moral persons in the original position will reach an agreement about two principles of justice (Rawls 1982, pp. 161–2):

1. Each person has an equal right to the most extensive scheme of equal basic liberties compatible with a similar scheme of liberties for all.
2. Social and economic inequalities are to satisfy two conditions: they must be (a) to the greatest benefit of the least advantaged members of society; and (b) attached to offices and positions open to all under conditions of fair equality of opportunity.

It is obvious that these principles are much broader than the economic version of the maximin criterion. The first principle emphasizes freedom. The second principle gives an unambiguous answer to the trade-off between equality and efficiency. Inequalities are acceptable if they work to the advantage of the worst-off members of society. A crucial point is the operationalization of the notions of advantage and benefit in this second principle (the so-called 'difference principle'). These are determined by the amount of primary goods available to the individuals. Primary goods are characterized as follows (Rawls 1982, p. 162):

(a) first, the basic liberties as given by a list, for example: freedom of thought and liberty of conscience; freedom of association; and the freedom defined by the liberty and integrity of the person, as well as by the rule of law; and finally the political liberties;

(b) second, freedom of movement and choice of occupation against a background of diverse opportunities;

(c) third, powers and prerogatives of offices and positions of responsibility, particularly those in the main political and economic institutions;

(d) fourth, income and wealth; and

(e) finally, the social bases of self-respect.

These primary goods are objective features of institutions. To use them as an indication of advantage, we have to construct an index of primary goods. But how to interpret such an 'index'? Economists have a tendency to interpret it as a kind of 'utility' function, possibly related to the notion of fundamental preferences (see, e.g., Kolm 1985). Rawls very explicitly rejects this interpretation. He argues that this notion of 'fundamental preferences' is plainly incompatible with the conception of a well-ordered society in justice as fairness. Indeed, 'in the circumstances of justice citizens' conceptions of the good are not only opposed, but incommensurable' (Rawls 1982, p. 179). They cannot be reduced to the metric of satisfaction or utility. Primary goods are important for the contractants in the original position, because they allow these free and moral persons to realize their own personal conception of the good. The index of primary goods is not a 'psychological' measure of satisfaction, its formulation is part of the contract in the original position (ibid., pp. 184–5):

An index of primary goods does not belong to theory in the economist's sense. It belongs instead to a conception of justice which falls under the liberal alternative to the tradition of the one rational good. Thus the problem is not how to specify an accurate measure of some psychological or other attribute available only to science. Rather, it is a moral and practical problem. The use of primary goods is not a makeshift which better theory can replace, but a reasonable social practice which we try to design so as to achieve the workable agreement required for effective and willing social cooperation among citizens whose understanding of social unity rests on a conception of justice.

Rawls' theory obviously is very different from the economic approach. It is *not* welfaristic, because it defines advantage in terms of an index of *objective* characteristics, the primary goods. Moreover, Rawls emphasizes the importance of individual freedom. These two features of Rawls' theory can be contrasted immediately with the limitations of welfarism, as sketched in section 3.1: the difficulty of giving a reasonable interpretation to the concept of 'welfare', and the conflict between welfarism (even in its weak Paretian form) and minimal libertarian values.

This does not mean that there are no problems with Rawls' theory (see, e.g., Kolm 1985, for a very sharp economic criticism). Different points of criticism will be used as starting points for the following sections of this review. In the first place, it is not always clear how to interpret the ordering of the principles: note, for example, that the 'basic liberties' are part of the list of primary goods. Libertarian thinkers have argued that Rawls' concept of freedom and the place of this concept in his construction of the just society are inadequate. We will comment on their criticism in section 4. In the second place it has been argued that, while Rawls undoubtedly has revived the (old) idea of the social contract, his interpretation of that social contract is not convincing. Many commentators have doubts about the argumentation that the basic principles necessarily would be chosen behind the veil of ignorance. Some alternative social contract theories are reviewed in section 5. Finally, the amount of primary goods available to an individual remains a 'resourcist' concept, that perhaps does not sufficiently take into account interindividual differences in needs. This leads us immediately to the recent work of Dworkin, Roemer and Sen.[35] This work is discussed in section 6.

4   Libertarian theories

We argued in the previous section that Rawls, much more than traditional welfare economics, emphasizes the importance of individual freedom. However, there are differing opinions about the interpretation of this concept of 'individual freedom' and about the extent to which it has to be respected. The libertarian interpretation is different from the one proposed by Rawls.

Contrary to what outsiders might believe when they follow day-to-day economic discussions, libertarianism occupies a minority position within the world of economic science.[36] It is true that the market is present everywhere, and that the superiority of the market procedure is one of the main tenets of libertarianism. However, as argued in the first section, respect for freedom is only one of the possible reasons to prefer the market mechanism and it seems fair to say that the quest for efficiency has been a much more important driving force for economists. The best-known exception to this general trend is Friedman (1962).

A typical welfare economic example of libertarian thinking is the book by Rowley and Peacock (1975). These authors explicitly complain about 'Paretian empire building' in economics. They define libertarianism as being 'concerned essentially, though not exclusively, with the maintenance and extension of individual freedom, defined as that condition of mankind in which coercion of some individuals by others is reduced to the minimum possible degree' (p. 78). Libertarians emphasize that human beings own themselves (including all personal talents and capacities). They fear government intervention, because it constitutes a violation of personal rights: for many libertarians, for example, there is no basic difference between income taxation and forced labour.

One feature of Rowley and Peacock's definition immediately catches the eye. What is meant by the extremely vague expression 'essentially, though not exclusively'? We touch here a basic problem of libertarianism. Libertarian thinking is perfectly internally consistent when it judges social states on the basis of their degree of freedom, and exclusively on that basis. But, as already argued in section 1, 'free' social states *may* involve a very unequal distribution of welfare, where some people are extremely wealthy and others near to starvation.[37] Whether this happens frequently is of course an empirical problem, and is doubted by some libertarians. Yet it seems somewhat precarious to rest a theory of justice on the presupposition that this problem would not occur. Only few people will accept such unequal distributions as 'just'. Or, if one restricts oneself to a narrow definition of 'justice',[38] few people will accept that only justice counts in the ethical judgement of social states. Introducing this ethical intuition into libertarian thinking then leads to the statement 'not exclusively' and to proposals for special arrangements for the very poor. But who is 'very poor' and what arrangements are sufficiently 'special' to be acceptable to libertarians? The point is that the admission of such exceptions makes a hole in the consistent fortress of freedom: it leads to the acceptance of a trade-off between different values and, as soon as one accepts the basic idea of trade-offs, one has to specify more carefully their exact range. Without such exact specification, the theory remains too vague to be really applicable.

Another important feature of the definition is its advocacy of an essentially negative concept of freedom (not being coerced). In fact, Rowley and Peacock even claim that positive freedom is the greatest enemy of negative freedom and that its advocates rapidly fall into a doctrine of authority. We will return to the relationship between positive and negative freedom(s) in section 6.2, where we will argue that the distinction is overdone by Rowley and Peacock (and other libertarian writers). But already here we can ask questions about the primitive notion of 'coercion'.

In the economic sphere, the notion of coercion can only sensibly be defined when one defines at the same time a set of legitimate property rights. Many libertarians start from the idea that the external world initially is unowned. People own themselves and therefore also are entitled to the fruits of their own labour. This includes (under certain conditions) objects from the (initially unowned) external world. Self-ownership therefore leads to a justification of private property. The legitimacy of property rights in this interpretation depends on the legitimacy of the initial appropriation of natural resources. Libertarians have not yet given a conclusive answer to the question of this initial appropriation. While it is not our intention to enter deeply into the philosophical discussions on property rights,[39] it is nevertheless interesting to mention the proposal made by Cohen (1986b). He does not deny self-ownership, but denies that from a moral point of view the external world can be considered as initially unowned. He argues that it is preferable to start from the assumption that the external world is *jointly* owned by all citizens. This means that people in a certain sense are trustees with respect to this external world. Each appropriation must be approved by the joint owners. Roemer (1986b) and Moulin and Roemer (1986) show that this assumption brings us very far into the direction of outcome egalitarianism. Their axiomatic approach translates the idea of entitlement into characteristics on the space of outcomes. Libertarians might claim that such outcome-orientated constructions are not appropriate to discuss matters of rights and entitlements. The notion of 'collective ownership of the external world', however, may become an important contribution to the debate on distributive justice.

This is also illustrated by Van Parijs (1988). He argues that libertarianism can only escape in a self-consistent way from the (for them) horrible consequences of this collective ownership by interpreting these consequences in terms of a decrease in personal freedom. But to give content to the idea of 'decrease in freedom' in this context, they have to include the possibility to dispose of (part of) the external world as an essential component of freedom. They then slip into a concept of *positive* freedom. Such a shift from negative to positive freedoms basically overthrows the libertarian construction and brings us very far into the direction of the non-welfaristic theories, which will be discussed in section 6. Before turning to these, however, we will first summarize some economic social contract theories.

5   Social contract theories

Libertarianism focuses on negative freedom, on the right of individuals not to be coerced. The freedom of others in this view is the only limitation to one's own individual freedom. Somewhat simplistically, one could say that social contract theories accept coercion, if the individuals have first unanimously (mostly tacitly) accepted it. If they have freely accepted a social contract, they have to obey its rules afterwards. We have noted in section 3 that the social contract idea has been reintroduced in political and economic philosophy by Rawls. Some economists have followed his lead but have given a quite different interpretation to the context of the social contract and to the characteristics of the contracting individuals. In this section we summarize the work of Buchanan and Kolm. Before turning to their social contract interpretations (sections 5.1.2 and 5.2.2 respectively), we will introduce the public choice school (section 5.1.1) and the theory of voluntary redistribution (section 5.2.1).

5.1   Buchanan: justice and the public choice school

5.1.1   The public choice school and the constitutional stage

Traditional welfare economics often implicitly assumed that its normative prescriptions would be automatically implemented by the government. This government then was seen as an 'ideal' economic agent, with as its only aim the fostering of the public good. During recent decades, this assumption has been questioned by the so-called 'public choice' school: these authors want to give an objective description and an explanation of the actual working of government (for an overview, see Mueller 1989).

They start from the idea that politicians and bureaucrats are driven by selfish motives. The political process is used by all kinds of pressure groups to foster their own interests. Very often the public discussion is conducted in the 'rhetoric of justice' but this rhetoric hides simple utility maximizing motivations. Much of the empirical work performed within the public choice school, has shown that this description of political life is a fruitful starting point to explain actual political mechanisms. Often these theories are used to cast doubt on all redistributive proposals. Indeed, who is to carry out any 'ideal' conception of distributive justice? If government is not an ideal and ethically motivated *deus ex machina*, then redistribution will reflect the power structure in society. It will be dominated not by ethical, but by purely selfish considerations.

But is it really true that there is no longer any scope for ethical thinking in this harsh world of selfish individuals? A negative answer to this question has been formulated by James Buchanan, who has become one of the most influential contemporary economic thinkers. He basically approaches the problem by drawing a clear distinction between two levels of decision-making: the constitutional and the post-constitutional stage. In earlier work (Buchanan and Tullock 1962; Buchanan 1975), he showed how people may decide about rules and institutions in a pre-legal state. In this pre-legal 'initial state of nature', property rights do not yet exist: there will, however, emerge a 'natural distribution', resulting in a certain sense from a war of each against all. This (Hobbesian) pre-legal state is characterized by the subjective uncertainty of individuals about the future development of society (an idea related to Rawls' veil of ignorance). On the basis of purely selfish motives, these individuals then will accept a system of property rights, simply to avoid the large 'defence and predation' costs associated with the state of nature. Such a system of property rights is a public good, with all the problems associated with public goods: each individual has an incentive to violate the contractual agreement and to become a free rider. In a certain sense, the most preferred position for everybody is for there to be a system of property rights, respected by everybody, except by the individual himself. But if everybody shows this same free-rider behaviour, then the contractual arrangement of course ceases to exist. And, given that everybody is selfish, this is what can be expected, unless there is an agency which protects the property rights. *All* people in the initial state of nature will therefore accept such an agency, i.e., accept the development of a 'protective state'.

As with all social contract theories, the basic ethical intuition in this construction is the strong emphasis on consensus: the fairness of the rules follows from the fact that all people agree about them. In formulating this idea of unanimity, Buchanan is strongly influenced by the work of the Swedish economist Knut Wicksell (1896). It leads to a purely procedural definition of what is ethically good: legitimacy can only be derived, at one level or another, from the voluntary consent of individuals. 'That which emerges emerges, and evaluative criteria can only be applied to processes of the interaction and not to the characteristics of the end-states that are generated' (Buchanan 1986, p. 273).

The unanimity criterion holds for decisions at the constitutional level, where the basic rules and institutions of society are determined. At this constitutional level, people may be aware that the general application of the unanimity rule may lead to huge transaction costs and to a severe loss of efficiency. Therefore, they may unanimously decide (at the constitutional level) that unanimity will not always be required for post-constitutional decision-making, for example on the provision of public goods. (This is worked out in Buchanan and Tullock 1962.) However, at the constitutional level, people will also be aware of the dangers resulting from an ever-growing state apparatus (Leviathan), and will formulate rules so as to constrain this coercing state agency. Moreover, for all constitutional changes the only ethically acceptable decision criterion again is the unanimity rule.

5.1.2 Justice at the constitutional level

Justice as such does not appear in the construction so far. In his recent work, Buchanan (1986) more explicitly addresses the question of justice: he emphasizes that his earlier analysis was essentially positive rather than normative, and that it was not his intention to support the 'justice' of the distributional results that emerged from his analysis. However, his theory of justice will also rely heavily on the idea of the two stages of decision-making.

Given the public choice description of the working of the state, Buchanan obviously cannot accept as just any redistribution through the actual political process. This political process is the main instrument for pressure groups to improve their own economic position at the expense of others. He emphasizes that an 'ideal' theory of justice cannot be realized in a social vacuum. When one wants to realize an ideal 'end-state', one does not merely distribute income: one has to *re*distribute income. There are utility losses involved in redistribution, because the wealthy people will be upset by the transfer process. More important, however, is the lack of ethical foundation of such redistribution: as noted earlier, the criterion of the legitimacy of change is consensus, and pure redistribution, defined in utility dimensions, cannot occur with general consent of all parties.[40] This position of course leads to a fierce defence of the status quo. Buchanan emphasizes that his position does not imply that the status quo is 'just' according to someone's private ethical values. These ethical values will differ among individuals, however, and nobody has the right to impose his own opinions on others.

However, such a cautious attitude is relevant mainly for post-constitutional decision-making. There is more room for justice considerations in the constitutional stage, where people contract about the rules of the game. It seems reasonable indeed that they will try to agree about *fair* constitutional rules. Since justice is defined by unanimity, and by unanimity only, Buchanan's theory as such is empty. By definition, the content has to follow exclusively from the opinions of the contractants in the natural state and nobody else (including the economist) has the right to condemn these opinions. However, the economist can try to gain some insight into what probably would result from free contracting at the constitutional stage.

Buchanan (1986) distinguishes four important factors to explain income differences: choice, luck, effort and birth. In so far as such differences are caused by the first three factors, he feels that few people would consider them as unfair.[41] The fourth factor is more problematic, however: 'Unfairness in the economic game described by the operation of market institutions within a legal framework of private property and contract tends to be attributed to the distribution of endowments with which persons *enter* the game in the first place, *before* choices are made, *before* luck rolls the economic dice, *before* effort is exerted' (Buchanan 1986, pp. 129–30, his italics). Given this basic assumption, people at the constitutional stage will agree about rules to correct for these unequal starting positions. In formulating these rules, of course, they will be very careful because they are aware of the dangers following from a powerful state apparatus. Therefore, they certainly will not aim at 'fine tuning', but they will formulate rules which quasi-permanently constrain governments as well as private parties. Three institutions then come to mind.

The first is the taxation of financial intergenerational transfers. Although interfering with the freedom of the donors, this is ethically acceptable because it corrects blatant inequities. The second institution is a publicly financed (not necessarily publicly provided) education system. The third institution is a set of rules to counteract overt discrimination in the allocation of job opportunities.

The institutions mentioned until now are set up to realize equality of opportunity and are not concerned about the resulting distributional end-states. Nothing in the structure of constitutional bargaining, however, necessarily forbids that people would try to avoid some 'unjust' end-states. But Buchanan doubts whether they will reach consensus about any such proposal. He suggests that the distributive rules of the market then will be accepted, because there is no alternative arrangement upon which unanimous agreement can be obtained. And he makes no secret of his own opinion in this regard: 'For my own part, I should remain relatively undisturbed about the distributional results of competitive market processes if rough fairness in the distribution of initial endowments and capacities could be guaranteed' (Buchanan 1986, p. 137).

The institutional rules proposed by Buchanan go further than the libertarian proposals. It stands to reason that application of the unanimity criterion indeed leads to the acceptance of collective provision of at least some public goods. When it comes to justice, however, Buchanan's ideas become rather speculative. Much of his analysis of justice is permeated by his (and the initial contractants') fear of Leviathan. This explains his strong plea for institutional arrangements only. Yet some people might doubt whether the proposed institutions suffice to reach justice. It is not obvious that contractants in the constitutional bargaining process would see no reason at all to correct for income differences following from luck. Many people could feel that turns of fortune are arbitrary from a moral point of view or, more selfishly, could want to insure themselves against bad luck. If this is true, some *redistribution* to avoid really horrible end-states could become acceptable.[42]

Another point refers to Buchanan's interpretation of 'equal opportunities'. In his interpretation, the creation of equal opportunities does not correct for differences in natural talent. It has been argued (for example, by Dworkin, as will be summarized in section 6.1) that compensation for such differences is indispensable for an ethically acceptable interpretation of the notion of 'equal opportunities'. Of course, if all initial contractants would share this ethical feeling, it is possible that they would consider this to be sufficiently important to overcome their fear of Leviathan. This would lead again to stronger redistributive policies.

Being based on the unanimity criterion, Buchanan's theory is open ended: surely, it does not give an answer to all ethical questions on distribution, and in ethical discussions other considerations may come into play. A more basic criticism of his theory asks about the ethical justification of the unanimity requirement itself. The unanimous agreement does not occur in a social vacuum: it presupposes a setting in which, for example, property rights have been defined. Therefore the justification of the structure of property rights again is crucial. We have seen that Buchanan for this justification refers to the 'natural distribution'. But can this Hobbesian state of nature, resulting from a war of each against all, indeed bear the ethical weight Buchanan seems to ascribe to it? If not, the unanimity requirement loses much of its ethical justification.

However, it remains an important contribution by Buchanan, and by the public choice school in general, to have emphasized that one cannot consider government as an ideal *deus ex machina* and that one has to be very careful when striving to realize ethical ideas through the actual governmental decision process. We return to this point in section 5.2.2.

5.2   Kolm: insurance, altruism and the Liberal Social Contract

It has been argued in the previous section that Buchanan's contractual theory does not go very far in correcting unequal distributions. The question arises how far one can go, if one wants to remain within a social contract framework and keep to the condition of unanimous consent. In his theory of the Liberal Social Contract,[43] Kolm (1985) broadens the scope of the social contract, and thus succeeds in justifying many redistributive policy measures. In defining this broader 'scope', Kolm has been inspired by the traditional theory of voluntary redistribution. Traditional Paretian welfare economics was primarily concerned with efficiency. Kolm (who had made already important contributions to the Paretian tradition) turned it into a consistent ethical theory, which can be interpreted as a version of contractual liberalism. We will first briefly comment on the welfare economic approach and then turn to Kolm's theory of the Liberal Social Contract. Note that we will use the traditional terminology ('liberal') when discussing Kolm's work.

5.2.1   The theory of voluntary redistribution

Traditional welfare theory by definition will only consider a redistribution as 'Pareto-improving' if it makes at least one individual better and nobody worse off. Given the traditional economic interpretation of the term 'better off', a redistribution of *utility* of course can never be a Pareto-improvement. However, this need not imply that one cannot argue for a redistribution of *income*. Indeed, it is possible that such income redistribution is valued positively, not only by the receivers, but also by the donors. They may have different motives for this positive valuation. Some of these motives will traditionally be called 'altruistic', others might be called 'selfish'.[44] On this basis one can construct a Paretian case for redistribution by government (for an overview, see Hennipman 1981).

The first motive is the altruistic one. It is a fact of life that people do care about others: it is not unreasonable to hypothesize that at least some wealthy people do care about the poor. Such altruism[45] may take different forms. The most obvious possibility leads to the introduction of other persons' utility into the utility function of the donor: donors then really care about the welfare of others. But donors may also be paternalistic. In that case it is the consumption by the poor of some specific commodities that enters the utility function of the rich. The distinction between these forms of altruism is crucial if we want to explain the ubiquity of transfers in kind, but for our basic question both forms of altruism are essentially equivalent. This basic question can be formulated as follows: since wealthy people are personally motivated to do something, why is private charity not sufficient to bring about a Pareto-optimal situation? Why do we need government intervention?

There are essentially two answers to this question. The first is a practical one: government can be assumed to have more information on who is really poor and to realize economies of scale in the process of helping these poor. There is a second and more fundamental answer. In this case, where the welfare (or the consumption level) of the poor enters into the utility function of the donors, this welfare (or consumption) level essentially is a public good. Therefore, there will be a free-rider problem. Every donor wants to see the poor people become less poor, but prefers at the same time that this increase in the utility (or consumption) level of the poor is realized through the help of others. If all (potential) donors follow the same reasoning, the resulting transfer to the poor will be suboptimal: the welfare of the donors (and of the poor, of course) will increase when they all are forced to give what they really want to give, but do not give spontaneously for strategic (free-rider) considerations.[46] Therefore, government intervention will lead to a Pareto-improvement.[47]

To understand better the preceding argument, it is useful to compare it to another possible form of altruism, where the donor wants to help the poor, because he feels morally obliged to do so. This can be baptized 'deontological altruism'. In this case, the act of giving is a purely private good and the case for government intervention becomes much weaker, since only the first (practical) reason remains valid. Even this reason seems to lose its validity in the case where rich people want to 'give' because they think that this will increase their reputation in society. This last motive will be seen by most as purely selfish, however, and we now turn to this class of motivations for income redistribution.

The most important of these selfish motives is the desire for insurance. If rich people realize that income changes may be caused by purely random factors, they will want to insure themselves against the possibility of bad luck. However, for many instances of bad luck private insurance markets will fail to exist. The creation of a social security scheme may then be a Pareto-improvement. Involuntary unemployment, leading to an unemployment compensation scheme, is an obvious example. *Ex post*, there will be a redistribution of income (from the working to the unemployed), but this redistribution follows from an (implicit) insurance contract. The unemployment compensation is equivalent to an insurance benefit; the taxes levied to finance these compensations can be seen as insurance premiums. Many other institutions in the labour market (e.g., seniority rights) can be interpreted in the same framework (see, e.g., Drèze 1979). Even these institutions are not sufficient to insure against all instances of bad luck, however. It therefore can be hypothesized that rich people will accept a government transfer scheme, which would guarantee at least a minimum income for everybody. Such a transfer scheme is a kind of insurance against extreme poverty. Its organization by government will be a Pareto-improvement.[48]

The theories sketched in this section undoubtedly can be helpful to explain the actual redistribution process in our Western societies. One may have doubts about the empirical importance of each of the motives taken separately, but it is to be realized that they all (from pure altruism to insurance) work together and interact in actual reality.[49]

However, the *ethical* status of this approach is less clear. The main reason to argue for this voluntary redistribution is the resulting increase in economic efficiency (welfare?), and the only ethical value involved is the Pareto criterion. We have commented already on the weakness of this criterion and, indeed, most of the relevant authors themselves are aware of this limitation. It is therefore suggested that 'Paretian' redistribution is only a first step, and that, after this step has been taken, we still need a Bergson-Samuelson social welfare function to choose the 'right' point on the Pareto-frontier. If one takes this second step, it is even possible to bypass the first one. We then are back in section 2 and none of the basic problems has been solved.

Moreover, many libertarians will already have problems with the first step: is it really acceptable to tax people for redistributional purposes with the pretext that they would be willing to give spontaneously, if only there would be no free-ridership?[50] It seems that such proposals can only get an ethical foundation within an explicit contractual framework. Such a framework is proposed by Kolm in his theory of the Liberal Social Contract.

5.2.2   *The Liberal Social Contract*

As all liberal thinkers, Kolm starts from the basic idea of the autonomy of the individual, leading to the ethical right to the product of one's own labour. This autonomy also implies the right to give up (or exchange) rights. A set of rights is legitimate if it follows from a transformation of another legitimate set of rights, and if the transformation itself was a legitimate process. Legitimacy follows from the voluntary agreement by all parties.

Now Kolm's theory takes its essential step. He argues that some voluntary agreements (contracts) will not arise spontaneously in the market place for a number of reasons, which have nothing to do with the desires of the potential contractants. Obvious examples are the presence of transaction costs, the lack of information, the difficulty to control the free-rider problem in a situation with public goods, the problem of externalities, the fact that one cannot draw a contract between persons who do not exist at the same time. And here begins the role of the political process:

> The political process is a social process that tries to achieve what direct free exchange was unable to do . . . The political philosophy that emanates from the liberty principle is: *any legitimate free agreement that would have been reached must be implemented* . . . Such an implicit agreement is called *a* Liberal Social Contract. *The* Liberal Social Contract is the name for the set of individual contracts and the principle itself . . . A Liberal Social Contract is a potential, putative, implicit, tacit legitimate agreement (Kolm 1987, p. 103).

And Kolm is explicit about the consequences of such a contract. Its implementation will require coercion: 'people must be forced to be free'. This coercion is legitimate, however, because it increases freedom, 'as if by removing a constraint which is what impedes the actual direct agreement'. This is a contractual theory of justice, since it derives the definition of legitimacy from the existence of voluntary exchanges between individuals. The voluntary exchanges may be *implicit*, however. Two further features of this version of contractualism must be noted. In the first place, a liberal social contract is an (implicit) agreement between real existing persons (and not a contract between zombies[51] in a kind of Rawlsian original state). This implies that the (tacitly) contracting parties are fully aware of their position in society. In the second place, each liberal social contract separately does not necessarily involve all individuals. Many decisions will only be relevant for a subset of citizens, for example, only those who will benefit from a given public good will enter into an agreement to provide (and finance) this public good. This second feature leads to a more flexible framework.

The obvious question now is: how do we know in practice the content of the (implicit) liberal social contracts? Here Kolm points to the results of economic, game-theoretical and philosophical analyses. The analysis of voluntary redistribution plays an important role in his construction of the role of government: he emphasizes both 'collective gift' (a version of altruism) and 'implicit insurance'. In his ethical construction, of course, the rationality of such interventions is *not* to increase 'welfare' or 'efficiency': he will interpret these liberal social contracts as an increase in the degree of freedom. And he goes further than the traditional welfare theory. In his view, compensation for past illegitimacies is an important ethical duty of government, leading to a tax-transfer system. He also considers the problem of natural resources: in his procedural framework, the 'right' allocation of such resources can only follow from unanimous agreement. Without predicting the outcome of this (implicit) bargaining process, he notes that unanimity will often require compensations from the receivers of resources to other people: in the Liberal Social Contract, these compensations will take the form of taxes. At least a part of all inheritances has to be interpreted as a 'gift from heaven' (which called back the donor) and, hence, as a natural resource: therefore, inheritance taxation will be one of the ingredients of the Liberal Social Contract.[52]

Kolm's theory undoubtedly gives some new and interesting insights in the basic tension between equality, efficiency and freedom. He works within a rights-based framework and, within this framework, goes a long way in justifying social institutions which redistribute income. This justification is new, precisely because it follows from a procedural ethical construction, and does not need any reference to end-state criteria. Some problems remain, however.

One might first raise the question whether the Liberal Social Contract is liberal enough. There can be no doubt that the theory is built up consistently from the principles of freedom. However, most libertarians will have problems when Kolm candidly admits that the Liberal Social Contract justifies some coercion. Kolm's answer could be that this coercion is not really coercion, if 'government' intervention only amounts to the realization of contracts, which would have been concluded spontaneously if there were no transaction costs. This requires in the first place that the government is perfectly informed about the true desires of the citizens. But we are in a world of imperfect information by definition, because otherwise there would be no need for the liberal social contracts. Who then is to decide about the exact content of the Liberal Social Contract in this framework, where it is not obvious on what ground somebody can claim to have more or better information than someone else? Perhaps this is not a fundamental problem, if we are willing to admit that government decisions indeed are imperfect, but accept that they nevertheless remain defensible if they are based as well as possible on the limited information available.

But this answer underlines the importance of a second problem: why would government officials be motivated to take the decisions which are best from a social point of view? Kolm (1985) emphasizes that the construction of a theory of justice only makes sense if there is somewhere an ethical desire in society. On this basis he defends his hypothesis of a benevolent government and devotes much attention to the detailed specification of the characteristics of such an ethically acceptable government organization. However, many libertarians will surely feel that he resurrects the old *deus ex machina* idea and underestimates the risks implied by the creation of strong coercive institutions. In a world of imperfect information, it might be very difficult to avoid manipulation by those who are in power.

From the other side, some could also claim that the theory does not go far enough in its advocacy of equality. However, Kolm is perfectly aware of this problem, and he introduces a broader ethical view through his theory of 'fundamental insurance'. He therefore sketches a situation where people do not yet know their earning capacity, their propensity to be sick, etc. In this kind of original position, people would probably accept a system of 'fundamental insurance', i.e., a system of transfers towards the handicapped or those with lower earning capacity (and, hence, lower incomes). This 'fundamental insurance contract' is *not* a liberal social contract, however, because it is not a contract between real, existing persons. Therefore, it will not necessarily have consequences for the liberal tax and transfer system. It will only become relevant when real, existing persons accept the ethical argumentation behind the 'fundamental insurance' idea and want it to be realized. In a certain sense, we then have a society with 'deontological altruists' and, as sketched earlier, a 'practical' argument for a liberal social contract. Of course, ethical thinking could also lead to 'pure altruism', where people really care about the welfare of others, and then we additionally have the 'collective gift' (public good) argument. It is therefore obvious that broader ethical views can enter the liberal system, but only through the opinions of the autonomous individuals. There is room for ethical discussion, but ethical dictatorship is not acceptable.

6   Non-welfaristic theories

The libertarian theories sketched in section 4 basically neglect the (end-state) distribution in their judgements of justice. The same is true for the social contract theories of Buchanan and Kolm. However, when people unanimously adopt a theory of justice, this theory can be implemented through a social contract. Even within these social contract frameworks, it therefore remains meaningful to think about 'end-state' justice, if only one does not impose one's opinions on society. Moreover, it is obvious that the criticism of welfarism, raised in section 3, does not necessarily lead to a rejection of all end-state theories: in fact, some of the most active critics of welfarism have proposed basing justice on end-state judgements, but looking at other variables than the welfare levels. In this section we will turn to the most influential of these non-welfaristic ethical theories.

A first theory is in the same spirit as Kolm's theory of fundamental insurance and is also strongly related to the no-envy framework reviewed in section 2.2. It was proposed by Dworkin (1981) in two papers which rapidly have become classics. We summarize it in section 6.1 and will also indicate some of its weaknesses. We then turn to Sen's theory of 'rights as goals' (section 6.2). This latter theory is a promising attempt to integrate freedom and equality into one consistent framework.

6.1   Dworkin and Roemer: equality of resources versus equality of welfare

In a first paper, Dworkin (1981) gives a penetrating criticism of welfarism. In the second paper, he then suggests an alternative interpretation of justice: the notion of 'equality of resources'.[53] Of course, a straightforward equal division of material resources would not be efficient, because of differences in tastes. For the division of these resources, Dworkin accepts the no-envy criterion, introduced by equity theory (see section 2.2), and also proposes an analogous market procedure.

We have mentioned already in the introduction that a simple equalization of resources cannot be 'just', because of differences in needs and effort. An analogous criticism has been raised in our treatment of equity theory. But Dworkin goes further than equity theory. He wants to find a solution for the problem that some (individual) resources are not transferable among individuals, i.e., cannot be distributed equally. He explicitly refers to differences in needs (e.g., being handicapped or not) and in productive capacities (natural talent). In Dworkin's view, the division of transferable resources has to compensate for these unequal 'starting positions'. Note that this interpretation of 'equal opportunities' goes much further than the one by Buchanan.

For Dworkin, the notion of 'income-fairness', as introduced by Pazner and Schmeidler (1978) (see section 2.2), is not acceptable as a compensation for differences in productive capacities. It leads to the slavery of the talented, and such a slavery is in conflict with the no-envy criterion. To compute the 'just' compensation for differences in talents, Dworkin therefore proposes as an alternative the idea of a hypothetical insurance market.

To describe this hypothetical situation, it is supposed not that people are wholly ignorant of what talents they have, but rather that they do not have any sound basis for predicting their economic rent – what income the talents they do have can produce. Each individual knows the aggregate productive capacity of society and in what income distribution it will result. But he is radically uncertain about his own position in that (known) income distribution.[54] The reasoning then goes as follows:

Assume that there is no monopoly in insurance, and that insurance firms offer policies of the following sort. Insurance is provided against failing to have an opportunity to earn whatever level of income, within the projected structure, the policy holder names, in which case the insurance company will pay the policy holder the difference between that coverage level and the income he does in fact have an opportunity to earn. Premiums will vary with the level of coverage chosen, must be the same for everyone at any particular coverage level, and will be paid, not out of the policy holder's initial stock of resources but rather from future earnings. (Dworkin 1981, p. 317)

Premiums and coverage levels will then be determined by this hypothetical market.

Dworkin argues that the division of transferable resources will be a 'just' compensation for the unequal division of non-transferable resources, if it mimics the *ex post* division, resulting from the hypothetical insurance market. He suggests that the instrument of a progressive income tax could be useful to realize such a copy of the hypothetical market outcomes in an actual social environment. The similarity between these ideas and Kolm's 'fundamental insurance' is obvious. If all people would agree that Dworkin's proposal is ethically appealing, then there is room for a liberal social contract, implementing such a progressive income tax.[55]

The idea of a hypothetical insurance market is an attractive one. It attacks the difficult problem of differences in needs and natural talents, and at the same time seems to avoid some problems of welfarism (for example, the subjectivity of personal preferences). Yet some important difficulties remain. Dworkin mentions the problem related to the simple equal division of 'property rights in the labour potential of society' (income fairness): the possibility of 'exploitation' of the talented. However, Roemer (1985) has shown that the hypothetical insurance mechanism does not solve this problem: it may lead (for a reasonable specification of the preferences) to a lower welfare level of the talented (and thus more exploitation) than the procedure where talented labour is owned equally by all people in society. And, worse still, it is possible that the insurance mechanism leads to a lower welfare level of the less talented people than they would reach in a situation with no compensation at all!

Roemer (1985; 1986a) also points to another problem, associated with the compensation for natural talents. If people are no longer responsible for their innate characteristics, it is not obvious how they can be held responsible for their preferences. The intuition is clear: when people have different preference structures, this must be due to some of their individual characteristics. The distinction between 'preferences' (for which people would be responsible) and 'talent' (for which they are not responsible) then becomes rather ambiguous. Moreover, taking into account *all* these characteristics finally leads to the 'fundamental preferences', discussed in section 2.3, which are the same for everybody. Hence a theorem: there is only one mechanism that equalizes resources (and compensates for innate characteristics) and that satisfies some reasonable properties; this mechanism distributes resources in such a way as to equalize utilities. Equality of resources (in Dworkin's sense) implies equality of welfare.[56]

Roemer confronts us with an important ethical difficulty. To quote his own words:

> The difficulty can be illustrated (if such is required) by taking an example from Dworkin (1981). He states that the equality-of-resource mechanism should be ambition-sensitive but not endowment-sensitive. A person is not entitled to the returns from a special endowment of resources he might possess, but he is entitled to returns from his ambition. But what is ambition? Is it the ability to work harder, or more persistently than the norm? That may be due to the possession of more adrenalin or endorphins than the normal person. Whatever ambition is, is there not some biological propensity which defines it, and should that propensity not be considered a resource? Or if differential ambition is due to differential external environments, surely that constitutes a difference in resources which resource egalitarianism should address. Dworkin also believes that the degree of risk a person wishes to bear is an aspect of his preferences, not his resources. But the same arguments can be given with respect to risk aversion as with respect to ambition. *At what point do we decide the person bears responsibility?* (Roemer 1985, p. 179)

6.2   Sen: rights and capabilities

The limitations of welfarism, sketched in section 3.1, are a good starting point to discuss the recent work of Amartya Sen. His theorem about the impossibility of a Paretian libertarian has been interpreted by some authors (for example Nozick) as an argument for a purely procedural theory of justice. Some libertarian theories in the same spirit have been reviewed in section 4 of this chapter. Sen himself, however, is not willing to draw such conclusions from his theorem. To argue against a purely procedural approach, he uses the argument which has been brought forward already many times in this review: the consequences of 'just' procedures may be really terrible. He refers to evidence which indicates that millions of people have died in famines in the recent past while there was no overall decline in food availability at all: the famines were caused by shifts in entitlements, that followed from the legitimate exercise of rights (Sen 1984a). It seems implausible that freedom has absolute priority in such life-and-death questions.

One can look at the same problem from a different (and more philosophical) angle and ask the question whether 'negative freedoms' are indeed only to be considered as 'constraints', within which social maximization takes place (if there is something left to be maximized). The latter position seems to imply that the amount of freedom is not a goal in itself and, hence, that no one is ever obliged to defend the 'negative' rights of someone else. Person A should not interfere with the freedom of person B (e.g., he should not black his eye), but what if he sees person C becoming aggressive towards B? Is A obliged to defend B? If yes, do we then not consider the realization of negative freedoms as a *goal* (instead of merely as a constraint)? Treating 'rights as goals' (Sen 1984b) has the advantage that we can also analyse in a coherent way trade-offs between different rights. Once we have a consistent objective function, we can answer questions such as: what is the right action for A, should he defend B against being beaten up, even if he therefore has to break into the house of D in order to use his phone to alert the police (Sen 1984b)?

Treating 'negative freedoms' as a goal, however, will surely not be sufficient to avoid the problem sketched in the first paragraph of this subsection: consequences may still be horrible. Given the problems associated with welfarism, it is preferable not to speak about 'welfare' consequences. However, consequences can also be described in terms of other variables. In this respect Sen proposes to admit 'positive freedoms' into our set of goals (for example the right to medical attention, the right not to be hungry). Despite the semantic similarity, this is a crucial step, which removes us from libertarianism.[57] Sen argues as follows:

Why should our concern stop only at protecting negative freedoms rather than be involved with what people can actually do? Should one be under an obligation to save the person who has been pushed into the river but not the person who has fallen in it? In deciding whether one is under an obligation to help a starving person, should one say 'yes' if the person has been robbed (with his negative freedom being violated), but remain free to say 'no' if he has been fired from his job, or has lost his land to the moneylender, or has suffered from flooding or drought (without any violation of negative freedom)? (Sen 1984a, pp. 314–15)

It is important now to give a concrete content to this notion of positive freedoms, without falling into the problems of welfarism. Sen (1985a; 1987) therefore introduces the idea of 'functionings': these functionings reflect what the person is succeeding in 'doing' or 'being'.

A functioning is an achievement of a person: what he or she manages to do or to be. It reflects, as it were, a part of the 'state' of that person. It has to be distinguished from the commodities which are used to achieve those functionings. For example, bicycling has to be distinguished from possessing a bike. It has to be distinguished also from the happiness generated by the functioning, for example, actually cycling around must not be identified with the pleasure obtained from that act. A functioning is thus different both from (1) having goods (and the corresponding characteristics), to which it is posterior, and (2) having utility (in the form of happiness resulting from that functioning), to which it is, in an important way, prior. (Sen 1985a, pp. 10–11)

'Positive freedoms' are then interpreted by Sen as the *capability* to function. He claims that the well-being and the living standard of individuals are determined by these capabilities (for example the ability to meet one's nutritional requirements, the wherewithal to be clothed and sheltered, the power to participate in the social life of the community – Sen 1979b).

The most interesting concept of 'equality' then refers to these basic capabilities. To define such 'equality', it is necessary to determine an *index* of these capabilities.[58] Like Rawls, Sen emphasizes that such an index is not equivalent to a utility function: *valuing* a life and measuring the *happiness* generated in that life are two different exercises (Sen 1985a, p. 12). It is, however, important to point to the differences between Rawls and Sen: the primary goods in the approach of the former are objective commodities, in the latter's theory the basic capabilities take into account characteristics of the individual. A giant will need more food than a dwarf to get the same capability to meet his nutritional requirements. Moreover, the procedure of introducing rights into the system of goals allows for trade-offs between these different rights. Sen therefore avoids the lexicographic ordering of principles which is proposed by Rawls.

It is possible that equality of basic capabilities cannot be realized. Moreover, such equality in any case is only a part of 'distributive justice'. Equality is not the only moral good, as was argued already in the introduction to this chapter. However, we can use the index of basic capabilities in any other function. It is possible to define a maximin (or leximin) criterion in terms of basic capabilities: this would allow us to introduce incentive considerations. It is possible even to define the social maximand as the sum of the different indices of basic capabilities: this brings us close to utilitarianism with 'broader' concepts of welfare and in that case gives a more concrete content to such a broad concept.

Sen's proposal to treat rights as goals is certainly a promising approach to structuring the social discussions around justice. Its integration of negative and positive freedoms makes it an appealing starting point to analyse the conflict between justice, efficiency and freedom. However, as it stands now, the theory of basic capabilities is formulated in a social vacuum and can therefore not be a fully adequate answer to the libertarian critique. What is the 'just' decision for society, if different citizens have different conceptions of the good? How must justice be 'organized', if we accept the criticism that government cannot be treated as an ideal *deus ex machina*? A complete elaboration of these questions will require a detailed specification of the trade-offs between the different rights, including a judgement on the acceptability and the limits of private property rights. It will also require a more thorough investigation into the concrete political and distributional implications of Sen's approach.

7   Conclusion

It cannot be the intention of this concluding section to summarize in a few lines the contents of this lengthy review. It seems useful, however, to sketch briefly the general picture and to suggest the main strengths and weaknesses of the economic approach.

This economic approach is influenced by the paradigm of the market. One cannot understand economic theories of justice without understanding economic theories on the working of the market system. This is often seen by non-economists as a basic weakness of the approach: they blame economists for their one-sidedness and sometimes argue that the emphasis on the market necessarily leads to a conservative bias. It is undoubtedly true that economists have not formulated a complete theory of justice – but who has? It is also true that mainstream economics is deeply embedded in the existing social structure. But, even taking into account these limitations, the economic understanding of the market mechanism may also be considered a basic advantage; at least, when one wants to formulate theories of justice, which are (immediately) relevant for our modern world, dominated as it is by that market mechanism. This is certainly true for the treatment of the 'incentive' problem. This problem has been studied extensively by economists. It has been neglected in this review, but is obviously important for the *practical* implementation of any theory of justice. Moreover, a better understanding of the market also seems important for the realistic formulation of the content of the basic principles of distributive justice.

Another important characteristic of mainstream economic theories is their consequentialist point of view. This approach even has a quasi-monopoly position in the field of so-called 'public economics', where criteria of justice are applied to concrete policy problems.[59] Such consequentialism may come into conflict with a deontological approach to human rights (see, e.g., Nozick). Yet, here also the criticism is not altogether convincing. Perhaps Nozick is right in claiming that 'consequences' should not be the *only* factor determining the 'rightness' of any economic action. However, it is hard to defend that consequences do not matter at all: in the review, we have several times given the example of large famines. Surely, a theory of justice should be *consequence sensitive*.

But what are the important variables to be considered when describing 'consequences'? The mainstream economic answer has been to concentrate on the welfare levels of the individuals in society. During the thirties and forties, it was almost generally accepted that these welfare levels could not be compared between individuals. The huge stream of research following the publication of Arrow (1951) has shown that under this informational assumption it is very difficult to formulate an attractive theory of justice. 'Equity' theory is the only elaborated attempt in the modern economic literature and it can be argued that some problems remain with this theory. Most welfare economists have chosen another route: they accept interpersonal comparability of welfare and try to give it an appealing interpretation. Once this is done, the way is paved for incorporating ethical considerations into the social welfare function framework. Utilitarianism has been resurrected and Rawls' difference principle has been (incorrectly) translated as the 'maximin' (or leximin) criterion. Mathematical formulae have been proposed, that cover both utilitarianism and maximin as special (extreme) cases, and allow for 'intermediate' values of inequality aversion. The ethical problem of distributive justice has thus been reduced to the choice of a single parameter in a mathematical function.

One immediately feels that this is somewhat too simple.[60] There are two aspects to the oversimplification. The first is the exclusive concentration on individual utility levels; this has been christened 'welfarism'. The emphasis on welfarism can be explained by historical (the utilitarian soil of economics) and methodological reasons (its mathematical tractability and the possibility of integrating positive and normative economics). Yet it seems to be the main weakness of mainstream welfare economics. In the review, we have argued that individual utility levels do not capture all considerations which are relevant for distributive justice. The only way out of these problems is to reinterpret 'utility', so as to incorporate these other considerations. But this leads immediately to the question of what is then the 'most interesting' reformulation of utility; and to answer this question, one has to take into account non-welfaristic arguments. The relaxation of welfarism therefore is a necessary step if we want to construct a more appealing approach to justice.

There is a second problem with the mainstream approach. What is the 'right' way to act if different citizens have different conceptions of justice? What if we replace the *deus ex machina* conception of the state with a more realistic picture of self-interested politicians and bureaucrats? What is the role played by ethical feelings in such a society? Forced redistribution seems to interfere with the basic autonomy of each human being. It appears that a theory of justice in one way or another should confront this basic problem. Mainstream welfare economics has largely neglected it.

The basic autonomy of the individual and the respect for property rights are the starting point for libertarian theories of justice. The legitimation of the existing set of property rights then becomes a crucial problem. Moreover, these theories have to face the famine example mentioned earlier. Simply making an exception for 'extreme poverty' does not solve the problem, unless one defines carefully the concept of 'extreme poverty' and specifies exactly the relevant trade-off between the avoidance of such poverty and the basic liberties. But this means that one no longer has a 'pure' libertarian theory.

A possible way to escape from these problems is the use of a social contract framework. The best known example in economics is the work of Buchanan. He argues that the socially acceptable definition of justice is formulated by the initial contractants in the natural state, characterized by the war of each against all. These contractants will unanimously agree about institutions which guarantee 'equal opportunities', but at the same time be very reluctant to hand over much power to a strong government. This implies that *re*distribution generally will not be accepted. Buchanan's approach therefore tends to lead to a defence of the status quo, i.e., the distribution as it follows from the unhampered play of market forces. Surely, not everybody will agree that this limited interpretation exhausts the concept of 'distributive justice'.

As such, the contractual framework is empty, however. It is possible that contractants would agree about a broader concept of justice and would therefore even accept pronounced redistributive policies. This idea has been worked out by Kolm. In his theory, the social contractants are real existing persons. Moreover, the Liberal Social Contract is to a large extent implicit. All contractual agreements, which cannot be realized because of transaction costs (including the free-rider problem and the problem of yet unborn generations), are part of the social contract and must be imposed by a coercive government. People must be forced to be free. A consistent exploration of the consequences of this idea (partly inspired by the mainstream economic theories of voluntary redistribution) leads to the conclusion that many redistributive measures are in the self-interest of all citizens.

Kolm's approach thus leads to a 'broader' concept of justice than that of Buchanan. However, it can still be argued that looking for a consensus among citizens necessarily leads to a minimalist conception of justice; it suggests a 'right' procedure for social decision-making which respects the basic autonomy of each individual, but remains rather poor as a guide for personal ethical thinking. At least some of us will feel that justice is more than respect for individual rights and also implies a quest for an organization of the world with more altruism and where more people can realize their human potentialities. Of course, social contract theories do not have the ambition to be a guide for personal ethical thinking and different ethical positions may find their place in the framework. Even within a libertarian framework, it certainly is not forbidden to try to convert others to an ethically richer position. If everybody has been converted, this richer conception of justice can be realized through a social contract. Or, as Kolm states: 'Fraternity reconciles liberty with equality' (1987, p. 120).

'Fraternity' as such remains a rather vague concept. We need a more elaborated ethical theory that can act as a pole of attraction, if we really want to contribute to the social discussions about distributive justice. Such a theory should be non-welfarist, for the reasons discussed earlier. Kolm and Dworkin formulate an idea of fundamental insurance, but, as Roemer has shown, there may be problems with the exact specification of the insurance mechanism. An attractive alternative approach has been proposed by Sen. Why not try to transcend the basic conflict between justice and freedom by integrating negative and positive freedoms into a system of 'rights as goals'? This indeed seems to suggest a way to formulate consistently the trade-offs between these different freedoms.[61]

Recent economic thinking undoubtedly has yielded valuable insights, which may be helpful to structure a rational discussion on distributive justice. However, all rational reconstructions will only reflect a part of the complex social reality behind the idea of distributive justice. One should therefore not be too optimistic about the outcome of the social discussions. Consensus will not be reached and 'justice' will be realized through continuous social conflict, in which the conflicting groups are driven by a complex mixture of self-interest and their own ethical interpretation of justice.

Notes

1 Recently, some economists have tried to 'test' empirically whether economic theories may be relevant to describe the actual opinions of people. But even in these writings, the influence of psychology and sociology is rather limited – see for example Kahneman, Knetsch and Thaler (1986), Schokkaert and Lagrou (1983), Schokkaert and Overlaet (1989) and Yaari and Bar-Hillel (1984). For an overview of the psychological and sociological work on justice, see Törnblom, and Arts and van der Veen, this volume.

2 In the economic jargon, cardinal measurement refers to measurement on an interval scale. If a set of numbers x represents the utility levels, a positive linear transformation of these numbers ($y = a + bx$) can also be used. The best known example of such a scale outside economics is the measurement of temperature (Celsius and Fahrenheit).

3 This policy rule only follows when individual utility functions are identical. If this is not the case, utilitarianism may have very unappealing distributional consequences. We return to this problem in section 2.3.

4 An interesting tale on the switch towards ordinalism is told by Cooter and Rappoport (1984). See Hennipman (1987) for a severe criticism of the Cooter/Rappoport story.

5 It is necessary to emphasize that Pareto himself certainly did not limit his theory to the concept of 'Pareto-efficiency'. See Kolm (1969, pp. 170–1) for a brief presentation of Pareto's 'true' ideas.

6 If A is not altruistic. We will return to that possibility in section 5.2.1.

7 The introduction of this function is usually attributed to Bergson (1938) and

Samuelson (1947). We will follow this tradition and terminology. Again, an early and important forerunner of the approach has been Pareto – see the discussion in Kolm 1969.

8 There is a basic problem of terminology here. Thinkers who defend a liberty-based social ethic are called 'liberals' in the continental and in the older English tradition. In recent Anglo-Saxon literature, however, the use of the term 'libertarian(ism)' has become widespread. Basically we will follow the latter convention, but make exception for those authors (such as Kolm 1985), who explicitly reject this term for their own theory.

9 In the original paper reference was made to the 'paradox of the Paretian *liberal*'.

10 This paragraph is the most technical of the review. It can easily be skipped by the reader who is not interested in the 'social choice' literature and is willing to accept that interpersonal comparability of welfare is necessary to give a real ethical content to the social welfare function.

11 One should be careful when blaming new welfare economists for this over-simplified position. The best among them were clearly aware of the problem. Samuelson (1947, p. 249) writes: 'It is not literally true that the new welfare economics is devoid of any ethical assumptions. Admittedly, however, its assumptions are more general and less controversial, and it is for this reason that it gives incomplete necessary conditions, whose full significance emerges only after one has made interpersonal assumptions. To refuse to take the last step renders the first two steps nugatory; like pouring out a glass of water and then refusing to drink.'

12 The definition of 'social welfare function' used by Arrow is somewhat more demanding than the Bergson-Samuelson function, introduced earlier. It has therefore been claimed (e.g. by Samuelson 1977) that the impossibility theorem does not hold for such Bergsonian social welfare functions. A suitable reformulation of the conditions, however, very soon resurrects the impossibility (see, for example, the recent treatments by d'Aspremont (1985) and Kemp and Ng (1987)).

13 We borrow this perspective from the many writings of Sen. See, for example, Sen 1985c for an easy, recent and explicit treatment of the problem. The link between social choice and moral philosophy is not always as clear as it should be: 'These misunderstandings about the content of social choice propositions are partly the fault of social choice theory itself. The language of social choice theory – though precisely formulated – has tended to be rather remote from the standard language of social and political philosophy, and the skill of the social choice theorist in obtaining technical results has not been quite matched by the inclination to discuss issues of interpretation' (Sen 1983, p. 17).

14 There is some terminological confusion in the literature. We will define our concepts as we proceed, and then stick to our own definitions.

15 We define a problem of 'pure distribution' as a problem not involving production. This implies that there is a fixed bundle of commodities, which is to be divided in a 'fair' way among a number of economic agents. We assume that commodities indeed are divisible.

16 Recently, an analogous fairness framework has also been used to discuss

different concepts of 'equality of opportunity'. For an overview, see again Thomson and Varian 1985.

17 Similar interpretations have been proposed by Harsanyi (1955), by Tinbergen (1975; 1978) and by Mirrlees (1982), who speaks about 'isomorphic' individuals. An alternative has been to start from the concept of 'just-noticeable difference' as a unit of measurement – see Ng (1975).

18 However, the leximin criterion has been independently proposed by Kolm (1972), who calls it 'justice pratique'.

19 Unit comparability does not imply level comparability. In fact, for a utilitarian comparison of two social states, only the differences in the individual utility levels for the two social states are relevant. This implies that the origins of measurement of these individual utility functions (and hence the utility levels) do not have any influence on the final welfare judgement.

20 The informational restrictions and ethical implications of the Arrowian framework are well explained in Sen's (1970b) classic. A recent and short treatment is in Sen 1985c. These ideas have been explored in the seminal papers by d'Aspremont and Gevers (1977), Hammond (1976) and Strasnick (1976). An early assessment can be found in Arrow (1977). Since then, the literature really has exploded. A (formal) overview, containing a complete list of references, is d'Aspremont (1985).

21 This is a 'rightist' specification within the terminology introduced in section 1.1.

22 An overview of different theoretical results is given by Atkinson and Stiglitz (1980). The recent literature contains many empirical applications of the approach. An interesting collection is Newbery and Stern (1987).

23 Another defence of utilitarianism starts from separability ideas – see, e.g., Gorman 1976; Mirrlees 1982; Boadway and Bruce 1984.

24 Starting with his influential papers (1953) and (1955). A collection of essays is Harsanyi (1976). A recent and concise overview of his ideas is Harsanyi (1982). Similar ideas have also been proposed by Vickrey (1960).

25 Rawls (1974; 1982) does not agree with this interpretation. We return to his own framework in section 3.2. See also Cullen, this volume.

26 A nice overview of the debate is given by the book of Sen and Williams (1982), containing contributions both by welfarists and non-welfarists, and an interesting introduction by the editors.

27 The example is from Arrow (1973), who also mentions the possibility of a strong taste for pre-phylloxera claret.

28 See Dworkin (1981) and Elster (1982) for in depth discussions of these and related problems.

29 Other examples are described and axiomatically analysed by Roemer (1986b).

30 One can claim that the example is not realistic, because the utility loss of 2 will normally be higher than the utility gain of 1. But this is not relevant for the point of the example, which is the limitation of welfarism to see beyond the utility numbers.

31 See, for example, the discussion between Ng (1981a) and Sen (1981), following the publication of Sen (1979a).

32 Despite his own statement that the example has had more attention than it deserves, and is now 'tired' – Sen 1983, p. 10.

33 A critical discussion of the literature until 1976 is in Sen 1976. For a more philosophical and less mathematical treatment, see Sen 1983.

34 See Sen 1983 for a critical discussion of this position. He argues that an ordering of social states need not be based on 'welfare', but could also start from the 'degree of consistency with the right procedures'. In that case the impossibility of the Paretian libertarian remains.

35 The problem is mentioned explicitly by Rawls himself: 'When we attempt to deal with the problem of special medical and health needs a different or a more comprehensive notion than that of primary goods (at least as presented in the text) will, I believe, be necessary; for example, Sen's notion of an index which focuses on persons' basic capabilities may prove fruitful for this problem and serve as an essential complement to the use of primary goods' (Rawls 1982, fn. 8).

36 If we define the world of economic science as the world of scientific journals and congresses.

37 At least when freedom is interpreted in its negative sense.

38 This often is the libertarian position, as described by Van Parijs (1987): 'Si une société, si riche soit-elle, laisse mourir ses indigents, j'ose croire que bon nombre de libertariens trouveront cela déplorable. Mais, pour autant qu'aucun droit de propriété n'ait été violé, il n'y a rien là *d'injuste* à leurs yeux' (p. 17).

39 See, for example, the huge philosophical literature concerning Nozick's interpretation of the so-called 'Lockean proviso' with respect to the initial appropriation of natural resources.

40 In fact, Wicksell (1896) himself reserved the unanimity criterion for allocation decisions, to be taken after a just distribution was reached by other means in a previous stage of decision-making. Moreover, in his view of the decision-making process it is a body of *representatives* that takes unanimously a *global* decision on all public goods.

41 In Buchanan and Tullock (1962), it is argued that the initial contractants might be willing to accept some redistribution of income as a kind of insurance against income uncertainty. We will return to this kind of argument in section 5.2.1.

42 We noted already that this possibility is mentioned explicitly in Buchanan and Tullock (1962).

43 We follow Kolm in using the term *Liberal* Social Contract.

44 It is important not to get confused by these adjectives: in all these cases, the redistribution of income leads to an increase in the utility of the donor. Therefore, from this point of view, they are all 'selfish'. Clearly, this raises some interesting philosophical questions about the exact interpretation of 'altruism'.

45 Although the traditional economic framework starts from the hypothesis that economic agents are mainly motivated by their self-interest, some economists have recently introduced altruistic motivations in their analysis. Important references are Collard 1978; Kolm 1969; 1984; and Margolis 1981. This

literature is beyond the scope of this review and we will only concentrate on some implications for redistributive government policies.

46 And under the hypothesis that the enforcement itself does not lead to a utility loss.

47 There exists a huge economic literature on the *voluntary* provision of such public goods: under some circumstances (e.g., a limited number of interested persons who have a close relationship) free-ridership will be restricted. Government intervention will be necessary only within communities with a certain size and impersonality. It is obvious that the most important problems of justice arise in the latter case.

48 Analogous ideas have been proposed to rationalize a redistributive income tax scheme – see, e.g., Varian 1980.

49 Still other selfish motives are treated in the literature. Rich people may be aware that an economy with fewer poor people might be more productive (an argument which was already prominent in the writings of Pigou and Marshall). Or they may fear that revolution and political upheaval will follow from extreme poverty (see, e.g., Brennan 1973).

50 It is exactly in this context that Rowley and Peacock (1975) use the term 'Paretian empire building'.

51 We follow again Kolm's terminology.

52 Other important aspects of the Liberal Social Contract, on which we will not comment here, are the macroeconomic policy and the legitimacy (under certain conditions) of government borrowing and debt.

53 Dworkin (1981, p. 283) is very cautious in his formulation: 'We shall be occupied, for the most part, simply in defining a suitable conception of equality of resources, and not in defending it except as such definition provides a defense.' However, in his reaction on Narveson (1983), Dworkin (1983) quite explicitly defends the importance of equality.

54 This of course is a 'veil of ignorance' idea, but the veil is thinner than in the approach of Rawls.

55 Of course for Dworkin the ethical appeal of this scheme does *not* hinge on such a unanimous approval, since he does not reason within a social contract framework.

56 The theorem of course assumes interpersonal comparability of welfare. If this assumption is not accepted (e.g., for the reasons discussed in section 3.1), then Roemer (1986a) proves an impossibility theorem: there is no mechanism with 'reasonable' properties that can equalize resources in the Dworkin sense.

57 Remember the position of Rowley and Peacock (1975) that positive freedom is the greatest enemy of negative freedom.

58 According to Sen, it is not necessary for such an index to reflect a *complete* ranking of 'bundles of capabilities'.

59 Newbery and Stern (1987) are quite explicit in their statements about the modern theory of taxation: 'The theory that this book will develop, apply, and discuss reflects and contributes to the modern theory of public economics ... The essence of the approach lies first in the formal modelling of consequences and second in the use of explicit value judgements to assess the consequences' (p. 5). For an alternative approach, see Kolm 1988.

60 One should be cautious in judging applied economic work, however. In actual political discussions, the objective of 'justice' is often reduced to 'less income inequality', without further nuances and without specifying the exact interpretation of 'less'. Doing sensitivity analysis within the welfaristic social welfare function approach (see (1) in section 2.3) is then a definite step forward. Moreover, if one wants to make the problems tractable, one mostly has to accept so many simplifying assumptions about the working of the economy, that the social welfare function probably is not even the worst part of the exercise.

61 From a methodological point of view, I want to mention explicitly the work of Roemer (1985, 1986a, 1986b). His proposal to axiomatize justice in the space of 'economic environments' seems to me one of the most promising suggestions in the recent economic literature.

4   Justice and the law

John Bell

1   Introduction

1.1   *Philosophical concerns in legal writing on justice*

Lawyers and legal philosophers have not been overly preoccupied with
the question 'what is justice?' Few works have been wholly dedicated to
the topic in recent years, and many of the articles do not have any great
innovative quality. In many ways this is symptomatic of the more practical way in which the topic is approached – not as a question of absolute
or abstract ideals to which the law should aspire, but as a matter of how
insitutions currently in existence should operate and how the rules of law
can be made to conform more closely to the values shared in the community in which it has to operate.[1] To this extent, legal writing on justice
rejoins the concerns of economic and sociological literature surveyed in
other chapters (see Schokkaert, and Arts and Van der Veen). On the
whole, lawyers are more concerned with achieving practical justice than
with philosophizing about it. As Pound put it (1951, p. 129),

lawyers are not required to conduct a sit-down strike until philosophers agree, if they
ever do, upon a theory of values or a definition of justice. Experience developed by
reason and reason tested by experience have taught us how to go far toward achieving
a practical task of enabling men to live together in politically organized communities
in civilized society with the guidance of a working idea even if that working idea is not
metaphysically or logically or ethically convincingly ideal.

The philosophical discussions which do take place are typically of a
derivative character, drawing on established authors in philosophy,
rather than creating much which is novel. Of course, some works do
overlap (see especially Finnis 1980, Hart 1961, Kelsen 1973, Luhmann
1973 and Perelman 1972). But for the most part works of authors such
as Rawls, Nozick, Ackerman, Habermas and existential philosophers
have been central to what is written. This chapter seeks to survey some of
the major jurisprudential works on the subject published in the last
twenty years, concentrating mainly on Western Europe.

1.2   *The meaning of justice*

Terminology: English is probably the worst language in which to present
European conceptions of the relationship between 'law' and 'justice'.

Other languages have two words for 'law': *lex/loi/legge/Gesetz* (viz. specific legal prescriptions contained in statutes, etc.) and *ius/droit/diritto/Recht* (viz. legal standards in general). Often the latter notion is linguistically connected to justice: *iustitia/Gerechtigkeit*. Rightness and legality are thus often connected concepts.

As will be seen in section 3, other terms such as 'equity' (in the biblical sense) are closely connected, though this term has such a specific legal meaning as to be often translatable preferably by the English notion of 'fairness'. 'Natural justice' has such a specific role in common law terminology (meaning roughly 'le fair-play') that it is avoided altogether here in anything but its very specific legal meaning (viz. the right to a hearing and to an unbiased judge). It is in the study of these more specific concepts that most understanding of lawyers' views on justice is to be gained.

Content: Perhaps the most used legal definition of justice comes from Ulpian in the third century AD: 'constans et perpetua voluntas ius suum cuique tribuendi' (Digest 1.1.10 pr). This notion of 'giving to each his own' brings forward the central elements of equal treatment and concern for how resources are allocated. While 'legal justice' in its restricted sense is usually limited to treating all according to their legal entitlements, lawyers are often concerned with how the law ought to allocate entitlements in the first place.

In a survey of the literature on justice, Voigt and Thornton (1984, Introduction) identify three types of values: social order (conformity to legal or other norms); social well-being (the public interest or common good); and individual freedom (individual autonomy). Discourse ordered around these different values produces different results. While the second and third set out goals which transcend the legal order, the first does not necessarily do so. Theories which concentrate on justice according to law can be agnostic as to the basis of the view of justice which the law embodies.

Passmore (Kamenka and Tay 1979, chapter 2) argues that one must differentiate civil justice, which would exclude no one from a calculation of what is just, from communal justice, which is limited to those obligations which result from belonging to a particular community. He also argues that one must distinguish social justice, which would seek to distribute goods on the basis of merit or other reasons (e.g. underprivilege), thus permitting redistribution of existing entitlements, from formal justice, which would not. He argues that civil justice and social justice expect too much of the notion of justice (as opposed to values such as charity, etc.) and that it is properly confined to the other two elements. Many authors reviewed here would contest the exclusion of social justice. For example Feinberg (1980) sees social justice as central, and Honoré (1987) defines 'social justice' as going beyond equal advantage, but treats it as central to his conception of justice. Nearly all authors, however, are concerned with the obligations of justice as they relate to a particular community. (In this the legal authors show resemblance to the sociologists described by Arts and van der Veen in the next chapter.) Concern for justice between communities or in relation to individuals from outside a community is typically confined to international law (Stone 1984), and concern for justice between generations is rare, but can be seen in Tammelo (1982, p. 110) and Barry (Kamenka and Tay 1979, chapter 3).

2   Justice as an abstract value

Two trends can be detected among the literature which does consider justice in the abstract, rather than in terms of the concrete operation of existing institutions. One trend looks at justice as an ideal which transcends ideas currently in society (2.1), the second limits itself to a consideration of justice as a socially determined value (2.2).

2.1   Justice as an ideal

Much of current jurisprudential literature is positivist in character and would deny the existence of an ideal of justice to which the law and legal institutions ought to conform (2.1.1). That body of literature which does seek to defend justice as an ideal grounds the content of this virtue in natural law, or through discursive or utilitarian justifications (2.1.2). Even within the camp of those who would seek to defend the ideal of justice, many would seek to narrow its claims and scope (2.1.3).

2.1.1   Positivism and justice

Positivism dominates much of legal philosophy at the present period. In a limited sense, positivism would simply deny any *necessary* connection between law and justice, since law is a human creation, identifiable from purely social sources of legislation, custom, case-law and doctrine. (See Hart 1961, chapter 8; Raz 1980, chapter 4.) This would in no way deny that the positive law seeks to achieve an extra-legal ideal of justice. It would merely state that law need not necessarily do so and its validity does not depend on conformity to justice. There are, however, wider claims made by some positivists who would seek to suggest that no values other than those which are socially determined can be demonstrated and that notions such as 'justice' are merely empty categories within which individual or collective preferences are expressed. It is this latter version of positivism which will be considered here.

The denial of a discoverable ideal to which reference is made by arguments of justice comes most strongly from those who would claim that values are merely emotive expressions of opinions. For example, Ross (1958, p. 274) states:

To invoke justice is the same thing as banging on the table: an emotional expression which turns one's demand into an absolute postulate. That is no proper way to mutual understanding. It is impossible to have a rational discussion with a man who mobilizes 'justice', because he says nothing that can be argued for or against.

For authors like Kelsen,[2] discussions under the heading of 'justice' involve conflicts of values the choice between which can only be made on the basis of 'emotional factors' and, at best, one can only get a majority viewpoint. As a result, the best one can achieve is a relative justice. If one wants to talk of 'objective' values, this can only be in the sense that collective values stand as independent of the individual member of the community (Grzegorczyk 1982, pp. 267–70). The conflict of views between individuals about what is just and the absence of an authentic arbiter between competing claims is thought to lend support to this view, because there is no ascertainable agreed point of reference to settle what is objectively just, so that individual views appear merely to be unsupported assertions. Existentialist and structuralist approaches would reach similar conclusions (see Blessing 1973, p. 249; Miaille 1978, pp. 315ff.).

The other concern of this group of authors is in the vagueness of the values which are associated with justice. For instance, the notion of 'give to each his own' has no real content without some decision about what belongs to particular individuals. Such decisions can be both good and bad, depending upon viewpoint. The same could be said for equality before the law (Kelsen 1973, pp. 13–15). Without some objective and independent reference-point for what is the correct distribution of property or the correct treatment of individuals, reference to 'justice' can only really mean 'justice according to law', where 'law' means the law of a particular community. In this way the problem of what is just is not a real problem (Marcic 1969, p. 175). Justice comes in as a matter of how legal decisions are made rather than what values go into the creation of legal norms (see Luhmann 1973). Even notions such as 'equity' which appear to appeal to values which transcend the law can be seen in fact as merely positive legal norms of a higher level which modify the operation of specific legal rules (Marcic 1969, pp. 179–89). The content of 'equity' as applied in the law is found in principles which are accepted within a particular legal community. As such, they need not import any higher notions of morality than the institutional morality of that legal system.

2.1.2   Grounding justice as an ideal

Those who would wish to assert the possibility of an ideal value of justice to which the law should aspire fall mainly into three camps. The natural lawyers offer an objective value or values from which the notion of justice may be defined. A more popular approach in recent years has been to suggest that values such as justice are not simply discovered, but are constructed. Such constructions are not, however, arbitrary or irrational, but can be justified in a way which makes sense of the basic values adhered to in a community (MacCormick 1982, p. 153). Such a discursive approach has much in common with the 'reflective equilibrium' of Rawls (1971). The two approaches to justifying an ideal view of justice are not incompatible and may be used in combination. A third approach has a longer history, basing justice on an assessment of utility or a similar value.

(a) Natural law approaches

A natural law approach is best defined as one which seeks to establish and justify principles of justice which have some independence from particular human communities. The ideas of justice found in any one community may be thought of as attempts to understand and express the requirements of an ideal justice to which the community aspires. Such an ideal forms the basis for criticism of the achievements of particular communities, whose achievements will never be more than approximations of the ideal. While authors may illustrate the plausibility of their views from particular societies, description of what a particular society believes does not exhaust the content of ideal justice (D'Amato 1984, p. 224; Del Vecchio 1955, chapter 13).

Justice and the moral law: A classical exposition of the natural law viewpoint would suggest that the law ought to adhere to the demands of the moral law (Dabin 1969, Part 3, chapter 3; Villey 1975, pp. 59–60). The precise content of this ideal is to be obtained from rational reflection, even though it is recognized that statements of what is just may not be capable of full articulation (Fikentscher 1977, pp. 6–7; Battifol 1979, p. 417). A provisional assessment is made in relation to a particular society and culture, even if no absolute standard can be claimed for such a method (Fikentscher 1977, p. 641). (No attempt is made to ground such an ideal purely on religious revelation.) Yet it is clear that justice is not the only moral virtue and merely represents a particular virtue. For some like Villey (1975, p. 63), justice is merely dealing with that part of the moral law which relates to dealings between individuals: giving to each their own. For others like Dabin (1969, p. 395), 'legal justice' (*la justice légale, richtiges Recht*) is merely the following of the rule of reason in the construction of legal rules and in the operation of institutions, a minimum to be contrasted with the highest ideals represented by 'just law' (*la loi qui consacre la Justice, gerechtes Recht*). (But this is contested by others like Finnis 1980, chapter 7.) Thus, even if the law does have a teleological character, aiming to achieve some ideal of justice, this may not include an obligation to achieve the most perfect form of justice (D'Amato 1984, p. 224; Zanfarino 1967). For this reason, most modern authors prefer to present justice not as an independent virtue, but as a way of realizing other values, such as individual rights or the common good.

Basis in the dignity of the individual: For many authors, the starting point for reflection is the central value of the individual in moral thinking. Each individual is an end in himself and must be treated as such, or, as Del Vecchio (1955, p. 63) puts it, I have to treat others as 'other *mes*'. This element of reciprocity provides a trans-subjective conception of justice: 'each individual must be recognized (by others) for what he is worth, and to each must be attributed (by others) what belongs to him' (Del Vecchio 1955, p. 67). The precise content of these principles is filled out by a proper understanding of what it is to treat another as an absolute, autonomous being. This expansion of the Kantian ideal is a widely held conception (e.g. Tebaldeschi 1979, chapter 7). Weinreb (1987) places the emphasis on the recognition of the awareness of each individual as a free actor as the basis of justice, which is an approach based more on the rights of the recipient than on his duties to others.

In order to establish what should belong to an individual and that to which he is entitled, some authors have developed theories of 'basic goods' necessary to the flourishing of any individual human life. Notable among recent authors in this area are Finnis (1980) and Grisez and Boyle (1982). As the latter (1982, p. 345) put it:

The basis for moral norms ... includes two types of propositions. One of them characterizes certain goods – 'goods' not in a moral sense but merely in the sense of things desired for their own sake – as constituents of human well-being or flourishing. The other kind of proposition specifies the manner in which human acts must be related to these human goods if the acts are to be morally right.

Practical reasoning in relation to the basic goods enables a correct understanding of what is morally right, and this can be applied to the moral virtue of justice. Thus, Finnis (1980, chapter 2) argues that we can identify certain basic goods. A first basic value, corresponding to the drive for self-preservation, is the value of *life*, including every aspect of the vitality (*vita*, life) which puts the human being in good shape for self-determination. *Knowledge*, as a concern for the truth, and *play*, enjoying an activity for its own sake, are non-instrumental goods, as is *aesthetic experience*, where what is sought after and valued for its own sake may simply be the beautiful form 'outside' one, or the creation and/or active appreciation of some work of significant and satisfying form. *Religion* involves finding answers to the ultimate order of things in the world, and man's place in it. For Finnis, *sociability* is also a non-instrumental value. Having friends or living in society are valuable in themselves, as well as being means of realizing the objectives of a particular individual. Human flourishing does not only involve achieving certain objectives, there is also concern about how this occurs. The value of *practical reasonableness* identifies the good of being able to bring one's own intelligence to bear effectively on the problems of choosing one's actions and lifestyle and shaping one's own character.

An alternative approach to justice is to posit certain individual rights, justified independently of utility, and to use respect for these as a yardstick of what is just. This view is seen in Dworkin (1978) and Sen (1985d), as well as in the philosophical writings of authors like Nozick (see Cullen, this volume). Rights are thus founded on a rational consideration of basic intuitions about human interests. The inviolability of the human individual is taken here as a starting point for reasoning, imposing on the State duties of respect and neutrality (see Nino 1980, pp. 418–21; 1984). Reasoning about what is just must take the rights thus developed as a starting point, and whether these rights are respected by a particular outcome is a criterion of whether it is just. On the other hand, others might argue that this is too individualistic a viewpoint, and that the individual must first be situated in society, before his or her fundamental interests can be assessed. Rights in this way would not have an absolute character, and would not be seen as antithetical to State action in the way some of the rights literature seems to suggest (Bagolini 1983, pp. 30–41).

Justice and the common good: Whereas some, such as Villey (1975), see justice as essentially a virtue pertaining to the organization of society and the protection of individuals, others such as Finnis see it as both an individual and a social virtue – a way in which the individual and the collectivity can ensure human flourishing in their society. For Finnis (1980, chapter 6), the common enterprise of life in a society committed to securing human flourishing requires certain ways of dealing with the common stock of resources, either by assigning them to particular individuals or by collective management for the common good. Needs, function, deserts, capacity, etc. form relevant considerations. No operation of the common enterprise can be allowed to swamp the individual and, to that extent, an individual cannot be required to do too much for the common good. Both Finnis and Grisez and Boyle would see individual liberty as part of any proper understanding of human flourishing. For them, the duty of the individual to help promote the common good is a way of realizing human flourishing and, in particular, the good of sociability. It does not thereby restrict improperly the diversity and freedom of individual action.

(b) Discursive theories
Leading among the theorists who try to ground arguments of justice in discursive methods of justification is Perelman (1972) (also Alexy 1989).

He argues that the method of conviction in moral argument is not by reference to some absolute, but by reference to standards accepted within an audience or community. He suggests that 'politically just laws and regulations are those that are not arbitrary, because they correspond to the beliefs, aspirations and values of the political community' (1972, p. 63). An unjust law is thus one which deviates from the customs and precedents of the community without due reason and thereby creates arbitrary discrimination (ibid. chapter 6, esp. p. 75). A similar approach is adopted by Tammelo (1977, p. 56; 1982, p. 23) who argues that absolute objectivity is impossible to obtain. Nevertheless, at a specific time and place, certain principles can be held to be established in an inter-subjective manner and this counts as objectivity. Such a basis might be thought not to provide a transcendent ideal of justice, but merely a social custom (see Samek 1981, p. 810). Stone (1965, pp. 327–8) argues that it may reproduce little more than the irrational views of a community. Such discursive justification is not, however, simply a matter of reflecting the existing views of the community, but rather offering arguments which the audience can be convinced to accept, given its present nature (Perelman 1972, chapter 5; MacCormick 1984, p. 153). This approach presupposes that disagreements about what is just are not radical and that there is, at least at root in any community, a basic agreement about the fundamentals of justice (see Schramm 1983).

Despite the more general claims of such an approach, it would not, in practice, often yield results which were more than local understandings of justice. Indeed, more recent writings of Rawls (1987) which might be thought to parallel this approach seem to suggest that a contractarian approach can only produce understandings which reflect the views of a particular society.

(c) Utilitarian and connected approaches
Some utilitarian approaches have long been connected with legal positivism, as in the case of Bentham. For them, utility provides a concrete measure which is less speculative than notions of natural law origin. While located in a concrete society, it sets an ideal which may not conform to the opinions current in it about what is just, and as such it provides a critical ideal. Although subject to much criticism, it continues to be defended and discussed in standard legal literature, though little is added which is not found in philosophical literature (Simmonds, chapter 1; especially Hart 1983, Essay 9; *L'Utile et le juste* 1981).

An alternative approach which links justice to the common welfare while respecting the autonomy of the individual is to be found in the economic analysis school of thought. The leading exponent of this approach is Posner (1981, chapters 3 and 4) who argues that the maximization of wealth is the correct test of what is just. Such a standard is neutral as between individual conceptions of the good life and yet provides the means for those conceptions to be fulfilled. Social resources are most efficiently used by those who value them most, which is tested by a person's willingness and ability to pay for the good. Such an approach differs from utilitarianism in its Kantian postulate that every person is an end in himself and so cannot be abused for the collective good. Respect for each person requires that inherited wealth or innate talents are seen as part of a person's entitlements and cannot be redistributed without their consent. But this view has been subjected to strong criticism (see Baker 1975, Calabresi 1980 and Dworkin 1980).

There are many who would argue that justice and utility are distinct standards for community decision-making. Utilities have to be compared between individuals, while this is not always true of justice. Equally, what is socially useful may not be the just thing to do (Campbell 1988, pp. 13–14).

2.1.3   Narrowing the claims of justice

As has been seen from references to Dabin and Villey above, the claims of justice are frequently narrowed in scope, because of the moral values it serves. The problems of justification of the content of justice lead a number of theorists to narrow the scope of the notion to make it more defensible. These narrowings can lead the notion to have merely a negative connotation, or to be essentially procedural or otherwise formal.

(a) Justice as a negative value
There are those who claim like Weinberger (1986, pp. 207–8) that:

I am of the opinion that *no one knows objectively and conclusively what is just, nor can it be proven*. However, at the same time, I am *quite convinced that it is possible to argue rationally about problems of justice* and it seems to me that *in some instances*, at least in relation to certain very plausible assumptions, *it is possible to show that something is unjust*.

Campbell (1988, p. 2) and Eley (Rechtsgefühl, pp. 155ff.) suggest similarly that we develop ideas by way of negative reaction to events, rather than by the elaboration of a positive ideal. In this way a fully developed theory of justice need not be articulated. As with Dabin (1969, p. 395), justice here seeks not so much to state an optimum as to deal with practical problems in the human condition as it is to be found.

A negative conception may be proposed not merely for epistemological reasons, but also on account of the social function which justice plays. Some authors argue that justice operates as a constraint on the liberty of individuals or on their use of power, rather than as a positive ideal (Larenz 1979, p. 44; Zanfarino 1967). The use of justice as a control of power is emphasized by Coing (1985, pp. 222ff.) and D'Amato (1984, chapter 10). In such views, notions of the 'just price' set limits as to what is permissible, rather than setting an ideal to which a transaction must conform (Larenz 1979, pp. 71ff., and below section 3.2.1 on justice in contracts).

Others such as Stone (1965, chapter 11), while accepting that no full statement of justice is possible, argue that one can state at least some directives of material justice and certain settled points about what justice involves. This goes further than a purely negative conception, while admitting the impossibility of a fully developed conception which is not controversial.

(b) Justice as formal justice
Authors may limit justice to formal considerations, notably of the procedure to be adopted in making decisions. Of course, authors may set out formal criteria for what may count as an argument of justice, e.g. universalizability (Tammelo 1971 and Steiner 1985), conformity to utility (see above, p. 121), or capacity to achieve social consensus (Zippelius and Kriele, in Rechtsgefühl, pp. 16ff. and 31ff.). The concept of procedural justice will be discussed fully in section 3.1.1 below. Here it suffices to point to views of justice which choose procedure as the substantive content of the concept. Stone (1984), for instance, argues that the mediation of mine and thine is worked out by having a constituency in which all can express their views and by a process which directs attention to the sociocultural situation of human beings. In particular, those who see equality before the law as the central part of the ideal of justice are more easily given to seeing procedural justice as the way in which justice is best secured (Coing 1985, pp. 229–31; Hart 1961, p. 155).

2.2   Justice as a socially determined value
Some of the foregoing approaches to justice as an ideal virtue might appear to lead to results which are little different from those argued for by philosophers such as Williams (1985), who suggest that meanings for the concept of justice vary from community to community without there having to be a general theory which will encompass all views. Sociological studies demonstrate the variety of the content and use of justice principles (see especially Eckhoff 1974, pp. 34ff.). The view that justice is a socially determined value leads to suggestions that it is equivalent to legal justice 2.2.1, that justice is a process and not an ideal 2.2.2, and that the more fruitful study of the subject is sociological, rather than philosophical 2.2.3.

2.2.1   Justice and 'justice according to law'
For some, like Marcic (1969), justice in a pragmatic sense is what is done according to law. The idea of giving to each his own expresses a relationship set up by law and the standard by which a situation is judged as 'just' or 'unjust' is that created by the law. Thus 'justice' (*Gerechtigkeit*)

is equivalent to 'conformity to law' (*Rechtsmässigkeit*) and, thus, 'validity according to law' (*Rechtsgültigkeit*) (Marcic 1969, p. 175). Tay (Kamenka and Tay 1979, chapter 4) suggests this would be the view, for example, of the common law which sees justice in terms of formal, procedural justice with the emphasis on the impartial application of law, and could apply to notions of equality before the law.

Such an approach might appear too restricted in that others would argue that legal justice has to be fitted into a structure of social justice and is necessarily parasitic on it. Legal justice would only be just if the social arrangements which the law enforces are themselves just according to the wider principles of social justice operative in society (see Sadurski 1983; and a similar point made from a Marxist standpoint by Földesi 1977). Unlike the former view, this approach would suggest that social standards of justice exist independently of what is embodied in law and can be used to criticize its provisions. Positive social morality can exist alongside positive law, even if both are merely conventional. This would be even more true for those like Feinberg (1980) and Stone (Kamenka and Tay 1979, chapter 5) who would want to argue that justice involves more than mere equality between citizens in their treatment under the law.

2.2.2   *Justice as a process, not an ideal*

Within current structuralist and other legal philosophy, the tendency has been to argue that, at least in the modern law, justice is not an ideal to be strived for in the way individual decisions are considered, but merely a social process within which the complexity of human relations can be handled. The principal exponent of this view is Luhmann (1973). He suggests that the indeterminacy in objectives of the economic model of activity in a complex society gives rise to a critical and evolutionary account of justice, rather than an absolute and perfectionist account. The contingency of human existence is handled not through an attempt to make it conform to a dimly perceived ideal. Instead, the desire for justice is itself an ineradicable feature of the world which must be managed. Jäger (1979) also argues that justice is not a standard, but a system of social direction for handling social situations. As part of the process of social decision-making, justice is a process for dealing with the complexity of the social facts and the demands made on the social system. In this, law cannot be seen in isolation, but as interdependent with other social systems and subject to change over time. The imperative of the justice process ('act justly') encourages consistency in the handling of these problems and the consideration of the 'adequate complexity' of the social situations which fall for decision.

Some like Dreier (1974) would criticize this approach as postulating for critical purposes too absolute an idea of justice. Dreier suggests that it is possible to deal with complexity within the issue of what is materially just relative to the particular institutional arrangements within which the problem falls to be dealt. However, Luhmann (1974) argues that the empty content of the formulae used to express justice cannot generate the substantive standards which Dreier and traditional authors require for handling questions of material justice.

2.2.3   *Justice as a subject for sociological, not philosophical inquiry*

(On this topic see further the discussion by Arts and van der Veen.)

If justice is a socially determined value which exists independently of the views of any particular individual, questions arise as to how society acquires its values, how individuals are socialized to accept those values, and what interrelationship exists between the views of individuals and of the collectivity. Such concerns are of a sociological kind, involving social sciences and psychology, rather than speculative philosophical accounts of what ought to be considered as just. Among the major strands in the large literature can be identified a number of ideas. First, the view that there can be different types of justice in different kinds of society and that it is useful to attempt a typology (Kamenka and Tay 1979, chapters 1, 4 and 7; Eckhoff 1974, pp. 34ff.). Some attempt to study how arguments of justice are used in society and how individuals come to acquire their sense of justice (Eckhoff 1974; Lautmann in Rechtsgefühl, pp. 257ff.).

The notion of the *sense of justice*[3] has been particularly discussed in German-speaking countries in recent years. While its origins lie in juris-prudential debates of the nineteenth century between Jhering and Rümelin (Meier 1985, pp. 1–11), it resurfaces as a suitable area for inter-disciplinary work between lawyers, philosophers and psychologists. Although Meier (p. 24) identifies both descriptive/empirical and nor-mative/dogmatic uses of the notion in the literature, the predominant trend is the former, though, having identified it, authors may then suggest that the law would be best if it conformed to it. This can build upon provisions of positive law. Certain legal systems refer specifically to the 'legal convictions' of the community as a standard for completing legal texts: for example, the new Dutch Civil Code, Introductory section, art. 7 (*de in het Nederlandse volk levende rechtsovertuigingen*), and Henf (1978, p. 351) found similar ideas in German judicial decisions.

The terms of the debate, as in the past, look to how the sense of justice in individuals is acquired – is it innate or is it the consequence of experi-ence of the law, i.e. does law follow or create this sense? Much of this literature demonstrates the way in which individual values are acquired by identification with values in society, in which the law has a distinct role. (See especially Eckensberger, Rehbinder and Lautmann, in Rechts-gefühl, pp. 71, 174 and 257, and Jakob (1980). But Ott (1986) argues that the psychological theories are limited in that they have no predictive ability.) Such a sense of justice forms a pre-understanding which motivates and structures the approaches of judges, lawyers and citizens to decisions on legal questions (Lampe and Eley, Rechtesgefühl, pp. 110 and 136; Bagolini 1980, pp. 30ff.). All the same, a number of authors would want to argue that the sense of justice is not to be equated with purely irrational and personal intuition. Following Riezler (1969), Kriele (Rechtsgefühl, pp. 23–5) suggests that there are three elements in the notion: (a) an intuition for what is legal; (b) a feeling for what the law should be; (c) a sense of what should happen according to law. Both (a) and (c) are the product of training and exposure to the law, so only (b) is purely subjective. Zippelius (Rechtsgefühl, p.16) argues that the structure of legal reasoning requires that justifications for decisions are capable of attracting the consensus of the legal and wider community, so that the notion of a sense of justice as used in law has an important objective element. But there has been criticism of the study of the sense of justice on the ground that it can do no more than reproduce views (rational and irrational) expressed in society, and that it cannot provide justification for social decisions (see Stone 1965, pp. 313–21).

Despite these external forces shaping and controlling personal senses of justice, both legal philosophers and psychologists insist that the sense of justice is not just mechanistically adopted from others, or developed by interaction with the social environment, but has an organic growth in which the individual makes an original contribution within the framework for thinking and expression provided by the social environment. (See Eckensberger, Rechtsgefühl, especially pp. 80–1 relying on the theories of moral development of Piaget. Lampe and Weimar make similar points in Rechtsgefühl, pp. 118–19 and 161–3, as do the legal philosophers Bagolini 1980, pp. 32–3, and Weinberger 1986, pp. 211–12.)

3   Justice as a concrete value

Much of legal writing is not addressed to the discovery of the appropriate values to be implemented by an appeal to justice, but to an analysis of the operation of existing legal institutions (3.1) and the values which they enforce (3.2). Both are the practical ways in which lawyers give effect to the values of justice and are linked to specific objectives and values which are often less contested than the value of justice itself. Such objectives take for granted an existing organization of society and so are more positivist than the critical analyses of justice discussed in section 2 of this paper.

3.1   The administration of justice

Justice according to law involves the existence and operation of legal institutions. Without adopting the common law view which takes adjudication as its central exemplar of justice (Kamenka and Tay 1979, chapter 4), the values of a fair procedure in the handling of claims and in the resolution of disputes according to law (3.1.1) and of equal access to legal institutions (3.1.2) may be seen as central concerns in the administration of justice.

3.1.1 Procedural justice

It is a central theme in much writing that justice involves the impartial application of legal rules without bias and in a way which treats all subjects of the law equally and entitles them to state their point of view. Three issues will be considered separately: (a) what values procedural justice involves; (b) how far any notion is limited to the law or to one culture influenced by a particular legal system; and (c) how far these values are realized in particular legal systems.

(a) Procedural justice: the values. Procedural justice is usually justified as a distinct virtue of a legal system. As Bayles (1990, p. 3) puts it: 'Procedure concerns the process or steps taken in arriving at a decision; substance concerns the content of the decision. The two are conceptually distinct, for one can use different procedures for the same substantive issue and the same procedure for different substantive issues.' A number of values can be discerned in this area, principal among which Bayles identifies as impartiality, an opportunity for each party to be heard, the requirement of reasons to be given for a decision, and the formal justice of consistent adherence to rules.

Although institutions of justice are imperfect, their function is to provide for the realization of that value and for the peaceful resolution of disputes which arise as to its requirements. If, as many think, the central issue of justice is the proper arbitration between *mine* and *thine* (Villey 1975; Stone 1984), then impartial (i.e. non-partisan) decision-making is the service which the law has to provide either in the distribution or in the correction of holdings of social resources (Coing 1985, pp. 229–30). Personal interest or animosity which may affect the outcome of a decision prevent the proper impartiality needed for the administration of justice.

The right to participate in the process of decision about one's entitlements under justice may be seen as a way of ensuring that all relevant considerations are brought into the conclusion (Stone 1984; Luhmann 1973) or, as Coing (1985, p. 230) suggests, it may be a way of ensuring that there is no abuse of power to the disadvantage of a particular individual.

Since even those who argue that justice essentially involves equal treatment would not deny the necessity to make relevant differences between individuals in a community (Hart 1961, chapter 8) the feature of equal treatment is closely connected to impartiality – it is what follows when there is no rational reason for alternative treatment (Raz 1986, chapter

9; Honoré 1987). The giving of reasons and adherence to previously stated rules are practical ways of avoiding arbitrariness and abuse of power in coming to social decisions. All the same, none of these procedures can ensure that the right decision is reached.

(b) Procedural justice: its universality. Attempts have been made to characterize certain values of procedural justice as peculiar to law, while others would argue that the values operate outside law and are in no way dependent on its example (see the debate between Ingram (1985) and Day (1985)). Most authors concentrate on the legal approach and presume its dominance, though this may involve going beyond formal resolution of disputes to include informal settlements (Coleman and Paul 1987, chapter 5). The formulations of procedural justice in terms of the maxims *nemo iudex in causa sua* and *audi alterem partem* are well developed in the common law and are argued by Tay (in Kamenka and Tay 1979, chapter 4) to be basic to its perception of justice. These values are, however, found in other, non-common law versions of justice, though their procedural expression might well differ (Coing 1985, p. 230). Sociological studies both inside and outside the common law would affirm these values of procedural fairness (Röhl 1987, p. 158). The common law procedure tends to adopt an adversarial model, which involves each party presenting a case orally with the judge adopting a passive role, and the trial is concentrated at a single time. In other systems, the judge has a more active role and the arguments of the parties are more typically written, with the interviewing of witnesses spread over a period of time. Studies conducted by Thibaut and Walker (1975) with participants from various legal cultures would give some indication that the adversarial model has an appeal beyond the confines of the common law. The feature they identified which made the model attractive was the control by the disputants over the process and over the decision-maker, rather than the domination of the officials seeking the right answer (Thibaut and Walker 1975, p. 119).

(c) Procedural justice: its effectiveness. The justification for procedural justice is often said to be the achievement of correct decisions, but there are other arguments more connected with fairness, such as the participation of individuals in making decisions (Bayles 1990, chapter 6). All the same, effectiveness remains an important issue for achieving justice in any case.

Effectiveness can be measured in terms of the efficiency both in achieving settled goals and in satisfying the requirements of the wider community. As will be seen in the literature on access to justice, the claims of the legal system to achieve procedural fairness have to go beyond the formal claims to look at the effective participation permitted to individuals. To determine the satisfaction of social needs, authors ask how far the legal model of justice fits the aspirations of various communities, as is shown by Thibaut and Walker (1975) and the 'sense of justice' literature (notably Rechtsgefühl).

3.1.2 Access to justice

As Habschied (in Storme and Casman 1978, p. 48) puts it,

> we will never reach a justice whose decisions are always conform to substantive truth. But what we can do is to guarantee each citizen fitting and equal treatment before the courts, and equal treatment for all the parties. They must have the same possibilities, the same chances, and the principle of 'Waffengleichheit' (equality of arms) should prevail.

Diverse issues may be identified in the implementation of this principle – there is the problem of equality of the parties before the court (the ability to pursue cases despite legal costs); there is the public interest in the work of lawyers and in the resolution of representative disputes; and there is the wider provision of legal advice to meet the legal needs of the community (Denti in Storme and Casman 1978, p. 175; Cappelletti and Garth 1978, Introduction).

The difficulty of concentrating on access to the court process is that it presupposes that all legal needs can be met in this way and that court resolution is what parties would seek, were they given the chance. As Röhl (1987, p. 485) points out, legal norms do not cover all aspects of social life, so that disputes about price fixing, or non-economic values (e.g., love, friendship, art or religion) or purely intellectual and scholarly debates are not regulated by law. It may not appear socially appropriate to invoke the law within particular relationships. Studies done of business relations suggest that this may be true within long-standing and continuing business dealings (Macaulay 1973, chapter 3). Something similar may occur within particular societies, so that some Eastern cultures would rely less on law than Western cultures (Röhl 1987, pp. 491–2; Cohen 1967, p. 54; Kawashima 1967, p. 41; cf. Liebermann 1981). Disputes frequently have to be of particular seriousness or of a specific type, or be understood by the participants in a particular way before the law is invoked.

Whether out of preference or to make up for the deficiencies of the legal system, there may be alternative social mechanisms for the resolution of disputes, which will affect the use that is made of legal institutions. Justice may well require the existence of such mechanisms in some social contexts and should, some argue, influence their operation (Hutchinson 1981; Coleman and Paul 1987, chapter 5).

Nevertheless, there may be defects in the way the legal system operates: legal needs may not be assessed correctly or met by the legal professions, and access to the courts may be practically impossible.

Legal needs. A major problem is that the legal way of looking at situations is not that necessarily shared in the wider community. A process of translation has to take place in order to identify the needs which the law can solve. The availability of persons able to provide such legal advice at times, places and prices which are realistic is a major problem of practical justice, and many criticisms are launched on all counts against the institutions of many Western countries (see Blankenburg 1976; 1980; Röhl 1987, pp. 496–9; Abel-Smith, Zander and Brooke 1973; Delivery of Legal Services 1976; Rechtsbedürfnis und Rechtshilfe 1978). Sociological studies, using market research interview techniques, suggest that there are many legally relevant problems which are not picked out by the legal system, either because the parties themselves do not see the legal possibilities or, indeed, lawyers are not able to elicit and identify them in interviews with potential clients (Röhl 1987, pp. 487–8). The concerns of legal professions are more with the problems of the middle classes (property, car accidents, family provision), rather than with the problems of the poor (landlord and tenant, welfare benefits, employment). While other institutions (unions, citizens' advice bureaux, etc.) may fill the gaps, the literature suggests that many legal entitlements are not effectively identified as capable of legal protection.

Access to justice. Habschied (Storme and Casman 1978, p. 57) argues that, without equality in access to the courts, there can be no equality of arms in legal battles. As the Access to Justice Project showed (Cappelletti and Garth 1978, Introduction), much attention has been paid to legal aid in the sense of funding lawyers to act for those who are unable to afford the economic cost of litigation. This involves lawyers receiving state funds for the work they do by private arrangement with the assigned client. Only in a few systems would public salaried attorneys be employed. In an earlier work, Cappelletti, Gordley and Johnson (1975, Part 1) argue that three justifications of these forms of legal assistance are current – the ideas of charity to those less fortunate in society, the political right of access to the courts, and the welfare right which requires the state to make social provision to ensure access. The third, much more than the first, requires the provision of social funds for legal assistance.

The Access to Justice Project also identifies modification of the court processes to permit test and class actions as ways in which the delivery of justice could be improved. In test actions, one case is brought to settle a point which involves many litigants and potential litigants. The point may be of small moment when each case is considered individually, but the frequency of it makes its legal resolution of social importance, as well as securing justice where individuals alone would be unlikely to succeed owing to costs (Arens 1976). The alternative is the class action by which a person or group sues on behalf of a class of persons who are not inividually identified, though the members of the class will benefit from the action.[4] While not going so far as a popular action (one brought to enforce the law by a person with no specific interest in the outcome) or having a public official to perform the same function, this does ensure that the entitlements of persons under the law are enforced with some degree of effectiveness.

3.2   Specific legal values
Although lawyers may not specifically refer to the value of 'justice' when applying the law, there are a number of ways in which aspects of justice may be involved. Specific legal problems are handled by reference to underlying principles derived from justice (3.2.1), and particular values are applied which represent aspects of justice (3.2.2).

3.2.1   Areas in which problems of justice arise
It could be argued that much of the law involves problems of justice and a complete survey cannot be attempted. However, certain specific aspects do attract considerable debate over the extent and manner in which justice has a role to play in the administration of the law.

As a general phenomenon, justice may not simply be expressed in specific legal standards but may also be used in the elaboration of the law as a whole. This may be either through the process of interpreting existing legal standards to make the application of concrete legal rules conform more to the requirements of justice, settled legal standards or in developing new standards to meet novel or changed social circumstances in which the law has to operate. Whether understood as a general principle of the positive law (Esser in Newman 1973, p. 299; Marcic 1969; Robbers 1980), or as importing of extra-legal standards (Dabin 1969, Part 3, chapter 3), justice has an important place in the development of the law by judges, and may be justified by the difficulty of relying on legislative intervention to meet all difficulties or novelties which may arise (Newman 1973, pp. 597–8, and national reports).

While this aspect is common to many areas of the law, there are more specific problems of justice which arise in the diverse branches of the law. Legal issues more frequently concern commutative justice, and there is far less theoretical concern with wider questions of distributive justice, such as how property or state benefits shold be allocated. All the same, issues of commutative and distributive justice may be integrally connected in legal problems. Among those recently attracting jurisprudential attention are (a) justice in contractual exchange, (b) corrective justice in tort and restitution, (c) justice in punishment, and (d) reverse discrimination.

(a) Justice in contractual exchange
In the area of contracts, legal literature is concerned with two connected issues: whether justice provides the basis for contractual obligations, and

the extent to which justice impinges on the substantive content of contracts, rather than just on the procedures by which they are made.

Among the currently discussed justifications for the enforceability of contractual obligations, justice plays a small role. The dominant justifications are the moral obligation to keep promises (Fried 1981; Lucas 1980, chapter 12) and that to fulfil the justified expectations which one has aroused in another, on the one hand, and the utilitarian concern for effectiveness of transactions on the other. The moral obligation to keep one's promises arises without direct reference to justice. It is an independent part of the moral code, though it may be that one has no such moral obligation where the promise is to do something unjust (Lucas 1980, chapter 12). Such a theory is often, but not necessarily, connected with the idea that the will of the parties makes a contractual obligation binding.

The justification based on expectations suggests that the disappointment of the person to whom a promise or inducement is given provides the real basis for an obligation to perform it, rather than the mere promise itself. There are various versions of this theory. Common in Anglo-American legal thought is the 'reliance theory', whereby obligations arise where acts of reasonable reliance take place (Atiyah 1986, chapter 2; Fuller and Perdue 1936). This would include situations in which contractual obligations arise in the absence of express promises. This approach is much criticized on the grounds that the obligation is normally considered as arising *before* reliance by the promisee has taken place. Indeed, it is usually considered as justifying that reliance. A more common expectation-based theory suggests that a contract gives rise to those obligations which are reasonably expected of the parties either because they were expressly promised or because they are what people reasonably expect in such situations (Baker 1979, p. 23). Such a theory would justify both importing obligations into a contract and correcting its express terms in line with reasonable expectations. Although not specifically justified in terms of justice, expectation theories have an undoubted connection to ideas of fairness and justice.

By contrast, utilitarian considerations about securing individual preferences and an efficient market are much less connected with justice. By and large the role of law is to facilitate and not to correct market transactions. Accordingly, as Rodota (1974, p. 41) points out, market views of justice are the ones typically imported into law. Some would go further and suggest that market justice is the only appropriate standard (Posner 1981, pp. 69–75). Most legal systems, however, do include mandatory rules about usury, contractual warranties, and minimum wages, which set an irreducible minimum and thus effectively operate a kind of distributive justice in transactions. To the extent that maximizing the wealth of the parties or society is not the only value, then such distributive goals of the law are defensible (see Kronman 1980; Ghestin 1980, ss181–7; di Robiliant 1987, pp. 34–6).

While these limitations do involve a concern with outcomes, positive law is generally concerned with the fairness of the procedure by which the result was reached. Following market ideas of value, some jurists argue that price is determined simply by reference to what people are prepared to pay. The law does not exist to set an independent standard of what is the appropriate *content* of a contract, rather it concerns itself with the procedure of transactions (Battifol 1979; Stone 1984; Coope 1988; but cf. Ghestin 1980, ss. 181–3; Brownsword 1988). As Fouillée put it, 'Qui dit contractuel, dit juste' (What is contractual is just). But such an extreme view is now rarely accepted (see Rouhette in Harris and Tallon 1989, p. 21). Given the problems of unequal bargaining power in the formation of contracts between professional sellers and non-professionals, such as consumers, most legal systems have qualified the principle of freedom of contract, in order to prevent the enforcement of unjust transactions (Zweigert and Kötz 1987, vol. II, pp. 9–11).

Reiter (1981, pp. 362-3) identifies three situations where the law needs to control injustice: where there is inadequate distribution of information among those in the market; where particular dominant contracting parties are not subject to normal market forces and so exercise abnormal power over others wishing to contract with them; and where the victims of unfair contractual power are too diffuse to exercise political or other pressure to ensure control is exercised over the dominant party. The law here imposes standards of justice which justify the correction or refusal to enforce agreements which parties have made. Although 'fairness' or 'justice' may be the expressed standard by which the law intervenes to limit freedom of contract, legal systems and jurists usually try to be more explicit in determining what justice involves, if only to ensure that legal certainty is respected.

Even when justice has this extensive role, it is usually only one value among many, and certainty and market efficiency will limit its scope (Eckhoff 1974, p. 128; Ghestin, in *L'Utile et le juste* 1981, p. 35).

(b) Corrective justice: tort and unjust enrichment
There is much debate about whether reparation for wrongs (tort) or for unjust enrichment (restitution) is simply a matter of corrective justice. Traditional theorists and sociological studies would identify the correcting of wrongs done as a central aspect of justice.[5] How far justice is involved in this area of the law depends on the basis for the obligations to make reparation.

Cane (1982, p. 30) argues that there are four notions of justice involved in tort. One may have an obligation of reparation because one has violated a right of another (the *rights basis*). This can arise even if no tangible harm has resulted, such as when a person has been wrongfully detained, or where her reputation has been attacked by a defamatory statement. More commonly, the basis for an obligation is *conduct*, where the moral fault of the tortfeasor justifies his duty of reparation. A person is obliged in fairness to correct the situation of another which his own wrong has caused (Zweigert and Kötz 1987, vol. II, chapter 17). Even though a person is not morally at fault, he may owe an obligation to make reparation if *fairness* requires that he bear the burden of a risk which he has created for his own benefit. Thus, if one person builds a reservoir on his land and it floods the land of his neighbour, the creation of the risk alone suffices to justify his duty to make reparation to his neighbour, even without proof of fault. (For a survey of risk theories, see Tunc 1981 and Starck 1985, ss. 26–89; also Zweigert and Kötz 1987, vol. II, pp. 347–61; cf. Fletcher, in Bayles and Chapman 1983, pp. 57ff.). This has been used to justify strict liability for accidents at work and on the roads. Employers and motorists create risks of which it seems only fair that they should bear the cost. A final justification of liability in tort is that based on the *need* of the victim. Tunc (1972) argues that social solidarity justifies the imposition of liability on a person, even in the absence of fault, in order to provide the victim with a solvent source of reparation. This would justify an obligation to make good losses for the acts of others for whom one is responsible (employees or children), or for operations which one undertakes, such as driving a car. Hamson (1973) counters this by arguing that fault alone provides a moral obligation of justice for imposing a duty to make reparation. Social solidarity might justify an obligation of *charity* to help the victim of misfortune, but justice is a more restricted concept.

These four bases offer different conceptions of justice. Disputes between theorists on each particular conception in part seek to widen or narrow the scope of justice. But other justifications for tort liability go beyond justice to other considerations, such as utility. Most important of these factors is loss-spreading in the community. Obligations of reparation are typically met by self-insurance or re-insurance, so the real cost of liability is spread throughout the community. Attaching liability to particular individuals is a way of spreading the cost of accidents. Another function of tort law could be to discourage accident-causing activity (Calabresi 1970). The economic analysis school would support this, seeing tort especially as being a matter of providing appropriate incentives to socially valuable (wealth maximizing) conduct (Posner 1977, chapter 3). This would be supported by the fact that persons can be held liable without any fault on their part.

The relationship between these utilitarian objectives and justice in tort law is the subject of much dispute. Some would argue that the values of corrective justice should exclude utilitarian justifications (Weinreb in

Bayles and Chapman 1983, p. 123). MacCormick (1982, chapter 11) agrees that the obligation of reparation is an obligation of corrective justice, but suggests that there may be other obligations of distributive justice requiring alternative social approaches both within tort law and beyond. Coleman (in Bayles and Chapman 1983, pp. 45ff. and 65ff.) goes further to suggest that obligations of reparation and liability recognized in tort may be compatible with corrective justice, but by no means suffice to justify particular rules of tort. Other principles, probably not of justice, are needed to explain why a victim has a claim of reparation, though justice may well be involved in determining the quantum of reparation due. While ideas of moral fault and risk-creation may provide strong arguments of justice, other conceptions of justice may have less force and the function of the law may have more to do with other arguments (Eckhoff 1974, p. 143; Atiyah 1987, Part 6).

On the whole, the area of unjust enrichment is more closely associated with justice. A person has an obligation to make reparation to another for the benefits which he has gained at another's expense or by that person's mistake. The unfairness consists in benefiting from one's own wrong, or taking advantage of another's mistake, or refusing to pay for acts done not gratuitously, but in the expectation of payment (Zweigert and Kötz 1987, vol. II, chapter 15).

(c) Punishment

There are long-standing debates between retributivists, deterrence theorists and reformers on the appropriate objectives of punishment (see Ten 1987; Walker 1980; Poncela in *L'Utile et le juste* 1981, p 59). These debates ask how far the punishment of criminals can involve considerations of deterrence and reform for the benefit of the community, rather than simply concerns to give the offender his just deserts, both in the objectives of the punishment system and in the measure of punishment.

The justice arguments focus on the place of retribution in punishment. Retribution involves either the restoration of a balance of liberty between members of society which the offender has breached (Finnis 1980, pp. 262–6), or the formal dissociation by society of itself from the offender (Lucas 1980, chapter 6). Such approaches would provide the justification and determine the quantum of punishment. Others, though not subscribing to this justification, might still wish to see retribution as a restriction on utilitarian arguments of deterrence in relation to the quantum of punishment. Retribution would provide a limit on strict utilitarian considerations of deterrence in the way a person were punished (Hart 1963, pp. 235–7). Thus, however effective a deterrent it might be, retribution would prevent capital punishment being used as the sentence for parking offences.

The dominant arguments in this area are typically utilitarian, focusing on the deterrence of the individual and others, and the reform of the offender. Even where such arguments are not the guide for deciding whether an offender should be punished and how much, they may have a strong influence on other features of the penal process. Desert alone is rarely the guiding feature in the decision to prosecute an offender. Utilitarian considerations of the cost and effectiveness of a prosecution will be very important. When it comes to designing the prison regime, then reform and deterrence will feature more importantly than desert. On the whole, justice in the form of retribution is only one of the considerations guiding the penal process, and that primarily in the decision to punish an offender.

(d) Reverse discrimination
The issue of reverse discrimination has mainly been discussed in the United States in connection with the treatment of racial minorities and of women. Much of the debate has centred on the justification of such action in relation to the value of equality (see Dworkin 1978, chapter 9; 1985b, Part 5). The departure from equality is frequently justified on the basis of justice (particularly compensation for past wrongs or ensuring distributive justice over time) (see Goldman 1979 for a survey). But there are also strong utilitarian arguments for such a practice to promote a more harmonious society. Justice is, therefore, not necessarily the dominant reason for the practice of reverse discrimination.

3.2.2   Values which express justice
The word 'justice' is frequently invoked in legal texts as part of a rule which the judge has to apply. Although the notion may, in such circumstances, have specific legal connotations, these are frequently by way of restriction on its apparent breadth and there is much scope for the incorporation of extra-legal understandings of justice in the way this standard is applied by lawyers. However, there is a reluctance to give too wide a scope for such a notion in the application of the law, since it may produce uncertainty and the danger of arbitrariness in the application of the law. Other terms with more specific legal meanings are used in preference, though they share with 'justice' an open-ended character. Among the most important notions in this context are (a) equity, (b) reasonableness, (c) equality, and (d) mercy.
   (a) Equity is usually defined, following Aristotle, as the value which corrects the law where it is in some way defective. As such, it has clear affinity to the idea of 'justice'. As with the notion of justice, some see equity as the means by which transcendent values are introduced to correct the law (D'Agostino 1978, chapter 1; Ripert 1953, no. 157), but the predominant trend of legal doctrine and jurisprudence is to see equity as a higher-order principle of positive law, whose content is defined by

the legal system itself (Marcic 1969, p. 179; Ghestin 1980, s. 185; Esser, in Newman 1973, pp. 303-4). For example, Henf 1978, pp. 349–51, suggests that the West German courts base their views on ideas of justice derived from the 'sense of justice of the people' (*Bewusstsein des Volkes*).

(i) *The function* of the concept was defined by Papinian as 'adiuvandi, vel supplendi, vel corrigendi juris civilis': helping in the understanding of what the law means, supplementing it when it is incomplete, and correcting the broad expression of legal rules to ensure they conform to the values of the legal system (Jestaz 1972, ss. 12–15; Hartkamp 1984, ss. 53–6; Newman 1973, pp. 590–1). In that some versions of positivism have encouraged the view that legal rules are fixed norms for action in situations, the corrective role of equity might appear an intrusion. But current legal philosophy would consider the legal system to be made up of standards of varying generality, not only rules, but also more general standards called 'principles' (Dworkin 1978, pp. 23–6). When this variety of legal norms is taken into account, then there is no such contradiction but merely the harmonization of different elements of the legal system (Henf 1978, pp. 314ff.). The concept of equity is merely a way in which the complex of principles underlying and justifying specific legal provisions can be brought to bear on their application (Rodota 1974, pp. 35–6; Henf 1978, p. 240). Nevertheless, these underlying values may have to give way to the precise expression of the concrete legal rule and may, thus, not be of full effect. The resulting pattern of equity's incorporation into a legal system through specific reference in particular legal rules or principles or in the more general principles of law used to interpret and elaborate specific legal norms will be fragmentary (Newman 1973, pp. 596–7). This pattern will both make specific some of the content of equity and ensure that it is not a pretext for unfettered judicial discretion.[6] Many studies would suggest that the use made of equity does not involve a critical approach to current social institutions, but rather the alignment of legal rules to the best implementation of the values of the existing system (Rodota 1974, pp. 38ff.; Marcic 1969, pp. 183ff.).

(ii) *The content* of equity is variously expressed (see Törnblom, this volume). A major approach is to define it as requiring a *proportion* or *balance* in the dealings between individuals – a dealing is equitable if the outcome for one is not out of proportion to the outcome for another (Villey 1975, p. 77; Finnis 1980, p. 163; Röhl 1987, p. 146; Ghestin 1980, ss. 182–3). From Henf (1978, pp. 188–9) and Battifol (1979, p. 412), among others, equity appears as an essentially negative principle, ruling out excessive disproportion, rather than requiring due proportion in transactions.

But proportionality must be judged from particular standpoints. Röhl (1987, p. 152) suggests four: inputs, equality of outcome, need, substantive justice of the transaction. For the most part, the literature, both doctrinal and sociological, looks to proportionality of inputs. As will be seen below, strict equality is almost never proposed, and the appeal to non-comparative notions of 'merit' is strongly contested. In a liberal, market economy, the notion of substantive justice of transactions as a corrective to what the market produces is not widely admitted, if at all. Equity considers proportionality taking for granted an existing pattern of distributions of social goods, rather than seeking to disturb it, and provides thus only a relative version of justice (Rodota 1974; Luhmann 1973; Röhl 1987, pp. 164–5). The sociological literature would suggest that, in individuals' conceptions of injustice, the lack of proportion between gains and losses is a major factor (Röhl 1987, pp. 147–52), and the jurisprudential literature seems to adopt much the same approach. Eckhoff (1974, pp. 92–8) suggests that such a balance will, nevertheless, tend to protect the weaker party by providing stability and a limit to greed by the more powerful, even if the transaction is not such as would result from pure distributive justice.

Newman (1973) argues that three principles of equity are of general application: good faith, honesty and generosity.

Good faith is commonly required by legal systems, for example by art. 1134, s. 3 of the French Civil Code, art. 242 of the West German Civil Code, art. 1374, s. 3 of the old Dutch Civil Code (now included in the wider concept of 'rightness and fairness' (*redelijkheid en billijkheid*) in art. 6.1.1.2, lid. 1 of the new Civil Code; arts. 1371, 1374 and 1375 of the Italian Civil Code). Good faith normally requires that a person fulfils the expectations which he has created (Newman 1973, pp. 301–2, 603, principle IV; Larenz 1979, pp. 79–85). Beyond that, it may require compliance with recognized standards of fair dealing, especially in matters such as the disclosure of material facts both before and during a contractual relationship, and in helping others to reap the due benefit from a contract (Newman 1973, p. 603, principle V).

Honesty requires that rights should be based on substance not form and that a person should not seek to abuse rules on formalities to secure an unfair advantage. Here the strict rights set up by legal rules are corrected by equitable principles (Newman 1973, p. 603, principle I). One might include in this connection the wider principle of the abuse of rights which many continental legal systems admit as an equitable corrective to strict legal rights (Esser, in Newman 1973, p. 301; Ghestin and Goubeaux 1982, ss. 693–740). Newman (1973 pp. 603–4, principles VIII and X) includes this under the notion of generosity, but this seems inappropriate.

Generosity would involve the foregoing of strict legal rights for the benefit of another, for example in the sharing of the burdens of misfortune. While Newman (1973, pp. 603–4) argues that principles requiring a person who has suffered a loss to mitigate the damage or prohibiting a person to take an advantage of a mistake unless they have changed their position in reliance fit within the notion of generosity, this would seem more positive than most authors would admit (Battifol 1979, p. 401; Kamenka and Tay 1979, chapter 2). It is more commonly admitted that equity may be invoked to prevent a person taking unfair advantage of the situation of social misfortune in which another is placed (Henf 1978, pp. 300–2).

'Equity' may be used as a term to cover other values discussed here. Henf's study of West German cases found 25% of uses related to equality of treatment, 50% to the character of past conduct, and 25% to effects on third parties (Henf 1978, p. 240). He concludes that it really provides a framework for handling the specific features of individual cases.

(b) '*Reasonableness*' is a term used frequently in common law legal culture, though it does have its equivalents elsewhere. Fletcher (1985) attributes the importance of the notion within the common law to the particular way in which it sets out its rules. Whereas continental systems might state a precise rule, and then use notions such as equity to limit its effect, the common law is likely to state a legal standard in terms of 'reasonableness', so that the two stages in reasoning are included within the rule itself (Fletcher 1985, p. 951). The notion thus serves to place limits on what might otherwise be strict legal rights. Yet, although incorporated in a legal rule, the term does not have a clear legal content, but rather enables a variety of relevant considerations to be brought into the application of the law. Consequently, MacCormick (1984, p. 143) suggests that 'reasonableness' is not a value in itself, but a 'value function' within which a variety of elements are considered. Figures such as 'the reasonable man' (or the Roman *bonus paterfamilias*) represent the community's standards and so 'reasonableness' seeks to express standards which are capable of consensus within the community (MacCormick 1984, p. 153).

(c) Equality is seen as one of the general principles of law (Buch 1971, p. 196). Many authors see the principle of deciding like cases alike and treating citizens equally as coextensive with justice (e.g. Hart 1961, p. 155; Radbruch 1950, p. 168). Those who consider that justice is merely established by comparing the law's treatment of one person with others could also be considered as supporting this (Sadurski 1983, p. 329). More commonly, these features are but one aspect of justice, the other being material justice, which would involve considerations of merit, need or other values (Fikentscher 1977, p. 191; Larenz 1979, pp. 37–44; Perelman 1972, p. 15; Feinberg 1980; Lyons 1984, pp. 78–92). Ott (1986, p. 379) argues that all equality principles are reducible to principles of distributive justice. While this aspect is contested, few contest that equality in the sense of egalitarianism does not form a legal value. Thus the concern of the law with material justice is of limited

effect and essentially negative, especially as existing distributions are usually left unchallenged. To that extent, even those who would argue for a wider scope for justice would give a very important place within that value to equality of treatment (Perelman 1971; 1977; Stone in Kamenka and Tay 1979, chapter 5; Stone 1965, p. 335; Battifol 1979, p. 406). For instance, Ott (1986, p. 374) concludes from a study of Swiss cases that distributive principles do not dominate judicial discussions, but concerns for equality of treatment do. It is the dependence of this notion of equality on pre-existing decisions about what is appropriate treatment in the first place that makes many contest the value of this aspect of justice at all (Bagolini 1980, p. 10; Marcic 1969, p. 175; Luhmann 1974; Lyons 1984, pp. 78–92).

(d) *Mercy* is usually seen as corrective to the law, and is not generally considered as part of justice. Not all moral virtues are covered by justice. Thus, even the application of law in the light of justice will not be morally virtuous (Coleman and Paul 1987, chapter 1; Battifol 1979, p. 401).

Conclusion

Legal justice is primarily conceived as the just application of established rules of positive law. Hence lawyers concentrate on the justice of procedures and access to the institutions for the administration of justice. Furthermore, there is the suggestion from some lawyers that the disinterested application of known rules through fair procedures has a value in itself, whatever the fairness of the rules applied. In a similar vein, the focus on corrective justice is a strong feature of legal writing. Taking a certain established distribution of social goods, the lawyers are concerned to differentiate between changes brought about by the normal operation of the market, chance, etc., and those brought about in unjust ways, calling for correction. In both the procedural and the corrective functions, legal justice serves to maintain justice within a social order which has been determined from outside.

Although this instrumental function of legal justice occupies most attention, it cannot totally describe the function of law. The social order which law serves does not come as fully determined. Established rules and procedures cannot cope with all the manifold situations and activities of individuals, nor with the changes which these undergo in time. The rules and procedures need modification and elaboration by those who administer them. In addition, the inability of legislators to foresee all different circumstances leads them to define legal standards in general and imprecise terms, leaving much scope for discretion in their application. As a result, legal justice must also address substantive questions about what are fair rules which should be applied to social situations (Bell 1983, chapter 2).

While such considerations of substantive questions of justice are part and parcel of legal justice, they will rarely be addressed in abstract form by lawyers. Problems arise and will be addressed in relation to specific branches of substantive law, in the interstices of the established rules. For that reason, legal theories of justice are more likely to appear fragmentary and specific, rather than abstract and general. Issues of distributive or redistributive justice will rarely be addressed as such, but will form the background for the solution of more concrete legal problems or for theorizing on specific areas of law. As a result, consideration of justice as an abstract value shows limited originality and deliberation.

By focusing on problems of justice within an established positive social order, legal writers are more readily drawn to basing arguments on what is discursively acceptable within the existing community and the 'sense of justice' which is prevalent therein. The social practice of legal activity thus shapes the way in which issues of justice are approached and the focus of interest which is adopted. This is not to say that philosophical, political, economic and psychological theories are ignored and cannot dialogue with law. It is merely that they predominantly dialogue in specific and not abstract ways.

Notes

1 For an explanation of why legal academics are rarely concerned with material (as opposed to procedural or formal) justice see J.R. Lucas, 'The Problem of Material Justice' (1985) *Archiv für Rechts- und Sozialphilosophie (hereafter ARSP)*, 24, 20. An interesting example is J.G. Murphy and J.L. Coleman (eds.) 1984, *The Philosophy of Law*, Toronto: Rowman and Allanheld, which has one page and one footnote specifically on 'justice'!

2 Kelsen 1973, esp. pp. 4 and 14. For a discussion of Kelsen's theory of justice, see R. Tur and W. Twining (eds.) 1986, *Essays on Kelsen*, Oxford: chapter 12 (J. Bjarup on 'Kelsen's theory of law and philosophy of justice') and chapter 13 (P. Pettit, 'Kelsen on justice: a charitable reading').

3 As was noted in the Introduction to this book, there is a difficulty with the proper English translation of the German word *Rechtsgefühl*. The phrase used here is one used by the authors themselves in translations, though 'sense of law' would sometimes be right, despite its unduly positivistic connotations in English.

4 Of the large literature on this area, see B. Garth 1982, Introduction: towards a sociology of the class action, *Indiana Law Journal* 57, 371ff.; Witsch 1975, Class actions, *Juristenzeitung* 277ff.; Groenendijk 1982, Die Wahrnehmung gebündelter Interessen im Zivilprozess, *Zeitschrift der Rechtssoziologie* 3, 240ff.

5 For a survey of the theoretical literature see Tunc 1981, ss. 119–25; also Stein and Shand 1974, pp. 84-6. On the sociological approaches see Röhl 1987, p. 161 (especially the discussion of the work of Macaulay and Walster 1971). The place and understanding of justice in this area may be quite variable among cultures: see Friedman 1985, who argues that the general expectation for compensation in the United States is more extensive than in other countries.

6 The French reinforce the point by reference to 'le bon juge Magneaud' who at the end of the nineteenth century invoked principles of equity to dispense with the application of strict legal rules in specific circumstances: see Jestaz 1972, ss. 11–15. See also the criticisms made of Lord Denning, Master of the Rolls, in England who frequently invoked 'equity' to similar ends: see J. Jowell and P. McAuslan (eds.) 1984, *Lord Denning: The Judge and the Law*, London: Sweet and Maxwell. Both those who consider equity to be a transcendent value and those who consider it to be purely positive argue that it is an open-ended concept, not one which permits judgment on an irrational basis: see D'Agostino 1978, p. 41; Marcic 1969, p. 183; Ott 1986, p. 381, thesis 4; Henf 1978, pp. 347–51 (though he notes at pp. 226ff. that the evidence adduced in judicial arguments is fairly minimal).

5 Sociological approaches to distributive and procedural justice

Wil Arts and Romke van der Veen

1 Introduction

Having examined the contribution of sociology to the treatment of justice, Rytina (1986, p. 117) came to the conclusion that justice is more often an implicit theme than an explicit object of study in sociology. A cursory glance at the history of sociological thought corroborates this statement, since ideas about justice certainly don't seem to have been central in the works of most early and classical sociologists. Nevertheless, most of the founding fathers touched upon concepts of justice from time to time and some of them dwelt on the subject at length.

If we take the works of several proto-sociological thinkers in the eighteenth century, we can discern an interest in justice as a social phenomenon that is of a more than passing nature. David Hume's *Treatise of Human Nature* (1739–40) and *Enquiry concerning the Principles of Morals* (1751) both explore the concept of justice extensively. In Hume's conception, ideas of justice and rules of justice are rooted neither in human nature nor in God's will (i.e., natural law), but rather in social life itself. They are first and foremost products of education and human conventions, albeit not 'mere' conventions. Justice is of the utmost importance for people living together in a society and no human society can do without rules of justice. Hume's conception of justice, however, is a very narrow one. For Hume, principles of justice mainly concern property rights. A contemporary philosopher of eighteenth-century Scottish Enlightenment, Adam Smith follows Hume diligently and elaborates on his work in his *Theory of Moral Sentiments* (1759) and *Lectures on Jurisprudence* (1762–4). But he puts much more emphasis on the historical dimension of justice. In the former book he especially goes into the origin of criminal law and in the latter he also treats the origin of property rights from the point of view of civil law.

Among the nineteenth-century sociologists Herbert Spencer is one of the earliest to concern himself explicitly with the problem of social justice. In his *Principles of Ethics* (1879–93) he treats this problem extensively. For him, social justice is identical to social equilibrium. Social justice is an essential precondition of social progress. For Spencer, the place of societies in social and moral evolution can even be determined by their characteristic attitudes towards, and conceptions of, justice. In militant societies ideas of inequality will dominate, while in industrial society ideas of justice will emphasize equality. In his view, a specific sense and conception of justice is the prerequisite and inevitable product of evolutionary progress. In the twentieth century, Hobhouse (1922) and Ginsberg (1965) attempt to elaborate on Spencer's ideas in a neo-evolutionist direction. In accordance with the spirit of the age, they strip his work on justice from the ideological root stock and the optimistic view of progress.

At the end of the nineteenth and the beginning of the twentieth century, the idea of justice features in the work of two of the most famous classical sociologists: Emile Durkheim and Max Weber. The main repository of Durkheim's account of justice is his *De la division du travail social* (On the division of labour in society) (1893). In this book, he relates types of law to types of social solidarity. For him, justice is first and foremost a moral sentiment and in the second place an institution. The form justice takes depends on the specific type of solidarity generated by the conditions of a particular society. The function of sentiments about justice and judicial institutions is to put constraints on the behaviour of the members of society. Unlike Durkheim, Weber used the term justice primarily to refer to the administration of justice and the problem of legitimacy. For him the issue of central importance to the study of justice is the bureaucratization of the administration of law. It is especially in his posthumously published *Wirtschaft und Gesellschaft* (Economy and Society) (1922) that this treatment of justice, as part of a more encompassing rationalization process, can be found.

Standing on the shoulders of these two giants of classical sociology, modern sociologists have been enabled to elaborate on work on justice in two directions. First, theory construction and research into social stratification has been of vital importance to the development of ideas regarding the social nature of justice. Second, the administration of justice has been the most important topic in a comparatively new branch of sociology that has prospered in recent decades, i.e., the sociology of law. Moreover, sociologists of law have shown a special interest in issues of procedural justice, while the sociologists of social stratification have concerned themselves with studying distributive justice. The development of research into justice in these two directions has meant that justice as a social phenomenon has become an *explicit* object of study in sociology.

In the next sections, we investigate the treatment of justice by modern sociologists in detail. We especially emphasize the sociological literature on this subject which has been published during the last two decades. In section 2, written by Arts, we examine distributive justice and the sociology of stratification. In this section we especially shed light upon two topics in sociology which are related to the theme of social justice: (1)

norms and values as social mechanisms which give guidance to the distribution of goods and status in society, and (2) the notions of social justice held by the public, or by specific social groups. In section 3, written by van der Veen, we look at procedural justice and bureaucratic performance. This topic was introduced into sociology by Max Weber and has received much attention in what we have come to call the sociology of law.

2   Distributive justice and the sociology of stratification

2.1   Introduction

Social inequality has always been one of the central problems in the field of sociology. A number of sociologists even go as far as defining sociology as the science of social inequality. This definition is incorrect and it is more accurate to assert that sociology as a science owes much to the study of social inequality, perhaps even its origin. In layman's terms the problem can be expressed by the question: 'Who gets what and why?' The normative counterpart of the above is commonly referred to as the problem of distributive justice and put simply, it is the question of: 'Who should get what and why?' The latter problem has especially been a source of normative studies by philosophers and lawyers but also for some interesting empirical and theoretical studies by sociologists. For example, classical sociologists such as Durkheim, Mosca, Pareto and Weber were already interested in finding a solution to it (Berting 1970). It was, however, not their main concern.

Although these classical sociologists professed to study a whole range of social phenomena, such as social inequality and distributive justice, over a whole spectrum of societies, in reality they concentrated on the so-called modern, industrial or democratic Western society. They investigated especially what has been called the 'Rise of the Western World', i.e., how the contemporary societies of Western Europe and North America came into existence as a result of an all-encompassing process of rationalization, which found its expression in secular trends of industrialization, democratization and modernization. Moreover, they studied the effects of these trends on the functioning of society, its social cohesion and, in the case of social stratification, its structure and legitimization. Their growing interest in the problem of distributive justice can be attributed to the development of a more embodying conception of justice in the nineteenth century. According to Hayek (1976, p. 197), it was only around the middle of the nineteenth century that people in the West began to adhere more systematically to the idea that social inequality could be subjected to a comprehensive evaluation in terms of justice and injustice.

The most important of the classical sociologists who managed to produce evenly balanced studies on social stratification and distributive justice was Emile Durkheim (1858–1917). Our treatment of the issue of distributive justice will begin with an examination of his contribution. We will then assess the reactions within sociology to his theories by examining the work of his supporters and his critics. In so doing we will provide an insight into two sociological topics, which are related to the theme of distributive justice: (1) norms and values as social mechanisms which direct the distribution of scarce goods and status in society, and (2) the notions of distributive justice held by the public at large, or by specific social groups within Western societies. Finally we will look at the predictions regarding the similarity or dissimilarity of perceptions of distributive justice between and within societies, which can be derived from these theories.

2.2   Durkheim's contribution

The main repository of Durkheim's account of social stratification and distributive justice is his *De la division du travail social* (1893). In this book, he relates types of law to types of social solidarity. For him, justice is as much a moral sentiment as an institution. The form justice sentiments and institutions take depends on the specific type of solidarity generated by the conditions of a particular society. The function of sentiments about justice and of judicial institutions is, in his opinion, first and foremost to put constraints on the behaviour of the members of society.

In a later book *Le Suicide* (1897), and especially in the section on anomic suicide, Durkheim alludes to his theory of social stratification almost in passing. His point of departure is the idea that human nature, in its essential qualities, is substantially the same among all men. Characteristic of the human condition is the fact that man's desires are infinite and his resources scarce. Such a state of affairs could easily result in feelings of morbid discontent. In order, therefore, that people be satisfied with life in general, a balanced *modus vivendi* must be reached which is based on the restraint of human desires. Human beings, however, are not endowed with a faculty by which to restrain their own desires, and they are therefore obliged to have recourse to a force exterior to them: namely society. Desires cannot automatically be restrained by society, they can be tempered only by a limit that is recognized as being just. Men would never consent to restriction of their desires if they felt justified in overstepping the assigned limit. Since, as already stated, they cannot impose such a law of justice upon themselves, men are obliged to have it imposed upon them by an authority which they respect, and to which they yield spontaneously. Society can play such a moderating role either directly and as a whole, or through the agency of one of its organs; for it is the only moral power which is both superior to the individual, and whose authority is accepted. Society alone has the power necessary to stipulate law and to set the point beyond which the 'passions' must not go, and it alone can determine the reward to be prospectively offered to every class of people who pursue an occupation, in the name of the common interest.

Durkheim presupposes that each society cherishes moral ideas (values, norms, laws, rules) which determine the extent to which occupations are perceived as being more or less valuable to society and thus prescribe the just standard of living for those individuals. Such moral ideas also pertain to minimum requirements for those at the bottom of the social hierarchy and maximum requirements for those at the top. Moreover, in each society we can discern moral ideas about which individuals ought to follow specific occupations and hold certain posts. Durkheim points out the fact that the precise contents of these ideas differ from society to society, but not in a haphazard way. Such moral ideas vary in accordance with the social conditions and the type of solidarity characteristic of a particular society (see further Green 1989).

2.3   Functionalism

Without always explicitly referring to him, most modern functionalist sociologists writing on social stratification follow the route mapped out by Durkheim. They place even more emphasis on the social valuation of occupations than Durkheim himself did. They assume that the differences in social rewards which can be discerned in a society and seem to be legitimized by the value system of that society are grounded in the differences in importance of occupations for the functioning of that society as a whole.

Parsons (1940, 1953, 1970) and Davis and Moore (1945, 1953) are particular examples of authors who developed functionalist theories of stratification in Durkheim's mould. (For an overview of the functionalist theory of stratification see Huaco 1966.) The starting point of such theory is the statement that social inequality is ubiquitous. Inequality is not only an inevitable social phenomenon, but it is also necessary for the survival and the balanced functioning of societies, for which it is a functional prerequisite. In order to survive, each society is obliged to allocate roles to its members, i.e., ensure that the right people occupy the right positions, and to motivate them, i.e., ensure that its members perform their respective occupational roles adequately. Occupations are not of equal importance; they can be ordered in a hierarchy, with those roles most central to the survival and prosperity of society occupying the highest ranks.

Each society needs coordination mechanisms to allocate roles to its members and motivate them by means of the differentiated distribution of rewards. The market and the political process are examples of such mechanisms, but their distributive outcomes are not stable enough to ensure success. Therefore, over and above these mechanisms, a third (institutional) mechanism functions with more telling effect. Law and tradition are the principal components of this mechanism, whose functioning ensures that appropriate social rewards are in a manner of speaking built into the various occupational roles. Rewards are institutionally transformed into rights, i.e., legitimate claims to rewards, and these rights are attached to occupations. When in a society legitimate claims to primary resources – such as power and influence, income and wealth, status and prestige – are distributed in a specific way, an ordering of society in strata comes into existence, whereby each stratum comprises individuals in equally rewarded occupations. In other words, a system of social stratification.

The functionalists assume that there is well-nigh perfect consensus among all segments of the population of a society concerning the functional importance of the various occupational roles and the legitimacy of the unequal distribution of primary resources, a consensus which is embodied in the very moral order of society and internalized by nearly all of its members. Moral evaluation, however, would be more likely to influence the distribution of prestige than the distribution of power and income. The market and the political process thus play a more important role in distributing the latter two resources. Therefore, the functionalists emphasize the prestige or moral reward that is inherent in various occupations or functions and not just the economic returns. Rytina (1986, p. 129) pointed out that this has crucial implications for conceptions of justice. If differentiated rewards in terms of prestige exist, they rest, according to functionalist theorists, on convergent evaluations of the moral standing of different positions in the division of labour. Thus differential rewards in terms of prestige imply that the inequality which arises from the division of labour is viewed by all as being just. Functionalists also assume that there is a direct connection between the institutional order of society and the way people think about justice. In the Western world, the institutional order of society, and especially the division of labour and the nature of social stratification, have changed considerably during the last few centuries. Therefore ideas of justice will have changed too.

If we want to characterize the transformation of traditional into modern society we can do that by pointing on the one hand to the expansion of legal institutions, the bureaucratization of law and the increase in procedural rules, and on the other, to the shift in value-orientation from particularistic to universalistic norms. The typical conception of justice in traditional society was mainly of a particularistic nature. Legitimate claims to social rewards were based on kinship and consanguinity. In modern society the typical conception of justice is first and foremost universalistic in nature. The legitimacy of claims to social rewards is now judged by impersonal standards, and especially standards of individual achievement (Sampson 1981, p. 113). In modern societies, we not only see that the allocation of occupational roles and the differentiated distribution of primary resources is increasingly based on achievement and less and less on the base of ascription, but also that egalitarian ideas have become more important. At the level of values, the modern societal community has become basically egalitarian in the sense that inequalities must be positively justified in terms of their significance for the society concerned.

An explanation for the systematic change in modern societies from ascription to achievement can be found in a hypothesis that relates technological evolution to value patterns. Such a hypothesis states that the technological progress modern societies have made has resulted in an increased need for more highly qualified actors in occupational roles. Modern societies are no longer in a position to waste human resources, a kind of profligacy that is characteristic of traditional societies with their rigid caste or class structures. A great deal of research has been done to test this hypothesis, and a classic study is Blau and Duncan's *The American Occupational Structure* (1967). They assume that objective criteria of evaluation that are universally accepted increasingly pervade all spheres of life and displace particularistic standards of diverse in-groups, as well as intuitive judgements and humanistic values which are not amenable to empirical verification. Their empirical findings were that, in the USA at least, the achieved status of a man, i.e., what he has accomplished, in terms of objective criteria, becomes more important than his ascribed status, i.e., the man's identity in terms of family origins. In their opinion this implies that superior status can no longer be directly inherited, but must be legitimized by actual achievements that are socially acknowledged. American follow-ups to Blau and Duncan's research can be found, for example, in Duncan, Featherman and Duncan (1973) and Hauser and Featherman (1977). However, in these research projects the central question of whether there is a consensus about the criteria governing the allocation of occupational roles and the allotment of social rewards has come no nearer to being answered than was the case in Blau and Duncan. Hauser and Featherman (1977, p. 49) merely remark that the question of whether or not the sociological facts of inequality and stratification in a given community are consensually validated and whether or not an individual's sense of distributive justice corresponds to these facts are interesting topics of research which concern the mechanisms of social change, but they don't treat those topics themselves.

2.4   Marxism

The aforementioned macro-sociological analysis of social stratification and distributive justice has been termed by Anthony Giddens (1982) the theory of industrial society. This tradition did not originate in Durkheim's work but can be traced back to the early nineteenth-century sociologists such as Saint-Simon and Comte. Giddens also perceives another main macrosociological analysis of modern society: Marxism. He terms this theoretical tradition the theory of capitalist society. Among other things, supporters of this theory have taken issue with the functionalists over the supposed changes in value patterns. For the Marxists, modern capitalist societies are not kept together by value consensus as much as by coercion. They contest the functionalist idea that values and moral ideals are the most important causal factors in social evolution. Nor do they accept that conceptions of justice and law play a significant role in the disruptive phases of social evolution which we call revolutions. In order to begin to understand what happens in a society we are first of all obliged to look at the mode of production that is characteristic of that society. This doesn't mean that in their opinion values and value orientations play no part whatsoever. They argue that moral principles and moral sentiments are, like the rest of the superstructure, grounded in the material foundations of a society in a manner which is not always uniform and straightforward (Lukes 1982, pp. 187–8). Notwithstanding this, values and value orientations can be important indicators of what is happening and changing in societies. The reason for this is that consensually held values, in the form of ideologies, have everything to do with class interests and are more or less functional or dysfunctional for particular modes of production.

Some Marxists agree with the functionalists' view that in modern capitalist societies there is a high degree of value consensus, even with regard to the prevalence of achievement criteria. The fact that most modern capitalist societies don't go to rack and ruin as a consequence of internal contradictions can be attributed to the part the superstructure and especially the ideology plays with respect to the legitimization of coercion (Abercrombie *et al* .1980, p. 29). By means of indoctrination, the dominant class of capitalists succeeds in ideologically controlling the working class. By acquiring an interest in and identifying themselves with the capitalist mode of production, workers adopt the dominant value system. In such a case, empirically found value consensus among the working class is to be attributed to so-called false class consciousness.

Other Marxists maintain that value consensus can only be found in the upper and upper-middle strata of society. For these theorists the idea that the working class has been systematically and successfully indoctrinated with the values of the dominant class does not hold. There is always sufficient revolutionary potential dormant in the working class, and by appealing to its own solidaristic ideology, the proletariat can at any time become conscious of its historical role and try to achieve hegemony over other classes (Larrain 1983, p. 82). This means that if we have a good look at the value orientation of members of the working class not only will we perceive an achievement pattern of distributive justice but over and above this we will find solidaristic principles of equality and need (see Malewski 1959).

An attempt to come to a synthesis of these two Marxist conceptions can be found in the so-called dominant-ideology hypothesis (Abercrombie *et al.* 1980). In Parkin's version of this hypothesis two value systems are singled out: a dominant and a subordinate system (Parkin 1972, pp. 92–3). Beside these two, a 'negotiated' version of the dominant system can be discerned, i.e., a version in which the dominant values are not so much rejected or disputed as modified by the dominated class in the light of, and as a result of, social conditions and the art of the possible. The specific appeal that will be made to a particular value system will depend on the nature of a situation. More specifically the hypothesis states that: in situations in which people are asked to evaluate the unequal allocation of occupational roles and allotment of social rewards in abstract terms, they will show a propensity to choose the dominant value system as a moral frame of reference. However, when in contrast people make decisions in concrete social settings and inevitably act according to these decisions, members of the dominated classes will either fall back on the subordinate value system or on the 'negotiated' version of the dominant system.

2.5 *Consensus or dissent?*

The debate between functionalists and Marxists discussed above cannot easily be settled by reference to the results of sociological research. It is not possible to conclude unequivocally that a high degree of consensus regarding the desirability of achievement values exists. The fact is that the results of sociological research in various countries have been acquired with the help of dissimilar measurement instruments and are not the same in character. When, for example, we compare similar research projects in the German Federal Republic and the United States we come to disparate conclusions. In the German city of Konstanz, Mayer (1975) finds strong agreement with respect to the achievement values that underlie and ought to underlie the allocation of occupational roles and the allotment of social rewards. Research carried out in an American town of comparable size (Muskegon, Michigan) by Rytina, Form and Pease (1970) yields other results. They found that the acceptance of the dominant American ideology ('equality of opportunity', 'meritocracy', etc.) was far from universal, even when the doctrines of that ideology were formulated in a highly abstract and vague manner. The degree of consensus decreased even further when the doctrines were specified in more concrete terms. Support for the dominant ideology was most pronounced among those who stood to gain the most from its implementation. Rytina *et al.* concluded that there seems to be less 'false class consciousness' than other social scientists tend to suppose.

When we take a close look at the vast body of research into justice evaluations of the distribution of income, we are confronted by the same kind of problem (for the USA: Jasso and Rossi 1977; Alves and Rossi 1978; Tallman and Ihinger-Tallman 1979; Hochschild 1981; Kluegel and Smith 1986; for Great Britain and the USA: Bell and Robinson, 1978; Robinson and Bell 1978; for the Netherlands: Hermkens 1983; Szirmai 1986; for Belgium: Lagrou *et al.* 1981; Overlaet and Lagrou 1981; Schokkaert *et al.* 1982). The research findings are not conclusive enough to settle the dispute. When it comes to the distribution of income, respondents agree with each other that achievement considerations should prevail over ascription. But as to the application of considerations of need and equality they differ. In the USA Alves and Rossi (1978) found that high-status respondents emphasize achievement, while low-status respondents deem considerations of need and equality as being as important. Tallman and Ihinger-Tallman (1979) reported evidence for the USA that lower-class respondents are more likely to advocate the use of an equality yardstick than upper-class respondents are. Robinson and Bell (1978) reported similar evidence for Great Britain. For the Netherlands Hermkens (1983) and for Belgium Schokkaert *et al.* (1982) come to the same kind of conclusion. In spite of an empirically found measure of disagreement due to class-specific views, they all are after all of the opinion that in modern Western societies people share an overarching consensually held achievement-orientated normative basis with which they judge the equitability of the distribution of income. In their opinion consent predominates dissent.

These empirical findings did not convince all theorists to the same degree. For some, especially the Marxists, the apparent consensus can be attributed to the fact that the questions asked were formulated in abstract terms. They are of the opinon that the observed agreement is an artifact of the measurement instruments used. Research that investigates the concrete distributive problems of everyday life results in findings which demonstrate that considerable differences in opinion exist especially in the lower strata of society (Mann 1970; 1973; Hyman and Brough 1975; Willman 1982; Tanner and Cockerill 1986). A tentative conclusion would be that considerable consensus exists with respect to abstract and general issues, but that with regard to the problem of distributive justice in everyday life we should speak of such a thing as 'parochial dissent'. In their opinion dissent predominates consent.

2.6   Exchange theory

A new frontal assault on the functionalist accounts of social stratification was launched by George Homans (1964), the founder of exchange theory. He accuses functionalists of introducing a holistic fallacy. Their error lies in the attempt to explain social stratification and conceptions of justice by referring to the needs of society rather than to human needs. Instead of looking at the functions and dysfunctions of status systems, sociologists should try to explain why and how status systems come into existence. Such an explanation would be based on hypotheses about the behaviour of men, and not about the behaviour of societies. It is one of the accomplishments of small-group research to explain how a status system, albeit on a small scale, emerges in the course of interaction between the members of a group. Homans (1974, pp 299–318) is of the opinion that small-group stratification phenomena bear so much resemblance to societal stratification phenomena that they must have been produced by the same processes in both domains. In small groups, members attain status in the public sphere of activity. It is in this sphere, in which services of different kinds and values are exchanged in a network including a large number of group members, that members become differentiated in status. In the public sphere, members often interact with, and express approval or respect for, others who are 'better' than they are by virtue of the services their betters perform. In the private sphere, i.e., that of leisure and 'social' intercourse in the narrow sense of the term, they are more likely to interact regularly with, and express a more intimate liking for, members who are approximately their equals in the public sphere. 'Social' peers are likely to be similar in values and abilities and, by interacting, are apt to become still more alike in their behaviour, even to the extent of developing styles of life distinct from those of their superiors and inferiors. Stratification in society at large develops in an analogous manner. In all stratified societies the individual's status is principally determined in the public sphere by their occupations and by the incomes their occupations secure. The greater the degree of parity between peers in public status, the more likely they are to interact in the private field, i.e., the sphere of leisure, of non-work environments. People who are roughly equal in public status also tend to become similar in other aspects than those of occupation and income which established their status in the first instance. This results in the development of social strata with relatively homogeneous occupational prestige factors, incomes and ways of life. It is thus that social stratification comes into existence in wider societies. This peer-group mechanism can explain the genesis of social stratification in all types of society as well as in small groups.

Homans' treatment of social stratification and justice forms part of a theory of social behaviour, which is grounded in ideas imported from economics and psychology (Homans 1961; 1974). An orientating statement is that social interaction can be conceived of as being an exchange of rewards and punishments. Such an exchange is presumed to be subject to the same laws as those which govern economic transactions. Human beings are motivated by the expected gains (rewards minus investments and costs) associated with alternative courses of action. However, moral considerations, and sentiments concerning distributive justice in particular, play their part. Such sentiments not only motivate people, but are also important factors in the stabilization of social relations.

At first sight it is remarkable that Homans adopts a Durkheimian concept as his starting point. The central idea of Marcel Mauss' *Essai sur le don* (The Gift) (1925) is that reciprocity is a pivotal mechanism of justice. Homans remarks that when we invest a great deal in an enterprise, we tend to feel that we are entitled to a considerable reward. The corollary is that we object when those who have only invested a little are substantially rewarded. If we interact with individuals whose investments are modest compared with the rewards received, we tend to conclude that equity in distributive justice has been violated. This is especially the case when we feel that we have made a net contribution to that largesse. Homans concludes that individuals employ a variant of Aristotle's proportionality rule in order to evaluate the outcomes of interactions between individuals. There is a general feeling that returns should be proportional to costs and investments. Although such a proportionality rule is generally accepted as being the most general conception of distributive justice, there is often difference of opinion with respect to the question of to what extent a distribution of social rewards is just in particular circumstances. An explanation for such divergence of opinion must be sought in the fact that actors do not place the same emphasis on the factors of reward, cost and investment. Ideas of distributive justice therefore differ from society to society, from group to group and in each society from one historical period to the other. Group members or members of a society will not exhibit a tendency to agree in their judgement of the equitability of a specific distribution of rewards unless they share the same social background, have had similar experiences in the past, and have similar lifestyles (Homans 1982, p. xv). Such homogeneity generates the same kind of expectations with regard to how each member ought to benefit from interaction within a particular group or society. In other words, the members hold a specific value system in common. A situation in which there is no balance between investments (such as age, sex, seniority, race, education, experience, etc.) on the one hand and rewards (income, prestige, popularity, etc.) minus costs (working hours, fatigue, unfavourable working conditions, etc.) on the other hand, leads to problems and frustration. When people not only perceive but also experience injustice, anger and aggression result.

Blau (1964b) has elaborated on Homans' ideas by applying them to institutional behaviour and permanent social relations. He introduces the concept of fairness, and remarks that it is more or less identical to Homans' concept of distributive justice. Fairness then refers to the equitability of rewards, according to the norms of a group (or society), for services rendered. His explanation, however, has a strong functionalist flavour, since according to Blau, the origin of ideas of social justice can be traced back to the relation between the societal needs for the performance of specific tasks on the one hand and the investment by people and groups necessary for the successful performance of these social functions on the other. Fairness norms function as a mechanism which matches consumer demands to productive capacity, since they provide differential incentives which encourage people to invest time and effort in attaining various societal goals. Fairness implies that those who invest a great deal in order to render services in high demand ought to receive correspondingly high social rewards. Unfair treatment can lead to strong disapprobation, which makes it costly to profit 'unfairly' from others who are in a weaker position.

After the early works of Thibaut and Kelley (1959), Homans (1961; 1974) and Blau (1964b) sociological exchange theory did not at first follow up the idea that justice sentiments motivate behaviour and stabilize social relations. Social psychologists, however, took these ideas on board almost immediately. What we have seen in the last few decades is a flourishing of social psychological theory construction and research, the so-called equity tradition, in which the ideas of Homans *et al.* have been pursued (see Törnblom, this volume). The growth of social psychological knowledge regarding distributive justice later influenced sociological work in its turn. Thus the application of exchange theory to distributive justice has been proceeding in a roundabout way.

What happened was that sociologists borrowed ideas from equity theory and other social-psychological theories to tackle once again the problems at the core of the sociological debate between functionalists and Marxists on social stratification and social justice. In eschewing approaches to these problems from the traditional holistic angle (functionalism and Marxism), and adopting an individualistic perspective instead, these theorists were hoping to find a short cut to scientific progress. Looking at the old problems from another angle might lead to a better formulation of these problems and to more informative solutions, i.e., theories with greater verisimilitude. For these theorists there are two questions of particular importance for solving the problems on hand. The first question concerns the way people come to choose particular justice principles or acquire a preference for specific distribution rules. The second question pertains to the moral judgement or justice evaluation of factual allotments and distributions of social rewards.

2.6.1 *Justice principles*

Several authors (Rescher 1966; Eckhoff 1974; Deutsch 1975; Sampson 1975; Miller 1976; Leventhal 1976b; Schwinger 1980) have tried to answer the question pertaining to the choice of justice principles. They agree with each other that this choice seems to depend mainly on the nature of the situation. In some cases, depending on the nature of a particular situation, an achievement or contribution principle will be chosen, while in others a need principle will dominate and again in others an equality principle will play the dominant role. The factor that is presumed to turn the scales is the common goal that underlies the interaction in a certain situation. In situations in which the primary goal is to facilitate and enhance productivity, the contribution rule is preferred. When concern for preserving harmony in a group is paramount, equality will be the dominant principle. The need principle will dominate, when the well-being of individuals is most salient. The research data reviewed by Cook and Hegtvedt (1983) and Deutsch (1985) broadly support the notion that different situational conditions influence the choice of justice principles. Hochschild (1981), for example, reports that in the United States egalitarian principles are especially supported within family life and politics, whereas achievement or contribution principles are more popular in the economic domain. Within those domains the relative preference for the competing principles of justice seems also to depend on other structural conditions. Kellerhals *et al.* (1987) showed for example that in Switzerland the goals that underlie interaction within the family, and therefore the choice of justice principles, depend not only on the nature of the situation, i.e., the family's characteristics, but also on other structural factors such as group cohesion, social integration and the way the behaviour of the family members is regulated.

2.6.2 *Justice evaluation*

Exchange theorists assume that people use principles of justice as standards to pass judgements on the fairness of the allotment of incomes and their distribution in particular situations. However, agreement between people on the choice of the abstract justice principles to be applied to a specific situation does not necessarily imply consensus on concrete justice judgements and vice versa (Hamilton and Rytina 1980, p. 1119). This is due in particular to three factors which we propose to examine in turn:

(a) subjective perception and appreciation;
(b) social comparison;
(c) social attribution.

(a) Even if people apply the same principles of justice, their dissimilar perception and appreciation of people's inputs and outputs can be the source of disagreement. However, a straightforward statement about the circumstances under which people will have (dis)similar perceptions and appreciations is not offered by exchange theory. Most of the theorists merely suggest that it is important to know whether people live and work under the same conditions, whether they have the same needs and whether they adhere to the same values. Homans (1974), for example, remarks that, since individuals' needs and values are the result of learning processes, those people who share the same experiences, i.e., have the same social background, will arrive at similar fairness judgements. Adams (1965) likewise argues that the process of socialization plays an important role in consensus building. He puts forward the hypothesis that the larger the cultural community people live and work in, the greater the number of individuals with a similar mode of perception and valuation of inputs and outputs. This hypothesis is not a very informative one, since it only states that people who adhere to the same values and have a similar outlook will pass the same judgements. What we do know, however, is that perceptions of social status and reward hierarchies are related to the location the observer occupies within these hierarchies. Wegener (1987) argues that people perceive their own social standing as well as their income on distorted continua. The subjective social position of an individual is perceived as approximately 'average', and this mis-perception corresponds with the perception of his or her subjective income as being approximately 'average' as well. It is sensible for the majority of individuals to experience this correspondence as being 'just' according to Homans' (1974) famous dictum that 'what is determines what ought to be'. Distributions which are stable over time acquire a sort of customary 'inertia'. This conviction of distributive justice becomes part of the normative culture of a society. A society in which the majority of the individuals believe that the society is organized according to just standards will exhibit a common value system. Thus, dissimilar percep-tions can also lead to consensus. What Wegener (1987) argues is that we believe the distributions of social goods to be just because we mis-perceive, in our own different ways, the distributions of these goods themselves.

(b) Dissent and consensus can also originate from differences in the way people compare themselves with others. People tend to avoid com-paring themselves with other people who are quite different or far away, especially when the results of the comparisons can be unpleasant, prox-imity and similarity are therefore crucial factors in comparison processes (Merton 1968). Because experienced injustice generates unpleasant emo-tions, people also have a propensity to avoid comparisons that might disconcert them. In some situations, however, people are forced to make 'realistic' comparisons and hence cannot avoid experiencing a feeling of injustice. In other situations it is much easier to steer clear of 'realistic' comparisons and their concomitant feelings of injustice. It is thus important to discover with whom or what people compare themselves and in what degree and under which conditions. Although this would seem to be a straightforward question, a straightforward answer cannot be found in the literature of exchange theory. Finding an answer apparently poses very complex problems. Goodman (1974), for example, has shown that people employ different modes of comparison simultaneously when they are asked to judge the fairness of income differentials. When Austin (1977) constructed a typology of social comparison processes he was hoping to create a measure of order in the chaos, but the irony is that in doing so he showed how complex comparison processes can be.

(c) Dissent with respect to fairness judgement can be caused not only by dissimilar perceptions, valuations and comparisons, but also by dissimilar attributions. In the analysis of fairness judgements it is important to know what people believe to be the causes of specific types of social inequality and who or what they hold responsible for those inequalities. Cohen (1982, p. 120) is of the opinion that much of the discord and many of the conflicts involving distributive (in)justice are rooted in dissimilar attributions. In attribution theory it is assumed that people are apt to some particularly frequent erroneous attribution tendencies (Kelley 1973, p. 123). Such erroneous tendencies involve, for example, a propensity to overestimate either the influence of dispositional (internal) factors or the influence of situational (external) factors. Attributions are generally of a self-serving nature. Dispositional attributions are employed for a person's or an in-group's favourable outcomes while situational attributions are applied to the favourable outcomes of out-groups. Social position and ideology also play their part. Conservative, middle-class and older people tend to make dispositional attributions for unfavourable outcomes of others while progressive, lower-class and younger people prefer situational attributions for those outcomes (Howard and Pike 1986, pp. 155–6). Nevertheless, consensus can be the result of a certain attribution style. Shepelak and Alwin (1986, p. 44), in any case, suspect that individuals attribute their levels of social reward to those situational and dispositional factors that, on the one hand, maintain and protect their sense of dignity and, on the other hand, maintain and protect the system of legitimized inequality in the distribution of social rewards. We are once more struck by how little we know about the social conditions under which such differential attributional tendencies emerge (Crittenden 1983, p. 442).

In order to overcome the problems mentioned above, Jasso (1980) constructed a 'new' theory of distributive justice. She avoids the complexities originated by processes of perception, comparison and attribution by measuring the just amount of a good directly. In this way she considers the way people come to a justice evaluation as given. She does not look at the afore-mentioned processes themselves, but only at their end product: the justice evaluation. For the construction of her theory she could fall back upon her earlier work on the specification of a justice evaluation function (Jasso 1978). This justice evaluation function that is at the core of her theory can succinctly be expressed as being the natural logarithm of the ratio of the actual amount of a good and the just amount of that good. Critical comments have subsequently led her to reformulate parts of the theory (Jasso 1981; 1983; 1986). An attempt to integrate several causal and disturbing factors in an encompassing theory has also been made by Markovsky (1985). His aim has been the construction of a multilevel theory of distributive justice. First of all he wanted his theory not only to account for the justice evaluation people make with regard to the goods they receive themselves, but also with regard to the goods other individuals and groups receive. The core of his theory is a social reference function. Just as was the case with Jasso, Markovsky solves the problems at hand in an indirect manner. His theory predicts the conditions under which people are likely to experience the allotment and distribution of scarce, coveted goods as just, but it does not specify the process by which people arrive at such a judgement.

In spite of the fact that we have to attach great importance to the work done by Jasso and Markovsky, we can ask in all conscience whether they are not begging the question. All of the preceding had to do with the difficulty of determining what is perceived as just and how subjective evaluation makes that difficult to establish. Transforming a dependent or endogenous variable into an independent or exogenous variable boils down to an evasion of the afore-mentioned problems and not to solving them.

2.6.3 *Social consequences of justice evaluation*

Jasso's theory is especially interesting in that it also takes the social consequences of justice evaluation into account. She is of the opinion that those social phenomena that are indicators of the degree of cohesion or integration of societies and social groups can be explained and predicted by looking at certain parameters of the distribution of justice evaluations in a particular group or society. In her opinion the dynamics of social life are the result of changes in the distribution of justice evaluations. She formulates several hypotheses in which the independent variables are statistical measures for the distribution of justice evaluations and the dependent variables are examples of the above-mentioned social phenomena, i.e., the indicators, such as the tendency for a social aggregate to disintegrate, the degree of dissatisfaction within it, the probability of violent revolutionary conflict breaking out, the rate and character of crime and incidence of psychiatric disorder in that aggregate, etc. These hypotheses, however, are not logically derived from the theory, but rather seem to be much more the results of the implementation of the theory as a heuristic device.

What she forgets to mention is that in an exchange theoretical context collective phenomena are not deemed to be directly linked together. Collective phenomena, such as distributions of justice evaluations in groups or societies, are the initial conditions from which the attitudes and actions of individuals arise. Under certain boundary conditions those individual attitudes and actions are transformed into collective phenomena such as justice norms or justice-motivated collective action (e.g., strikes, revolutions, revolts). The reason for this omission of Jasso is perhaps that within exchange theory very little work has been done till now in exploring collective justice phenomena (Rytina 1986, pp. 144–7).

2.7   Mavericks

Functionalism, Marxism and exchange theory are not the only major traditions in the analysis of Western societies. The hermeneutic tradition, for example, starting with Weber, provides us with interesting ideas about justice. Unlike Durkheim, however, Weber used the term justice not in the sense of distributive justice, but primarily to refer to procedural justice and, above all, the administration of justice and the problem of legitimacy. For him, the central issue in the study of justice was the bureaucratization of the law administration. In this section, however, we will confine ourselves to issues of distributive justice. In the hermeneutic tradition very little has been done to theorize and investigate these issues. But a number of important studies on the problem of distributive justice have been written by lone wolves such as W.G. Runciman and Barrington Moore, jun. Their work does not fit into the above-mentioned theoretical traditions, and in this section we will attempt to summarize their ideas as briefly and concisely as possible.

In his *Relative Deprivation and Social Justice* (1966) Runciman attempted to analyse the relation between inequalities and the feelings of relative deprivation to which they give rise. More specifically, he tried to analyse the attitudes to social inequalities in twentieth-century England. As a point of departure, he first posed the empirical-theoretical question, 'What is the relation between institutionalized inequalities and the awareness of resentment of them?' and subsequently the normative question, 'Which, if any, of these inequalities ought to be perceived and resented – whether they are or not – by the standards of social justice?'

In order to find an answer to the first question, he drew on reference group theory and the notion of relative deprivation. The central idea he derives from these theoretical conceptions is that feelings of deprivation people experience are not a simple function of their objective situation, but depend largely on the frame of reference with which they evaluate their situation. Social inequalities which give rise to feelings of relative deprivation have to be analysed as inequalities between comparative reference groups and membership groups. Runciman concludes from his empirical research that as far as economic inequalities are concerned, the choice of comparative reference groups is limited. People tend to compare themselves with those peers who live and work in the vicinity. Runciman found that people feel themselves much less relatively deprived than could be expected from their objective situation. He attributes this to their myopia.

For an answer to the second question Runciman invokes the help of Rawls' theory of justice. He tries to show that a modified version of this contractual conception of justice can demonstrate in principle what kinds of grievances could be vindicated as being legitimate and what reference group choices could therefore be described by this standard as being 'correct'. This is an important achievement for two reasons: first, because the notion of social justice is somehow implicit in every account of how people feel about social inequality; second, because such a theory makes it possible to distinguish between feelings of relative deprivation which can and which cannot be properly described as a sense of envy rather than the perception of an unfulfilled right.

According to Runciman (1967) the idea of a social contract is especially important for the analysis of social stratification and distributive justice in society at large. Individualistic principles of distributive justice such as Homans' proportionality idea are only in evidence in small face-to-face groups. This point of view is shared by Barrington Moore, although he takes Homans' notion as a starting point. For his macro-sociological study *Injustice. The Social Bases of Obedience and Revolt* (1978) Moore needs a complementary device, which he finds in the notion that people create, in the course of history, an implicit and sometimes explicit social contract. Principles of distributive justice are part of this ever-changing contract.

Moore's book has two parts. The first part concerns the existence of an implicit contract between rulers and ruled relating to universal problems of social coordination. This contract contains the norms of justice and, by implication, the criteria for identifying injustice. In a second, closely related part, he looks at the circumstances in which social orders whose apparent effect is to produce unjustified suffering acquire moral authority. In this context, he also examines the factors – psychological, social and cultural – that enable moral outrage against injustice to be expressed and facilitate action to eliminate the unjust exercise of authority.

In connection with social differentiation and social stratification Moore distinguishes two contradictory principles of justice. One is a general notion of equality based on what consumer units need: a sense that every person or household should receive 'enough'. The other is a principle of inequality based upon some ranking of the value of different tasks and social functions. Attempts to reconcile them take the form of notions of distributive justice in which the extra reward is accounted for in terms of the extra investment of effort, skill, or some other quality that performance of the task requires. Violations of any of these principles and disputes over these principles can be and are sources of moral anger, and prior to that of a sense of social injustice, and can and do lead to breaking of the social contract.

2.8   Conclusion

Both functionalism, as the theory of industrial society, and Marxism, as the theory of capitalist society, are predominantly holistic and deterministic in nature. Societal evolution expressed as either the functionalist's logic of industrialism, or the Marxist's logic of history, determines which principles of justice eventually will be chosen, which perceptions of distributive justice will occur and what will be the behavioural consequences of those choices and perceptions in which Western societies. The principal causal factor in both theories is the technological stage in which each particular society finds itself. This does not mean that there is a one-to-one relationship between the material conditions of a society and its value pattern or ideology. It does mean, however, that economic and technological constraints will eventually force people to embrace certain principles of distributive justice. Providing they are in a quite similar technological and economic stage, Western societies will exhibit similar choices of justice principles and judgements of fairness and people will act according to those principles and judgements. Both functionalism and Marxism would predict that in this latter case the rough patterns of choices and perceptions of justice that can be discerned within those societies will show a high degree of similarity. They differ, however, in their predictions as to the particular degree of consensus regarding principles and perceptions of justice to be found within those societies. Functionalism forecasts a high level of consensus whereas Marxism foretells that consensus and discord will depend not only on the logic of history but also *inter alia* on the level of class consciousness.

In turn, exchange theorists lean more towards the individualistic and voluntary. In their opinion, all people will always and everywhere use the same kind of proportionality principle when judging the fairness of the societal allocation and distribution of scarce resources. However, people will specify this principle in a different way from society to society, from group to group and within these societies and groups from time to time. The question of which principles will be chosen and which judgements will be passed can be answered by reference to the statement that says that principles and judgements are, first and foremost, the products of a combination of circumstances. Therefore, it is very difficult to predict which *specific* principles will be chosen and which *specific* judgements will be passed by *particular* people in *particular* circumstances. Much more extra knowledge about intial and boundary conditions is necessary to make accurate predictions. Exchange theory does predict, however, that we will find less consensus between and within Western societies than functionalists, and even Marxists, suppose. There will be a wide scale of *particular* choices and *specific* judgements regarding distributive justice. A monocausal explanation or a simple causal model of perceptions of distributive justice is not, contrary to functionalist and Marxist belief, a feasible option. In their opinion justice is, like beauty, in the eye of the beholder.

3   Procedural justice and the sociology of law

3.1   Justice and the law

The problem of procedural justice, i.e., the question of which rules, procedures and organizations are used to guarantee justice in society and the question of whether, and if so to which degree, people deem these institutional arrangements just, is the central issue in this section. One of the fields of sociological study which concentrates explicitly on the problem of procedural justice is that of the sociology of law. The theme of the administration of justice and the related problem of legitimacy was introduced into sociological thought by Max Weber. His concept of bureaucratic administration, that describes in an ideal-typical way an effective institutional arrangement for the administration of justice that is characteristic for the modern era, has been widely influential in the treatment of this subject. It has informed normative discourse as well as studies of government administration. In answering the first question regarding procedural justice, Weber describes the characteristics of modern officialdom (Gerth and Mills 1948, pp. 196–8).

1. Fixed and official jurisdictional areas are generally ordered by rules, that is, by laws or administrative regulations.
2. The principles of office hierarchy and of levels of graded authority imply a strictly ordered system of superordination and subordination in which there is a supervision of the lower offices by the higher ones.
3. The management of the modern office is based upon written documents.
4. Office management presupposes thorough and expert training.
5. Official activity is the primary task of the official.
6. The management of the office follows general rules, which are more or less stable and exhaustive.

The second question he answers by referring to the submission of bureaucratic administration to democratic control. In a constitutional state this guarantees, according to Weber, the legitimacy of its administration.

In contemporary studies, the theme of procedural or bureaucratic justice can mainly be found in studies concerning legislative or administrative agencies and the application of the law. The central questions in these studies are: 'Can social change be effectuated through the law?' and, 'How do the governmental institutions that administer the laws function?' These two questions are related. Effectuating social change through the law depends (among other factors) on the way governmental institutions function. Tomasic (1986, p. 99) is pessimistic regarding the progress made in the study of these two topics: 'In regard to the issue of social change, we seem to have progressed little beyond Roscoe Pound's discussion of 1916 concerning *The Limits of Effective Legal Action* ... the key governmental institutions through which change comes about, namely the legislature and administrative agencies, have received little direct attention.'

In the study of governmental institutions we can observe a recent shift in attention. The 'classical theory of bureaucracy assumed conformity [to the law] as self evident, [whereas] modern approaches tend to emphasize the many degrees of freedom and discretion if not arbitrariness within and among various units of administration' (Kaufmann *et al.* 1986, p. 13). By this shift the dominance of the classical Weberian theory in the sociology of law is slowly being eroded.

The classical theory expresses itself in the sociology of law in what Tomasic (1986, p. 99) calls the dominance of the legalist paradigm, 'which focuses attention upon lawyers and the courts'. Little attention is paid to non-legal institutions and the functioning of the law is too often interpreted in a command model, which does not call the daily routines of legal and administrative agencies into question (cf. Tomasic 1986; Feeley 1976; Abel 1980).

Feeley (1976) wrote an interesting critique of what he calls the 'received concept of law'. This is characterized by the law-as-command notion. In Feeley's view, this notion is too static and 'so preoccupied with a criminal law model that it ignores other forms of laws' (Feeley 1976, p. 504). Law is seen as a coercive system, while coercion is in fact only one of its functions. Abel (1980, p. 826) likewise rejects the original, legalist paradigm as being exhausted. Both Abel and Feeley call for concepts of law-making and the administration of law which are more social-scientific. The functioning of the law in society is the central topic in such an approach. It redirects the study of law from the courts, lawyers and criminal law to public policy and administrative law. A central problem in the public policy perspective on law is the instrumental use of the law.

The importance of a public policy perspective on law has been stressed by Nonet and Selznick in their book *Law and Society in Transition*. They write: 'to make jurisprudence more relevant and more alive, there must be a reintegration of legal, political and social theory' (Nonet and Selznick 1978, p. 3). To achieve this they present a 'recasting' of jurisprudential issues in a social science perspective. They distinguish three 'basic states of law in society: (1) law as the servant of repressive power, (2) law as a differentiated institution capable of taming repression and protecting its own integrity, and (3) law as a facilitator of response to social needs and aspirations'. They call these three types of law respectively repressive, autonomous and responsive. Central in this typification is the role of purpose. 'There is a repressive instrumentalism in which law is bent to the will of governing power, there is a withdrawal from purpose in the striving for autonomous law and there is a renewal of instrumentalism, but for more objective public ends, in the context of responsive law' (ibid., p. 15).

Each type of law is connected to a specific type of administration which Nonet and Selznick label, following Bennis (1966; 1973), as prebureaucratic, bureaucratic and postbureaucratic. Bureaucratic administration is hierarchically structured, rules are fixed and the decision-making process is routinized and allows for little delegation. 'Postbureaucratic' administration is goal-orientated, based on substantive instead of formal rationality, and the decision-making process and the interpretation of rules is contextual (Nonet and Selznick 1978, p. 22). These types can well illustrate some of the problems we will later discuss.

For our discussion, the models of autonomous and responsive law are the most relevant. Central in autonomous law (or the Weberian ideal-type) is its emphasis on procedural justice and (therefore?) elaborate legal rules. The administration of the law is characterized by strict adherence to the rules (and is therefore vulnerable to formalism and legalism) and narrow delegation (ibid., p. 16). In responsive law, in contrast, emphasis is placed on substantive justice and on more loose rules which are subordinated to principle and policy. The administration of the law in this model is purposive and there is broad delegation, but administrative agencies are accountable to purpose (ibid.) In the model of responsive law, procedural justice is subordinated to substantive justice. Needless to say, Nonet and Selznick favour a system of law inspired by their model of responsive law, because it better fits the goals and functions of modern society and public policy. At the same time, the dangers inherent in a responsive model are clear, since without sufficient (democratic) control it can become a modern variant of repressive law, with *ad hoc* and particularistic rules and an opportunistic use of discretion. Disputable though it may be, Nonet and Selznick's classification of types of law is nevertheless an inspiring instrument for research and discussion. The models of autonomous and responsive law illustrate the problems the modern welfare state encounters. On the one hand the welfare state is goal-orientated and thus substantive justice plays an important role in social policy; on the other hand the welfare state is a constitutional state in which procedural justice plays a prominent role.

A social science or public policy perspective on law directs attention to aspects of the making and administration of law that do not fit the dominant conception based on an autonomous or bureaucratic model of law. In his book *The Limits of Law* (1980), Allott stresses two aspects of law – law as communication and law as a social phenomenon – which are often neglected. If the law is interpreted as a system of communication instead of as a system of coercion and social control, then the reception, interpretation and acceptance of the law by the public become highly problematic (Allott 1980, pp. 73–98). Secondly, he argues, the functioning of the law is dependent on its social environment (ibid., pp. 99–120). Friedman (1975; 1985) operationalizes this in the concept of legal culture. The legal culture of a society is highly influential on the effectiveness of law. According to Allott, the failure to appreciate such communicative and social aspects of the functioning of the law explains the ineffectiveness of many laws.

The relation between social environment and the functioning of the law is the main theme in the work of the legal anthropologist Sally Falk Moore. She has studied the role played by legal or administrative rules in daily social interaction, and introduced the concept of the 'semi-auto-nomous social field'. The semi-autonomy of different social fields is typical for Western societies. Complete autonomy from, or complete dominance of, social fields by the law or the state are unthinkable. 'Since the law of sovereign states is hierarchical in form, no social field within a modern polity could be absolutely autonomous from a legal point of view. Absolute domination is also difficult to conceive, for even in armies and prisons and other rule-run institutions, there is usually an underlife with some autonomy' (S.F. Moore 1978, p. 78). Thus, social interaction is never completely regulated by law, it is only one of the factors determining social interaction. This observation again calls the instrumentalist interpretation of the functioning of law into question. As Moore writes: 'the ongoing competitions, collaborations and exchanges that take place in social life also generate their own regular relationships, rules and effective sanctions . . . The ways in which state enforceable law affects these processes are often exaggerated and the way in which law is affected by them is often underestimated' (ibid., p. 80).

A public policy perspective on law or more attention for the function-ing of the law in its social environment directs our attention to the administration and to the public. Only recently has a body of literature begun to emerge which concerns itself with the functioning of administrative organizations and increasingly provides valuable insights into the administration of the law. These studies focus on the administrative agencies which are the key institutions in the administration of justice.

Questions concerning social justice are related to the law in many ways. First they are related to the way the law is modelled. For example: 'To what extent do considerations of social justice have to be incorporated in the law? Do the "ethics of justice" require complex legal rules or is social justice better served by more general rules?' Second, the nature of social justice effectuated by the law is dependent on the manner in which the law is applied by administrative agencies, which in turn influences the public's attitude towards governmental agencies and thus the relationship between officials and clients. The attitude of the public towards questions of social justice in general, or to use Friedman's term 'the legal culture', is a third way in which problems of social justice are related to the law. In the following paragraphs we briefly review these three relations.

3.2 Law-making and social justice, the dilemma of procedural and substantive justice

According to Fuller, the law has its own 'inner morality'. This 'inner morality of the law' is predominantly procedural in character and is incompatible with the instrumental use of law. He formulates this morality in the following points: (1) legal rules should be general rather than specific, (2) treatment should be in accordance with rules, (3) rules should be promulgated, (4) rules should be intelligible, (5) rules should be relatively stable over time, (6) rules should be consistent, (7) rules should not be retroactive, and (8) conduct in accordance with rules should be reasonably performable by individuals (Fuller 1964). Fuller claims that the inner morality of law is an intrinsic asset of the law, which may not be violated for instrumental purposes (cf. the responsive model of law). Moreover, Fuller claims that law is primarily a product of social interaction and not vice versa (cf. Schuyt 1985), which implies that the instrumental use of the law is limited, because it must (more or less) accord with the rules of social interaction. This confronts us with a fundamental dilemma in the relation between justice and the law. Procedural justice limits the instrumental capacities of the law, whereas substantial justice calls for more responsive laws which stand in a strained relation with the inner morality of law.

In his study of the implementation of a wage-price freeze, entitled *Regulatory Justice*, Kagan wrote: 'As long as we demand justice, legal complexity will be our fate' (Kagan 1978, p. 182). Considerations of social justice tend to push regulation towards a more selective approach because a selective approach provides more opportunities for the redress of social inequalities and social problems. Selectivity, however, implies legal complexity.

Goodin takes issue with this view and states that, 'a system of loose legal principles is better adapted than rigid rules for capturing the wide range of ethically significant considerations in any particular situation' (Goodin 1979, p. 80). The ethics of justice demand loose, general or vague legal rules because there will be few cases which are alike in all relevant respects (cf. Dworkin 1977b, p. 14–80). 'The focus then is on equity, treating cases differently only in proportion to the ethically significant differences between them' (Goodin 1979, p. 86). A just system of legal rules, according to Goodin, would become too complex. Beyond a certain point, detailed exceptions and qualifications can become a source of confusion.

Thus the law is trapped between two competing criteria, the need for certainty, to avoid arbitrariness and to promote predictability and thus procedural justice on the one hand, and the need for flexibility, in order to guarantee substantive justice on the other (cf. Goodin 1979, pp. 84–5). The development of the legal system in most Western countries is in the direction of a growth of complex and protective regulation (cf. Bardach and Kagan 1982). Different sources can be pointed to as being the cause of this development:

> political pressure towards precision (Goodin 1979; Goodin and Le Grand 1986);
> the logic of regulation, which is 'the natural tendency to follow things to their logical conclusion' (Bardach and Kagan 1982, p. 19);
> the administrative need for certainty; in order to be able to implement regulation, administrative agencies need a certain amount of standardization (Gunsteren 1976; Goodin 1979, p. 89);
> a public need for certainty and predictability (Hart 1961, p. 127).

Goodin's plea for 'loose laws' fits Nonet and Selznick's model of responsive law. Responsive law is directed at substantive justice and therefore rules are more general and subordinated to principle. Autonomous law, in contrast, has elaborate rules to which have to be adhered to strictly.

The advantages and disadvantages of loose laws *vis-à-vis* legal complexity seem however to be dependent on the subject and goal of regulation. Bardach and Kagan (1982) see more advantages in loose laws and flexible enforcement than in, as they call it, 'tough legalism'. Their study, however, concentrates on the regulation of business and with this in mind their conclusion becomes understandable:

while legalism and other expressions of regulatory toughness may sometimes be appropriate – indeed, unavoidable – for dealing with the minority of bad apples, they may be self-defeating in dealing with the majority of good apples. Although the scope of the problem is unknown, it is likely that in a very large number of cases regulatory toughness in its legalistic manifestation creates resentment and resistance, undermines attitudes and information sharing practices that could otherwise be cooperative and constructive, and diverts energies of both sides into pointless and dispiriting legal routines and conflicts (Bardach and Kagan 1982, p. 119).

However, one might say that legal complexity can also enhance the legitimacy of the law and does not necessarily have to diminish compliance and social responsibility (cf. Friedman 1985). Regulation of entitlement in social security will probably always lead to complex laws, but can nevertheless satisfy the public need for substantive justice. An important difference between business regulation and social security is that the latter does not seek (or at least seeks to a lesser extent) to change behaviour. Most rules in social security regulation have an administrative character. The discussion about law-making and the ethics of justice can therefore profit from a more differentiated theory about forms and functions of regulation and from a better insight into the functioning of the law.

The discussion about law-making and social justice is based on a 'top-down' view of regulatory enforcement (cf. Diver 1980). It concentrates on the rationality of the structure of the law. In the preceding paragraph we have, however, argued for a more contextual or social scientific interpretation of the functioning of the law. This means that the discussion about law-making or the modelling of the law has to be related to the actual administration of the law and, as suggested, the type and function of the law. In the next paragraph we will concentrate on the administration of the law, and its (social) effectiveness (cf. Gilbert and Specht 1974, pp. 26–65).

3.3   The administration of justice, the crucial role of officials

The daily functioning of the administration is dependent on four factors:

1. the form and functions of the law;
2. the structure of the administrative organization;
3. the role and functioning of the administrative official; and,
4. the relation between officials and clients.

We will give a short overview of these four topics.

3.3.1   Rules and the administration of justice

Legal rules are often interpreted as setting limits to the discretionary powers of administrative officials. However, 'the dichotomy between rules and discretion is useful but should not be taken literally. Elimination of all discretion by a rule is rare, and in a great many situations it is probably undesirable as well' (Handler 1979, p. 10). So within the boundaries of administrative law there is often discretionary leeway for the administrative official, which exerts great influence, as we will see, on the final results of the administration of the law (see Mashaw 1983, p. 9).

The fact that the discretionary power of officials cannot be entirely eliminated, and thus the fact that procedural justice will therefore always be dependent on officials, is related to a fundamental dilemma in legal classification. Classification in the law is necessary to reduce the complexity and diversity of social relations and social reality. But the words and notions used in the law are more or less situational, which implies that their meaning is related to the context of a specific case. This implies that legal rules are always to a certain extent vague and uncertain and so do not fully direct the decisions of officials.

Thus rules can also create leeway for discretion, since they are more or less vague, contextual, voluminous and/or contradictory (see Mashaw 1983; Lipsky 1980; Bardach and Kagan 1982; Pynoos 1987; Burke 1986). The extent of such discretion and the way in which it is used depends on a number of different variables. The first and foremost is the organizational structure of administrative agencies (cf. Blau 1955).

3.3.2   Bureaucratic organization and the administration of justice

Davis (1971), who argues for the elimination of all 'unnecessary' discretion, sees organizational structures as the most important check on the discretionary power of officials. The way in which supervision of subordinates by superiors is organized is an essential factor in the extent of discretionary power enjoyed by officials and the way in which they can use this power and thus essential for procedural justice (Davis 1971, p. 143). However, control of administrative officials, or street-level bureaucrats as Lipsky calls them (street-level bureaucrats are the officials that are in direct contact with the public) is more difficult than Davis suggests. Measurement and control of their performance is very difficult. 'Simply stated, it is extremely difficult to monitor most social service activity (i.e. to obtain reliable information about decision making so that performance can be evaluated); and if an activity does not readily lend itself to monitoring, supervisory officials lack the necessary information to assert control' (Handler 1979, p. 18). Thus 'the inability to measure street-level bureaucrats' performance has widespread implications for controlling the agencies' (Lipsky 1980, p. 53).

Not only the organizational structure, but also the nature of the bureaucratic role creates leeway for discretion. We are reminded that administrative officials are involved in daily contacts with the public. They are confronted with the problem of being obliged to make decisions on a mass basis, according to the rules, while being faced with the necessity to provide individual responses to the problems of their clients. Thompson (1975) calls this dilemma 'the problem of administrative compassion'. This dilemma accounts for the fact that administrative officials will always try to create some discretionary latitude. They need that latitude (cf. Burke 1986).

3.3.3   The official and the administration of justice

We can distinguish three main types of administrative organization. Each defines the role and functioning of officials in a different way:

the bureaucratic organization, which is characterized by a hierarchical structure, internal rules, narrow delegation and strict monitoring of officials' behaviour;
the professional organization, which is characterized by an interpersonal structure and in which the emphasis is on the application of knowledge rather than on rules; and,
the discretionary organization, characterized by contextual interpretation of cases, (some) organizational independence and a 'loose' or goal-orientated application of rules (cf. Mashaw 1983; Nonet and Selznick 1978; Van Groenendaal 1986).

All administrative agencies exhibit some of the characteristics of each of these three ideal-types. Precisely which characteristics are dominant depends on the rules that are to be administered, the organizational structure, the role of administrative officials and their relations with clients (for more about the critical role of the organization see Weaver 1977; Breyer 1982; Katzmann 1980; Wilding 1982; Gronow and Hegner 1980; Adler and Asquith 1981).

Mashaw systematizes these three types of organization and the role of officials in three models of bureaucratic justice (Mashaw 1983, p. 31):

Model	Legitimizing values	Primary goal	Structure of organization	Cognitive technique
Bureaucratic rationality	Accuracy and efficiency	Programme implementation	Hierarchical	Information processing
Professional treatment	Service	Client satisfaction	Interpersonal	Clinical application of knowledge
Moral judgement (discretion)	Fairness	Conflict resolution	Independent	Contextual interpretation

Kagan (1978, p. 95) presents a somewhat different typification of what he calls modes of rule application by officials. His model is based on two dimensions: the emphasis placed on the realization of organizational ends and the emphasis placed on adherence to rules. This produces the following model:

		Emphasis on realization of organizational ends	
		+	−
	+	Judicial mode	Legalism
Emphasis on adherence to rules	−	Unauthorized (professional) discretion	Retreatism

We have dubbed 'unauthorized' discretion 'professional' discretion. Legalism, the judicial mode, and professional discretion correspond to Mashaw's bureaucratic rationality, moral judgement and professional treatment respectively. We can now introduce a fourth type in Mashaw's model based on Kagan's mode of retreatism. This retreatist mode is characterized by the (supposed) inapplicability of the rules, the avoidance of problems in the daily routine and an indifferent attitude of administrative officials. If Allot's thesis that many laws are ineffective owing to underprovision of the necessary requirements for effective law and overambitiousness of the legislature holds (Allott 1980, p. 287), then this fourth type is an important one.

3.3.4   The relation between officials and clients and the administration of justice

The relation between administrative officials and clients is an important factor influencing the decisions of officials. The 'distance' between clients and officials is one aspect of this relation. If officials never actually see their clients, but only acquire a picture of them on the basis of administratively relevant papers (cf. Mashaw 1983), that picture will tend to be abstract. Contextual interpretation (or a judicial mode of rule application) will hardly be possible and therefore the mode of rule application will be legalistic. Lipsky points to a second aspect of the distance between clients and officials: 'the people with whom street-level bureaucrats regularly interact are not among their primary reference groups, affecting the degree to which client satisfaction has priority' (Lipsky 1980, p. 81). This can promote a more retreatist or legalist mode of rule application.

However, it is often necessary for officials to acquire an unambiguous picture of the client. This is a necessary condition for making contextual interpretations of the rules and the clients' situation. When it is impossible to acquire such a clear picture (for example because of obstruction by the client or problems of privacy) the mode of rule application by officials will shift in the direction of a legalist or a retreatist style. The possibility of monitoring clients depends of course also on the 'category' of clients of an agency. There can be more or less differentiation in the client population of an agency. Strong differentiation in the category of clients an official meets makes a legalist interpretation of the rules difficult for there are always idiosyncracies in the situation of the client. Homogeneity in the client population (in respect to the relevant variables) creates the possibility of a more legalist mode of rule application. There can also be important differences in the attitude of clients towards the administrative official. As Lipsky pointed out, clients are often non-voluntary. In his opinion this can have the effect that agencies become less responsive to their clients, because 'they have nothing to lose by failing to satisfy clients' (Lipsky 1980, p. 55).

Concerning the administration of justice, we can now draw some conclusions. The law can never fully direct the decision-making process of officials. Officials will always have some discretion. The organization has to control this discretion, but creates leeway for discretion itself. The more instrumental social policy is, the more these problems will be felt. These problems threaten procedural justice in law and policy. Officials come to play a crucial role in the administration of social policy, so citizens will become more dependent on the decisions of officials. It is therefore crucial to gain further insight in these decision-making processes and the mode of rule application of officials.

3.4   Legal culture; towards 'total justice'?

As we already stated, the law is dependent on its social environment and vice versa. The social environment of the law can, according to Friedman, be conceptualized in the notion of a legal culture. The term legal culture is used to 'describe a number of related phenomena. First, it refers to public knowledge of and attitudes and behavior patterns toward the legal system . . . These attitudes differ from person to person, but one can also speak of the legal culture of a country or a group, if there are patterns that distinguish it from the culture of other countries or groups' (Friedman 1975, p. 194).

The pattern Friedman points to as being specific for Western welfare states (in particular the USA), is one that he describes as a development towards a notion of total justice. This total justice is characterized by, as Friedman calls it, generalized expectations of justice and plural equality. Generalized expectations of justice imply that 'people expect to be treated – by government, people and institutions – as valid, total human beings; they expect to be assessed and respected as unique individuals. Justice (as now understood) means ignoring one's race or religion, and allowing nonconforming life-choices, within certain limits of tolerance' (Friedman 1985, p. 144). This generalized expectation of justice is accompanied by a general expectation of recompense. 'If calamity strikes, somebody should make amends through money damages or other forms of compensation' (Friedman 1985, p. 144). The generalized expectation of justice is reflected in a notion of plural equality. This means that 'every person has the right not to suffer any handicap or disadvantage, in life or law, because of "immutable" characteristics (race, sex, physical disability, old age), or because of way of life, or because of those mixtures of choice and birth called ethnicity and religion' (Friedman 1985, p. 107). So the modern notion of equality develops in the direction of a broad, social definition, whereas it primarily used to mean equality before the law, a formal sense of equality. Legal culture develops in the direction of this 'total justice', it is a trend, 'it may buckle and bend, but it will not go away . . . it seems to be here to stay' (Friedman 1985, p. 152).

The development towards total justice in legal culture has two important consequences for the subject under discussion: procedural or bureaucratic justice. First, it creates what may be called 'legitimization problems': government will never be able to meet all the demands of the public. Friedman, however, redefines these problems. He states that arguments about a legitimization crisis can be turned upside down (Friedman 1985, p. 30). The consequence of the notion of total justice is a critical public. It will use the law and it will critically monitor the decisions of administrative officials. So, the 'overuse' of the law can be seen as a sign of legitimacy instead of as a sign of crisis. A critical public, in this interpretation, can be seen as a necessary and correcting power in modern welfare states, which are legally complex and differentiated. This attitude of the public fits the many degrees of freedom and discretion in the administrative system we described above.

The second consequence of the development towards 'total justice' has been elaborated by Sampson (1981), although he does not use Friedman's concepts. Differentiation of regulation is reflected in a process of social differentiation. Sampson defines this social process as a development from a particularistic form of social organization towards a more universalistic form. Particularistic forms of social organization are characterized by the centrality of primary social bonds (e.g., family relations). Universalistic forms of social organization are characterized by an emphasis on more temporary, secondary group-ties (e.g., educational level, gender). Sampson suggests that the consequences of this development are paradoxical:

The effort to extend universalism has produced what appears to be a new kind of particularism. If the earlier era emphasized particularism based on primary-group bonds, this new era is beginning to stress particularism based on more secondary bonds, that is, the less personal and non-familial ties of human association including gender, race, sexual preference and consumer status. People are cast together into the same particularistic category and warrant special treatment because of their secondary qualities. Paradoxically, the extension of universalism is giving rise to new forms of particularism and introducing further dissensus about the proper conception of justice. (Sampson 1981, p. 116)

This means that the principles of (formal) equality and individual accomplishment which fit in a more universalistic social organization will be eroded and a new particularistic interpretation of social justice will arise: 'deserving will be linked to group membership and not invariably to individual accomplishment' (Sampson 1981, p. 123).

Sampson points to a fundamental dilemma in the notion of total justice. The generalized expectation of justice leads to a strong emphasis on, for example, the equity of the law (interpreted in the sense of plural equality). Equity in the (modelling and administration of the) law, combined with the notion of plural equality, can lead to very differentiated and detailed laws. This can (and often will) contradict the 'ethics of justice' (reinterpreted in terms of Friedman's legal culture). Every new rule or regulation will create new inequalities, for no rule can capture the wide range of particular situations. These problems enhance the strained relation that exists between procedural and substantive justice.

We can, however, also use more prosaic theories to explain the 'law explosion'. Schuyt (1989) mentions four possible explanations:

First, twenty-five years of economic growth have increased university enrollment, especially in law faculties after 1965. The postwar baby boom contributed to the increased production of lawyers. Because the ideology of professional autonomy allows lawyers to decide whether to render legal aid, many young lawyers have been able to find work within the 'market for welfare and well being'. Second, increased state intervention increased the legalization of social relations and thus the opportunities for legal work. Third, the dissolution of long-standing social bonds (work into unemployment, marriage into divorce, etc.) multiplied the rapidity of status change. Law is mobilized when people change their status (whether legally or socially). Fourth, economic activity has shifted from the production of goods to the production of services. Compared to medical services, legal services still constitute a very small part of this market.

3.5   Conclusion

In the attempt to find the links between the administration of the law and procedural and substantive justice we seem to have complicated matters instead of making them less opaque. Sociolegal research into administrative agencies has revealed the intricacies of the administrative process. The type of bureaucratic justice on which administrative behaviour is based depends on numerous variables. The influence exerted by each on the specific type of bureaucratic justice we will encounter in administrative agencies can be diverse. Nevertheless, insight into the administrative process will prove to be a valuable instrument in evaluating (the results of) governmental policy. The social scientific approach towards the law sheds new light on the important role which is played by the administrative officials and the public.

As has been illustrated, the developments in law and social policy, the developments in the administration of law and the developments in legal culture all create problems in guaranteeing procedural justice on the one hand and effectuating substantive justice on the other hand. These problems seem to increase. Drawing more general conclusions concerning the (social) effects of the law (of which social justice is one aspect) is seriously hampered by the fact that the majority of the studies concern themselves with one specific law or one specific field of governmental intervention (cf. Schuyt 1985, p. 121). What has been made clear, however, is the fact that analysis of governmental intervention through the law (which is the most common form of government intervention) is obliged to go beyond the simple 'law-as-command' model and is also obliged to call the Weberian ideal-type of bureaucracy, which assumes conformity to the law as self-evident, into question.

6 The social psychology of distributive justice

Kjell Törnblom

1 Introduction

[The] return to an ancient theme can be viewed as no more than a belated recognition of a deeper truth that our forerunners saw clearly: Almost any theory of society is likely to be a theory about justice as well, even if the analyst protests against that interpretation. Any substantial theory of society must explain social order and conflict. It does so through its explanations of social control, while these must focus implicitly or explicitly on whether members of a society believe its social arrangements are reasonably just. Such a focus is necessary, for that belief will affect somewhat the willingness to maintain the society, or to destroy it. (Goode 1978, p. 329)

Apart from reminding us about the great significance of justice as a theoretical issue and a social problem, the above quotation emphasizes the importance of a social psychological approach to the topic. That 'Justice is in the eye of the beholder' is widely recognized by social psychologists. Unfortunately, it appears that the fundamental wisdom contained in this simple proverb is too often neglected in various contexts of everyday life. Markovsky (1986) noted that although social policy debates are frequently influenced by the literatures of philosophy, political science and economics, sociological and psychological insights are generally left aside: 'The argument is over what political/economic system is most just, ignoring the complex cognitive factors which play on perceptions of justice, and ignoring the complex social factors which play on such cognitions. Without belittling attempts at formulating social policy prescriptions, [a favourable outcome of these attempts] is contingent upon understanding the cognitive and social structural factors that lead a society's members and policy makers to form a particular evaluation . . .' (Markovsky 1986, p. 3).

An attempt will not be made here to define the concept of justice. This would appear to be a 'hopeless and pompous task' (Reis 1984, p. 38), 'is beyond the capacity of any scientific analysis' (Goode 1978, p. 336), and 'is not the business of psychological studies of justice phenomena' anyway (Mikula 1984, p. 205). Past research has convincingly shown that the notion of justice seems to mean different things to different people and in different circumstances. 'Justice is like a greased pig, it yells loudly but is hard to catch'.[1] In any event, the perennial search for the true meaning of justice has not been particularly fruitful, and it is likely that 'there is no true or essential justice beyond its socially constructed meanings' (Markovsky 1986, p. 1). Indeed, as we shall see below, justice appears in different shapes (in thought and action); it is conceived in terms of, and operationalized into, a number of different justice principles the particular forms of which are affected by historical, cultural, societal, situational and individual factors.

The social psychology of 'distributive justice' covers a wide range of issues which attract the interest of a growing number of theorists and researchers. The scientific literature on the topic is impressive. A new multidisciplinary journal (*Social Justice Research*) solely devoted to justice research has recently been founded, and the quantity of journal articles, chapters, contributed volumes (in chronological order: Berkowitz and Walster 1976; Mikula 1980c; Lerner and Lerner 1981; Greenberg and Cohen 1982a; Messick and Cook 1983; Folger 1984a; Bierhoff, Cohen and Greenberg 1986; Cohen 1986c; Masters and Smith 1987; Vermunt and Steensma in press; Wosinska and Ratajczak in press) and monographs (in chronological order: Walster, Walster and Berscheid 1978; Lerner 1980; Sampson 1983; Deutsch 1985; Skarzynska 1985; Zaborowski 1986; Kellerhals, Coenen-Huther and Modak 1988a; Lind and Tyler 1988; Wosinska in press) that have been published since the early 1970s make attempts to keep abreast with the literature a real challenge. As the present review is restricted to the space of a chapter (rather than a book) it deals primarily with work addressing central theoretical issues and dwells very little on studies of an applied nature.

Apart from the introductory and concluding sections, this review is organized into four major parts. Section 2 features a description of equity theory, the formulation of which paved the way for a multidimensional conception of justice (section 3) and for the more sophisticated contingency approaches of today (section 4). As distributive justice is a problem of no less importance when negative rather than positive outcomes are to be allocated, and as most theory and research has focused on the latter problem, a separate discussion (in section 5) has been devoted to the relationship between those two processes. The concluding section touches upon some developing research topics and proposes some future lines of research. Finally, in view of the aims of this book, I have tried to spell out a number of implications for social policy debates and prescriptions of the research on the different topics dealt with in this chapter.

It should be noted that this review exclusively focuses on *distributive* justice (i.e., the perceived fairness of the shape or end-state of outcome allocation), while *procedural* justice (i.e., the perceived fairness of the process of outcome allocation) has been neglected. Apart from space limitations there are two main reasons for leaving out this important and highly relevant topic. First, two excellent reviews have been published recently (Tyler 1987; Lind and Tyler 1988). Secondly, it seems that the input to the area by European social psychologists is quite modest in comparison to their American colleagues.

2   Equity theory

The notion of distributive justice was introduced to a sociological audience by George Homans (1958, 1961), recognizing that the term was coined by Aristotle in his *Nichomachean Ethics* (1962, translation). Homans' analysis of distributive justice was carried out within the context of his exchange theory and derives from the frustration-aggression principle in behavioural psychology (Homans 1982). Empirical research on distributive justice gained momentum when Adams presented his equity theory in 1965. Adams' analysis built primarily on the seminal social exchange formulations by Homans (1958, 1961, 1974) and Blau (1964a, 1964b), as well as on Festinger's social comparison and cognitive dissonance theories (1954 and 1957, respectively). Another major boost to the area of distributive justice, or equity, was provided by Walster, Berscheid and Walster in 1973 with the publication of their article 'New directions in equity research'.

Equity theory generated an exponentially increasing growth of publications during the two decades following Adams' formulation (Adams and Freedman 1976). 'As a model for generating research, the equity-theory framework has been exemplary . . . [and] . . . The range of content areas to which it has been applied is quite broad . . .' (Shaw and Costanzo 1982, p. 107). But at the same time the theory inspired more complex and broader conceptions of distributive justice (e.g., the 'contingency approaches' discussed below), as researchers began to respond to its various limitations.

It appears that equity theory presently enjoys a significantly reduced following in favour of alternative and multifaceted conceptions of justice (according to which equity is only one among several possible justice criteria). It seems reasonable to assume that equity calculations would be particularly encouraged and prevalent (as a basis for judging fairness) within social systems whose modes of allocating desired (and scarce) resources give priority to such principles as contributions or merit in their compensation (and provision of incentives) for socially valued contributions and efforts by individuals and groups.

2.1   Description

A fundamental tenet of equity theory is that it views interpersonal relationships in terms of exchange transactions involving various kinds of resources. People make certain investments (inputs or contributions) in return for which they expect to receive certain rewards (outcomes). 'It is assumed that equitable interdependence creates interpersonal attraction which functions to produce group cohesiveness' (Hogg and Abrams 1988, p. 98). When people's social rewards are proportional to their costs and investments, the situation is just or equitable (Homans 1961). This state of affairs is conducive to the establishment and maintenance of a social relationship. When rewards are perceived to be insufficient or oversufficient a situation of inequity prevails. This condition is assumed to produce psychological discomfort (or distress) as well as a desire to terminate the relationship or, at least, to make changes in the direction of equity. Furthermore, people are presumably interested not only in their own equity, but also in equity for others.

The notion of equity is often conceptually symbolized and defined in terms of a mathematical equation as follows:

$$\frac{Op}{Ip} = \frac{Oa}{Ia} \qquad \text{(Adams 1965, p. 281).}$$

Equity obtains when person p's ratio of outcomes (O) to inputs (I) is equal to that of person a. A person is assumed to experience *in*equity (injustice) if s/he perceives a discrepancy between his/her and another person's outcome/input ratios. (Similar formulae have previously been proposed by Sayles 1958; Patchen 1961; and Homans 1961.)[2] *Outcomes* are defined as 'the positive or negative consequences [i.e., 'rewards' or 'costs'] that a scrutineer perceives a participant has incurred as a consequence of his relationship with another', while *inputs* are 'the participant's contributions to the exchange, which are seen (by a scrutineer) as entitling him to rewards or costs' (Walster, Berscheid and Walster 1973, p. 152). Positive and negative inputs are called 'assets' and 'liabilities' respectively.

Equity theory, as formulated by Walster, Berscheid and Walster (1973), 'consists of four propositions designed to predict when individuals will perceive that they are justly treated and how they will react when they find themselves enmeshed in unjust relationships' (p. 151). These propositions contain some of the theory's major assumptions about the nature of Man, the behaviour of groups and the consequences of inequity. First, people are assumed to be basically self-interested creatures, in that they strive to maximize their own rewards. Second, people's self-interested nature is tempered, because groups need to maximize collective reward which, in turn, necessitates members adhering to an equitable system of reward allocation.[3] Third, perceived inequity and subsequent distress, as well as distress and the intensity of resulting equity-restoring attempts, are assumed to be positively and linearly related.

The individual's perceptions of equity and inequity are based upon his/her expectations concerning the amount of outcomes that are considered commensurate to particular inputs. These expectations are, in turn, commonly assumed to originate from social comparison processes.

The implication of the rule of justice is that men compare themselves with each other in terms of their investments as well as in terms of the rewards they receive from their services and expect differences in the latter to correspond to differences in the former. Their satisfaction depends not only on the absolute amount of reward they receive for their services but also on the fact that the expectations raised by these comparisons are not disappointed. (Blau 1964a, pp. 194–5)

Thus, perceived discrepancies between the perceived actual and the perceived ideal (expected) match between inputs and outcomes is assumed to result in subjective experiences of inequity.

Adams (1963) emphasizes that the conception of equity is historically and culturally determined, and that 'In order to predict when an individual will experience inequity, under given conditions of inputs and outcomes, it is necessary to know something of the values and norms to which he subscribes – with what culture or subculture he is associated' (p. 425). Using Japan as a contrasting example to the United States, he notes that inputs conceived in terms of type and amount of work are not everywhere related to salary as an outcome. Pay may instead be determined by factors like seniority, heritage, family conditions, etc.

As the experience of inequity (a special case of cognitive dissonance) is assumed to be uncomfortable, the individual becomes dissatisfied (discontented or distressed) and is motivated to reduce or eliminate it (especially when facing unfavourable inequity). Boulding (1962, p. 81) makes a distinction between personal and political discontent. Political discontent is based upon dissatisfaction with the external environment (in which case the person is not to blame for discrepancies between actual and expected outcomes), while personal discontent is experienced when the individual assumes personal responsibility for the perceived inadequacy of outcomes. Only the first type of discontent is relevant to the notion of injustice (inequity).

Finally, a number of suggestions have been offered about the ways in which inequity may be reduced or eliminated. Adams (1965) found empirical evidence for the following six methods of reducing inequity: altering one's inputs, altering one's outcomes, cognitively distorting one's inputs and outcomes, leaving the field, altering or cognitively distorting Other's inputs and outcomes, and changing one's comparison object (Adams 1965, pp. 295–6, also offered half a dozen hypotheses about the conditions determining the choice among the six modes of restoring equity). Recognizing that the mode of equity-restoration will, in part, depend upon whether the person is a victim or a beneficiary of inequity, Blumstein and Weinstein (1969) suggested that (1) the beneficiary will attempt to raise the rewards of the victim, and (2) the victim will attempt to lower the rewards of the beneficiary. These general propositions invite elaborations, and the contributions of Walster, Berscheid and Walster (1973) contain more detailed suggestions. According to these authors, the harmdoer (i.e., the person who causes inequity) may either compensate the victim (as suggested by Blumstein and Weinstein) or reduce his/her own outcomes to the victim's level (i.e., self-deprivation). Another class of equity-reducing techniques is psychological distortion of the input–outcome proportionality by derogating the victim (e.g., by devaluating the victim's contributions), minimizing his/her suffering (e.g., underestimating or denying the harm done to the victim), and denying one's responsibility for the victim's inequitable situation (e.g., by assigning the harmdoing to someone else). The victim may retaliate against the harmdoer or accept his/her apologies (i.e., forgive the harmdoer).

Most empirical research on equity theory predictions has focused on the resolution of inequity (or restoration of equity), and the experiment has been the most frequently used method. Cook and Hegtvedt (1983) have selectively reviewed the experimental evidence from reallocation and productivity studies (in the latter of which subjects were over or underpaid on an hourly or a piece rate basis). An extensive coverage of research on equity theory may also be found in a dissertation by Kumar (1986).

2.2   *Typologies of justice and injustice*

As a person's response (or lack of response) to inequity is affected by its (subjective) nature and magnitude, a systematic set of predictions will be facilitated by the construction of a typology of equity and inequity.

The notion of 'comparison' (i.e., the assessment or evaluation of a person's resemblance to other(s) – a social comparison – or to himself at another point in time – a temporal comparison) serves as the basis for a number of typologies of justice and injustice. The way comparison is conceptualized not only affects how equity and inequity will be defined (and what consequences these states will have), but also provides a framework within which various types of equity and inequity may be differentiated. Adams (1963) was inspired by Festinger's (1954) theory of social comparisons which addresses the individual's needs to evaluate his/her opinions and abilities. However, Adams extended the scope of Festinger's theory with regard to the objects of comparison. In equity theory comparisons concern Self's and Other's inputs (which may subsume not only opinions and abilities, but also task performance, expended effort, needs, a variety of achieved or ascribed person characteristics, etc.) as well as outcomes (e.g., reward and punishment, a category which Festinger did not consider).

Equity will exist under two conditions, according to Adams (1965): (1) when person P's inputs and outcomes are identical to those of person O, and (2) when P's inputs are higher (or lower) than O's and P's outcomes are correspondingly higher (or lower) than O's. By dichotomizing the values of inputs and outcomes Adams (1963) generated a typology containing six types of equity and ten types of inequity. Felt inequity is assumed to be greater when P's and O's inputs and outcomes are both dissimilar than when only one or other is dissimilar. In addition, over-payment is presumably more tolerable for P than underpayment. On the basis of the above assumptions Adams was able to distinguish among three magnitudes of felt inequity, thus providing a partial rank ordering among the sixteen types encompassed by his typology. As a positive linear relationship is proposed between the magnitude of felt inequity and intensity of affective and/or behavioural responses, the establishment of a rank order among types of inequity is obviously a crucial step toward the goal of predicting the intensity of psychological and behavioural equity-restoring processes.

The status-value approach to equity or distributive justice (Anderson *et al.* 1969; Zelditch *et al.* 1970; Berger *et al.* 1972) emphasizes the nature of justice evaluations, focusing on the status significance of characteristics ('any feature or aspect of a person that might be used to describe him, such as energy, height, or skin color'; Berger *et al.* 1972, p. 128) and goal-objects ('any object, tangible or intangible, that an actor might want, or that might satisfy some need, such as shelter, income, or a title'; ibid.) rather than their consummatory value (as is typical for exchange formulations of distributive justice). Fundamental to the status-value formulation of distributive justice is the proposition that an exclusive reliance on local comparison (in which a person compares him/herself with another particular person – a typical approach in research guided by Adams' equity theory) results in incomplete and incorrect identification of types of justice and injustice. Referential comparison (involving a particular category of people which serves as a reference group or a generalized Other with which P compares his/her own as well as O's situation) gives a different and more accurate meaning to both justice and injustice: 'A "just" state in local comparison sometimes is "unjust" viewed in terms of referential comparison' and vice versa, and 'Even two states that are "unjust" in both views are seen as quite different *kinds* of injustice in referential as opposed to local comparison' (Berger *et al.* 1972, pp. 123–4). For example, Adams (1963) claimed that a situation is equitable (just) if P's and O's inputs are equally low and their outcomes are identical (e.g., both P and O receive, say, $15 an hour). This is a reasonable conclusion when the situation is assessed through a local comparison. However, a referential comparison might very well reveal that both P and O are inequitably rewarded (i.e., underpaid or overpaid, which is quite possible if the relevant generalized Other is paid respectively $17 or $13 an hour for the same input).

Additional types of comparison have been discussed by Weick (1966), Pritchard (1969), Levine and Moreland (1987) and Masters and Keil (1987).

Berger *et al.* (1972) assume that the comparing individual, P, will develop prescriptive expectations that s/he and O (one or more Others) are entitled to goal-objects (outcomes), on the basis of their status characteristics (inputs), similar to those received by members of a relevant reference group. A comparison of the 'expected' with the 'actual' allocation of goal-objects (the values of which are dichotomized) for P and O generates a typology of the sixteen situations previously identified by Adams (1963). However, the 'new' typology corrects those instances in which Adams misclassified just and unjust states. It also allows for a distinction between individual injustice (injustice for self as well as for other) and collective injustice,[4] facilitating the analysis of justice processes on two different levels (see Anderson *et al.* 1969). A few years later Törnblom (1977a) made some further elaborations by simultaneously considering local and referential comparisons of inputs and outcomes.[5] This resulted in additional distinctions among different just and unjust situations within the framework of an extensive typology. These types were ordered in terms of magnitude of injustice by means of a set of propositions. (See also Törnblom 1982, for some methodological implications of this typology.)

Distinctions among unjust as well as just situations are crucial for a successful exploration of the connections among terms in a complex chain of events: type and magnitude of injustice vs. type and magnitude of distress vs. type and magnitude of justice restoring psychological and behavioural responses. 'What are the ramifications of different types and degrees of inequity for the continuation of exchange relationships? Does inequity lead to a termination of an exchange, or are there conditions under which exchanges will be continued even though they are inequitable?' (Blalock and Wilken 1979, p. 228). So far, few attempts have been made (two exceptions are Anderson *et al.* 1969 and Weick and Nesset 1968) where specific justice-restoring behaviours are systematically connected to specific types of discontent or injustice.

2.3   Critique and limitations

The origin of many recent theoretical and empirical developments within the area of distributive justice can be traced to a multitude of reactions against the limitations of equity theory. This fact does not demean the value of the theory: 'Although it has been much criticized in recent years, it is appropriate to recognize its extraordinary stimulative value to research and the unusual research creativeness of its adherents . . . it [has] had a major influence in social psychology' (Deutsch 1985, p. 30). Space does not allow a complete coverage of the many critical assessments to be found throughout the abundant literature (e.g., Cook and Yamagishi 1983; Deutsch 1985; Farkas and Anderson 1979; Furby 1986; Hook and Cook 1979; Jasso and Rossi 1977; Pritchard 1969; Tajfel 1982; Utne and Kidd 1980; Weick 1966; Weick and Nesset 1968). Instead, comments will here be selectively restricted to four issues: ideological implications, the subjective character of equity/inequity, qualitative aspects of equity/inequity, and the assumed linearity between felt inequity and equity-restoring behaviour. Not all of the statements below should be taken as a critique of equity theory. Some are meant as a commentary about issues that are in need of increased theoretical and empirical work.

2.3.1. Ideological implications. Any solution to the problem of just distribution of resources has consequences for the welfare of human beings. As social scientific theory may be utilized as an ideological tool for political purposes, one is well advised to consider the likely consequences of translating equity (or any other) theory into praxis or of treating its component propositions as normative rather than as a reflection of a particular economic system in a particular sociohistoric context. A potential danger with the adoption of equity as a basis for distributional policy and ideology is that it is likely to breed and provide justification for social inequalities. Thus, the desirability of alternative solutions to the problem of (scarce) resource distribution ought to be obvious. Certainly, those who favour equity as a universal solution to the distribution of scarce resources must reconcile themselves to the fact that their position may be instrumental to the preservation and perpetuation of social inequality, a condition which is likely to have severe negative effects on the life chances of the disadvantaged. The reluctance to reduce or abolish inequality is often justified on the basis of a commitment to social order and stability which is, in turn, frequently and erroneously assumed to be dependent upon the equity principle of reward in proportion to contributions.

On the other hand, those who dislike the equity principle, consider it unethical, and/or realize that equity theory is unlikely to be an accurate characterization of all social relations at any given place and point in time may, therefore, favour distribution according to an alternative criterion, say, the need or equality principle. However, they may sooner or later have to face the chilling reality of an increasing scarcity of resources for sustenance, a situation in which there is simply not enough for everyone to go around. Thus, the adoption of different distribution principles will present different problems to be analysed and resolved. The ideological basis and the likely conservative consequences of equity theory as a basis for social policy have been discussed by other social psychologists (e.g., Martin and Murray 1983; Sampson 1983; Deutsch 1985). The justification of social inequality by sociologists of the functionalist approach to social stratification (e.g., Davis and Moore 1945) immediately comes to mind in this context, as does the ensuing lively debate arising from the opposition by conflict theorists (e.g., Dahrendorf 1950).

2.3.2. The subjective character of equity/inequity. Adams and Freedman (1976) underscored the need to improve our ability to quantify the magnitude of inputs and outcomes, and thus of inequities. Even though some inputs (e.g., hours of work) and some outcomes (e.g., amount of money) are easy to quantify objectively, others are not (e.g., input in the form of effort or advice, and love or status as an outcome). In addition, a complicating state of affairs concerning all resources (inputs as well as outcomes) is that their values are subjectively appraised by allocators and recipients alike. The subjective value of a given resource is contingent upon factors such as the recipient's need for it (i.e., its marginal utility), its scarcity, and the identity of the person who provides it.

Considering social exchange as an on-going process composed of interdependent phases (Burgess and McCarl Nielsen 1974; Levinger and Huesmann 1980), the lack of consensus between the exchange partners' subjective evaluations of their own as well as their partners' inputs and outcomes may result in considerable complexities in predicting the direction of their interpersonal relationship (Törnblom 1977c).

Finally, the assessment of equity/inequity may be influenced by a recipient's perception of the intentionality or motivation behind exchange transactions (e.g., Goranson and Berkowitz 1966; Leventhal, Weiss and Long, 1969; Garrett and Libby 1973). The particular resource, *per se*, is frequently less significant than the perceived motives behind the exchange. 'It is not the gift, but the thought, that counts.' Thus, the exchange of resources of unequal value (or of resources that are normally not interchangeable – see below) are occasionally permitted. Excellent discussions of the impact of attributions on the assessment of and on responses to inequity may be found in chapters by Cohen (1982) and Utne and Kidd (1980).

2.3.3. Qualitative aspects of equity/inequity. Equity theory needs to be elaborated not only in its quantitative aspects (e.g., the meaning of proportionality – how much input is required for how much outcome), but also in qualitative terms. Consider, first, the possibility that an inequitable situation may be created because an *inappropriate kind of resource* is presented (or taken away). The particular contribution made by an individual which may lead to a claim of allocation according to contributions (merit) may involve a variety of resources. One may acquire merit by contributing money, goods, information, services, etc. Then, if a person's contribution consists of service, for example, should it be considered meritorious when love is allocated or when the allocation involves money?

Not only is the determination frequently problematic of how appropriate the interchange of particular resources is, and thus the assessment of its equitableness (as reciprocation with an inappropriate resource may create inequity), but individuals also differ in their subjective perceptions as to what constitutes a fair exchange. Increasing the amount of an inappropriate resource may not be sufficient to create, maintain, or restore equity. The results of studies by Teichman (1971) and Donnenwerth (1971) may be taken as indirect support of this proposition. Both studies were conducted within the framework of Foa's (1971) resource theory featuring a six-category resource classification system. Teichman (1971) found lower degrees of satisfaction the more dissimilar the resource of reciprocation was to the provided resource. Similarly, Donnenwerth (1971) found higher intensity of retaliation and more residual hostility in negative exchanges the more dissimilar the resource of deprivation and the resource of retaliation.

The question of whether or not a particular contribution will serve as a legitimate basis for the reception of a share of that which is distributed by merit has been raised by Adams (1965). He proposed two criteria: the existence of the contribution has to be 'recognized' by at least one of the parties to the exchange, and its possessor has to perceive it as 'relevant' to the exchange, Kayser and Lamm (1980) have suggested that personal characteristics and actions are relevant if they are perceived as causally important for the production of outcomes, variable and under the person's control. Törnblom and Foa (1983, p. 171) concluded 'that the relevance of a contribution may also depend on the relationship between the resource of contribution and the resource of allocation'. Indeed, a vignette study by Kreveld, Vermunt and de Vries (1985) showed that Dutch subjects favoured recognition as an outcome for devotion to work, pay for poor working conditions, while productivity was not associated with a preference for any particular kind of outcome.[6]

A second cause of felt inequity (or injustice) might be that *the adopted justice principle is inappropriate*. Although this may 'objectively' result in over or underreward (as judged by an outside observer against an equity criterion), the recipient's sense of injustice might *not* be caused by the 'inappropriate' amount of reward, *per se*, as much as by the fact that a distribution principle s/he considers just (e.g., equality) was not applied. Although much theory and research have been devoted to reactions to violations of the equity principle, there is an absence of a parallel effort with regard to other justice principles.

Third ('qualitative') inequity might also be experienced owing to the *inappropriate way in which an outcome is presented* (or an input is made). One might, for example, feel unjustly treated if the reward (regardless of the type of resource or distribution principle involved) for one's contributions is handed over with a frown rather than a smile. One may also experience injustice if, for instance, the expected outcome is not freely given but has to be requested.[7] The literature on 'procedural' justice contains the most detailed discussion of the relevance of the procedure or process of outcome distribution to justice and injustice (e.g., see Lind and Tyler 1988 and Tyler 1987, for excellent reviews). Further ideas may be gained from other sources, e.g., Kahn and Tice (1973) on stated intentions, Moscovici (1976) on 'behavioural styles', Lee and Ofshe (1981) on 'demeanours', and Törnblom (1988) on type, intent and mode of outcome allocation. (See additional comments under section 4.2.6.)

2.3.4. The assumed linearity between felt inequity and equity-restoring behaviour. A basic assumption in equity theory is that felt inequity/distress, justice motivation, and equity-restoring (overt and/or covert) behaviour are linearly related (see, for instance, Walster, Berscheid and Walster 1973). This hypothesis (especially with regard to favourable inequity) has been challenged by a number of researchers (e.g., Goodman and Friedman 1971; Lawler 1968a; Pritchard 1969; Cohen 1974; Lerner 1975, 1977; Moore 1978; Greenberg and Cohen 1982b; Steensma et al. 1981; Wilke and Steur 1972; Wosinska 1983). This led Huseman, Hatfield and Miles (1987) to formulate a theoretical extension of equity theory via a proposed mediating 'equity sensitivity construct' (hypothesized to be a trait rather than a state). They proposed that 'individuals react in consistent but individually different ways to both perceived equity and inequity because they have different preferences for (i.e., are differentially sensitive to) equity' (p. 223). People may be placed along a continuum of these preferences ranging from 'benevolents' (those who experience distress unless their outcome/input ratios are smaller than that of a comparison Other) through 'equity sensitives' (those who feel distress unless their and Other's ratios are equal) to 'entitleds' (those who are distressed unless their ratio is greater than Other's).

Not only individual but also situational variables are likely to modify an individual's sensitivity to inequity. Pritchard (1969), for example, argued that the likelihood of inequity experience varies positively with the psychological closeness of the relationship between participants (provided one person's gain is the other's loss). The results of a study by Lamm and Kayser (1978a) appear to support this contention. Subjects recommended equitable allocations to friends with unequal contributions of effort, while equality was preferred for acquaintances. This result was explained by reference to an assumed norm of mutual support among friends, according to which the neglect to obtain positive outcomes is more detrimental to a friendship than to less intimate relationships. However, other researchers (e.g., Austin 1980) have found that both friends and strangers overlook differences in merit when they perform poorly and prefer equal allocation. And, directly opposite to Pritchard's proposition, still others have observed subjects to allocate outcomes equitably to strangers but equally to friends (e.g., Mikula and Schwinger 1973; Mikula 1974b; and a host of other theorists who posit equality as the most appropriate form of justice in close relationships, for instance, Deutsch 1975; Greenberg 1983; Kidder, Fagan and Cohn 1981; Lerner 1975; Törnblom 1988).

Several researchers do recognize the possibility that equity-restoring responses might not be forthcoming. Leventhal (1976a), for instance, has suggested that this may happen when the recipient is unimportant to the source of injustice, when the perceived probability that justice can be restored is low, when necessary remedies are too costly or unpleasant, and when the magnitude of injustice is too small to bother with. Hassebrauck (1987) found that subjects are more likely to try to restore equity when they attribute their experienced inequity distress to the underlying inequity rather than to other causes. Explanations for the absence of a linear relationship among felt inequity, distress, and equity-restoring behaviour, with special focus on the victimizer, have been offered by Lerner (1980) and Deutsch (1985).

2.3.5. Conclusion. Although an impressive amount of existing research has found that people often do act in congruence with their 'justice motivation' to restore equity, few studies have attempted to specify systematically the conditions (particularly situational ones – see Thomas 1973) which affect this tendency in either direction (some exceptions are Leventhal and Michaels 1969, 1971; Leventhal, Michaels and Sanford 1972; Leventhal, Weiss and Buttrick 1973; Lane and Messé 1971; Wicker and Bushweiler 1970). On the other hand there is an abundance of parallel efforts to be found in studies on the relationship between attitudes and behaviour. Variables like competing motives, method of attitude formation, the general activity level of the individual, his/her level of competence, reference group support, normative constraints, behavioural consequences, opportunity to act and unexpected events (to mention a few) have been found to affect the attitude–behaviour relationship. It might be a good idea for equity researchers to take advantage of the lessons learnt within that research domain about topics of similar nature and, therefore, of mutual interest.

3   Allocation principles and subrules

One of the most serious limitations of equity theory is, as previously mentioned, that distributive justice is solely conceived in terms of proportionality (the exact meaning of which is unclear) between contributions and rewards (or inputs and outcomes). There is no doubt that resources *are* frequently allocated on the basis of equity considerations and that people perceive this to be appropriate and just. However, man does not live by equity alone (Weick 1966), nor is man an equity theorist by nature (Sampson 1975). Equity theory may certainly be highly relevant to some social relations in some sociohistorical contexts, but it is likely to be entirely inappropriate in others.

The persistent focus on the equity or contribution principle in early social psychological studies on distributive justice does not imply, however, that discussions of other allocation principles are lacking. The philosophical literature, for example, contains a rich tradition of treatises on different principles in the elusive search for the 'true' nature of justice (e.g., Nozick 1975; Rawls 1971; Rescher 1966). Philosophical treatments of justice have, according to Buchanan and Mathieu (1986), primarily been concerned with metaethical and normative questions: the former involves 'the meaning of terms used in moral discourse as well as the rules of reasoning and/or methods of knowing by which moral beliefs can be shown to be true or false' (p. 12), while the latter type of question has to do with 'what people ought to do, in contrast with what they in fact do' (p. 12).

In contrast to the normative (or prescriptive) approach of philosophy, social psychological approaches are typically descriptive and explanatory, focusing on questions such as 'under what conditions is justice or injustice perceived?' and 'how do people or groups respond to perceived injustices?' (Markovsky 1986, p. 2). Within social psychology an approach variously called the 'contingency' (e.g., Lansberg 1981), the 'classification' (e.g., Lamm, Kayser and Schwinger 1981) or the 'multiprinciple' approach (e.g., Mikula 1980a) presently dominates the justice area. Researchers in this tradition generally agree that the contribution principle is applied and considered just in some allocation situations, but that a variety of additional principles (qualitatively different from equity) are perceived as more appropriate in other situations.

The recognition of additional allocation principles has, no doubt, resulted in increased conceptual and theoretical refinements in social psychological analyses of distributive justice problems. However, insufficient empirical research has been devoted to the analysis of other rules than the contribution, equality and need principles. Perhaps the reason for this lacuna is to be found in the claim by some theorists of the 'multiprinciple' approach (e.g., Leventhal 1976b, p. 212; Schwinger 1980, p. 98) that those three principles are considered to be the most 'important' justice rules. It is doubtful, however, that there is any empirical foundation for such a claim. Its validity is, of course, contingent upon the question 'Important to whom, where, and when?' Lacking full knowledge of people's naïve conceptions of justice, a host of additional justice principles may readily be added to the list of 'important' principles. Indeed, a number of justice theorists have considered more than the contribution, equality and need principles in their discussions (e.g., Lerner 1981; Leventhal 1976a; Reis 1984; Törnblom 1977c).

Social psychologists typically want to explore people's actual evaluations and applications of allocation principles, i.e., to identify the conditions under which a given allocation principle is applied and considered just, and to examine what consequences the application of a given principle may have for different types of social relationship: a task group's productivity, group members' satisfaction, and so forth. Given this focus on the personal sense (i.e., the subjective aspects) of distributive justice and injustice, a fruitful starting point is to assess just how differentiated and complex people's justice conceptions are, rather than providing a list of as many conceivable justice principles as possible. Are people able to, and do people generally, conceive of distributive justice in terms of many or in terms of limited principles, singly or in combinations?

There appears to be no research attempting to determine the number of different principles in terms of which adults[8] are able to understand, define and implement justice in different contexts. The most common strategies of research are to present fictitious outcome distributions or describe various allocation rules to subjects who are asked to evaluate their justness. In other types of studies the researcher collects data on how subjects actually, or intend to, allocate outcomes in various situations. Unfortunately, subjects are not always instructed to make *just* allocations, in which case motives other than justice may account for their allocation decisions. Neither of these research strategies are well suited to produce information on the scope of people's conceptions of justice.

A step toward that end, however, was taken by Reis (1984) in an empirical study aimed at identifying the dimensions in terms of which people understand justice. Subjects were asked to rate (on a ten-point scale) the similarity of all possible pairs (=136) of 17 principles (which had been derived from the literature in various disciplines). Three dimensions underlying the similarity judgements were extracted by means of a multidimensional scaling technique (see Table 6.1): (1) Complex entitlement-determining procedures favouring long-term gratification versus simple outcome-focused rules favouring immediate gratification; (2) status–assertion versus status-neutralization; and (3) self-focused perspective versus group–other perspective (Reis 1986, pp. 201–2).

An interesting implication from Reis' research is that information about a person's location on the above-mentioned three dimensions (and perhaps others) might reveal a great deal about the complexity of his/her conception of justice, i.e., in terms of what kinds of principles the person is able to conceive of distributive justice. To this end, one may want to

Table **6.1** *A three-dimensional categorization of distributive justice norms. (Source: Reis 1986, p. 202.)*

	Self-perspective		Group/other perspective	
	Procedural focus Long-term gratification	Outcome focus Immediate gratification	Procedural focus Long-term gratification	Outcome focus Immediate gratification
Status assertion	Criterion-referenced exchange: proportionality	Hedonic self-interest: own needs	Impersonal exchange: laws, actions, not intentions	Self-preservation attenuated by group concern: own needs if resources scarce
Status neutralization	Self-centred idealism: own moral principles	Paternalism	Universal idealism: good for its own sake, help without return	Nurturance and solidarity: needs, equality

'investigate how personality and situational variables affect the relative salience of these dimensions as well as an individual's location along the axes' (Reis 1984, p. 51). Indeed, the results of a study conducted by Reis indicated that subjects who highly endorsed the Protestant Ethic (PE) exhibited a less differentiated and a less complex evaluation of the similarity of the 17 justice principles than did subjects with low PE endorsements. This implies that the commonly observed 'preference of high PE subjects for equity may be a sign of their relative simplicity in evaluating possible alternatives, rather than a generic preference for proportionality over other choices' (ibid., p. 55).

3.1   Classifications of principles

Other theorists have tried to create logical order among the various principles, 'sorting' them into categories according to some conceptual property they have in common. Anderson (1969), for example, distinguished between two main categories of principles, based upon exclusive and inclusive criteria of evaluation. Principles in the former category are those which require differential evaluations of recipients to determine their outcomes. The contribution principle is a good example in that recipients must be evaluated, for instance, in terms of their inputs toward a group goal. Inclusive criteria encompass allocation principles that emphasize recipient characteristics which are shared by all within a given social system (e.g., group membership), and on the basis of which each recipient has a right to obtain an equal share of available resources.

Anderson argues that values stressing inclusive criteria are strong within the Swedish labour movement, for example, but weak within the American for which exclusive criteria are more typical.

Noting that fair treatment of individuals may result in unfair allocation of outcomes among groups, or vice versa, Brickman *et al.* (1981) proposed a two-way classification of justice principles (similar to that by Anderson) according to their micro or macrolevel orientation. These authors contend 'that people have preferences for the overall shape of the outcome distribution *per se*, and not only for the microlevel principles by which such outcome distributions may be produced' (p. 174). Thus, it appears that the microjustice criteria people use to judge the justice of rewards to individuals or subgroups (e.g., need and contribution) are different from those used to assess the aggregate fairness of reward distribution in a social system as a whole, i.e., macrojustice criteria of 'System-level rules . . . [specifying things like] . . . whether there should be a guaranteed minimum income, or a ceiling on income, or a limit to income inequalities' (Mark 1980, p. 6). In other words, even though each recipient unit (be it individuals, groups or social aggregates) may receive what it deserves on the basis of some input dimension (in which case microjustice prevails), the total shape of the resource distribution across all constituent units of the macrosocial system (in which case only the distributive properties of the outcome dimension are relevant) may be judged unjust.

The theoretical significance of this classification lies in its implications with regard to the considerable likelihood of conflict when justice is demanded at both levels simultaneously. Thus, conflict may occur when justice is sought for the individual group member as well as for his/her membership group as a whole. The importance of making explicit the distinction between the micro and macrolevels in justice research has been noted by a number of other theorists, e.g., Eckhoff 1974 ('retributive' vs. 'distributive' justice – see below); Cohen 1979 ('individual deserving' vs. 'distributive justice'); Jasso 1983 ('the just reward function' vs. 'the just reward distribution'); and Markovsky 1985 ('personal' vs. 'collective' justice).

In his frequently cited book on justice, Eckhoff (1974) makes a distinction between two types of justice principles: (1) those which are concerned with reciprocation (a total of four principles;[9] see p. 30) and (2) those concerned with allocation, i.e., 'the process which takes place when something is dealt out' (p. 205) (five principles;[10] see pp. 31–9). He uses 'retributive' justice as a common term for the first type and 'distributive' justice for the second. Retributive justice principles aim at reciprocity and balance in the relationship between two individuals or between two groups or aggregates of people. In the case of distributive justice, however, there is no limit to the number of recipients who can be involved. Both types of justice are based on ideas of *equality*, in that retributive justice principles require that 'the exchanged values shall have equal weight if balance is to be restored' (p. 31), while distributive justice principles demand that recipients must be treated equally. It should be noted that retribution refers to exchange relationships while this is not the case with distribution. The latter term refers to 'the manner in which a set of elements is grouped . . . [and which] can come about through – or be influenced by – allocation processes' (p. 205). Also, the meaning Eckhoff gives to the term retribution is different from its conventional usage among social psychologists (i.e., allocation of negative outcomes).

Eckhoff makes a further distinction among principles of the distributive kind: (1) two of them (objective equality and equal opportunity) do not require recipient characteristics to be taken into account, while (2) the remaining three (subjective, relative and rank order equality principles) do.[11] That recipient characteristics may be considered in connection with principles of equality might seem odd. First, most justice researchers commonly apply other labels in such instances (e.g., equity, need, contribution, proportionality). Secondly, just as some equity theorists have been criticized for their tendency to view other justice principles as instances of the equity principle rather than as separate principles (the need and quality principles, for example, may be viewed as equity principles, if need and group membership are conceived as inputs), so might the attempt to categorize the equity and need principles as types of equality appear equally unwise from a theoretical point of view. However, it is important to bear in mind that equity theorists view resource transactions as reciprocal exchanges in which proportionality between inputs and outcomes is a requirement for equity/justice (a condition which excludes situations in which resources are 'merely' or unconditionally dealt out, that is, allocated), while Eckhoff's classification of principles accommodates both allocation ('distributive justice') and reciprocation ('retributive justice') and makes no *a priori* claim that outcomes and the individual characteristics deemed relevant for some of the allocation principles should be proportional.

3.2   Subrules

Eckhoff is not alone to conclude that equality is what justice is all about. Messick and Sentis (1983, p. 68) argue that 'This fact may be occasionally overlooked, for example, by researchers who differentiate *equality of outcome* from *equality of outcome per unit input* (equity). The issue is not whether equality is important but on what dimension the equality should be established' (my italics). In addition to the two equality principles just mentioned, the following four are important (at least in these authors' opinion): equal excess or equality of outcome above a minimum level, equality in psychic profit from exchange, procedural equality or equality in the application of rules and procedures, and equality of opportunity.

Obviously, equality as a principle for the distribution of benefits and harms may be expressed in several (and often incompatible) ways. This is true for other principles as well. The contribution (or equity) principle may refer to contributions of effort, achievement, ability and so on. Similarly, distribution according to an individual's needs may be based on a number of criteria, three of which may perhaps be considered especially important: biological, basic and functional needs[12] (see Benn and Peters 1959, pp. 144–7). Thus, allocation principles which are described generally and vaguely as 'The same for everyone', 'To everyone according to his/her contributions', and 'To everyone according to his/her needs', for instance, are wide open to a variety of interpretations and must be formulated more precisely to permit systematic research and to hinder arbitrary practical applications. Yet, even though most reports of empirical research do contain imprecise terms like equality, contribution or need as labels for allocation principles, it is usually possible (but cumbersome) to examine how they were operationalized to find out which particular version of a given principle, here called subrule, was involved. Nevertheless, justice theorists might have to incorporate possible consequences that the distinction among subrules may have for their theoretical models.

That increased conceptual clarity appears necessary was empirically demonstrated by a study in which subjects' justice evaluations of the equality and contribution principles were shown to vary with the way these were formulated, i.e., in terms of by which subrule they were represented or operationalized (Törnblom and Jonsson 1985). Further evidence indicating that subjects do distinguish and differentially evaluate subrules of the equality and contribution principles, respectively, may be found in a number of studies (e.g., Brickman 1977; Brickman *et al.* 1981; Kayser and Lamm 1980; Lamm and Kayser 1978a, 1978b; Lamm, Kayser and Schanz 1983; Schmitt and Montada 1982 – see review in Törnblom and Jonsson 1985). Thus, although a particular equality subrule may be considered just in a given situation. It is quite possible that another subrule of the equality principle is held to be unjust. Expressed in other words, the realization of equality in resource allocation through the application of a given subrule may simultaneously violate other subrules of equality, i.e., produce *in*equality from the perspectives of other subrules. For example, outcome allocation based upon equality of results may require *in*equality of opportunity and/or *in*equality of treatment.

These findings have important theoretical as well as practical implications. It may be theoretically misleading to make statements about the perceived justice of a resource distribution according to *the* equality or *the* contribution principle, unless the specific version of these is specified. Conclusions based upon a comparison of the results from two studies on the perceived justice of the equality principle, for instance, may be entirely misleading unless equality was operationalized into the same subrule in both.

From a practical or social policy orientated view, there are a number of reasons why increased attention to the subrules of the various justice principles appears warranted. In the political arena, for example, the variety of ways in which the principles of equality, contribution, need, etc. may be interpreted set the stage very effectively for deceptive slogans and platforms which, in turn, may (deliberately or non-deliberately) be used to manipulate and exploit groups of the constituency. In most democracies, at least, equality constitutes an honorific ideal imbued with great instrumental value in attempts to accord legitimacy to a political party. However, equality of opportunity, for example, is most often an entirely different species of 'equality' than is equality of results. The application of the former rule may serve conservative motives in that it tends to justify and maintain existing social inequalities (or to create new ones), while the latter may serve radical purposes in that it focuses on a redistribution of given resources (e.g., wealth and/or power) such that everyone will end up with equal amounts in the long run.

Owing to the diffuseness of the terms equality and contribution, as well as need and other principles of distribution, it is quite possible to set up arrangements for a social order compatible with one principle by using the vocabulary of another as a disguise. Thus, voters may easily be led into an erroneous assumption that the party they vote for is championing that version of equality which they favour and consider just.

With regard to resource allocation on a global level, it is vitally important to bridge culture-specific interpretations of justice principles. No matter how much agreement there is among nations as to the desirability of distributive justice, conflicts will always occur in the absence of shared consensus about the general principle which best represents justice or, worse, in the presence of miscommunication resulting from ignorance about each other's interpretation of a principle about which agreement has been reached (i.e., shared consensus about which subrule should be the legitimate representative of the principle in question).

3.3   Consequences of applying a principle
Social psychologists have taken a special interest in two issues which emerge as a natural result of recognizing the existence of several different justice principles rather than just one. At the heart of one of those issues lies a desire to explain the common observation that an individual, a group or a collectivity may consider a particular allocation principle to be just in one situation but not in another, or that several individuals,

groups or collectivities may disagree about the principle they consider just in a particular situation. Subsequently, researchers attempt to gain knowledge about the conditions which affect the justice evaluation of allocation principles and about the factors that determine what justice principle will be used as a criterion for resource distribution in different situations.

The other issue revolves around a second common observation, namely that the operation (as well as the evaluation and violation) of different principles may result in different (positive as well as negative) consequences for an individual's satisfaction with his lot, a group's effectiveness in performing a joint task, the socio-emotional climate among group members, the power and prestige order among group members, intergroup relationships, etc.

Fig. 6.1 is a diagrammatic representation of the two research issues.

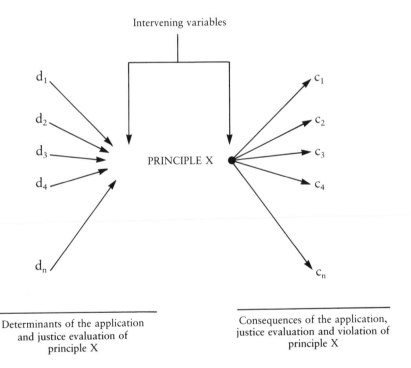

Determinants of the application and justice evaluation of principle X

Consequences of the application, justice evaluation and violation of principle X

Fig. 6.1 Diagrammatic representation of two major research issues: determinants and consequences of justice principles

d = determinant (e.g. characteristics of the recipient, the allocator, the social relationship, the social context)

c = consequence (e.g. for personal welfare, self-esteem, social relationships, a group's power and prestige order, task efficiency, intergroup relations, etc.)

(Of course, various intervening variables may modify the effect of a determinant or the consequence of applying a justice principle.) A separate section (section 4) will be devoted to the first-mentioned issue (depicted in the left-hand part of Fig. 6.1) as much more theoretical and empirical work has been produced in response to this as compared to the second topic. The present section will focus on the second issue (the right-hand part of Fig. 6.1), briefly describing what we know about the various kinds of positive and negative consequences that the application[13] of different justice principles may have (see also previous reviews by Leventhal 1976a; Mikula 1980b; Mikula and Schwinger 1978; Schwinger 1980).

Deutsch (1985, pp. 133–63) has summarized the results of six experiments (conducted by him and his students) on the effects of four distribution principles: the winner takes all, the proportionality (i.e., contribution or equity), the equality and the need principles. American college students served as subjects and were asked to distribute money in five experiments and grades in one. I will here briefly describe the findings about the effects of the four principles on task performance, and on attitudes toward the tasks, the distributive systems and the other group members. As the series of studies[14] under Deutsch's leadership were guided by and integrated within a relatively coherent and systematic theoretical framework, it is convenient to let the summary of his findings serve as an organizing structure within which results from other studies, when relevant, may be incorporated and compared.

Task performance. There were no different effects of the various distribution systems on productivity as long as individual or group task performance did not depend on social cooperation. However, when effective performance was contingent upon cooperation the operation of the equality principle resulted in the highest and the winner-takes-all principle in the lowest degree of productivity. There were some indications that 'the greater intragroup cooperation induced by the equality as compared to the proportionality [i.e., contribution] system can be detrimental to individual performance on mental tasks requiring sustained individual concentration' (p. 157). Other studies have found that outcome allocation according to contributions resulted in the most effective task performance (e.g., Lawler 1971; Steiner 1972; Weinstein and Holzbach 1973). Deutsch and his research group also found that there was no relationship between the justice evaluation of a distribution principle, or the experience of working under a preferred system, and subjects' actual performance under that principle.

Attitudes toward the task. The experimental tasks were considered more interesting and pleasant under the operation of the equality rule than under the other distribution systems. The equality principle also led to the highest motivation to perform well and to increase the group's performance, as well as to the lowest motivation to excel over the other group members. According to other studies, on the other hand, people seem prone to believe that group members would be the most task-orientated when the contribution principle is applied (Kayser 1983).

Attitudes toward the distribution systems. Subjects in groups which were characterized by face-to-face contact and interaction developed increased liking for the equality principle. It was considered the most enjoyable, most just, and most preferred principle of all except the contribution principle. Most subjects exposed to the contribution principle continued to favour this principle over the others.

Attitudes toward group members. 'The subjects in the equality and need conditions reported having cooperative feelings toward one another; those in the winner-takes-all and proportionality conditions reported having competitive feelings toward one another; and those in the two control or choice conditions felt more personal involvement with the other group members than did subjects in the other conditions' (Deutsch 1985, p. 158). One control condition was Rawls' (1971) 'the veil of ignorance' principle (see Cullen, this volume), and the other was called 'the known performance'. In both conditions subjects chose their own principle, in the former before and in the second after they had received feedback about their performance scores (subjects had no choice in the four experimental conditions). A number of additional studies have shown that equal distribution of outcomes may promote group solidarity and interpersonal harmony (e.g., Deutsch 1968; Steiner 1972). When contributions are employed as a criterion for resource allocation, the development of affective bonds among group members may be impaired (e.g., Bales 1955; Sampson 1969).

A few studies have shown that subjects are able to make various kinds of attributions about affective group features on the basis of the distribution principle that is operative. Greenberg (1983) showed that observers inferred higher degrees of liking, closeness and friendship between two persons who divided a restaurant check equally relative to persons who applied the contribution principle. Kayser (1983) examined inferences from five principles: need, equality, contribution, competition and injury/hindrance. Subjects considered the need principle to result in the most cooperative and intimate group climate and progressively less so with regard to the remaining principles (in the listed order). Further, interaction effects were found when the type of distributed resource was varied: higher states of cooperation and intimacy were inferred from equal than from need distributions of money, while the reverse was found for particularistic resources (love and service). Whereas Deutsch and associates did not find any significant sex differences, Kayser's results indicated that females attributed higher degrees of cooperation and intimacy than males when the need and equality principles were applied. However, the opposite was true for the remaining four principles.

The finding by Deutsch that a distribution system may have a different effect on productivity when performance depends on cooperation than when it does not, and by Kayser that men and women may make different inferences about the impact of an allocation principle alerts us to the possibility that the consequences of *applying* a principle may be modified by a number of intervening variables (as indicated in Fig. 6.1). Mikula (1980b), for instance, argued that a principle's situational appropriateness is a crucial factor. The application of a principle when and where it is considered inappropriate will certainly have different consequences than when it is appropriate. The interesting question is, however, given an appropriate and just allocation principle, how its consequences may vary when different factors are introduced. The cultural and historical contexts are likely to define the boundaries within which various personal and situational factors will modify the impact of applying a particlar justice principle. Also, people's justice evaluations of a resource distribution may have significant consequences for a number of social phenomena (see, for example, the review of Jasso's work by Arts and van der Veen, this volume).

Owing to the obvious importance for social policy-making of knowledge about the consequences (real as well as attributed) of different distribution systems, continued research in a wide variety of settings and contexts is certainly warranted. To quote Leventhal (1976a, p. 131): 'In most settings, existing allocation practices tend to support existing patterns of recipient behaviour. To change recipients' behaviour, the distribution of rewards and resources must be changed ... allocation decisions have profound effects on individual and group welfare ... [and] determine the fate of groups and organizations.'

The theoretical and pragmatic utility of future research would be enhanced by systematic and explicit attention to the question 'What type of positive or negative consequences does the application of a given justice principle in the distribution of what kind of resource have for what, for whom, when, where, and from whose point of view?' A typology of consequences (as well as of determinants – see next section) may serve as a useful framework within which cumulative research can be planned and findings systematically organized.

4   Contingency approaches: determinants of justice principles

4.1   Predominance of one or of several justice principles?

The recognition that justice may be defined in terms of any one of several separate criteria or principles (rather than in terms of a single equity/contribution/proportionality rule) led to the question 'Under what circumstances will a particular principle emerge as a value and guide for allocation and constitute the basis for assessing the fairness of a particular resource distribution?' This question appears to result from two implicit assumptions: (1) that different justice principles are dominant in different situations, and (2) that a person's conception of justice in a particular situation is exclusively based upon the one principle which happens to be dominant in that situation. These assumptions seem to underlie the multidimensional approaches of most contingency theorists (e.g. Deutsch 1975; Lerner 1975; Mikula and Schwinger 1978; Greenberg and Cohen 1982b; Kayser, Feeley and Lamm 1982; Kayser, Schwinger and Cohen 1984; Törnblom and Jonsson 1985).

A less common but, perhaps, equally plausible assumption is that people make compromises, i.e., that the fairness of outcomes is determined by weighting and combining two or more principles. For example, political theorists (e.g., Raphael 1970) have observed that the Welfare State combines the need and contribution principles (i.e., once the basic needs of everyone are satisfied, people may compete for additional rewards). According to Leventhal's (1976b) theory of justice judgement (to be discussed below) the individual determines a recipient's entitlement by combining separate justice rules into an overall estimate. A study by Debusschere and van Avermaet (1984) indicated that compromises do occur, at least between the equality and contribution principles, but that computational complexity lowers the amount of compromising in favour of the equality principle. Compromises were also observed in a study by Griffith (1989), and her re-examination of other research suggested 'that compromise solutions may be more prevalent than has been widely recognized'. This is due to the fact that allocations satisfying an ordinal conception of the equity or contribution principle, i.e., mere approximations of Adams' (1965) ratio conception, are frequently regarded as an allocation 'in the spirit of equity' (cf. Elliott and Meeker 1984).

Sampson (1976) views the issue of choice among justice principles from a rather unusual angle. However, he restricts his discussion to the equality and contribution principles, and it is not clear whether his, what we may call 'dialectic', approach is applicable to other principles as well. Sampson argues that we might miss the point by asking whether people are motivated by one or the other of the two conceptions of justice or by trying to unravel the conditions under which one or the other will predominate. He suggests that justice might result from a balancing between the two, and that too much of one principle would constitute a violation of justice. Sampson's hypothesis is that 'as either the differentiating tendencies of equity or the homogenizing tendencies of equality were to become excessive, the opposing process would enter as a kind of self-protective feedback circuit' (p. 470).

As most research of the contingency approach is based upon the premise that just behaviour is typically guided by a single dominating principle, the nature of which varies from situation to situation, greater attention will be given to this line of work in the following.

The main impetus to this approach was provided by Lerner (1975), Deutsch (1975) and Leventhal (1976a) in the United States, and by Mikula and Schwinger (1978) in Europe. The works of Lerner and a few other theorists focus on the interaction between factors which presumably influence justice conceptions (see section 4.3 for more details). Leventhal's work spans more than one approach, and is discussed in more than one context. Deutsch, Mikula and Schwinger, and many others tend to examine the effects of a single determinant or analyse the additive effects of several separate and simultaneously salient determinants.

For example, in his frequently cited 1975 article Deutsch analysed the effect of different group goals, holding type of group orientation constant. He proposed that groups that are cooperatively orientated towards economic productivity are likely to favour the contribution principle, in the sense that resources, roles, and means of production should be allocated to those who are able to use them most effectively. However, the need or equality principle will guide the distribution of consumer goods in such groups. Solidarity-orientated groups (for which the creation or maintenance of enjoyable social relations is the primary goal) are assumed to prefer equal distributions and, finally, caring-orientated groups are thought to favour the need principle.

Deutsch (1975) carries his analysis a step further by elaborating each of these general propositions into a number of more specific ones. First, in order to explain why one orientation comes to dominate others, he offers the hypothesis that 'the typical consequences of a given type of social relation tend to elicit that relation' (p. 147). Then, if certain features are present in a given situation (e.g., competition and impersonality), it is likely that a particular type of orientation (e.g., economic) would emerge. Thus, the connection between group orientation and the choice of distribution principle, and between group orientation and situational features, implies, according to Deutsch, that the greater the degree of a particular feature, the greater the likelihood that a particular distribution principle will be used. For example, 'the more impersonal the relations of the members of a group are, the more likely they are to use equity' (p. 148).

The assumption that social groups of various kinds can be meaningfully characterized in terms of a single dominant justice principle has been challenged by Goode (1978). He argues that Deutsch's proposition about equality as a dominant principle in solidarity-orientated groups, the primary goal of which is enjoyable social relations, 'cannot apply to concrete groups or relationships, but simply to the various *phases* or social *occasions* in almost any group or organizational life, when the goal is simply to engage in enjoyable social relations' (p. 351). Similar points have been raised by Leventhal (1976b, p. 219) and Mikula (1980b, p. 137).

The next section contains an overview of research on some of the several factors that may influence the application and justice evaluation of various allocation principles. The reader may also consult earlier reviews, e.g., Cook and Hegtvedt (1983), Leventhal (1976a), Mikula (1980b), and Mikula and Schwinger (1978). Apart from giving an idea about the variety of determinants researchers consider important, these overviews provide answers to the question 'What allocation principle(s) are likely to be activated by a particular state or value of factor X?' For example, the social relationship among group members has frequently been found to influence the choice of a distribution principle in such a way that the contribution principle is preferred or activated in a competitive and equality in a cooperative relationship.

4.2   Factors affecting the evaluation and choice of justice principles

Social psychologists have examined the effects of a large number of factors on the choice and perceived justness of various distribution principles. It should be noted at the outset, however, that the choice of a factor for investigation has far too often been made arbitrarily. In the absence of a theory suggesting at least some general and tentative criteria to guide the identification of the most significant factors that are likely to predict people's justice behaviour, the researcher's choice of a particular factor is likely to be largely determined by his/her idiosyncratic notions and preferences. As a result, the list of more or less unrelated factors exposed to empirical scrutiny is likely to grow infinitely, thereby defeating our purposes. At the present stage, it appears that most of us are still resting on our laurels from the 'discovery' that the choice and evaluation of a justice principle is context specific. It is now time to move ahead in the direction of specifying the most important and powerful contextual factors or aspects as they apply to justice-related behaviours. In order to push the research frontier forward, this endeavour must also produce some theory-based conclusions about the ways in which these contextual factors interact and modify each other's impact on the choice and justice evaluation of allocation principles. There are good reasons for Graziano (1987, p. 291) to argue that context is 'the largest single obstacle to our theoretical understanding of equity, social comparison, and judgements of justice'.

Factors that appear to determine (or at least be associated with) the evaluation and choice of a distribution principle may, for the moment, be grouped into at least six general categories to the extent that they are relevant to the characteristics of the actor, the contribution, the social relationship, the sociocultural and historical context, the outcome or the outcome allocation:

1. The actors involved in situations of resource (outcome) allocation may be described as recipients, allocators or both. Actors may be individuals, groups or aggregates of people.
2. One or more actors may make contributions (i.e., make performances of various kinds and/or possess various ascribed and/or acquired characteristics) which may have a bearing on how resources are to be allocated on their own personal behalf or as representatives of a group.
3. Various types of social relationship may prevail among actors.
4. Contributions and outcome allocations occur within a social, cultural and historical context.
5. Actors may receive outcomes (resources) of various sorts.
6. Outcome allocations and/or allocation procedures may be effectuated in a number of different ways, for different purposes, and according to various criteria (distribution and/or procedural principles).

Outcome allocations and allocation procedures as well as the criteria (principles) according to which they are effectuated may be evaluated in terms of, and applied because of, their acceptability, appropriateness, desirability, (distributive and/or procedural) justness, instrumentality for reaching goals other than justice, etc., for the individual or for the group or aggregate. In addition, the actor and/or observer may (on behalf of his/her own situation and/or that of other people) exhibit various behavioural and/or psychological reactions to the evaluation and/or application of a principle governing the outcome allocation and/or allocation procedure.

It is impossible, within the space of this chapter, to give a full description of existing research on the determinants of various justice principles. This would require at least three questions to be considered: 'Which are the factors that affect the choice and justice evaluation of distribution principles?', 'Under what conditions do these factors affect choices and evaluations?' and 'In what ways do these factors affect choices and evaluations?' A thorough examination of these issues is not possible in the present context, as the list of determinants exposed to research is considerable. Finally, some of the determinants have commanded extensive interest, resulting in a very large number of studies. Therefore, this presentation will be confined to only a few instances of each of the six categories listed above. Moreover, in some cases the number of studies cited will be limited. Instead, the interested reader will find some additional references to relevant research following the discussion of extensively examined determinants.

4.2.1   Characteristics of the actor

The most commonly examined demographic actor characteristics which have been shown to influence the choice and evaluation of a justice principle are sex and age. A common observation with regard to the sex variable is that men prefer the contribution principle while women favour equality. However, as a thorough review by Major and Deaux (1982) of research on individual differences[15] in justice behaviour shows, a closer scrutiny reveals that the impact of sex varies with the type of research paradigm used. When the allocator is not a co-recipient, very few sex differences are found. When allocations are made to oneself and others, women take less for themselves than men do, women with superior performance prefer equality while men allocate according to contributions, and both men and women with inferior performance prefer the contribution principle. However, these results have been modified by a number of situational factors (e.g., sex composition of the group, self-presentational concerns, etc.). When allocations to oneself and others are decided by the group as a whole, women prefer equality and men allocate according to arbitrary power differences in a game setting, while both sexes divide equally when inputs are performance-based in non-game group allocation settings. The general conclusion reached by Major and Deaux is that sex differences 'occur primarily when the allocator is also a recipient of his or her allocations' (p. 51). The interested reader is advised to consult already available reviews for descriptions of specific studies and the various theoretical explanations pertinent to sex differences (e.g., Austin and McGinn 1977; Bierhoff, Cohen and Greenberg 1986; Furby 1986; Leventhal 1973; Major and Deaux 1982; Mikula 1980b. Some relevant research: Bowden and Zanna 1978; Kahn, Nelson and Gaeddert 1980; Kidder, Bellettirie and Cohn 1977; Lane and Messé 1971; Leventhal and Anderson 1970; Major and Adams 1983; Mikula 1974a; Reis and Jackson 1981; Wender 1987a, 1987b).

There appears to be considerable disagreement among theorists as to whether or not age differences exist in conceptions of justice. In cases where differences have been observed, suspicions have been voiced that these differences might be mediated by other factors. Cognitive-developmental theorists, for example, have been criticized by Graziano (1987) for not acknowledging that differences in children's justice judgements may be better explained by the social context of judgements rather than age-related cognitive ability differences.

Review authors have reached different conclusions: Deutsch (1983; 1985) contended that age differences appear to exist and that these may be partly explained by differences in cognitive development and in socialization effects; Berg and Mussen (1975), Hook and Cook (1979) and Major and Deaux (1982) seem to agree that age differences are real, although our understanding of them is incomplete; Montada (1980, p. 258) concluded that the published results of all 'developmental studies are consistent in reporting age differences' but 'Exactly which differences occur is an issue that is far from being resolved'; Krebs (1982) assumes that age differences exist in that 'as children acquire an understanding of increasingly complex principles of justice, they become increasingly able to apply those that are most appropriate [i.e., foster the greatest justice] to particular situations'; Walster and Walster (1975) argued that evidence is mixed; Cook and Hegtvedt (1983) claimed that the effects of age are inconclusive; and Mikula (1980b) concluded that available evidence does not point toward any age-related preferences for certain justice principles.

Research has largely been confined to children and adolescents to the neglect of more mature age groups. In general, younger children (up to the age of six) seem to follow a principle of self-interest or equality in resource allocations while, presumably owing to increased cognitive abilities (e.g., Hook and Cook 1979) and development of higher-level moral reasoning (e.g., Damon 1977), more complex rules like the contribution and need principles gradually become more common with increasing age. (See Keil and McClintock 1983, for a more detailed review of thirty-one studies concerned with children's allocation behaviour.) Data from a study concerning hiring and dismissal in a work setting (Törnblom in prep. b) indicate that age differences in justice conceptions may be rare (at least in Sweden) among age groups ranging from 25 to 80 (some relevant additional research: Gerling and Wender 1981; Gunzburger, Wegner and Anooshian 1977; Lane and Coon 1972; Lerner 1974b; Leventhal, Popp and Sawyer 1973a; Mikula 1972; Simons and Klaassen 1979; Wender 1986, 1987b).

A number of actor characteristics other than demographic ones have also been examined, for instance, level of concrete operational thought (Wender 1987b), level of efficiency at work and material needs (Skarzynska 1985), occupation, salary, political preference, and education (Vogelaar and Vermunt 1991), and focal perspective (Skarzynska, in press; Törnblom, Mühlhausen and Jonsson, in press).

Relatively few studies have examined the effects of personality variables. Wahner (1986) found that control ideology (beliefs about how much the average person is able to influence his/her needs and achievements) and political ideology (political party sympathy) affected justice evaluations. Persons with low control ideology considered the need principle to be most just and the equality and contribution rules unjust. The reverse held true for subjects with high control ideology. Right-wing political sympathizers favoured the contribution rule, while left-wingers preferred the need principle. Other studies have examined the correlation between justice behaviour and personality variables like the Protestant Ethic (e.g., Greenberg 1978a), Machiavellianism (e.g., Blumstein and Weinstein 1969), and achievement motivation (e.g., Uray 1976). See reviews by Cook and Hegtvedt (1983), Major and Deaux (1982), Mikula (1980b) and Sampson (1980) for further details.

The importance of greater emphasis on personality and social character variables has been underscored by Sampson (1980, p. 290): 'It is difficult, for example, to argue persuasively that all persons are motivated by equity considerations if our research demonstrates important individual variation in motivation as a function of personality and social character' (see also Huseman, Hatfield and Miles 1987). However, Major and Deaux (1982) concluded from their review of individual differences in justice behaviour that it is doubtful 'that there are any individual difference variables that will predict justice behaviour regardless of the situation' (p. 71).

4.2.2 Characteristics of the contribution

The reader may recall (from section 2 on equity theory) that the contribution principle seems to be preferred when contributions (inputs) are 'recognized' and 'relevant' (Adams 1965), and when they are seen as 'causally important for the production of outcomes', 'variable' and 'under the person's control' (Kayser and Lamm 1980). Additional factors readily come to mind – factors which are of particular importance in the process of causal attribution, i.e., the naïve explanation of how relevant contributions were accomplished. For instance, the contribution may be intentional, it may be under the actor's voluntary control (e.g., achieved characteristics, such as effort – as opposed to ascribed ones, like sex or skin colour), and affected recipients may hold a particular actor to be responsible for the contribution. These kinds of 'internal' attribution, in which case a particular contribution is seen as directly caused by the individual, are likely to increase the probability of adopting an allocation principle based on some proportionality between a person's characteristic and receipts (e.g., the contribution rule). If the contribution is attributed to some cause external to the individual, such as luck or chance, there is little or no obvious reason for making distinctions among recipients. In such cases, unequal resource distributions among recipients are likely to be regarded as unjust.

The relationships between cognitive mediating factors, such as causal attributions about the accomplishments of contributions, and choice among justice principles have been scarcely researched (for exceptions see Shepelak 1987; Stolte 1983; Wittig, Marks and Jones 1981). It is, however, an important topic of inquiry (cf. Utne and Kidd 1980; Cohen 1982), and research efforts along these lines are likely to be made in the future.

A few studies indicate that allocation rule evaluation and preference may vary with the nature of the contribution (e.g., whether it is positive or negative, consists of effort, ability, quality or quantity of performance, etc., is accomplished by omission or commission, is independently or collectively produced, or whether it results in the 'production' or accumulation of love, status, or money, etc. for subsequent allocation).

Some studies have used a research design involving (direct or indirect) exchange situations and others have dealt with pure distribution situations (where information about individual contributions – if any – are lacking or assumed to be irrelevant). Unfortunately, it is frequently difficult to disentangle the separate effects of the nature of the contribution and the nature of the outcome. If, for instance, the contribution consists of an insult or poor performance and the outcome of social disapproval or fines, is the choice or evaluation of an allocation principle affected by the nature of the contribution or the nature of the outcome? (See section 2.3.3 for additional comments.)

In addition, a distinction is rarely made between two facets of a contribution, namely the input (e.g., ability or effort), *per se*, and the outcome of the input, i.e., the performance outcome (e.g., quality or quantity of work) – the latter of which must not be mistaken for the outcome or reward to be distributed. As Griffith (1989) has noted, performance outcomes are a direct function of inputs, i.e., a particular performance is always based on some measure of ability and/or effort (except in the case of chance games and the like), but few studies provide subjects with information about both aspects (an interesting exception is a study by Overlaet 1989). Indeed, the concepts of input and performance outcome are typically confused in the literature. A related and common mix-up exists between performance outcome (e.g., quality or quantity of work) and the material or immaterial resource produced or accumulated by the performance outcome (money, service, status and goods, for instance). 'There should be a more careful examination of how the performance outcome produces the resources for distribution or even if the performances are related to the production of the resources to be distributed' (Griffith 1988[16]).

Intuitively one would assume that the relative size of the contribution will affect the choice of allocation principle. Contrary to what at first might be taken for granted, however, the allocator-recipient with the largest contribution frequently opts for outcome distribution according to the equality principle, while the low contributor prefers the contribution principle (e.g., Leventhal and Lane 1970; Mikula 1972; 1974; Mikula and Schwinger 1973; Shapiro 1975). However, the reason for violating a seemingly appropriate and legitimate justice principle (i.e., the contribution principle), thus obscuring the presumed relevance and influence of a contribution characteristic (i.e., size), apparently has to be sought in motives other than justice. These motives may confound, compete with and overpower, or act to mediate, the effect of contribution size on the choice of allocation rule. Accordingly, researchers have discussed alternative motives like the desire to maintain a positive self-image (Andrews and Valenzi 1970; Friedman and Goodman 1967) and self-presentational concerns (Morse, Gruzen and Reis 1976; Mikula 1975;

1977; Reis 1981; 1984; Schwinger 1980). There may also be instances in which outcomes are equally allocated rather than according to contributions due to difficulties in assessing their sizes (Leventhal 1976b).

There is some evidence which indicates that the 'behavioural modality' (cf. McKinney 1971; Herrmann 1971; Törnblom 1971) in which contributions are made may affect distribution principle preference. Extending Kahneman and Tversky's (1982) study on positive affective reactions, Landman (1987) found that subjects attributed more intense negative affective reactions, as well, when something was accomplished (contributed) through action rather than through inaction. One of several plausible explanations, following Weiner's (1980) attributional theory of emotion, is that it may be easier to attribute the result of a contribution achieved by inaction (as compared to action) to external (rather than internal or personal) factors. If this reasoning is extended to the preference of distribution principles, one would expect inaction, or omission to do something, to be associated with a preference for equality, while the contribution principle is likely to be preferred when contributions are produced through action, or commission (see Törnblom and Jonsson 1987).

4.2.3 Characteristics of the social relationship[17]

Several studies indicate that an individual's justice conception and choice of distribution principle is influenced by the prevailing social relationship among actors (e.g., Austin 1980; Benton 1971; Greenberg 1978b; Griffith and Sell 1988; Kellerhals, Coenan-Huther and Modak 1988b; Lamm and Kayser 1978b; Lamm, Kayser and Schanz 1983; Lerner 1974b; Mikula 1974b; Mikula and Schwinger 1973; Morgan and Sawyer 1967; Shoeninger and Wood 1969). For instance, Lerner (1974b) showed that the equality rather than the contribution principle was preferred in the context of teams. Other researchers (e.g., Hassebrauck 1984) have obtained corresponding results when examining the effect of social relationship conceived in similar manners (e.g., its intimacy, cooperativeness, duration, interdependence or similarity).

Several explanations have been advanced to findings of the kind described above. Cooperative relationships (such as a team) are frequently perceived as units characterized by positive affective qualities, solidarity, mutual respect and cohesiveness. On the other hand, competitive social relationships are commonly thought of as 'aggregates' of people with a diversity of more or less conflicting interests and associated with neutral or negative affective qualities. In general, the application of the equality principle in resource allocation is considered appropriate within cooperative relationships as it is assumed to be conducive to the creation or maintenance of solidarity, harmony and status similarity among recipients. The contribution principle is assumed to encourage status differentiation, conflicting interests and a negative affective social climate – qualities which are more or less common within competitive relationships.

Also, 'teams' are usually more enduring over time than 'non-teams'. In the former case equality is assumed to dominate while the contribution principle is emphasized in the latter (McClintock and van Avermaet 1982). Consistent with these suggestions, studies have shown that subjects (with large contributions) who anticipate future interaction may favour equality, while subjects (regardless of contribution size) who do not expect further interaction may prefer allocations according to contributions (e.g., Shapiro 1975; Grumbkow *et al.* 1976).

Contrary to conclusions of the kind just mentioned, however, one may easily recall everyday experiences suggesting that equality is not always implemented or considered to be the most just distribution principle in *Gemeinschaft*-like relationships. A number of researchers have made similar observations (e.g., Goode 1978; Lerner 1974b; Kayser and Lamm 1981; Lamm and Kayser 1978a; Mikula 1980b; Schwinger and Nährer 1982). A study by Lamm and Kayser (1978a) indicated that friends might prefer unequal allocations when unequal inputs result from unequal expenditure of effort. Acquaintances, on the other hand, ignored effort differences and allocated benefits equally. The authors suggested that a 'friendship norm' may have been operative, prescribing friends to do their best in the interest of the relationship. A person violating this norm forfeits his/her rights to an equal share of the collectively produced outcome. It is possible, judging from a study by Benton (1971), that such a friendship norm may not develop until later stages in life. In this study children preferred contribution-based allocations with non-friends, while equality was favoured for friends and neutral relationships. It is also possible that the equality principle is sometimes as much preferred for a cooperative as for a competitive situation (see Törnblom and Jonsson 1987).

An alternative explanation to the preference for inequality (e.g., the contribution principle) in the context of friendship, teams, unit relations, and the like, may be gathered from Lerner (1981), who argued that the sentient person's focal awareness is a crucial determinant in his/her choice of an allocation principle. When the *relation* among people who have convergent goals and are engaged in a unit relationship is focalized, equality in allocation will constitute justice. Should the acquisition process (i.e., the activity required to accomplish the convergent goals) be focalized or made salient, allocation according to the contribution principle will represent what is just. (If, on the other hand, people in a unit relation have divergent goals, equality of status is predicted to be dominant when the relation is figural, while the principle of justified self-interest will assume dominance when process is the salient aspect.)

In sum, it appears that the empirical evidence for a positive relationship between equality in the allocation of outcomes and *Gemeinschaft*-like relationships is inconclusive. Perhaps the findings from relevant studies are only deceptively inconsistent, however, owing to the possibility that some of these focused on the relation among participants while others were inadvertently concerned with the process of goal-accomplishment (cf. Lerner 1981). Apparently, research of a more rigorous and systematic nature is badly needed in connection with this determinant, not least because of its obvious importance and implications for social policy-making. A basic requirement for further research is a generally agreed typology which enables the identification of the most fundamental characteristics descriptive of different, social or interpersonal relationships (see efforts in this direction by Lerner 1975; 1977; Lerner, Miller and Holmes 1976; Wish, Deutsch and Kaplan 1976; Wish and Kaplan 1977[18]).

4.2.4 Characteristics of the social, cultural and historical context

Only relatively tentative conclusions can be made about the nature of national or cultural differences in conceptions of justice in resource allocation. The present scarcity of cross-national or cross-cultural studies is unfortunate, especially if it is true – as Mikula and Schwinger (1978) have argued (at least in cases where a group-specific allocation principle has not yet developed) – that justice principles in the superordinated social system (or culture) will heavily influence justice conceptions in subordinated systems. Surely, this is a reasonable assumption, as individuals and groups operate under various constraints of social and cultural origins.

A review by Gergen, Morse and Gergen (1980) suggested that Americans are more likely to distribute resources according to the contribution principle than are Europeans. Consistent with this proposition, Törnblom, Jonsson and Foa (1985) found that Swedes preferred equality more than Americans who preferred the contribution principle more than Swedes. The preference order among the three principles investigated was equality, need and contributions for Swedes, while it varied with the allocated resource for Americans. Swedes also differentiated more among the principles than did Americans. Kahn, Lamm and Nelson (1977) compared the preferences of American and German students and found that the American students were more positive to an allocator who favoured the contribution principle when his/her inputs were low and the equality principle when inputs were high. Mikula (1974a) compared the allocation decisions of Austrian and American students, while the latter were studying in Austria. Contrary to Gergen, Morse and Gergen's (1980) conclusion, Americans were slightly more likely to use the equality principle. The allocation preferences of second-grade German

and Turkish school children were compared in a picture-story study by
Wender (1987a). The contribution principle was preferred over the need
principle by Turkish children when coins were allocated, while the German children favoured allocations according to needs. Murphy-Berman
et al. (1984) found that Indians preferred the need principle to a greater
extent than did Americans who tended to endorse the equality or contribution principles.

A meaningful understanding of the documented differences among
nations with regard to preference for justice principles requires a careful
analysis of those societal and cultural differences in value-orientations
and other elements that may have a bearing on people's justice conceptions (cf. DeVos and Hippler 1969; Gergen, Morse and Gergen 1980; C.
Kluckhohn 1951; F. Kluckhohn 1953; Price-Williams 1985; Robinson
and Bell 1978; Rokeach 1973; Williams 1970). This was attempted by
Murphy-Berman *et al.* (1984) and Törnblom, Jonsson and Foa (1985).
However, further cross-national research is clearly needed, not only
because of the present scarcity, *per se*, of systematic investigations but
also, as Major and Deaux (1982, p. 59) put it, 'Given the considerable
implications of differing justice systems for international harmony, it
seems important to pursue this area of research further.'

A number of propositions have been advanced (usually by sociologists)
as to why societies would differ in their emphasis on distribution
principles. Most of these writings are purely theoretical. A study by
Tallman and Ihinger-Tallman (1979) is an exception. They predicted that
with societal development, the emphasis on a distributive justice criterion
will change from equality to proportionality. More specifically, a growing complexity in the division of labour and a higher development of
social structures were hypothesized to make an emphasis on proportionality norms more likely and on equality less likely. Data from Mexico
and the US supported these hypotheses.

In a similar vein, Lenski (1966) suggested that technologically
advanced societies will tend to distribute available goods and services on
the basis of power, while the need principle will predominate in technologically primitive societies. Rescher (1966) argued that unless the characteristics of a society's economy of goods are considered, the relative
merits of various distribution principles cannot be appropriately assessed. Presumably, the need principle is likely to be preferred in an
economy of scarcity, and equality in an economy of abundance (see
Greenberg 1981 for a review of empirical evidence). Equal shares may be
feasible when resources are abundant but not when they are scarce. Also,
on the (probably erroneous) assumption that egalitarian societies are less
productive, less (relative to more) affluent societies could not afford to let
equality in resource distribution predominate (Gans 1974). Further,
societies that live by hunting will tend to be egalitarian because they have

no use for private property (ibid.) and because egalitarianism functions as a form of insurance against anyone being left without a share of the collective resources (Moore 1978).

The relationship between the institutional context in which an allocation takes place and choice of justice principle has been the focus of a few studies. The results of a previously mentioned German study (Wahner 1986) suggested that the need principle is considered more just in a political than in a business (industrial single enterprise) context; in the latter context the principle of justified self-interest was viewed as most just. Törnblom and Foa (1983) reviewed American, German and Swedish studies on the effects of institutional context on the choice of justice principles. Overall the need and equality principles were preferred for intrinsically (or social relations) and caring (or welfare) orientated contexts, while equality assumed dominance for economically orientated ones. Data from a field study by Prentice and Crosby (1987) suggested that the contribution principle is the most endorsed justice rule in the workplace, while those who considered evaluations of deservingness to be relevant in the home context tended to favour the need principle. Also, a study by Hochschild (1981) matched the institutional domains of socialization with the equality principle, market with the contribution or self-interest principles, and politics with the equality principle.

Finally, Stolte (1987) has contributed an interesting analysis to show how different structural-exchange exigencies are likely to generate five justice norms (discussed by Eckhoff 1974): equal opportunity, equality, status/rank inequality, need and equity.

4.2.5 Characteristics of the outcome

Several theorists have argued that the quantity of the available outcome will affect the choice of allocation principle. Walster and Walster (1975) argued that the equality principle will be preferred when the amount is small. This proposition is probably valid if equality is operationalized as 'equality of opportunity' (in which case the role of distributing procedures comes to the fore); it seems unreasonable to apply either 'equality of treatment' or 'equality of results' if resources are sufficiently scarce to be useless if equally shared or if they are not divisible. Instead, as Greenberg (1981) has noted, sociohistorical accounts (e.g., Calabresi and Bobbitt 1978) and experimental evidence (e.g., Coon, Lane and Litchman 1974; Greenberg 1979; Lane and Messé 1972; Karuza and Leventhal 1976; Katz and Messé 1973; Leventhal et al. 1973b) indicate that principles focusing on needs and efficiency will be given priority. When resources are sufficiently abundant to fulfil everyone's needs or desires, however, the issue of distributive justice is unlikely to arise at all. According to Rescher (1966), however, a situation of abundance might paradoxically result in an 'economy of felt insufficiency'. The reason is that people's expectations are likely to rise with increasing prosperity, with the consequence that their 'levels of "tolerable minimality" are revised drastically upward' (p. 994) and the economy of abundance 'becomes treated as an economy of scarcity' (p. 106).

Several studies suggest that the justice evaluation and/or choice of a distribution principle is affected by the nature of the allocated resource (e.g., Foa and Stein 1980; Kayser, Feeley and Lamm 1982; Kayser, Schwinger and Cohen 1984; Kreveld and Beemen 1978; Schmitt and Montada 1982; Schwinger, Nährer and Kayser 1982; Törnblom, Jonsson and Foa 1985). Martin and Harder (1988), for instance, found that subjects rated the contribution principle as most important for the distribution of financially related rewards (e.g., profit sharing, office space, company cars), while equality among individuals, equality across groups, and personal need were most important for socio-emotional rewards (e.g., help for an employee's spouse, friendliness). A review by Törnblom and Foa (1983) suggested that equality might be the most preferred principle for the allocation of love, goods and services, while the contribution rule is most appropriate for status. The equality and need principles appear to be equally endorsed for information, while both the equality and contribution rules seem to be acceptable for the distribution of money. Because the nature of the reviewed studies differ in various ways, however, it is too early to draw any firm conclusions about the ways in which type of resource and allocation principle might be related. In general, relatively little research effort has so far been devoted to examining the impact various characteristics of the allocated outcome may have on the evaluation and choice of justice principles.

4.2.6   Characteristics of the outcome allocation

Leventhal (1976b) has suggested that the equality principle will dominate when harmony and solidarity are sought among recipients, that the contribution principle will be weighted heavily when effective performance is emphasized, and that liking and responsibility for others will make the needs principle salient (see also Deutsch 1975 for similar conjectures). One may, of course, voice objections to such unconditionally stated propositions. For example, it seems gratuitous to claim that the shouldering of responsibility for a recipient's welfare would elicit need-orientated allocations. Of course this may depend on whose needs are recognized (e.g., those of a child or a prisoner) and on the nature of the allocator's responsibilities (e.g., those of a parent or a prison guard).

However, research has shown that instructions to allocate outcomes with the intention of motivating the recipients to accomplish various goals (including justice) result in the choice of different allocation principles. Mikula (1973), for example, found that Austrian allocators preferred the equality principle to a greater extent when they were instructed to satisfy the recipients than when they were asked to be just. In a study by Vermunt and Lerner (1987), Canadian and Dutch subjects role-played a supervisor in an industrial plant. Canadians gave the highest bonus (i.e., deviated from the contribution rule) when asked to provide motivation to meet a deadline, and the lowest bonus (i.e., conformed to the contribution principle) when they were instructed to pay according to productivity. No significant differences were obtained for the Dutch sample. Nelson and Dweck (1977) instructed 4-to-5-year old children to share a reward 'as they wanted' or 'so it would be right for doing this much work'. Self-interested shares resulted in the first instance, while distributions were based upon contributions in the second case.

In most studies of the above kind it is difficult to separate the normative and instrumental aspects of allocation. For example, even though the desired goal is increased productivity, the allocator's conception of justice is still likely to affect her choice of distribution principle. Would she not ask herself: 'What is the most just way to reward workers in order to motivate them to increase their productivity?' Thus, a simple comparison of the choice of allocation principle in response to instructions to be just with choices under different guidelines does not appear to be a particularly fruitful research strategy.

The allocation of outcomes may be executed in a number of ways, and it seems reasonable to assume that the manner or mode in which outcomes are allocated would affect the quality and intensity of recipients' cognitive, evaluative and/or behavioural responses to a particular allocation event. The act of allocation may, for instance, convey cues on the basis of which recipients make attributions about the purposes with the allocation. A resource given with reluctance or accompanied by a frown, for example, is likely to be differently interpreted and less appreciated or valued than a resource given without hesitation or with a warm smile. Research in other areas, e.g., social influence and role theory, has attended to this facet (cf. Moscovici 1976, on 'behavioural style'; Lee and Ofshe 1981, on 'demeanour'; Sarbin and Allen 1968, on 'role enactment'). So far the topic has only been given scant attention within the area of distributive justice (an empirical study has been conducted by Mikula, Petri and Tanzer, submitted; discussions may be found in Törnblom 1988 and Törnblom and Jonsson 1987). Perhaps the main reason for the lack of attention to issues of this kind is that they are considered more properly to fall within the province of procedural justice, the concern of which is the various aspects of the process of outcome distribution. (See further comments under section 2.3.3.) Also, some studies (e.g., Grumbkow, Steensma and Wilke 1977) have found that subjects are more likely to adhere to the equality principle when allocation is public (i.e., known) as compared to private (i.e., secret).

Finally, a body of literature with a focus on the sign of outcome allocation has recently begun to emerge. The basic topic of interest is whether or not justice is conceived in different terms in the context of negative as compared to positive outcome allocation. Since the sign of outcome allocation may modify the impact of many of those factors whose effects on positive outcome allocation have already been discussed, a more detailed presentation of this research will be found in section 5.

4.3   Integrative theoretical models

As justice theorists began to identify an increasing number of justice principles as well as factors that seem to activate these principles, a definite need emerged to construct a theoretical framework capable of integrating propositions and research findings. Existing propositions are largely unrelated, scattered, and address different levels of analysis – from psychological and social psychological to macrosociological and historical. In the absence of a body of interrelated propositions, or even a manageable inventory of existing propositions (a demanding but probably worthwhile task to undertake) as a basis for such a framework, some attempts have been made at constructing models confined to the combination of a rather limited set of determinants, where each combination is assumed to activate a different justice principle. With two exceptions, the models to be described below basically restrict their attention to the social relationship among participants as a situational determinant influencing people's definitions of justice and their choice/ evaluation of an allocation principle.

A model developed by Lerner (Lerner 1975; 1977; Lerner, Miller and Holmes 1976) to predict which justice principle will be employed in the allocation of resources is based upon the combination of two social relationship dimensions: (1) the 'object of perception', other people with whom one interacts are viewed particularistically as unique persons or universalistically as impersonal and substitutable occupants of social positions (cf. Parsons' 'pattern variables', 1951); and (2) one's 'perceived relationship' to these person(s), which is categorized into three types according to the degree of psychological distance between the subject and object persons. This continuum ranges from identity relations (sameness, i.e., little or no distance, characterized by identification or empathic involvement with other people) to unit relations (similarity, i.e., short distance, perception of cooperative relationship and belongingness with others) to non-unit relations (difference, i.e., the most distant type, where competition and antagonism between participants are salient). Each of the six interpersonal relationships, as generated by cross-cutting the two dimensions, is assumed to result in the development of a particular form of justice (see Table 6.2). For example, in the case of a unit relationship the equality principle will presumably be used when the other is viewed

Table **6.2** *Forms of justice. (Source: Lerner 1975, p. 15, Table 1.)*

Object of Perception	Identity	Perceived relationship Unit	Non-unit
	Perception of O as self	Perception of similarity, belonging with O	Perception of contesting interests and personal differences related to the claims
Person	NEEDS	PARITY	LAW, DARWINIAN JUSTICE
	Perception of self in O's circumstances of need	Perception of equivalence with O	Scarce resources, with equally legitimate claims within the 'rules'
Position	ENTITLEMENT, SOCIAL OBLIGATIONS	EQUITY	JUSTIFIED SELF-INTEREST

as a person but the contribution principle is seen as more appropriate when the other is treated as an occupant of a position (cf. Carles and Carver 1979).

A few years later, Lerner (Lerner and Whitehead 1980; Lerner 1981) extended his model by combining the three types of perceived relationship with three kinds of process, i.e., 'emergent activities', or relationship among the goals of the participants with respect to resource acquisition – 'vicarious dependency' (identity), 'convergent goals' (unit), 'divergent goals' (non-unit). As each kind of process may occur in all three relations, and as either the relation or the process may be focal in a given situation (leaving the other to constitute the ground or a limiting condition), eighteen types of 'interpersonal encounters' are generated. Justice is assumed to take a different form in each of these encounters. Thus, for instance, justice will take the form of equality when the relation is focal among people who have convergent goals and are engaged in a unit relationship. If people in a unit relationship have divergent goals, a principle of justified self-interest is predicted to be dominant when process is the salient aspect.

A model presented by Greenberg and Cohen (1982b) is based upon two (independent) dimensions in terms of which social relationships may be described: interdependence and intimacy (see Fig. 6.2). Interdependence is defined as 'the degree to which participants in a social exchange have control over each other's resources' (p. 444), while intimacy refers to 'the closeness of the social bond between individuals' (ibid.). In addition, these two dimensions are proposed to reflect a single

218   *Kjell Törnblom*

unifying dimension of potential conflict over resources, i.e., 'a concern for self-interest in distribution relative to other-interest' (p. 445). Greenberg and Cohen suggest that various social relationships (of which strangers, bargainers, friends and marrieds are discussed) may be mapped along this dimension. For instance, friendship may be characterized by a relatively high degree of intimacy but a low degree of interdependence. In such a relationship person's and other's interests tend to converge, resulting in a relatively low degree of conflict over resources. Once located along the dimension of potential conflict over resources, different social relationships may be linked to different justice principles. So, for example, friends are expected to define justice in resource allocation in terms of the equality principle.

In the view of Kayser, Feeley and Lamm (1982) and Kayser, Schwinger and Cohen (1984), certain characteristics of social relationships are, in the mind of a naïve observer, interdependent with specific allocation principles. Four characteristics are distinguished (see Table 6.3), each comprising five elements: (1) the cognitive/motivational orientations of the actor (partner, unit, self competition and aggression); (2) the affective climate of the relationship (ranging from very positive to very negative); (3) the types of resource most frequently exchanged (particularistic, universalistic and mixtures of both kinds); and (4) the typical direction of transactions (giving, taking away and both combined). Different transaction principles are associated with different combinations of elements from the four characteristics, resulting in five psychological constructs or configurations. 'These configurations are central parts of laymen's theories on the functioning of groups . . . [and constitute] . . . an instru-

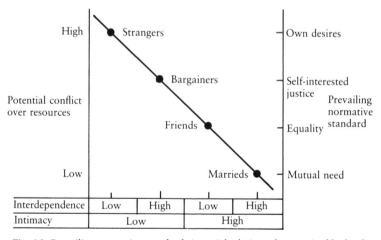

Fig. 6.2 Prevailing normative standards in social relations characterized by levels of interdependence and intimacy. (*Source:* Greenberg and Cohen 1982b, Fig. 12.1.)

Table **6.3** *The five configurations of social relationships in contract theory. (Source: Kayser, Schwinger and Cohen 1984, p. 436, Fig. 1.)*

Cognitive/ motivational orientations of the actors	Partner's welfare: partner	Welfare of the relationship: unit	One's own welfare: self	Relative advantage: competition	Other's harm: aggression
Affective relationship	very positive	positive	neutral	negative	very negative
Most important resource classes	particul.	particul.[a] univers.[b]	univers. particul.	univers. particul.	particul.
Typical direction of transaction	giving	giving	giving and taking	taking	taking
Transaction-principle	need principle	equality principle	contribution principle	maximal difference	maximal harm

Notes:
[a] Particularistic resource classes
[b] Universalistic resource classes

ment for the ordering (classification and regulation) of groups' (Kayser and Schwinger 1982, p. 48). However, elements from all relationship characteristics need not enter into the layman's perception at any given occasion; thus, his/her 'analysis' may vary from deep to shallow.

There is some evidence suggesting that observers are able to make inferences about the prevailing social relationship (in terms of the different configurational elements) on the basis of the transaction principle in use, and vice versa (see Kayser 1983; Kayser, Schwinger and Kayser 1981; Schwinger, Nährer and Kayser 1982; related research findings are reported by Austin 1980; Clark 1981; Clark and Mills 1979; Greenberg 1983; Mills and Clark 1982; Törnblom, Fredholm and Jonsson 1987; Törnblom and Fredholm 1984).

Mikula and Schwinger (1978) attempt to 'demonstrate how one must proceed in the derivation of predictions concerning the choice of a justice principle, if one starts with a multi-dimensional concept of justice' (p. 235). They focus their analysis on what effects different affective group climates (positive, neutral and negative) have on the choice of the contribution, equality and need principles, as well as on the consequences the adoption of each principle have for the group climate. These two determinants are then integrated in an analysis of their simultaneous impact on the choice of an allocation rule. The consequences of applying a principle are assumed to carry the greatest weight as a determinant when the situation is unclearly structured. Mikula and Schwinger predict 'that in unclearly structured situations the equality principle will be employed most frequently in positive groups, while the contribution principle will be the one used in neutral and negative groups, provided the necessary preconditions are fulfilled' (p. 242).

The theory 'justice judgement', formulated by Leventhal (1976b), assumes that the individual combines several justice principles to arrive at an overall estimate of a recipient's deserved outcomes. This idea is illustrated by the equation

$$\text{Deserved outcomes} = w_c D \text{ by contributions} + w_n D \text{ by needs}$$
$$+ w_e D \text{ by equality} + w_o D \text{ by other rules,}$$

where D stands for deservingness and w for weight. The term $w_n D$ by needs, for example, stands for the weight attached to the needs principle in comparison to the other principles and an estimate of the outcomes deserved on the basis of that principle. Thus, Leventhal's conception of how people assess distributive justice is different from that of the previously mentioned theorists, all of whom assume that a single principle governs the distribution at any particular occasion. To arrive at a final assessment of outcome justice ('deserved outcomes'), the individual is assumed to go through a four-phased justice judgement sequence: a weighting phase, during which the individual 'must decide which justice rules to use and how much weight to give them' (p. 215); a preliminary estimation phase, during which 'the amount and type of outcomes the receiver deserves on the basis of each applicable justice rule' is assessed (p. 215); a rule combination phase, during which the equation is used 'to obtain a final overall estimate of the amounts and types of outcomes deserved by the receiver' (p. 215); and an outcome evaluation phase, during which the justice of the actual outcome is assessed by comparing it to the deserved outcome.

The underlying assumption of Lansberg's (1981; 1984) 'congruency' approach is that the degree of ambiguity about the evaluation and choice of a justice principle varies inversely with the degree of congruency among the institutional, situational and individual factors affecting the choice. Assessments of congruency/incongruency require the individual to engage in cognitive operations which appear partly to overlap with those taking place during the 'weighting' phase of Leventhal's (1976b) 'justice/judgement sequence'. During this phase the individual presumably decides, on the basis of various determinants, how much weight to give each justice principle. Thus, Lansberg's model seems to complement that part of Leventhal's theory of justice judgement.

Although predictions about the certainty by which a given justice principle will be chosen requires knowledge, a priori, about whether or not a factor actually is a determinant of that particular principle, Lansberg's (as well as Leventhal's) approach leads to interesting questions about the nature of conflict (incongruency) and conflict resolution in situations where different kinds of incongruency (conflict) among determinants may exist/occur – issues that have received scant attention by justice researchers. Under what conditions, for example, will a factor of a given category carry more weight for the choice of a justice principle than conflicting factors of other relevant categories?

4.4   Conflict among determinants and among principles

Let us, for purposes of clarity, make a distinction among three types of conflict with regard to factors determining the choice of justice principle: (1) situations in which a single determinant leads to different justice principle choices for different recipient categories; (2) situations in which two or more determinants dictate different justice principles for a single recipient category; and (3) situations in which two or more determinants prescribe different justice principles for different recipient categories.

The first type of conflict is exemplified by the third assumption in Komorita and Chertkoff (1973, p. 153) which predicts that recipients who are strong in resources are likely to favour the contribution principle, while those who possess little would opt for equality. In this case, the effects of a single determinant (self-interest) are different when considered from the perspectives of two different recipient categories (highs and lows in resource strength). If additional (congruent or incongruent) determinants had been recognized, one would need to know why and how self-interest had come to assume dominance. It is interesting to note that a prediction directly opposite to that of Komorita and Chertkoff has been posited and empirically supported in cases where self-interest (e.g., self-presentational motives) as well as other-interest (e.g., social responsibility norms) are salient (e.g., Berkowitz 1972; Reis 1984; Shapiro 1975. See also discussions of the 'politeness ritual' in Mikula 1974b; Mikula and Schwinger 1973; 1978; and Schwinger 1980). The main reason for opposite findings seems to be that Komorita and Chertkoff dealt with competitive situations while others focused on cooperative ones.

Obviously, the first type of conflict deals with conflict between recipient perspectives rather than with conflict among allocation principle determinants. However, the remaining two types focus on situations in which two or more conflicting determinants are simultaneously salient. For example, an individual level determinant (like self-interest) may stand in conflict with an equally dominant situational determinant (like group solidarity) in that each dictates different justice principles.

Full-scale analyses of conflicts of the *second* type are typically (deliberately or non-deliberately) avoided by assuming that one of the determinants somehow overpowers the other(s). Specifications of the conditions under which a particular determinant may assume dominance over others are generally lacking. Instead, most researchers take their starting point at a later stage in the justice deliberation process. The approach of virtually all studies is to examine the effects of manipulating a given factor assumed to influence the choice of a justice principle. Such research is guided by a question like 'Under what conditions will a particular justice principle be preferred over others?' or, more specifically, 'What principle will be adopted, considered just, etc., when determinant X is predominant or salient?' The studies reviewed in the preceding section belong to this category. Unfortunately, this approach will contribute little to answer the question 'Under what conditions will the influence of determinant X overpower the influence of other determinants in the choice of a justice principle?' A few influential theoretical frameworks appear to function as models for the former line of inquiry (e.g, Deutsch 1975; Lerner 1975; 1981; Leventhal 1976a) but none for the latter.

The scarcity of research on situations containing two or more conflicting allocation principle determinants (i.e., the second and third type of conflict) has been noted by Cook and Hegtvedt (1983, pp. 226–7): '(a) Isomorphism between individual and group goals is typically assumed; (b) often only a single goal is operationalized at a time. . . .' However, a few theorists have analysed the commonly occurring conflict between factors on the individual (micro) and collective (macro) levels (e.g., Brickman *et al.* 1981; Elliot and Meeker 1984; 1986; Jasso 1983; Markovsky 1985; Meeker and Elliot 1987) and attempted to specify some conditions under which determinants on the individual or the collective level may predominate. However, most of this work seems to emphasize the reactions of a single individual or recipient category.

No research seems to exist with regard to the third and more complicated type of conflict involving two or more conflicting determinants, the thrusts of which have different implications from the perspectives of two or more recipient categories. A preliminary theoretical analysis has been attempted by Törnblom (1988). This analysis is restricted to two types of individual determinants (self-advantage and other-advantage orientation) and two types of collective determinants (socio-emotional and task-orientated group climate) dictating justice principles with different implications from the perspectives of two recipient categories (persons responsible and non-responsible for positive as well as negative outcomes). Different types of conflict may be distinguished within this framework on intra and interpersonal as well as intergroup levels. Finally, some propositions concerning conflict resolution on the interpersonal level are suggested. Before this model is exposed to empirical test, it is likely to need further development.

The occurrence of conflicts among determinants is a fact of everyday life which warrants serious attention. By taking account of simultaneously operative justice principle determinants we take the opportunity to examine the dynamics inherent in the resolution process relevant to this kind of conflict. It is important to gain an understanding of the processes that precede a possible general consensus on a given allocation principle or a compromise among competing principles.

5   Distributive vs. 'retributive' justice

Up to this point only positive outcome allocation has been discussed. This is merely a reflection of the present research emphasis within the area; it does not imply that justice considerations in the context of negative resource allocation[19] are theoretically less complex or intriguing or a less important social problem. People frequently have to put up with negative outcomes in a wide variety of situations and institutional contexts. Such aversive circumstances (1) may come in different shapes (e.g., as punishment, deprivation, burden, cost, loss, etc.), (2) may be realized in different ways (e.g., by delivering harms or by withholding or withdrawing benefits), and (3) may involve different types of resource (e.g., money, love, esteem, power, freedom, health, citizenship, employment, information, goods, services, etc.).

Results from theoretical and empirical investigations within several research domains appear to be in surprising agreement about asymmetry in people's responses to positive and negative experiences, in that greater weight is assigned to negatives (unpleasant outcomes) than to positives (pleasant outcomes). Rook (1984) found that negative social interactions (problematic ties with others) have a more potent impact than positive social interactions (supportive ties); more intense emotional responses were attributed to unhappy decisions than to otherwise equivalent happy decisions in a study by Landman (1987); research by Hamilton and Zanna (1972), Hodges (1974), and Richey, McClelland and Shimkunass (1967) suggests that negative information about others is weighted more heavily than positive information; Fiske (1980) found that negative traits have greater impact than positive traits on impression formation; people weigh potential losses more heavily than potential gains in risk-taking situations (Slovic and Lichtenstein 1968); and Abelson and Kanouse (1966) found that subjects attributed heavier weight to negative than to positive information in others' evaluations of an object.

An understanding of how people think about justice in connection with the allocation of negative in comparison to positive outcomes would appear to be of equal (or perhaps greater) importance to social psychologists and policy-makers alike. For example, as Murphy-Berman *et al.* (1984, p. 1271) noted, 'in the West in the 1980s, budgetary cutbacks are increasingly common and the impact of these cutbacks on those in need is a significant social issue'. Indeed, if people's justice conceptions concerning the allocation of positive outcomes are different from their conceptions in the context of negative outcome allocation, a number of serious implications of this knowledge arise for politicians and other decision-makers.

Existing justice models place their focus on positive outcome allocation, but it seems that their component propositions are meant to be equally relevant and valid for negative outcome allocation as well. However, no reasons are offered as to *why* no differences are assumed to obtain between the two. As long as it is unknown whether or not fundamental differences do obtain between various phenomena associated with positive and negative outcome allocation (e.g., with regard to justice evaluation of allocation principles, reactions to injustice, etc.), it is theoretically unsound and perhaps potentially dangerous in a pragmatic sense to work under any pretences in either direction. Thus, research on this topic is fully warranted.

A number of theorists have lamented the gaps in our knowledge about the negative side of resource allocation (e.g., Cook and Hegtvedt 1983; Deutsch 1983, 1985; Greenberg *et al.* 1985; Griffith 1989; Griffith and Sell 1988; Hamilton and Rytina 1980; Hogan and Emler 1981; Kayser and Lamm 1980; Lamm *et al.* 1983; Meeker and Elliot 1987; Mikula and Müller 1983; Miller and Vidmar 1981; Murphy-Berman *et al.* 1984). I have speculated elsewhere (Törnblom 1988) about the reasons for the scarcity of theoretical and empirical research on negative outcome allocation, frequently designated as 'retributive justice' (e.g., Hogan and Emler 1981). However, one can now discern a growing theoretical interest in exploring the forms of justice associated with the distribution of negative resources and circumstances, and research has recently begun to emerge which compares the choice of justice principles for positive and negative outcome allocations. Results from several studies have shown that an allocation principle may be preferred equally for both positive and negative outcome allocation, preferred for one but not for the other, or not at all preferred. Such inconsistent findings clearly call for a model which explicitly addresses the question under what conditions a given allocation principle is considered more, less or equally just for positive and negative outcome allocations.

Inconsistent findings with regard to positive vs. negative outcome allocation are only to be expected, however, considering that existing studies differ in a number of ways, e.g., in design and methodology, subject and target person characteristics, relationship among recipients and between recipient and allocator, number of recipients, institutional context, type of allocated resource, mode of accomplishing the outcome allocation (e.g., giving, withholding, taking away), type/intent/result of outcome allocation (e.g., distribution, reward, profit; retribution, punishment, cost), production of outcomes (e.g., joint effort, luck, gift), and nature of the task – to mention a few.

The present review focuses on research dealing with more than one allocation principle, excluding issues such as the quantitative fit between crime and punishment or the amount of retaliation subsequent to unfavourable inequitable outcome distribution. In most of the studies money was the only type of outcome allocated to participants in a dyad, and subjects usually responded to vignettes in their capacity of non-recipient outside observers. In some of the reviewed studies subjects were not instructed to evaluate the outcomes in terms of their justness; instead preferences, behavioural intentions or normative responses other than justice were recorded. Nearly all studies have limited their attention to the equality and contribution principles.

Most of the existing research appears to be guided by the question 'Under what conditions and to what extent does the allocation of positive and negative outcomes follow the same or different justice principles?' Indeed, the results of several studies suggest that a number of factors may have different impact on the choice and evaluation of justice principles for positive and negative outcome allocation.

Four vignette studies examined whether the *type of social relationship* among recipients is a variable that might have a different impact on the choice of justice principles for positive as compared to negative outcome allocation. Lamm and Kayser (1978a) asked German male university students to decide how much money two fictitious males working on a joint task should receive or pay subsequent to a successful or an unsuccessful project. When the two partners were described as 'acquaintances', subjects preferred the same principle, i.e. equality, for both positive and negative outcome allocation. When they were described as 'friends', however, subjects favoured equality for positive outcome allocation and the contribution principle for negative. Törnblom and Jonsson (1985, 1987) asked Swedish female students at a school of nursing to evaluate the fairness of distributing or withholding monetary bonuses according to the equality and contribution principles in a sport context. Equality was considered the most just principle for both positive and negative outcome allocations when recipients were described as a 'soccer team'. When recipients were 'competing runners', equality was favoured for negative outcomes while the contribution and equality principles were about equally preferred for positive outcomes. Finally, Griffith and Sell (1988) instructed American male and female college students to distribute or withdraw money to/from two cooperating or competing fictitious partners who had performed unequally on a task (of unspecified nature). Performance differences were explained to result from differences in ability in one experimental condition and from differences in effort in another. No explanation was given in a third condition. 'Cooperation' was not associated with any differences between amounts of outcome in positive and negative outcome allocation. (In both cases allocations were closer to the equality than to the contribution principle in the no information and ability conditions, but closer to contributions when performance was due to effort.) However, allocations were closer to the contribution principle in all three 'competition' conditions for both positive and negative outcome allocations. In addition, negative allocations were significantly closer to 'perfect equity' than were the positive. No sex differences were observed.

Input-related individual factors were the main focus of seven vignette studies and of one experiment concerned with negotiations (Kayser and Lamm 1980; Lamm and Kayser 1978b; Lamm *et al.* 1983; Meeker and Elliot 1987; Overlaet and Schokkaert 1986; Schokkaert and Overlaet 1989; Törnblom *et al.*, in press; Törnblom, in prep. b). German male and female upper-level high school students were asked, in the study by Kayser and Lamm (1980), how much money two similar persons should receive or pay subsequent to the success or failure of a joint project. When success and failure resulted from high and low ability, respectively, subjects preferred equality for both positive and negative outcome allocations. But when success and failure were due to high and low *effort*, respectively, they favoured the contribution principle for positive but equality for negative outcomes. Using a similar design, Lamm *et al.* (1983) found that German male and female high school students recommended both gains and losses to be allocated according to the equality principle. Lamm and Kayser (1978b) conducted an experiment on the effect of negotiations on the allocation of two team members' jointly attained gains and losses subsequent to task performance. When performance feedback was lacking, the German male university student subjects favoured equality rather than effort and ability contributions as a criterion for both positive and negative outcome allocation. When performance feedback was given, positive and negative outcomes were allocated according to effort rather than ability contributions. Male and female American undergraduate subjects, in Meeker and Elliot's (1987) study, preferred the contribution principle for positive outcome allocation when recipients made high contributions and/or had low waste, while equality was favoured for negative outcome allocation. Schokkaert and Overlaet (1989) conducted a vignette study with first-year economics students in Belgium. When input differences between two workers resulted from unequal effort, the contribution principle was preferred over the equality principle for the distribution of profit; but when input differences were attributable to differences in ability, equality was considered the most just criterion. Exactly opposite findings obtained when a loss was to be shared. Similar results to those obtained for differences in effort inputs had been obtained in an earlier study by Overlaet and Schokkaert (1986). Törnblom *et al.* (in press) found that Swedish male army draftees believed that a male recipient who is responsible for positive or negative conduct (resulting in the consequences to be meted out) would consider it just to give non-responsible persons as much reward (days of leisure) as he receives but unjust to impose equal amounts of punishment (days of confinement) on them. Non-responsible persons were believed to consider equality as just for positive outcome allocation, but for negative outcomes subjects were divided: 52% attributed positive and 48% negative justice evaluations of the equality principle. Hassebrauck (1985) found that age had a differential impact on the choice of justice principles for positive and negative allocations. German children between the ages of four and six watched a puppet show in which the actors received candy as rewards and chore assignments as punishment. Children in each age cohort agreed that the equality principle was more appropriate than the contribution principle for positive outcome allocation. Four and five-year-olds favoured equality when punishment was imposed, while the contribution principle obtained the highest endorsement among six to eight-year-olds. However, Törnblom (in prep. b) found no consistent age-related differences among Swedish males and females between the ages of 25 and 80. In general, all age groups favoured the contribution principle in a work context (where positive and negative outcome allocations were operationalized as employment and dismissal, respectively).

Schmitt and Montada (1982) conducted a study in which German employers, social workers, trade union members and streetwalkers judged the justness of the equality, contribution and need principles for the delivery or withdrawal of four types of resource in three social contexts. Overall, the need principle was considered most just for privileges (i.e., participation in decision-making/house confinement) and equality for symbols (i.e., praise/blame) in both positive and negative outcome allocation. Partial agreements were obtained for money/goods (i.e., bonus/fine) and 'positions' (i.e., promotion/dismissal). For these resources both the need and contribution principles were viewed as just for positive outcomes, but only the need principle for negative allocations. Although money was the only type of resource employed in a cross-cultural study by Murphy-Berman *et al.* (1984), we may still take notice that both American and Indian males endorsed the need principle to a greater extent for the allocation of negative outcomes (a pay cut of 200 dollars/rupees to be distributed between two employees) than for positive outcomes (dividing a bonus of 200 dollars/rupees).

Two studies (Steensma *et al.* 1977; Grumbkow 1977) showed that Dutch male college students, workers, and supervisors at a public utility organization recommended both monetary bonuses and fines to be allocated according to contributions. However, a majority of the subjects participating in a study by Grumbkow (1985) preferred equality for positive but both equality and contributions as criteria for negative outcome allocation.

In sum, subjects considered the same principle to be just for both positive and negative outcome allocation in fifteen cases (equality was preferred for both in eleven and the contribution principle in four), whereas different principles were favoured for positive and negative outcomes in fourteen cases. The general picture emerging from these studies is that (1) there is considerable disagreement among studies as to whether the contribution principle is considered more, less, or equally just and appropriate for positive as compared to negative outcome allocation, (2) there is slightly less disagreement about the equality principle; it was considered equally just in about 60% of the conditions, more just for positive outcomes in 30%, and less just in 10% of the various conditions, (3) there is some agreement with regard to the relative ranking of the equality versus the contribution principles for positive outcome allocation (equality took priority over contributions as a criterion for allocation in fifteen conditions; the opposite was found in eight conditions, while no differences were obtained in two), and (4) agreement is a bit lower with regard to the relative ranking of these two principles for negative outcome allocation (equality was considered more appropriate in fourteen studies while the opposite was found in nine, and no differences in one).

Considering these divergent findings, there is clearly a need for a detailed analysis of the properties in terms of which existing research studies differ and which, in turn, may explain the inconsistent results. To this end, a more precise and rigorous terminology needs to be developed and adopted to facilitate distinctions among phenomena which have different implications for how people respond to positive and negative outcome allocations. (See Törnblom 1988 for a suggested conceptual framework pertaining to the types/intents/results of outcome allocation, the modes of accomplishing outcome allocation, and the types of outcome.) Further, not only is more systematic research warranted with regard to direct comparisons (under different circumstances and within the context of a coherent theoretical framework) between positive and negative outcome allocation, but we also need to bring our knowledge about justice conceptions in the context of negative outcome allocation *per se* up to par with what we know about the allocation of positive outcomes (see Griffith 1989). In addition, it appears desirable to break the present tendency to restrict attention to the equality and contribution principles.

6   Concluding remarks

This review has pointed to several important developments in, limitations of and policy implications of social psychological theory and research on distributive justice. A few very brief comments may be appropriate at this point about some areas of investigation which deserve attention, and to which European researchers have made significant contributions, but which have been neglected here owing to space constraints and the particular structure of the chapter.[20] I will conclude by suggesting a few of the many interesting research questions that seem worthy of future investigation.

6.1   Some additional noteworthy research topics

In their review of research on distributive justice, Cook and Hegtvedt (1983, p. 233) concluded that 'The precise nature of the relationship among injustice, multiple distribution rules, and individual and collective reactions to injustice remains to be addressed both theoretically and empirically.' Among the topics that have not been included in this review are collective reactions to injustice as well as justice conceptions on the level of intergroup relations. The works by Martin and her co-workers (e.g., Martin and Murray 1984; Martin *et al.* 1984; Martin *et al.* 1988) may serve as a good starting point for those interested in the relationship between collective behaviour and distributive injustice (see also, for instance, Moore 1978; Taylor and Moghaddam 1987; Taylor *et al.* 1987; Webster and Smith 1978). The focus of much of the research on justice in intergroup relations is placed upon how group members distribute resources to members of their own group and an outgroup (see Billig 1976; Ng 1981, 1984, 1986; Ng and Cram 1987; Rabbie and Horwitz 1969; Rabbie 1982; Sherif *et al.* 1961; Sherif 1966; Tajfel *et al.* 1971; Tajfel 1978; Turner 1980). Interesting attempts have also been made to compare justice processes on the interpersonal and intergroup levels and to explore whether or not it is possible to make extrapolations from interpersonal to intergroup relations (cf. Caddick 1980; Syroit, in press; van Avermaet and McClintock 1988). It seems, however, that research about justice on the collective and intergroup levels has yet to move beyond the limited context of the contribution principle to the complexities introduced when the impact of multiple distribution rules are to be considered.

Whereas much of the work on the relationship between injustice and individual as well as collective action focuses on the disadvantaged and their attempts, or lack thereof, to improve their situation, an interesting line of research by Montada and his research team in West Germany (e.g., Montada *et al.* 1986; Montada and Schneider 1988) is concerned with relative privilege. Of particular interest are those circumstances in which one's own privilege causes uneasiness (rather than pleasure) which, in turn, may lead to 'existential guilt' and attempts to cope with one's (often undeserved) position of advantage. (Existential guilt is defined as 'an intra- and interindividually varying disposition to react with feelings of guilt to perceived differences between one's own favorable lot or position (i.e., one's own privileges) and the unfavorable lot of others', Montada *et al.* 1986, p. 126.) Some of the questions guiding Montada's research are 'When do they "plead guilty" to having taken advantage undeservedly? and, When do they apply various defensive strategies to justify the status quo?' (ibid., p. 140). No comments are needed as to the considerable social significance of this work.

Over a dozen years ago Adams and Freedman (1976) lamented the lack of research on the phenomenological quality of distress caused by inequity. Different types of inequity (and distributive injustice in general) are likely to result in different types of distress which, in turn, are likely to result in different kinds of behaviour. Therefore we need to know more about (1) the nature of distress, i.e., the different ways in which distress may be experienced, (2) the relationship of different types of distress to injustices caused by the violation of different distributive justice principles, and (3) the relationship of different types of distress to psychological and behavioural reactions to distress. This knowledge is important for the prediction of the manners in which (and the intensity by which) victims of different types of injustice will attempt to reduce or eliminate injustice. Creative research studies related to some of these issues have been conducted in Austria by Mikula. One line of this research (Mikula 1986, 1987; Mikula and Schlamberger 1985) has examined and compared victims' and observers' cognitive responses to injustice. Mikula and his collaborators are also in the process of exploring the unjust events people commonly experience in their everyday lives, as well as the conditions necessary for an event to be perceived as unjust (Mikula 1988; Mikula *et al.* 1988).

6.2   Suggestions for future research

In the introductory section of this chapter it was pointed out that research within the area of procedural justice falls outside the scope of this review owing to the relative scarcity of European contributions. Some American research has indicated that procedural aspects of distribution may be more important to the individual than the final shape of the distribution, i.e., that the fairness evaluation of a particular resource distribution is affected by the fairness of the procedures by which the distribution was brought about. European replications are certainly warranted to examine the generality of this and other findings. A number of interesting queries may be generated, e.g., does the degree of importance of distributive versus procedural aspects and their perceived fairness vary with the social context in which they occur, the nature of the resource distributed, the individual versus the collective levels, positive versus negative resource allocation, and so forth? Do people react differently to distributive as compared to procedural injustice? Do people differentiate more among distributive or procedural justice principles? In general, a concentrated effort to map out the relationship between distributive and procedural justice should prove highly valuable to both fields of research.

Another interesting topic deals with the means of production. According to what justice criteria should the means of production (rather than the resources of consumption) be distributed? Does the manner in which a resource is produced affect people's conceptions about justice in resource distribution? These and related types of question are seldom asked by researchers within the area of distributive justice. Nevertheless, attention appears warranted to the ways in which the organization of production (and the hierarchy of power) is related to the distribution of the produced resources (cf. Cohen and Greenberg 1982, pp. 33–4). One of the issues subsumed under this topic would concern the relationship between justice in the distribution of (access to ownership of and/or decision-making control over) the resources (or means) of production and justice in the distribution of the resources of consumption (i.e. 'distributive justice'). In the opinion of Rescher (1966, p. 89), 'Any theory of distributive justice that fails to make provision for a principle of production of goods and merely insists upon the fairness and equity of distribution of such goods as lie at hand is gravely deficient ...' There is, for instance, surely a 'difference between dividing a pie that ... [a person] has baked and dividing a pie that has drifted gently down from the sky' (Wolff 1977, p. 207).

Perhaps the current tendency to confine the analysis of distributive justice to the domain of consumption is related to the way in which work or labour is conceived in (at least) most present Western industrialized societies: work is instrumental, considered to be an input, a means to securing a steady pecuniary income for the fulfilment of one's sustenance needs and various pleasures in life. It is not a mere coincidence that equity theory mirrors this view, and that most initial empirical work within this tradition employed research designs that modelled this reality, representing work by various kinds of experimental 'tasks' and income by a monetary 'reward' (no matter how trivial its amount). Thus, the individual is cast in the role of a consumer, justice considerations revolve around the way consumer goods (the outcomes of labour) are distributed, and the contribution principle appears to be the most logical standard against which justice should be judged. Although later work expanded this narrow conception of justice by adding other justice principles (as we have seen), the initial focus on the domain of consumption has been retained, however. Had work been conceived of as an outcome, a reward, an end in itself (e.g., a creative activity, a realization and expression of human nature), the individual as a producer (rather than consumer) would have been the natural emphasis, and issues relevant to the sphere of production (rather than consumption) would have been the likely targets of people's justice considerations.

In a recent review of the theoretical directions within mainstream social psychology McMahon (1984) argues that justice researchers must explain why they are interested in justice norms rather than in other kinds of norms or norms in general: 'Are the issues being discussed generally applicable to normative dynamics or peculiar in some way to justice norms?' (p. 131). Related questions to be answered when attempting to define the scope of a theory of distributive justice are 'When is justice a topic of concern for the individual (the group, or whatever the relevant unit of analysis might be)?' 'Why and under what conditions do people make justice evaluations and/or use justice as a standard for their conduct (i.e., behave justly)?' Although it does not provide a direct or full answer to these questions, a good starting point for ideas is Stolte's (1987) article in which he leans on structural exchange theory and symbolic interaction theory to describe (1) the process through which justice norms form, and (2) how and why justice norms vary.

Similarly, it is not clear if and in what way(s) justice evaluations of a distribution principle differ (in terms of their determinants and consequences, for example) from other types of moral evaluations or from non-moral evaluations (Jonsson and Törnblom, 1984b). Indeed, in most studies it is extremely difficult to determine exactly what type of evaluation was elicited from subjects. If justice evaluations are a different species from other types of evaluations (which we must assume is a prevalent belief among justice theorists), then the hows and whys need to be explicitly stated. In addition, the possible interdependence between justice evaluations and other kinds of evaluations should be systematically investigated. It is likely, for example, that the justice evaluation of a distribution principle will vary positively with its perceived conduciveness to fulfilling the evaluator's self-interests (e.g., Greenberg 1981).

Related issues (mentioned in section 3) revolve around our ignorance about the complexity and the size of the range of justice criteria or principles in terms of which people may define and evaluate distributive justice. Do people use a single criterion at a time or a mixture of different criteria? Is the restricted focus of present-day researchers on the contribution, equality and need rules valid and justifiable, or should additional principles be given equal or more attention? Increased knowledge is needed about the composition of people's justice standards, and we need to know more about the range of justice principles that figure in the heads of people and/or guide their conduct.

A large section of this chapter (i.e., section 4) was devoted to a description of theory and research concerned with identifying factors that appear to affect the evaluation and application of justice principles, while less space was allotted to the sparse research on consequences of applying different justice principles (section 3.3). An impression emerging from this literature is that a moratorium is warranted on research testing this or that arbitrarily chosen 'determinant' in isolation from others, while freed energy should instead be canalized (1) towards a concentrated attempt at constructing a meaningful inventory of existing findings about factors that appear to affect our justice conceptions, and (2) towards more research investigating the various consequences the application of different justice principles may have when serving as criteria for the allocation of various types of resources (other than, and in addition to, money).

While existing research, then, has given high priority to a mapping of the factors that activate various justice principles and quite low priority to examining the consequences of applying a given principle, it seems that no attention has been given to a third topic worthy of serious attention: whether or not the violation of different distributive justice principles may result in different cognitive, affective and behavioural consequences (see previous comments on the phenomenology of distress). For instance, will the violation of the contribution principle evoke quantitatively or qualitatively different reactions as compared to the violation of the equality principle? If so, why is this the case, under what circumstances will this happen, and what implications does this have for interpersonal relations and the structure and dynamics of social groups? The lack of interest in the violation of justice norms is a bit surprising, particularly against the background of highly relevant research on role conflict by role theorists. The existence of conflicting justice norms in many choice situations frequently implies that conformity to one norm necessarily results in the violation of another. How does the individual deal with such dilemmas (e.g., Mikula and Korytko 1989; Törnblom 1988)? Is the violation of a particular justice principle considered to be more or less serious than the violation of others? To this date, research concerned with consequences of violating justice has been conducted largely within the framework of equity theory, thus being confined to the contribution principle. However, the application of a given justice principle will inevitably violate other justice principles. As different groups in a society frequently subscribe to different principles, and as justice for the individual may collide with justice for the group or society as a whole, problems of different degrees of severity are likely to arise. Situations of this kind place actors involved with social policy planning on the horns of a dilemma which nevertheless has to be faced squarely.

Acknowledgements
I am grateful to Uriel Foa, Wanda Griffith, Gerold Mikula, Melvin Lerner and, in particular, Klaus Scherer for their useful comments.

Notes

1 Origin unknown to this author.

2 As Adams' (1965) formula cannot adequately handle negative inputs, Walster, Berscheid and Walster (1973) proposed a more complex equation as a remedy. Since then, a number of attempts have been made to arrive at further improvements (e.g., Alessio 1980; Anderson and Farkas 1975; Cosier and Dalton 1983; Farkas and Anderson 1979; Harris 1976, 1983; Jasso 1978, 1980, 1981, 1983, 1986; Jonsson and Törnblom 1983a, 1983b, 1984a; Markovsky 1985; Messick and Sentis 1979; Moschetti 1979; Romer 1977; Samuel 1976a, 1976b, 1978; Theriault 1978; Vecchio 1982; G.W. Walster 1975, 1976; and Zuckerman 1975).

3 However, Yamagishi (1984) argued that people may sometimes care less about maximizing the collective reward than about their own short-term interests, even though this is often harmful to their long-term interests (cf. the 'tragedy of the commons' – Hardin 1968). This is more likely to happen with increasing strength of the conflict between self-interests and collective interests, and the less the benefits of acting toward collective interests can be experienced.

On the other hand, 'enlightened self-interest' is a notion that frequently appears in philosophical discussions, an idea that involves a merging of one's personal interests with those of others. Owing to the interdependence among members of a group or a society 'the general interest is itself a crucial part or aspect of one's self-interest' (Rescher 1987, p. 31). Conduct guided by 'selfish (narrow) self-interest' not only may have negative consequences for the welfare of others but, ironically, is also likely to be ultimately self-defeating to the subject person him/herself, as those who are negatively affected may turn against him/her. As self-interest is part and parcel of human nature, perhaps the most intelligent and productive (as well as moral) alternative is to enlighten oneself about the needs and interests of others, in order to make those part of one's own. Thus, the only viable type of self-interest may be this 'enlightened' (wide) self-interest, whether or not one is genuinely concerned about the welfare of others.

4 For additional forms of (in)justice, see Weick and Nesset 1968; Austin and Walster 1975; Cook and Parcel 1977; Crosby and Gonzalez-Intal 1984.

5 These comparisons include comparison between (1) expected and actual outcomes (termed 'outcome designations'), (2) P's and O's inputs vs. those typical for the reference group, (3) P's and O's inputs, and (4) P's and O's outcomes.

6 The resource of allocation has also been shown to be related to a person's social orientation and to the choice of allocation principle. The results of a study using Polish male and female university students (Grzelak 1985) indicated that type of social orientation (individualism, altruism, equity, competition and cooperation) varies with the outcome involved (money, control and work). The relationship between resource (type of outcome) and choice of allocation principle is further discussed in section 4.2.

7 A study by Törnblom (in prep. a) showed that subjects' attributions of friendship between two persons varied depending on which of four modes of giving

and receiving resources was involved (giving-giving, requesting-giving, giving-requesting, and requesting-requesting).

8 However, a number of studies have examined children's justice conceptions (e.g., Damon 1975, 1977; Hook and Cook 1979; Gerling and Wender 1981; Mikula 1972; Simons and Klaassen 1979; Wender 1986).

9 'Good shall be repaid by good', 'hurt can be repaid by hurt', 'a wrong shall be righted' and 'someone who has received a beneficial service must expect certain disadvantages or burdens to be imposed on him in return' (Eckhoff 1974, p. 30).

10 'Objectively equal amounts to each' (the term 'objective' is here used in the sense that recipient characteristics are irrelevant to any given outcome distribution in which each person receives the same *amount*, but not necessarily the same *kind* of outcome; it seems that this principle might encompass equality of outcomes at any given allotment occasion as well as 'equal results', i.e., equality of the accumulated total outcomes), 'subjective equality of transfers' (encompassing the need principle as well as equal results, the latter in the sense that recipients should be brought to the same level of subjective outcome value), 'relative equality' (in which case recipient characteristics are considered, commonly labelled the equity or contribution principle by social psychologists), 'rank order equality' (a variation of the contribution principle) and 'equal opportunity' (see Eckhoff 1974, pp. 35–8).

11 The most important recipient characteristics are need, fitness, desert, status and position, all of which may be criteria for distributions which have nothing to do with equality (see Eckhoff 1974, p. 38).

12 'Biological needs' have to do with survival, 'basic needs' with the relative notion of a bare minimum for a 'decent' sort of life, and 'functional needs' with requirements that have to be satisfied for a person to be able to do his/her job (see Benn and Peters 1959, pp. 144–6).

13 Although a large number of studies have investigated the consequences of violating the equity or contribution principle, there appears to be no research comparing the consequences of violating different justice principles.

14 Unfortunately, as these studies are only briefly described in his book (Deutsch 1985), a closer examination of their details is not possible.

15 Major and Deaux (1982, pp. 62–70) have organized existing explanations to individual differences in justice behaviour into three main groups: (1) normative explanations (i.e., people adhere to different justice norms), (2) interaction orientation explanations (i.e., people differ in their interaction objectives), and (3) cognitive explanations (i.e., people differ in their perceptions of inputs, performance evaluations, performance attributions, reward expectancies and their perceptions of outcomes).

16 Griffith, W.I. Personal communication, 13 September 1988.

17 Parts of this section are adopted from Törnblom and Jonsson (1989, pp. 28–31).

18 It may be noted that their typology of social relations incorporates power differentials, an important relationship dimension which has been widely neglected in theories and research on distributive justice (e.g., Austin and Hatfield 1980; Cohen 1986a; Cook and Hegtvedt 1986; Homans 1976; Morgenthau 1974).

19 As the term 'retribution' is more narrow than 'negative outcome allocation' in
   its connotations, it appears wiser to use the latter label as it can more easily
   accommodate a wide variety of concepts, e.g., deprivation, cost, burden, loss,
   punishment, retaliation, etc. (see Törnblom 1988 and Griffith 1989 for fuller
   discussions of prevailing terminological confusions).

20 A more extensive and detailed presentation of theory and research on justice
   will be found in Törnblom and Griffith (in prep.).

7 Interdisciplinary theory and research on justice

John Bell and Erik Schokkaert

1 Introduction

The various chapters of this volume represent differing ways of considering the question of justice. To caricature the positions somewhat, one could say that for philosophers it is a problem of moral rightness. For economists, it is a problem of the efficient realization of social choice. For lawyers, it is a problem of conformity to rules. For social psychologists, it is a matter of individual reactions in interpersonal relations. And for sociologists, it is a mixture of all the preceding points of view. The positions are not necessarily contradictory, but they are not always easy to correlate.

All the same, within the Western European and American tradition of thought, some common assumptions can be detected. Moreover, apparently conflicting approaches may turn out to be complementary. In this chapter, we highlight certain features of the discussion and point out some possibilities for further interdisciplinary research.

2 What is justice?

Justice is a measure of the acceptability of certain outcomes of human relationships or situations. Two elements are essential. Justice concerns *interpersonal* relationships, i.e. the way we organize our (large or small) communities. Moreover, justice gives rise to *rights* and *duties*. Therefore it is a more important feature of some social relationships such as between state and citizen, business and client, employer and employee, than others. In contrast, love and respect are more appropriate standards for family relationships and friendship.

2.1 Justice and other virtues
2.1.1 Charity
Justice is not the only virtue of interpersonal relationships. For instance, the requirements of justice and charity are typically seen as distinct. In their usual interpretation, a person is free to be charitable, but has a moral duty to be just. Both virtues have consequences for the distribution of social goods, and they will frequently benefit the disadvantaged in the

community. They may also have equalizing effects on holdings, though the requirement of equal treatment is much weaker in the case of charity. All the same, the reasons for such distributions and their moral necessity are different. It is important to define the respective domains of justice and charity. For instance, many authors argue that a certain degree of redistribution is necessary for reasons of *justice*. For Nozick and other libertarian thinkers, however, this is a basic confusion of ideas. For them, ideas about redistribution belong to realms other than justice, since they denote an approach to problems other than that based on strict respect for existing holdings of resources (entitlements).

2.1.2   Fraternity

The issue of *justice versus fraternity* is clearly seen in the way in which the relevant community for the operation of justice is defined. Once we take a specific group of human beings to be the body among whom justice must operate, then we delimit those whose demands and needs are relevant in discussion of questions of justice in the distribution of resources or the correction of wrongs. The outsiders are treated not on the basis of justice, but on the basis of fraternity or other moral considerations. Though this might most obviously be applied to questions of help to developing nations or to those who suffer from disasters, it also applies to immigration and to the way in which foreigners are treated within a country. By restricting the scope of a community in a particular way, it is possible to avoid certain issues as relevant to the debate about justice. But, of course, the definition of the relevant community is in itself dependent on our conception of justice. If we treat all who might be affected by decisions as relevant participants in the distribution of a resource, then this might enlarge significantly the community within which justice has to be shown. For instance, the decision to burn fossil fuels will affect both future generations in the using country and the citizens of other countries who suffer from the resulting emissions in the form of acid rain, etc.

2.2   Forms of justice

Two main forms of justice appear in the literature: corrective or commutative justice on the one hand and distributive justice on the other hand. Redistributive and contributive justice are closely linked to the latter.

2.2.1   Corrective justice

The principal characteristic of corrective justice is the requirement of action to correct a situation resulting from a wrong done. For instance, one person has broken a promise and another has suffered loss as a result. Justice may require the promise-breaker to correct the loss by providing compensation to the victim.

The characterization of a changed situation as an injustice worthy of correction involves some assessment of the value of the prior holdings, of the nature of the event causing the loss, and of the obligation of the beneficiary or cause of the event to make good the loss. For instance, if I am in business and operate more efficiently than you, so that you lose customers to me, I am not thereby required to make good the loss, but am treated as a praiseworthy member of a capitalist society. The loss caused and the method of its infliction are not treated as some form of wrong without further factors, such as unfair competition or breach of undertaking.

The issue of corrective justice appears almost exclusively in the legal and psychological approaches to justice. It focuses predominantly at the microlevel, or at the level of legal institutions designed to regulate inter-individual relationships. However, it might also be applied to some dealings between the individual and society. Thus, it could be envisaged that punishment should be considered as correction for past wrongs being paid back to the victim (society). Such an approach would have obvious implications for deterrence or reform theories of punishment.

2.2.2   Distributive justice

Distributive justice is the principal concern of the discussions in philosophy, economics, sociology and psychology. Basically one can distinguish between three forms of distributive justice. The first two forms both refer to the allocation of new resources. First there is the distribution of some fortuitously acquired bounty (the so-called 'manna from heaven') to which there are no prior entitlements. Second, and most commonly, there is the question of how one distributes the benefits of some collectively created resource, and indeed how one identifies what resources are created collectively.

Authors typically argue that resources of the first kind are most appropriately allocated on the basis of equality or need, since no one individual has a fundamentally stronger claim to such a resource than any other. By contrast, where the resource is created by the contribution of the existing resources or efforts of individuals, then the entitlements generated by these factors may be important criteria for the just allocation of the resource.

This second form of distributive justice is closely connected with the notion of contributive justice, i.e. whether individuals are required by justice to make contributions for the benefit of the whole community. Unless there is such a requirement, then an individual ought to be entitled to any new resource in proportion simply to his or her contribution. The idea of contributive justice has, however, little place in the literature.

Indeed, the bulk of the literature in Western Europe and North America discussed in this book starts from individualistic presuppositions in which the notion of the 'community' has no real place.

The allocation of new resources is the main point of interest for the psychological research. Entitlement-orientated philosophical and economic theories also have a tendency to limit the domain of distributive justice to these first two forms. Other authors however include *redis*-*tributive* justice as a third form of distributive justice. Redistribution involves some reallocation of existing entitlements. In essence, the approach is to deny the justice of existing holdings and thus to treat them as needing corrective treatment. Between individuals, one may challenge the way in which resources were acquired, and at the societal level, one may argue that certain modes of acquisition do not give rise to a genuine entitlement. In this respect three questions are especially important: the rightness of the initial appropriation of natural resources, the rightness of different compensations linked to differences in natural abilities and the rightness of acquisitions and inheritance.

It is important to stress that, for those who are critical of current distributions of entitlements, the distinction between distributive and redistributive justice is not relevant (and may even be dangerous). In their view, such redistribution is the only way to realize justice. Redistribution infringes no legitimate entitlements, merely illegitimate ones. Thus, to divide justice issues into those concerned with distribution and those with redistribution is not merely a formal structuring device. Its introduction already suggests a substantive position.

2.3   *Justice: formal or substantive?*

Sometimes a distinction is made between formal and substantive theories of justice. The implications of this distinction depend on the meaning that is given to the notion of formal justice. Various authors label their theories as 'formal', though not all of these are appropriately called 'formal'. One interpretation of the concept is represented by the discursive schools of thought. These authors want to set out the formal characteristics which any argument of justice must display. Their theories permit any content to be given to the ideal of justice by participants in justice-discourse, but require certain formal characteristics for any valid argument. This interpretation of formal justice basically is one possible approach to the problem of moral epistemology. One could say that this is a kind of 'methodological' notion of formal justice, still allowing for various substantive interpretations. On the other hand, it might well be argued that the methodological requirements of such discourse theories already determine the substantive principles which may emerge, albeit indirectly.

Another interpretation of 'formal justice' is popular among lawyers:

legal justice is then conceived as the just application of established rules of positive law. Most people will agree that this is a necessary condition for social justice. A few lawyers would go further, however, and claim that this formal justice exhausts the concept of social justice in general. Of course, this is no longer a purely methodological stance. In fact, this interpretation of formal justice is really a theory of substantive justice – and one which is hardly defensible.

The interpretation of justice as the just application of the law is sometimes called 'procedural justice', because it indeed has the consequence that procedure becomes the substantive content of justice. The notion of procedural justice is, however, beset by terminological confusion. The concept of procedural justice itself relates to the issue of whether justice offers results or methods for achieving results. How far does justice demonstrate the desirability of certain outcomes, and how far is it concerned simply with the methods by which results are arrived at?

The importance of procedural justice in judicial decisions is intended to satisfy concerns about the justice of a result which runs counter to what one side claims to be its entitlement. In a society where there can be genuine disagreement about what justice demands, then abiding by an agreed method is likely to allay some feelings of discontent. It could be said that following a procedure respects the autonomy of individuals and treats each person as worthy of receiving explanations for decisions reached. We may also follow a procedure for prudential reasons, in that by listening to all sides in an impartial way, we may reach the best solution.

In a non-judicial context, other interpretations have been given to the notion of procedural justice. It has been argued, for instance, that the use of philosophical devices such as the social contract or the Rawlsian idea of the original position in a certain sense also leads to a procedural theory. However, such theories are procedural in a very limited sense only: the use of these devices has the objective not of establishing procedures for arriving at decisions, but of offering neutral methods of justifying results. While procedural in form, they are really ways of trying to assess the justice of outcomes. Contrary to the legal interpretation of procedural justice, the real concern of these philosophical approaches is the fairness of a result, not the design of a procedure.

A purer procedural theory of distributive justice is proposed by libertarians such as Nozick: they accept the *market as the right procedure* to realize distributive justice. In their approach, the theory of the initial entitlements to property rights in a sense exhausts the theory of justice: the final distributive outcome does not matter, as long as the property rights of all individuals have been respected. This is to be contrasted with other philosophical theories, which do not want to accept the justice of the market procedure as such, but instead consider property rights and market relationships as part of the basic institutions of society which have to be critically scrutinized.

It is useful to compare the libertarian procedural theory of distributive justice with the legal theory of right procedures. Although most liberal legal systems include some rules which go against the free working of the market, they largely work within the context of a market system, which they treat as given. This does not imply as such that they would accept the justice of the market outcomes, only that they do not question these outcomes. Libertarians go further: they definitely state that the market procedure *by definition* leads to just outcomes. In this way, they enlarge the legal concept of procedure.

2.4 Justice as a positive or negative virtue

Whereas theories of distributive justice mostly have a positive ideal, those focusing on corrective justice are more concerned with avoiding injustice. Moreover, psychological research seems to suggest that the perceptions and views of individuals identify what is unjust more sharply than what is just. The question then naturally arises whether it is necessary to cherish justice as a positive ideal. Does it not suffice if we avoid the creation or perpetuation of social injustice? Certainly, it will be easier to reach consensus about some specific cases of injustice. This may lead to an almost undisputed minimal level of justice, though it is likely to be a consensus over a limited range of issues. But again, restricting the scope of justice to such minimal 'consensus' level is in itself a substantive position, with which many people would disagree.

3 The structure of justice research

Interdisciplinary discussions are often impeded by terminological confusions. Some illustrations are given in section 3.1. In section 3.2 we try to structure the field of justice research along two dimensions: the micro/macro and the descriptive/normative dimension. Any attempt to structure the differences between the approaches of the various disciplines is apt to be superficial and one-sided. However, it is a useful first step if we want to explore the possibilities of interdisciplinary research.

3.1 Some terminological confusions

Scientific disciplines derive their identification partly from the use of a differentiated jargon. This is unavoidable but it does not make interdisciplinary contacts easier. It even occurs that one and the same book is interpreted quite differently by different disciplines. This obviously has become the fate of Rawls' *Theory of Justice*, whose enormous influence can be judged from its appearance in all the previous chapters. One can see differences in the emphasis by different disciplines; in the case of economists there is even an unmistakable misinterpretation when they formulate the difference principle in terms of utility.

A long list of confusing terms could be drawn up. It suffices to point out a few. 'Utility' is a term with differing connotations in the philosophical literature, and yet it has a very special meaning in economic terminology. Many philosophical usages make 'utility' equivalent to 'the collective welfare' which is different from the use which would be made of the same term by economists. This divergence in usage can lead to difficulties in interdisciplinary work. The concept of 'entitlement' is sometimes understood in psychological work in terms of 'merit', whereas in some philosophical work, such as that of Nozick, it has the sense of 'existing holdings'. As has already been seen, 'procedural justice' also admits of interpretations which are by no means of the same character.

The term *equity* deserves special mention, because it is used to denote elaborated and highly influential theories. Equity theory has been one of the path-breaking approaches in psychology; economists have also proposed a theory of equity. The two theories are not related; they do not even have anything to do with each other. Things are made worse by the fact that 'equity' has a specific meaning in legal writings also. Some legal interpretations of equity in terms of proportionality remind us of the psychological theory but other interpretations are completely different. The least one can say is that care is needed when using this word in interdisciplinary contacts.

Terminological differences are not merely problems of translation. There are undoubted linguistic difficulties with concepts developed in one language as they are transposed into others, e.g. the concept of *Rechtsgefühl* mentioned in the Introduction. But most interdisciplinary problems are not of this kind. It is necessary for collaborators from different disciplines to pay attention not merely to the words used, but also to their connotations within other spheres of discourse, and to fix on common usages for the particular project. Care to use words which will not confuse researchers from outside the discipline can also prepare the ground for mutual understanding. On the whole, however, awareness of the problem, rather than standardization will be the main requirement for any researcher.

3.2   Micro or macro, ideal or description

In Table 7.1, we position the justice theories of the different disciplines along two dimensions. The first relates to the difference between *ethical and descriptive* approaches. The former treat justice as a critical ideal for judging social relations and outcomes, the latter see it merely as a description of standards currently applied in society. The second dimension relates to the *micro/macro* distinction: the question whether the focus of

Table 7.1.

	MICRO		MACRO	
POSITIVE (DESCRIPTIVE)	PSYCHO-LOGY	SOCIOLOGY	public choice	sense of justice, access to justice
		exchange theory	functionalism, Marxism, administration	ECON-OMICS	LAW
NORMATIVE (ETHICAL)		PHILO-SOPHY	theories of justice	

justice should simply be at the macro level of the design of social institutions, and how far it ought also to be concerned with the dealings between individuals. It is certainly worthwhile stressing that concentration on the macro level does not, of itself, involve the attribution of independent significance to the community. Most justice theories current in Western Europe and North America merely describe the design of social institutions in instrumental terms, as means for realizing the objectives of self-concerned individuals, rather than as dimensions to human living valuable in their own right. This is not true of all theories (e.g., that of Finnis) and the revival of communitarian thinking may provide greater emphasis in future on the role of the community in questions of justice.

One can safely put the psychological approach in the upper left-hand corner: it is firmly anchored in the tradition of describing actual perceptions of justice and injustice, rather than setting out to criticize these. Some exceptions notwithstanding, it also concentrates on interindividual (micro) relations. With the same degree of safety, we put philosophy in the lower right-hand corner: it is ethical in inspiration and, at least since Rawls, is about the basic institutions of society. A large part of law and economics is also located in the macro/ethical box. However, when lawyers talk about the 'sense of justice' or about 'access to justice', they seem to slip into the descriptive approach; and the same is true for the economic theories of public choice and real government behaviour. The sociological approach can be characterized as descriptive. Almost by definition, it is mainly orientated towards social institutions; however, the framework of exchange theory leads to a micro theory. The area of micro/ethical discussion is found in legal writing. For example, it occurs in discussion of the duty to provide compensation for wrongdoing, or the duty to keep promises or contracts.

The table immediately suggests where there are close similarities between the different disciplines. Most of these have already led to intensive contacts 'within each box': between exchange theorists and psychologists, between social philosophers and normatively orientated economists (and to a lesser extent lawyers), between sociologists, political scientists and public choice economists. In section 4 we will try to argue that the approaches in different boxes may be complementary.

4   Complementarities between the different approaches

Let us start from the structure of Table 7.1. We have noted already that interdisciplinary work is easy (and has been done) within any of the boxes of the table. There is much less contact between disciplines and theories from different boxes. This is a pity, because in fact the different approaches are largely complementary. In section 4.2 we will try to show that ethical theories may inspire and guide empirical research; in section 4.3 we will argue that empirical insights are important for the construction of better normative theories. Before we turn to these substantial points, however, we will discuss some ideas which most scientific theories (in the different boxes) have in common. The acceptance of these common presuppositions in a certain sense differentiates the scientific from the non-scientific (more emotional) approaches in everyday life.

4.1   Common presuppositions of scientific theories of justice

Everyday discussions about justice abound with references to broad principles such as 'equality', 'desert' or 'needs'. Often these principles are used without even defining them in a concrete way. All scientific theories on the contrary start from the (indeed self-evident) point that the *real difficulties arise not so much in agreeing to abide by any of these principles, but in deciding what those concepts really mean and how to assign priority between them.* If the concepts are empty categories, then it is unclear how far they are helpful in resolving the practical problems over which people are in dispute.

The idea of equality occupies a special position in current Western theories of justice. It operates as a formal starting point in that there is an assumption that each individual in society is worthy of equal consideration. There is also the view that each citizen has the right to equal participation in the process of the distribution of resources. This is frequently expressed as a Kantian position that each person is an end in his own right, rather than a means to the end of serving others or society as a whole. In legal thought equality, even in corrective justice, requires equal application of the rules and the treating of each disputant as of equal value as a subject of the law.

Such a starting point has at least two consequences. It rules out aristocratic or other hierarchical views of society which could justify alternative and unequal treatment of individuals. It also rules out certain allocations which discriminate between individuals for reasons which are not connected with any coherent theory of justice. These are the so-called 'arbitrary' considerations.

Although this notion of equality is almost universally accepted, it remains only a purely formal starting point. Indeed the '*non*-arbitrary' considerations justifying discrimination between individuals may take any form, dependent on the proposed theory of justice. There is no consensus at all about what is the relevant object to be distributed (equally). Economic and philosophical models offer ways of measuring welfare, utility, income, resources, opportunity, needs and even rights and entitlements. The psychological comparisons made by individuals show a similar diversity of approach. On the whole, attention is paid to economic values, but status and other goods could equally be the object of justice.

Given these different points of departure in a discussion of what is just, there is room for fundamental conflict and disagreement about the justice of particular solutions. The complexity of human situations necessitates some simplification if a meaningful discussion of justice is to take place. But such a simplification inevitably magnifies fragments of individual situations, and comparisons made on that basis may well prove unacceptable or unsatisfactory. The lack of agreement on one predominant feature of situations in the light of which justice is to be measured suggests that one may need a plurality of features in order to satisfy individuals.

This *idea of plurality* is a second common presupposition of all scientific theories. It is essential of course in the empirical descriptive approaches. Yet all interesting normative approaches also start from this basic question: what can be the meaning of justice in a world of diverging opinions about what is a good society? Plurality may require the acceptance of a variety of methodologies and even of outcomes. All the same, some limits must be set in order to achieve comparability of results. At the same time, absolutist positions almost by definition make scientific or philosophical discussion impossible. Holding these ideas in necessary tension, we may say that any research must be open to as wide a range of solutions as possible. At the same time, the results must be reached by methods which are adequately rigorous.

4.2   Limitations of empirical research on justice

Some social scientists have the tendency to reject all approaches which we collected in the 'ethical' boxes of Table 7.1. They claim that the search for the right concept of justice is elusive: during many centuries people have tried to convince each other about a specific concept, without ever reaching consensus. They then propose to describe only the actual opinions, rather than try to formulate ethical standards. We do feel that this is an extreme and one-sided position.

Justice is not found simply in reportive statements of what particular people consider to be just or unjust. A theory is required capable of being used in the design of social institutions and in resolving particular practical issues. Some critical judgement is needed to produce such a theory. Even in the exercise of empirical research, some critical judgement is required. Ethical theories may well serve to inspire both the choice of empirical research and the exercise of critical judgement.

In the first place, empirical observations have to be fitted into a structure capable of providing conceptual clarity and having organization. Prescriptive theories of justice will offer such constructive frameworks.

Attention to ethical theories is also necessary because human behaviour is motivated by much more than justice considerations alone. Self-interest obviously is often the most important driving force. And we mentioned already at the beginning of this chapter that, even if we concentrate on moral considerations in interpersonal relationships, other behavioural standards (such as love or respect) may be more relevant than justice under some circumstances. Moreover, answers to justice questions as well as real behaviour may be influenced heavily by perception biases, by lack of information and by own-situation-induced myopia. All this leads to the conclusion that in most studies it is extremely difficult to determine exactly what type of evaluation was elicited from the subjects. Empirical data will thus not provide sufficient clarity for analysis and exploration. All the same, analysis may require us to distinguish and define explicitly these different motivations and perceptions. In particular, if we want to get a better insight into justice as a distinct motivation, these distinctions are essential. This implies that, in one way or another, we have to transcend our immediate observations and make use of analysis made at a more theoretical or philosophical level. A theoretical distinction between justice and other human motivations will typically be ethically inspired. Devices such as the veil of ignorance have been introduced exactly to create a position, where ethical (justice) considerations would dominate the other motivations. Though aware of the potential distortion which a particular ethical theory may bring, an empirical researcher can fruitfully make use of the analysis of justice issues made in ethical writings.

The most important perceptual bias is the one caused by a person's own position within a given institutional framework. There is by now overwhelming evidence that the global social context exerts an important influence on people's attitudes and reactions. There is also a strong presupposition that these attitudes and reactions often are orientated towards the continuation of the status quo, even among those who do not occupy highly ranked positions in the present situation. The concept of ideology is crucial here. Does the fact that many people in economic situations accept a desert or equity principle for the just distribution by itself imply that these are the absolutely just principles? For those who believe that justice is about the basic institutions of society, such a conclusion would be hardly acceptable, because the reactions of the actors merely reflect the consequences of one way of organizing society (the actual one) and turn them into the definitive ethical rule. A seemingly more prudent position is that actual answers and attitudes are not necessarily just, but that at the same time one should give up the quest for a Utopian ideal concept of justice. Concretely this also produces a conservative position. Indeed, this position tends to deny the importance of justice as a critical ideal. Yet this ideal has undoubtedly always been one of the most important driving forces for social change.

The question of the relationship between attitudes and the social system in which one lives is a difficult one. It reappears in one form or another in all schools of thought (very explicitly, for instance, in the Marxian discussions) both in epistemological and in ethical theories. It cannot be our ambition to state a definitive answer. But it must be obvious that ethical theorizing (so far as it is possible) may be a very important contribution to this debate. At least, it may make social scientists more critical of the data on which their conclusions are drawn.

4.3   The basis of ethical judgements

While we feel that the importance of ethical thinking about justice must be stressed, social scientists have a point with their relativistic approach: it is true that there has never been and probably will never be a consensus among philosophers. Although ethical theories are powerfully persuasive, their main practical contribution at the macro level is in structuring the debate on the principles of justice which should be adopted, and in making different argumentations more transparent. The strength and underlying assumptions of the various arguments are clarified and this improves the quality of the discussion. The insights of the social sciences contribute to this debate, and their contributions, particularly in the analysis of intuitions on justice, should be integrated into the process of ethical theorizing.

This leads us to the question of the basis of ethical judgements. Two extreme views must be discarded immediately as possible bases for interdisciplinary research. At one extreme we have the most idealistic interpretations (such as the Aristotelian or traditional natural law approaches). We have emphasized already that these do not carry much favour among social scientists and present-day philosophers. In a world of diverging opinions one should start from the fact that there is no consensus about any of these absolute theories, but one would like to get some better insight into the reasons for these disagreements and into the way to solve them. At the other extreme stands the interpretation that our human sense or intuition of justice is an irreducibly emotional or subjective response to a situation. In this view (in which the whole idea of this book does not make much sense) there is no intersubjective ground to establish the rational foundation of a critical notion of justice.

An interesting middle course between these two extremes is offered by the Rawlsian idea of reflective equilibrium. This can be interpreted broadly, without necessarily leading to the device of the original position. In this broad interpretation, it refers to the constant dialogue between (empirical) intuitions and findings and theories: theories are revised on the basis of empirical intuitions and observations, primitive empirical intuitions are critically scrutinized on the basis of the theoretical principles. The process ends when we reach an equilibrium where there is consistency between our theoretical principles and our intuitions and observations. Contrary to the extremely subjective views, this idea at least encourages discussion of the seriousness of opinions and the depth of convictions found in initial opinions on justice, abstracting from the contingent features of particular advantages, to be derived from specific outcomes. Contrary to the absolute views of justice, the corrective to existing perceptions or claims does not derive from an absolutely given external ideal. The idea of reflective equilibrium gives priority to consistency and coherence in thought, rather than to specific ideals of the good.

In this interpretation, empirical work by social scientists is eminently useful for the formulation of an adequate ethical theory. Since most of the concepts used in modern theories of justice are subjectively defined, it is important to be able to understand both why individuals measure certain outcomes in particular ways and why they give priority to some values, rather than to others. Most theories take as a fixed starting point the fact that people adopt certain positions with regard to particular outcomes, and then ask how these competing demands may be reconciled. If the areas of preference formation and preference articulation were more thoroughly studied, it might be perceived as more legitimate to discount certain preference statements as too culturally conditioned or inadequately expressed.

In this respect two specific points may be noted. It is common in philosophical writings to sharpen the intuition and illustrate the argumentation by presenting little (or grand) stories in which a justice problem arises. This fits nicely into the idea of reflective equilibrium, of course. However, rarely if ever is taken into account the psychological finding that intuitions about justice principles may be highly dependent on the social environment in which the story is situated. This finding should lead to some caution in the interpretation of stories. One could perhaps even suggest the more far-reaching conclusion that ethical theories themselves should distinguish between different social situations. Certainly the empirical basis for theoretical judgements about justice needs to be more articulated.

A second remark relates to the implementation of ethical theories of justice. All empirical results from the different disciplines in the 'descriptive' boxes of Table 7.1 show that the practical application of pure principles is fraught with difficulties. People will not understand and/or accept the principles, State or other institutions and bureaucracies will try to (mis)interpret the principles in their own interest, lack of consensus may lead to sharp and possibly disastrous social conflicts. If ethical theories are formulated to be showered from the ivory tower of philosophy upon the people in society, they should take into account these difficulties: insights from the social sciences may be very helpful in reaching a balanced and realistic view of what is possible and what will probably remain Utopian for ever.

5   Liberty and efficiency: constraints on justice?

It is sometimes claimed that the pursuit of (especially distributive) justice is constrained by the importance of other social objectives (see the Introduction). One of these is liberty, another is the efficiency of social cooperation.

The philosophical literature, in general, suggests that it is better to include the problem of the conflict between liberty, efficiency and justice within the definition of justice itself, rather than to see it as an external constraint on the pursuit of justice. Whether this is correct or not is a matter for debate. It is clear that relationships have to be established between justice and a number of values, but these relationships may be distinct in different areas. The relationship between justice and economic efficiency in establishing wage incentives may be very different from that appropriate to the allocation of hospital beds to patients. Such differences may make the process of establishing a single relationship between the various values of justice, efficiency, liberty and so on rather problematic. As a result, it may be better to treat the values of liberty and efficiency as external constraints on a theory of justice. Such a formal arrangement of the problem does not, however, make the resolution of particular conflicts any easier.

Freedom is essential to libertarian theories, of course. But we have mentioned already that the freedom of the individual to choose his/her lifeplan and the fundamental subsidiarity of the functions of the social institutions are also basic presuppositions of the rest of the modern justice literature. The Rawlsian and welfarist literature which dominates contemporary debate takes the problem of justice to be the reconciliation of individual wants within a world of limited resources. The function of social institutions is to provide mechanisms for fulfilling these wants and not to decide upon collective objectives which will favour certain lifeplans at the expense of others. Such a theory of individualist, pluralist, liberal neutrality dictates the nature of the issues which are discussed under the heading of 'justice'. The notion of community and collective programmes as valuable in themselves is not seen as a basis for discussing aspects of justice. This individualistic view of course lessens the conflict between liberty and justice.

The conflict does not disappear altogether, however. Indeed, a theory of justice is ultimately a justification of certain basic institutions and a ground for corrective social action which forces people to behave in a certain way, and may thus be contrary to individual freedom. Social contract theories try to resolve the tension between freedom and justice by suggesting that the principles forced on individuals are those which they would (under certain circumstances) rationally agree to. Of course, this social contract approach is far from universally accepted.

The trade-off between liberty and justice is not exclusively an ethical problem. Feelings of freedom and loss of freedom are essentially subjective and culturally conditioned. Empirical research into the opinions and motivations of citizens may therefore be very helpful to judge the importance of the tension between these feelings and justice and to suggest ways to overcome it.

Another possible conflict is between justice and efficiency. It is often said that over-concern with justice in the distribution and redistribution of resources could lead to a reduction in cooperation or at least in the efficient production of the wealth and resources on which the welfare of the society depends. Again this problem is typically treated as part of the definition of justice itself. This is clear for the economic theories of social welfare functions and, indeed, for all theories with a utilitarian background. But the Rawlsian difference principle and the libertarian belief in the market also take into account efficiency considerations in a quite explicit way.

Again, the potential contribution of the social sciences must be emphasized. Indeed, they should investigate whether there is in reality indeed a conflict with efficiency. Economic theories usually accept that the conflict exists and try to estimate the magnitude of the efficiency losses. Some psychologists and sociologists, however, claim that more justice will increase efficiency: they argue that people will be more motivated to work when they live in what they themselves perceive as a just environment. These divergent interpretations have enormous consequences for practical and political judgements. It seems that here lies a crucial point for further interdisciplinary contacts.

6   Conclusion: possibilities for interdisciplinary research

This volume shows the richness of the ideas about justice, which have been proposed by the different disciplines. Each one of these contributions throws an interesting light upon the problem, starting from a specific intellectual background and making use of a specific jargon and a specific technical apparatus. However, this volume also shows that interdisciplinary contacts have been rather rare and seldom fruitful. This is not only due to the terminological confusions. More essential are the differences in world view and the differences in methodological requirements and presuppositions, not to say sheer ignorance or arrogance. In this chapter we have tried to show that more interdisciplinary contacts are possible and even necessary.

In Table 7.1 we have structured the field across the descriptive/ethical and the micro/macro dimensions. It is obvious that each of the boxes in the table contains a rather homogeneous set of approaches. Indeed, within each box, there have been intensive contacts. It is interesting to see how the boxes partly cross the boundaries of the disciplines: exchange theory sociologists have a closer intellectual relationship with social psychologists than with their Marxian colleagues; normatively orientated economists feel better at ease with consequentialist philosophers than with their own public choice colleagues.

The contacts between boxes have been much more limited, however. Nevertheless, we have argued that the approaches in different boxes are largely complementary. Ethical theories may inspire, guide and relativize the findings of empirical work. Empirical findings may inspire, guide and relativize ethical constructions. The questions are different and must remain different, but the answers are interrelated.

A number of areas might be fruitful for interdisciplinary research. The technique of game theory is studied not only in economics, but also in psychology, sociology and philosophy. It offers a possible dimension to the study of the choice of criteria of justice in the absence of consensus. Equally, the choice of a specific problem area, such as the allocation of wage increments among a professional group, might help to focus both on the criteria for such allocations (ability, past performance, future promise, etc.) and the consequences for morale, efficiency, and disputes arising from the exercise itself. Although such studies would be primarily empirical, it would be a way of testing ethical intuitions about the requirements of justice and refining them in a concrete way.

We all want to understand the theoretical notion of justice. But at the same time we all care about the world. Anyone who takes seriously his/her own personal notion of justice, will want to realize it, i.e. make the world more just in his/her opinion. The scientific work presented in this volume should help us to put our own personal position in perspective without losing our own ethical drive. In a pluralistic world this is only possible if we emphasize the importance of mutual understanding and respect as cornerstone of justice. Or is this another value?

Bibliography

Abel, R.L. 1980. Redirecting social studies of law. *Law and Society Review* 14, 429–43.

Abel-Smith, B., M. Zander and R. Brooke 1973. *Legal Problems and the Citizen*, London: Weidenfeld and Nicolson.

Abelson, R.P. and D.E. Kanouse 1966. Subjective acceptance of verbal generalizations. In S. Feldman (ed.), *Cognitive Consistency*, New York: Academic Press.

Abercrombie, N., S. Hill and B.S. Turner 1980. *The Dominant Ideology Thesis*, London.

Ackerman, B.A. 1980. *Social Justice in the Liberal State*, New Haven/London: Yale University Press.

Adams, J.S. 1963. Toward an understanding of inequity. *Journal of Abnormal and Social Psychology* 67, 422–36.

1965. Inequity in social exchange. In L. Berkowitz (ed.), *Advances in Experimental Social Psychology*, New York: Academic Press, pp. 267–99.

Adams, J.S. and S. Freedman 1976. Equity theory revisited: comments and annotated bibliography. In L. Berkowitz and G.W. Walster (eds.), *Advances in Experimental Social Psychology*, New York: Academic Press.

Adler, M. and S. Asquith 1981. *Discretion and Welfare*, London.

Ake, C.F. 1975. Justice as equality. *Philosophy and Public Affairs* 5, 69–89.

Alessio, J.C. 1980. Another folly for equity theory. *Social Psychology Quarterly* 43, 336–40.

Alexy, R. 1989. *A Theory of Legal Argumentation: The Theory of Rational Discourse as Theory of Legal Justification*, Oxford: Clarendon Press. A translation of Alexy 1978. *Theorie der juristischen Argumentation: Die Theorie des rationalen Diskurses als Theorie der juristischen Begründung*, Frankfurt am Main: Suhrkamp.

Allott, A. 1980. *The Limits of Law*, London.

Alves, W.M. and P.H. Rossi 1978. Who should get what? Fairness judgements of the distribution of earnings. *American Journal of Sociology* 84, 541–64.

Anderson, B. 1969. Teoretiska synpunkter på rättvisa och jämlikhet (Theoretical considerations on justice and equality). *Sociologisk Forskning* 6, 27–40.

Anderson, B., J. Berger, M. Zelditch Jr and B.P. Cohen 1969. Reactions to inequity. *Acta Sociologica* 12, 1–12.

Anderson, N.H. and A.J. Farkas 1975. Integration theory applied to models of inequity. *Personality and Social Psychology Bulletin* 1, 588–91.

Andrews, I.R. and E.R. Valenzi 1970. Overpay inequity or self-image as worker: a critical examination of an experimental induction procedure. *Organizational Behavior and Human Performance* 5, 266–76.

Arens, P. 1976. Das Problem des Musterprozesses, *Jahrbuch fr Rechtssoziologie und Rechtstheorie* 4, 344ff.

Aristotle 1962. *Nicomachean Ethics*. M. Ostwald (trans.), New York: Bobbs-Merrill (The Library of Liberal Arts).

Arrow, K. 1951. *Social Choice and Individual Values*, New York: Wiley. Revised 1963.

1973. Some ordinalist-utilitarian notes on Rawls's theory of justice. *Journal of Philosophy* 70, 245–63.

1977. Extended sympathy and the possibility of social choice. *American Economic Review* 67, 219–25.

Atiyah, P.S. 1981. *Promises, Morals and the Law*, Oxford: Oxford University Press.

1986. *Essays on Contract*, Oxford: Oxford University Press.

1987. *Accidents, Compensation and the Law*. 4th edn by P. Cane, London: Weidenfeld and Nicolson.

Atkinson, A.B. 1970. On the measurement of inequality. *Journal of Economic Theory* 2, 244–63.

Atkinson, A.B. and J. Stiglitz 1980. *Lectures on Public Economics*, London: McGraw Hill.

Austin, W. 1977. Equity theory and social comparison processes. In J.M. Suls and R.L. Millers (eds.), *Social Comparison Processes*, Washington DC: pp. 279–305.

Austin, W. 1980. Friendship and fairness: effects of type of relationship and task performance on choice of distribution rules. *Personality and Social Psychology Bulletin* 6, 402–7.

Austin, W. and E. Hatfield 1980. Equity theory, power, and social justice. In G. Mikula (ed.), *Justice and Social Interaction. Experimental and Theoretical Contributions from Psychological Research*, New York: Springer-Verlag.

Austin, W. and N.C. McGinn 1977. Sex differences in choice of distribution rules. *Journal of Personality* 45, 379–94.

Austin, W. and E. Walster 1975. Equity with the world: the cross relational effects of equity and inequity. *Sociometry* 38, 474–96.

Bagolini, L. 1980. La giustizia nella crisi, 57 *Rivistà internazionale di filosofia del diritto* 57, 3ff.

1983. *Giustizia e Società*, Rome: CEDAM.

Baker, C.E. 1975. The ideology of the economic analysis of law. *Philosophy and Public Affairs* 5, 3ff.

Baker, J. 1979. From sanctity of contract to reasonable expectation. *Current Legal Problems* 17–39.

Bales, R.F. 1955. Adaptive and integrative changes as sources of strain in social systems. In A.P. Hare and E.F. Borgatta (eds.), *Small Groups: Studies in Social Interaction*, New York: Knopf.

Bardach, E. and R.A. Kagan 1982. *Going by the Book: The Problem of Regulatory Unreasonableness*, Philadelphia.

Baron, R.A. 1977. *Human Aggression*, New York: Plenum.

Barry, B. 1973. *The Liberal Theory of Justice: A Critical Examination of the Principal Doctrines in A Theory of Justice by John Rawls*, Oxford: Clarendon Press.

1975. Review of Robert Nozick's *Anarchy, State, and Utopia*. *Political Theory* 3, 331–6.

1977. Justice between generations. In P.M.S. Hacker and J. Raz (eds.), *Law, Morality, and Society: Essays in Honour of H.L.A. Hart*, Oxford: Clarendon Press, pp. 268–84.

1978. Circumstances of justice and future generations. In R.I. Sikora and B. Barry (eds.), *Obligations to Future Generations*, Philadelphia: Temple University Press, pp. 204–48.

1979. Justice as reciprocity. In Kamenka and Tay (eds.) 1979, pp. 50–78.

1982. Humanity and justice in global perspective. In J.R. Pennock and J.W. Chapman (eds.), *Nomos XXIV: Ethics, Economics, and the Law*, New York and London: New York University Press, pp. 219–52.

1989a. *Democracy, Power, and Justice: Essays in Political Theory*, Oxford: Clarendon Press.

1989b. *A Treatise on Social Justice, Vol. 1: Theories of Justice*, Hemel Hempstead: Harvester-Wheatsheaf.

Barry, B. *et al.* (eds.) 1983. Symposium on Ackerman (1980). *Ethics* 93, 330–90.

Battifol, H., 1979. *Problèmes de base de philosophie du droit*, Paris: LGDJ.

Baumol, W. 1986. *Superfairness*, Cambridge, MA: MIT Press.

Bayles, M.D. 1990. *Procedural Justice: Allocation to Individuals*, Dordrecht: Reidel.

Bayles, M.D. and B. Chapman 1983. *Justice, Rights and Tort Law*, Dordrecht: Reidel.

Beitz, C.R. 1975. Justice and international relations. *Philosophy and Public Affairs* 4, 360-89. Reprinted in Blocker and Smith (eds.) 1980, pp. 211–38.

Bell, J. 1983. *Policy Arguments in Judicial Decisions*, Oxford: Oxford University Press.

Bell, W. and R.V. Robinson 1978. An index of evaluated equality: measuring conceptions of social justice in England and the United States. *Comparative Studies in Sociology* 2, 235–70.

Benn, S.I. and R.S. Peters 1959. *Social Principles and the Democratic State*, London: George Allen and Unwin.

Bennis, W.G. 1966. *Changing Organizations*, New York.

1973. *Beyond Bureaucracy: Essays in the Development and Evolution of Human Organization*, New York.

Benton, A.A. 1971. Productivity, distributive justice, and bargaining among children. *Journal of Personality and Social Psychology* 18, 68–78.

Berg, N.E. and P. Mussen 1975. The origins and development of concepts of justice. *Journal of Social Issues* 31, 183–201.

Berger, J., M. Zelditch Jr., B. Anderson and B.P. Cohen 1972. Structural aspects of distributive justice: a status value formulation. In J. Berger, M. Zelditch Jr and B. Anderson (eds.), *Sociological Theories in Progress*, vol. 2. Boston: Houghton-Mifflin.

Bergson, A. 1938. A reformulation of certain aspects of welfare economics. *Quarterly Journal of Economics* 52, 314–44.

Berkowitz, L. 1972. Social norms, feelings, and other factors affecting helping behavior and altruism. In L. Berkowitz and E. Walster (eds.), *Advances in Experimental Social Psychology*, vol. 6. New York: Academic Press.

Berkowitz, L. and E. Walster (eds.) 1976. *Equity theory: Toward a General Theory of Social Interaction. Advances in Experimental Social Psychology*, vol. 9. New York: Academic Press.

Berting, J. 1970. *Reciprociteit en Gelijkheid*. Sociologen over Sociale Rechtvaardigheid, Meppel.

Bierhoff, H.W., E. Buck and R. Klein 1986. Social context and perceived justice. In H.W. Bierhoff, R.L. Cohen and J. Greenberg (eds.) 1986.

Bierhoff, H.W., R.L. Cohen and J. Greenberg (eds.) 1986. *Justice in Social Relations*, New York: Plenum Press.

Billig, M. 1976. *Social Psychology and Intergroup Relations*. New York: Academic Press.

Blalock, H.M. Jr and P.H. Wilken 1979. *Intergroup Processes. A Micro–Macro Perspective*, New York: The Free Press.

Blankenburg, E. 1976. Rechtsberatung als Hilfe und Barriers auf dem Weg zum Recht, *Zeitschrift für Rechtspolitik*, 93ff.

1980. Mobilisierung von Recht, *Zeitschrift der Rechtssoziologie* 1, 3ff.

Blau, P.M. 1955. *The Dynamics of Bureaucracy*, Chicago.
  1964a. Justice in social exchange. *Sociological Inquiry* 34, 193–206.
  1964b. *Exchange and Power in Social Life*, New York: John Wiley.
Blau, P.M. and O. D. Duncan 1967. *The American Occupational Structure*, New York.
Blessing, M. 1973. Aspekte existentiellen Rechtsdenkens. Thesis, University of Zurich.
Blocker, H.G. and E.H. Smith (eds.) 1980. *John Rawls' Theory of Social Justice: An Introduction*. Athens, OH: Ohio University Press.
Blumstein, P. and E. Weinstein 1969. The redress of distributive injustice. *American Journal of Sociology* 74, 408–18.
Boadway, R. and N. Bruce 1984. *Welfare Economics*, Oxford: Basil Blackwell.
Boulding, K.E. 1962. Social justice in social dynamics. In R. Brandt (ed.), *Social Justice*, Englewood Cliffs, NJ: Prentice-Hall Inc., pp. 73–92.
Bowden, M. and M.P. Zanna 1978. Perceived relationship, sex-role orientation, and gender differences in reward allocation. Paper presented at the annual meeting of the American Psychological Association, Toronto.
Brenkert, G.G. 1979. Freedom and private property in Marx. In Cohen *et al.* 1980, pp. 80–105.
Brennan, G. 1973. Pareto desirable redistribution: the non-altruistic dimension. *Public Choice* 14, 43–68.
Breyer, S. 1982. *Regulation and its Reform*, Cambridge, MA.
Brickman, P. 1977. Preference for inequality. *Sociometry* 40, 303–10.
Brickman, P., R. Folger, E. Goode and Y. Schul 1981. Microjustice and macrojustice. In M.J. Lerner and S.C. Lerner (eds.), *The Justice Motive in Social Behavior: Adapting to Times of Scarcity and Change*, New York: Plenum Press.
Broekman, J.M. 1986. Justice as equilibrium. *Law and Philosophy* 5, 369–91.
Broome, J.A. 1978. Choice and value in economics. *Oxford Economic Papers* 30, 313–33.
Brown, A. 1986. *Modern Political Philosophy: Theories of the Just Society*, Harmondsworth: Penguin.
Brownsword, R. 1988. Liberalism and the Law of Contract, *ARSP* Beiheft 36, 86–100.
Buch, H. 1971. L'Egalité dans les principes générauz du droit. In H. Buch *et al.* (eds.), *Egalité*, Brussels: Bruylant, vol. I, 196ff.
Buchanan, A.E. 1982. *Marx and Justice: The Radical Critique of Liberalism*, Totowa, NJ: Rowman and Littlefield; London: Methuen.
Buchanan, A. and D. Mathieu 1986. Philosophy and justice. In R.L. Cohen 1986.
Buchanan, J. 1975. *The Limits of Liberty*, Chicago: University of Chicago Press.
  1986. *Liberty, Market and State*, Brighton: Wheatsheaf Books.
Buchanan, J. and G. Tullock 1962. *The Calculus of Consent*, Ann Arbor: University of Michigan Press.
Burgess, R.L. and J. McCarl Nielsen 1974. An experimental analysis of some structural determinants of equitable and inequitable exchange relations. *American Sociological Review* 39, 427–43.
Burke, J.P. 1986. *Bureaucratic Responsibility*, Baltimore.
Caddick, B. 1980. Equity theory, social identity, and intergroup relations. In L. Wheeler (ed.), *Review of Personality and Social Psychology*, Beverley Hills, CA: Sage Publications, vol. 1.
Calabresi, G. 1970. *The Cost of Accidents*, New Haven: Yale University Press.
  1980. About law and economics: a letter to Ronald Dworkin. *Hofstra Law Review* 8, 553ff.

Calabresi, G. and P. Bobbitt 1978. *Tragic Choices*. New York: W.W. Norton.
Campbell, T.D. 1988. *Justice*. Basingstoke and London: Macmillan Education.
Cane, P. 1982. Justice and justifications for tort liability. *Oxford Journal of Legal Studies* 2, 30–62.
Cappelletti, M. and B. Garth 1978. *Access to Justice*, Milan: Giuffrè.
Cappelletti, M., J. Gordley and E. Johnson 1975. *Towards Equal Justice: A Comparative Study of Legal Aid in Modern Societies*, Milan and Dobbs Ferry: Giuffrè.
Carles, E.M. and C.S. Carver 1979. Effects of person salience versus role salience on reward allocation in a dyad. *Journal of Personality and Social Psychology* 37, 2071–80.
Cavalli-Sforza, L.L. and M.W. Feldman 1981. *Cultural Transmission and Evolution: A Quantitative Approach*. Princeton, NJ: Princeton University Press.
Chagnon, N.A. and W. Irons (eds.) 1979. *Evolutionary Biology and Human Social Behavior: An Anthropological Perspective*, North Scituate, MA: Duxbury Press.
Clark, M.S. 1981. Noncomparability of benefits given and received: a cue to the existence of friendship. *Social Psychology Quarterly* 44: 375–81.
Clark, M.S. and J. Mills 1979. Interpersonal attraction in exchange and communal relationships. *Journal of Personality and Social Psychology* 37, 12–24.
Cohen, G. A. 1981. Freedom, justice and capitalism. *New Left Review* 126, 3–16.
    1985. Nozick on appropriation. In *New Left Review* 150, 89–105.
    1986b. Self-ownership, world ownership and equality. *Social Philosophy and Policy* 3, 77–96.
Cohen, J.A. 1967. Chinese mediation on the eve of modernization. In D. Buxbaum (ed.), *Traditional and Modern Institutions in Asia and Africa*, Leiden: Brill, pp. 54ff.
Cohen, M. et al. (eds.) 1980. *Marx, Justice, and History*, Princeton, NJ: Princeton University Press.
Cohen, R. L. 1974. Mastery and justice in laboratory dyads: a revision and extension of equity theory. *Journal of Personality and Social Psychology* 29, 464–74.
    1979. On the distinction between individual deserving and distributive justice. *Journal of the Theory of Social Behaviour* 9, 167–85.
    1982. Perceiving justice: an attributional perspective. In J. Greenberg and R.L. Cohen 1982, pp. 110–60.
    1986a. Power and justice in intergroup relations. In H.W. Bierhoff, R.L. Cohen and J. Greenberg (eds.), *Justice in Social Relations*, New York: Plenum Press.
Cohen, R.L. (ed.) 1986c. *Justice: Views from the Social Sciences*, New York: Plenum Press.
Cohen, R.L. and J. Greenberg 1982. The justice concept in social psychology. In J. Greenberg and R.L. Cohen 1982.
Coing, H. 1985. *Grundzüge der Rechtsphilosophie*, 4th edn, Berlin: de Gruyter.
Coleman, J. and E.F. Paul (eds.) 1987. *Philosophy and Law*, Oxford: Blackwell.
Collard, D. 1978. *Altruism and Economy*, Oxford: Martin Robertson.
Cook, K.S. and K.A. Hegtvedt 1983. Distributive justice, equity, and equality. *Annual Review of Sociology* 9, 217–41.
    1986. Justice and power. An exchange analysis. In H.W. Bierhoff, R.L. Cohen and J. Greenberg (eds.), *Justice in Social Relations*, New York: Plenum Press.
Cook, K.S. and T.L. Parcel 1977. Equity theory: directions for future research. *Sociological Inquiry* 47, 75–88.
Cook, K.S. and T. Yamagishi 1983. Social determinants of equity judgments: the problem of multidimensional input. In D.M. Messick and K.S. Cook 1983.
Coon, R.C., I.M. Lane and R.J. Lichtman 1974. Sufficiency of reward and allocation behavior. *Human Development* 17, 301–13.

Coope, C. 1988. A Comment on Brownsword. *ARSP* Beiheft 36, 101–22.

Cooter, R. and P. Rappoport 1984. Were the ordinalists wrong about welfare economics? *Journal of Economic Literature* 22, 507–30.

Cosier, R.A. and D.R. Dalton 1983. Equity theory and time: a reformulation. *Academy of Management Review* 8, 311–19.

Crittenden, K.S. 1983. Sociological aspects of attribution. *Annual Review of Sociology* 9, 425–46.

Crosby, F. and A.M. Gonzalez-Intal 1984. Relative deprivation and equity theories. Felt injustice and the undeserved benefits of others. In R. Folger 1984.

Dabin, J. 1969. *Théorie générale du droit*, 3rd edn, Paris: Dalloz. 1st edn 1944 translated as General theory of law, in K. Wilk and E.W. Patterson (eds.) 1950, *The Legal Philosophies of Lask, Radbruch, and Dabin*, Cambridge, MA: Harvard University Press, pp. 225–470.

D'Agostino, F. 1978. Dimensioni dell'equità, Turin: Giappuchelli.

Dahrendorf, R. 1959. *Class and Class Conflict in Industrial Society*, Stanford, CA: Stanford University Press.

Daly, J. 1988. Marx, justice and dialectic. *Irish Philosophical Journal* 5, 72–110.

D'Amato, A. 1983. Legal uncertainty. *California Law Review* 71, 1–55.

1984. *Jurisprudence: A Descriptive and Normative Analysis*, Nijhoff, Dordrecht.

Damon, W. 1975. Early conceptions of positive justice as related in the development of logical operations. *Child Development* 46, 301–12.

1977. *The Social World of the Child*, San Francisco: Jossey-Bass.

Daniels, N. 1975a. Equal liberty and unequal worth of liberty. In Daniels 1975b, pp. 253–81.

Daniels, N. (ed.) 1975b. *Reading Rawls: Critical Studies on Rawls' A Theory of Justice*, New York: Basic Books; Oxford: Blackwell.

Darwall, S.L. 1980. Is there a Kantian foundation for Rawlsian justice? In Blocker and Smith (eds.) 1980, pp. 311–45.

D'Aspremont, C. 1985. Axioms for social welfare orderings. In L. Hurwicz, D. Schmeidler and H. Sonnenschein (eds.), *Social Goals and Social Organization: Essays in Memory of Elisha Pazner*, Cambridge: Cambridge University Press, pp. 19–76.

D'Aspremont, C. and L. Gevers 1977. Equity and the Informational Basis of Collective Choice. *Review of Economic Studies* 44, 199–209.

Davis, K. and W.E. Moore 1945. Some principles of stratification. *American Sociological Review* 10, 242–9.

1953. Reply and comment, *American Sociological Review* 18, 394–7.

Davis, K.C. 1971. *Discretionary Justice, A Preliminary Inquiry*, Baton Rouge, IL.

1975, *Police Discretion*, St Paul, Minn.

Day, P. 1985. Procedural Justice. *ARSP* Beiheft 21, 51ff.

Debusschère, M. and E. van Avermaet 1984. Compromising between equity and equality: the effects of situational ambiguity and computational complexity. *European Journal of Social Psychology* 14, 323–33.

Del Vecchio, G. 1955. *La Justice*, Paris: LGDJ.

Delivery of Legal Services 1976. *Law and Society Review* 11, 2nd series.

DeMarco, J.P. 1980. Rawls and Marx. In Blocker and Smith (eds.) 1980, pp. 395–430.

Deutsch, M. 1968. The effects of cooperation and competition upon group process. In C. Cartwright and A. Zander (eds.), *Group Dynamics*, New York: Harper and Row.

1975. Equity, equality and need: what determines which value will be used as the basis of distributive justice? *Journal of Social Issues* 31, 137–49.

1983. Current social psychological perspectives on justice. *European Journal of Social Psychology* 13, 305–19.

1985. *Distributive Justice: A Social-Psychological Perspective*, New Haven, CT: Yale University Press.

DeVos, G.A. and A.A. Hippler 1969. Cultural psychology: comparative studies of human behavior. In G. Lindzey and E. Aronson (eds.), *The Handbook of Social Psychology*, Vol. 4. Reading, MA: Addison-Wesley.

Diver, C.S. 1980. A theory of regulatory enforcement. *Public Policy* 28, 257–99.

Donnenwerth, G.V. 1971. Effect of resources on retaliation to loss. Unpublished doctoral dissertation. University of Missouri, Columbia, Missouri.

Dreier, R. 1974. Zur Luhmanns systemtheoretischer Neuformulierung des Gerechtigkeitsproblem, *Rechtstheorie* 5, 189ff.

Drèze, J. 1979. Human capital and risk-bearing. *Geneva Papers on Risk and Insurance* 12, 1–22.

Duncan, O.D., B.L. Featherman and B. Duncan 1973. *Socioeconomic Background and Achievement*, New York.

Dworkin, R. 1977a. Justice and rights. In R. Dworkin, *Taking Rights Seriously*, London: Duckworth, pp. 150–83. A revised version of Dworkin's review of Rawls (1971), which is also reprinted in Daniels 1975b, pp. 16–53.

1977b. The model of rules. In Dworkin 1977a, pp. 14–80.

1978. *Taking Rights Seriously*, London: Duckworth. Second edition.

1980. Is wealth a value? *Journal of Legal Studies* 9, 191–226.

1981. What is equality? Part 1: Equality of Welfare, Part 2: Equality of Resources. *Philosophy and Public Affairs* 10, 185–246 and 283–345.

1983. In defense of equality. *Social Philosophy and Policy* 1, 24–40.

1985a. What justice isn't. In R. Dworkin 1985b, pp. 214–20.

1985b. *A Matter or Principle*, Cambridge, MA and London: Harvard University Press.

Eckhoff, T. 1974. *Justice: Its Determinants in Social Interaction*, Rotterdam: Rotterdam University Press.

Eijsbouts, W.T. 1986. Over de taal van het beleid. In J.W. de Beus and J.A.A. van Doorn (eds.), *De Geconstrueerde Samenleving*, Meppel, pp. 49–61.

Elliot, G.C. and B.F. Meeker 1984. Modifiers of the equity effect: group outcome and causes for individual performance. *Journal of Personality and Social Psychology* 46, 586–97.

1986. Achieving fairness in the face of competing concerns: the different effects of individual and group characteristics. *Journal of Personality and Social Psychology* 50, 754–60.

Elster, J. 1982. Sour grapes – utilitarianism and the genesis of wants. In A. Sen and B. Williams 1982, pp. 219–38.

1985. *Making Sense of Marx*, Cambridge: Cambridge University Press.

Farkas, A.J. and N.H. Anderson 1979. Multidimensional input in equity theory. *Journal of Personality and Social Psychology* 37, 879–96.

Feeley, M.M. 1976. The concept of laws in social science: a critique and notes on an expanded view. *Law and Society Review* 10, 497–523.

Feinberg, J. 1970. Justice and personal desert. In J. Feinberg, *Doing and Deserving: Essays in the Theory of Responsibility*, Princeton, NJ: Princeton University Press, pp. 55–94.

1980. *Rights, Justice and the Bounds of Liberty*, Princeton, NJ: Princeton University Press.

Festinger, L. 1954. A theory of social comparison processes. *Human Relations* 7, 117–40.

1957. *A Theory of Cognitive Dissonance*, Evanston, IL: Row, Peterson.

Fikentscher, W. 1977. *Methoden des Rechts in vergleichender Darstellung*, vol. 4 (Tübingen: Möhr).

Finnis, J. 1980. *Natural Law and Natural Rights*. Oxford: Clarendon Press.

Fishkin, J.S. 1983. *Justice, Equal Opportunity, and the Family*, New Haven and London: Yale University Press.

Fiske, S.T. 1980. Attention and weight in person perception: the impact of negative and extreme behavior. *Journal of Personality and Social Psychology* 38, 889–906.

Fiske, S.T. and S.E. Taylor 1984. *Social Cognition*. New York: Random House.

Fletcher, G.P. 1985. The Right and the Reasonable. *Harvard Law Review* 98, 949–82.

Foa, U.G. 1971. Interpersonal and economic resources. *Science* 71, 345–51.

Foa, U.G. and G. Stein 1980. Rules of distributive justice: institution and resource influences. *Academic Psychology Bulletin* 2, 89–94.

Földesi, T. 1977. Die Arten der gerechtigkeit. *Annales Universitatis Scientiarum Budapestiensis* 19, 17ff.

Foley, D. 1967. Resource allocation and the public sector. *Yale Economic Essays* 7, 45–99.

Folger, R. (ed.) 1984. *The Sense of Injustice: Social Psychological Perspectives*. New York: Plenum Press.

Fried, C. 1981. *Contract as Promise*, Cambridge, MA: Harvard University Press.

Friedman, A. and P. Goodman 1967. Wage inequity, self-qualifications, and productivity. *Organizational Behavior and Human Performance* 2, 406–17.

Friedman, L.M. 1975. *The Legal System: A Social Science Perspective*, New York.

1985. *Total Justice*, New York: Prentice-Hall.

Friedman, M. 1962. *Capitalism and Freedom*, Chicago: University of Chicago Press.

Fuller, L. 1964. *The Morality of Law*, New Haven, CT.

Fuller, L. and L. Perdue 1936. The reliance interest in contract damages. *Yale Law Journal* 46, 52–96, 373–420.

Furby, L. 1986. Psychology and justice. In Cohen 1986c.

Gans, H.J. 1974. *More Equality*, New York: Vintage Books.

Garcia, J.L.A. 1986. Two concepts of desert. *Law and Philosophy* 5, 219–35.

Garrett, J. and W.L. Libby Jr. 1973. Role of intentionality in mediating responses to inequity in the dyad. *Journal of Personality and Social Psychology* 28, 21–7.

Gauthier, D. 1974. Justice and natural endowment: toward a critique of Rawls' ideological framework. *Social Theory and Practice* 3, 3–26.

1985. Bargaining and justice. *Social Philosophy and Policy* 2, 29–47.

1986. *Morals by Agreement*, Oxford: Clarendon Press.

Geras, N. 1985. The controversy about Marx and justice. *New Left Review* 150, 47–85.

Gergen, K.J., S.J. Morse and M.M. Gergen 1980. Behavior exchange in a cross-cultural perspective. In H.C. Triandis and R.W. Breslin (eds.), *Handbook of Cross-Cultural Psychology*, vol. 5. Boston, MA: Allyn and Bacon.

Gerling, M. and I. Wender 1981. Gerechtigkeitskonzepte und Aufteilungsverhalten von Vorschulkindern. *Zeitschrift für Entwicklungspsychologie und Pädagogische Psychologie* 13, 236–50.

Gerth, H.H. and C.W. Mills 1948. *For Max Weber: Essays in Sociology*, London.

Gewirth, A. 1971. The justification of egalitarian justice. *American Philosophical Quarterly* 8, 331–41.

Ghestin, J. 1980. *Droit civil: le contrat*, Paris: LGDJ.

Ghestin, J. and J. Goubeaux 1982. *Droit civil: introduction*, 2nd edn, Paris: LGDJ.

Giddens, A. 1982. *Sociology: A Brief but Critical Introduction*, London.

Gilbert, N. and H. Specht 1974. *Dimensions of Social Welfare Policy*, Englewood Cliffs, NJ.

Ginsberg, M. 1965. *On Justice in Society*, New York.

Goldman, A.H. 1979. *Justice and Reverse Discrimination*, Princeton, NJ: Princeton University Press.

Goldman, A.I. and J. Kim (eds.), 1978. *Values and Morals: Essays in Honor of William Frankena, Charles Stevenson, and Richard Brandt*, Dordrecht, Boston and London: Reidel.

Goldman, H.S. 1980. Rawls and utilitarianism. In Blocker and Smith 1980, pp. 346–94.

Goode, W.J. 1978. *The Celebration of Heroes: prestige as a Control System*, Berkeley, CA: University of California Press.

Goodin, R. 1979. Loose laws: the ethics of vagueness versus the politics of precision. *Philosophica* 23, 79–96.

    1985. Negating positive desert claims. *Political Theory* 13, 575–98.

Goodin, R. and J. Le Grand 1986. Creeping universalism in the welfare state: evidence from Australia. *Journal of Public Policy* 6.

Goodman, P.S. 1974. An examination of referents used in the evaluation of pay. *Organizational Behavior and Human Performance* 12, 170–95.

Goodman, P.S. and A. Friedman 1971. An examination of Adams' theory of inequity. *Administrative Science Quarterly* 16, 271–88.

Goranson, R.E. and L. Berkowitz 1966. Reciprocity and responsibility reactions to prior help. *Journal of Personality and Social Psychology* 3, 227–32.

Gorman, W. 1976. Tricks with utility functions. In M. Artis and R. Nobay (eds.), *Essays in Economic Analysis*, Cambridge: Cambridge University Press, pp. 211–43.

Gouldner, A.W. 1960. The norm of reciprocity: a preliminary statement. *American Sociological Review* 25, 161–78.

Graziano, W.G. 1987. Lost in thought at the choice point: cognition, context, and equity. In J.C. Masters and W.P. Smith (eds.), *Social Comparison, Social Justice, and Relative Deprivation. Theoretical, Empirical, and Policy Perspectives*, Hillsdale, NJ: Erlbaum.

Green, S.J.D. 1989. Emile Durkheim on human talents and two traditions of social justice. *The British Journal of Sociology* 40, 97–117.

Greenberg, J. 1978a. Equity, equality, and the protestant ethic: allocating rewards following fair and unfair competition. *Journal of Experimental Social Psychology* 14, 217–26.

    1978b. Allocator-recipient similarity and the equitable division of rewards. *Social Psychology* 41, 337–41.

    1979. Scarcity and the distributive fairness of natural resource allocation. Paper presented at the meeting of the Southwestern Psychological Association, New Orleans, March 1979.

    1981. The justice of distributing scarce and abundant resources. In Lerner and Lerner 1981.

    1983. Equity and equality as clues to the relationship between exchange participants. *European Journal of Social Psychology* 13, 195–6.

Greenberg, J. and R.L. Cohen (eds.) 1982a. *Equity and Justice in Social Behavior*. New York: Academic Press.

    1982b. Why justice? Normative and instrumental interpretations. In Greenberg and Cohen 1982a.

Greenberg, J., M.M. Mark and D.A. Lehman 1985. Justice in sports and games. *Journal of Sport Behavior* 8, 18–33.

Griffith, W.I. 1989. The allocation of negative outcomes: examining the issues. In E.E. Lawler and B. Markovsky (eds.), *Advances in Group Processes* vol. 6, Greenwich, CT: JAI Press.

Griffith, W.I. and J. Sell 1988. The effects of competition on allocators' preferences for contributive and retributive justice rules. *European Journal of Social Psychology* 18, 443–55.

Grisez, G. and J. Boyle 1982. *Life and Death with Liberty and Justice*, Notre Dame, IN: Notre Dame University Press.

Groenendaal, T. van 1986. *Dilemma's van regelgeving: de regularisatie van buitenlandse werknemers 1975–1985*, Alphen a.d.: Rijn and Utrecht.

Grumbkow, J. von 1977. Verdeling van positieve en negatieve beloningen. *Mens en Onderneming* 31, 285–94.

   1985. Power strategies and the equitable allocation of positive and negative sanctions. Mimeo.

Grumbkow, J. von, E. Deen, H. Steensma and H. Wilke 1976. The effect of future interaction on the distribution of rewards. *European Journal of Social Psychology* 6, 119–23.

Grumbkow, J. von, H. Steensma and H. Wilke 1977. Toewijzen van beloningen in aanwezigheid van de proefleider. *Nederlands Tijdschrift voor de Psychologie* 32, 495–500.

Grunow, D. and F. Hegner (eds.) 1980. Welfare or Bureaucracy? Problems of Matching Social Services to Clients' Needs, Cambridge, MA.

Gruter, M. and P. Bohannan (eds.) 1983. *Law, Biology, and Culture: The Evolution of Law*, Santa Barbara, CA: Ross-Erikson.

Grzegorcyzk, C. 1982. *La théorie générale des valeurs et le droit*, Paris: LGDJ.

Grzelak, J.L. 1985. Money isn't everything: differential effects of type of values upon social orientations. Department of Psychology, University of Warsaw, unpublished manuscript.

Guest, S. and A. Milne (eds.) 1985. *Equality and Discrimination: Essays in Freedom and Justice*, ARSP, Beiheft 21, Stuttgart: Steiner.

Gunsteren, H. van 1976. *The Quest for Control*, London.

Gunzburger, W.W., D.M. Wegner and L. Anooshian 1977. Moral judgment and distributive justice. *Human Development* 20, 160–70.

Haarscher, G. 1986. Perelman and Habermas. *Law and Philosophy* 5, 331–42.

Habermas, J. 1973. Wahrheitstheorien. In H. Fahrenbach (ed.), *Wirklichkeit und Reflexion: Walter Schulz zum 60. Geburtstag*, Pfullingen: Neske, pp. 211–65.

   1983. *Moralbewusstsein und kommunikatives Handeln*, Frankfurt am Main: Suhrkamp.

Hamilton, D. and M. Zanna 1972. Differential weighting of favorable and unfavorable attributes in impression of personality. *Journal of Experimental Research in Personality* 6, 204–12.

Hamilton, V.L. and S. Rytina 1980. Social consensus on norms of justice: should the punishment fit the crime? *American Journal of Sociology* 85, 1117–44.

Hammond, P. 1976. Equity, Arrow's Conditions and Rawls' Difference Principle. *Econometrica* 44, 793–800.

   1982. Utilitarianism, uncertainty and information. In Sen and Williams 1982, pp. 85–102.

Hampshire, S. 1982. Morality and convention. In Sen and Williams 1982, pp. 145–57.

Hamson, J. 1973. Reply to Tunc, *Cambridge Law Journal* 52.

Handler, J.F. 1979. *Protecting the Social Service Client: Legal and Structural Controls on Official Discretion*, New York.

Hardin, G. 1968. The tragedy of the commons. *Science* 162, 1243–8.

Harris, D. and D. Tallon 1989. *Contract Law Today*, Oxford: Oxford University Press.

Harris, R.J. 1976. Handling negative inputs: on the plausible equity formulae. *Journal of Experimental Social Psychology* 12, 194–209.

1983. Pinning down the equity formula. In D.M. Messick and K.S. Cook (eds.), *Equity Theory: Psychological and Sociological Perspectives*, New York: Praeger Publishers.

Harsanyi, J.C. 1953. Cardinal utility in welfare economics and in the theory of risk-taking. *Journal of Political Economy* 61, 434–5.

1955. Cardinal welfare, individualistic ethics and interpersonal comparisons of utility. *Journal of Political Economy* 63, 309–21.

1975. Can the maximin principle serve as a basis for morality? A critique of John Rawls's theory. *American Political Science Review* 69, 594–606. Reprinted in J.C. Harsanyi (1976).

1976. *Essays on Ethics, Social Behaviour and Scientific Explanation*, Dordrecht, Boston and London: Reidel.

1982. Morality and the theory of rational behaviour. In A. Sen and B. Williams 1982, pp. 39–62.

Hart, H.L.A. 1961. *The Concept of Law*, Oxford: Clarendon Press.

1963. *Punishment and Responsibility*, Oxford: Oxford University Press.

1973. Rawls on liberty and its priority. In Daniels 1975b, pp. 230–52 (references in chapter 2 are to this version); and in Hart 1983b. *Essays in Jurisprudence and Philosophy*, Oxford: Clarendon Press, pp. 223–47. See the response in Rawls 1982b.

1983a. *Essays in Legal Philosophy*, Oxford: Oxford University Press.

Hartkamp, A.S. 1984. In *Asser's Handleiding tot de Beofening van het Nederlands Burgerlijk Recht: Verbintnissenrecht* vol. 1, 7th edn, Zwolle: Tjeenk Willink.

Harvey, J.H., W.J. Ickes and R.F. Kidd (eds.) 1976, 1978, 1981. *New Directions in Attribution Research*, vols. 1–3, Hillsdale, NJ: Erlbaum.

Hassebrauck, M. 1984. Die Beeinflussung von Reaktionen auf distributive Ungerechtigkeit durch die Art der Sozialbeziehung. *Zeitschrift für Sozialpsychologie* 15, 278–89.

1985. Retributive und distributive Gerechtigkeit im Aufteilungsverhalten von Kindern. *Zeitschrift für Entwicklungspsychologie und Pädagogische Psychologie* 17, 164–71.

1987. The influence of misattributions on reactions to inequity: towards a further understanding of inequity. *European Journal of Social Psychology* 17, 295–304.

Hauser, R.M. and B.L. Featherman 1977. *The Process of Stratification. Trends and Analysis*, New York.

Havelock, E.A. 1978. *The Greek Concept of Justice: From Its Shadow in Homer to Its Substance in Plato*, Cambridge, MA and London: Harvard University Press.

Hayek, F. 1976. *The Mirage of Social Justice*, London: Routledge and Kegan Paul.

Heider, F. 1944. Social perception and phenomenal causality. *Psychological Review* 51, 358–74.

Henf, F. 1978. Billigkeit und Zivilrichterliche Argumentation. Thesis, Kiel University.

Hennipman, P. 1981. De verdeling in de Paretiaanse welvaartstheorie. In P.J. Eijgelshoven and L.J. van Gemerden (eds.), *Inkomensverdeling en openbare financiën*, Utrecht: Het Spectrum, pp. 128–70.

1987. A tale of two schools: comments on a new view of the ordinalist revolution. *De Economist* 135, 141–62.

Hermkens, P.L.J. 1983. *Oordelen over de Rechtvaardigheid van Inkomen*, Amsterdam: Cobra.

Herrmann, T. 1971. 'Prescriptive' and 'proscriptive' conformity as a result of childhood training. *European Journal of Social Psychology* 1, 140ff.

Hewstone, M. (ed.) 1983. *Attribution Theory: Social and Functional Extensions*, Oxford: Blackwell.

Hobhouse, L.T. 1922. *The Elements of Social Justice*, London.

Hochschild, J. 1981. *What's Fair? American Beliefs about Distributive Justice*. Cambridge, MA: Harvard University Press.

Hodges, B. 1974. Effect of valence on relative weighting in impression formation. *Journal of Personality and Social Psychology* 30, 378–81.

Hof, H. 1983. Verhaltensforschung zum Recht. *Rechtstheorie* 14, 349–73.

Hogan, R. and N.P. Emler 1981. Retributive justice. In Lerner and Lerner 1981.

Hogg, M.A. and D. Abrams. *Social Identifications. A Social Psychology of Intergroup Relations and Group Processes*, London: Routledge.

Homans, G.C. 1958. Social behavior as exchange. *American Journal of Sociology* 63, 447–58.

1961. *Social Behavior. Its Elementary Forms*, New York: Harcourt Brace. Revised edn 1974.

1964. Bringing men back in. *American Sociological Review* 29, 807–18.

1974. *Social Behavior. Its Elementary Forms*, New York. Revised edition.

1976. Commentary. In Berkowitz and Walster 1976.

1982. Foreword. In Greenberg and Cohen 1982a.

Honoré, A. 1987. *Making Law Bind*, Oxford: Oxford University Press.

Hook, J.G. and T.D. Cook 1979. Equity theory and the cognitive ability of children. *Psychological Bulletin* 86, 429–45.

Howard, J.A. and K.C. Pike 1986. Ideological investment in cognitive processing: the influence of social statuses on attribution. *Social Psychology Quarterly* 49, 154–67.

Huaco. G.A. 1966. The functionalist theory of stratification: two decades of controversy. *Inquiry* 9, 215–40.

Husami, Z.I. 1978. Marx on distributive justice. In Cohen *et al.* 1980, pp. 42–79. See reply in Wood 1979.

Huseman, R.C., J.D. Hatfield and E.W. Miles 1987. A new perspective on equity theory: the equity sensitivity construct. *Academy of Management Review* 12, 222–34.

Hutchinson, A.C. 1981. The formal and informal schemes of the civil justice system: a legal symbiosis explored. *Osgoode Hall Law Journal* 19, 473ff.

Hyman, R. and I. Brough 1975. *Social Values and Industrial Relations*, Oxford.

Ingram, P. 1985. Procedural equality, *ARSP* 21, 39ff.

Jäger, R. 1979. Die Gerechtigkeit: Masstab oder Steuerungssystem? Thesis, Munich University.

Jakob, R. 1980. Gerechtigkeit und Gerechtigkeitsvorstellungen. *ARSP* Beiheft 13, 155ff.

Jasso, G. 1978. On the justice of earnings: a new specification of the justice evaluation function. *American Journal of Sociology* 83, 1398–419.

1980. A new theory of distributive justice. *American Sociological Review* 45, 3–32.

1981. Further notes on the theory of distributive justice. *American Sociological Review* 46, 352–60.

1983. Fairness of individual rewards and fairness of the reward distribution: specifying the inconsistency between micro and macro principles of justice. *Social Psychology Quarterly* 46, 185–99.

1986. A new representation of the just term in distributive-justice theory: its properties and operation in theoretical derivation and empirical estimation. *Journal of Mathematical Sociology* 12, 251–74.

Jasso, G. and P.H. Rossi 1977. Distributive justice and earned income. *American Sociological Review* 42, 639–51.

Jestaz, P. 1972. Equité, in *Encyclopédie Dalloz*, Paris: Dalloz.

Jhering, R. von 1884. Über die Entstehung des Rechtsgefühls, *Österreichliche Juristenzeitung* 7. Reprinted 1986 by Jovene in Naples.

Jonsson, D.R. and K.Y. Törnblom 1983a. *Interpreting the Linear Equity Formula: A Comment on Harris et al.*, Technical report no. 5, Resources and Relations series, University of Göteborg.

1983b. *The Elusive Equity Equation: In Search of a Generalization of Adams' Ratio Formula*, Technical report no. 6, Resources and Relations series, University of Göteborg.

1984a. *The Integration of Two Formal Approaches to the Assessment of Fairness*, Technical report no. 6, Resources and Relations series, University of Göteborg.

1984b. *The Conception of Justice: Towards a Coherent Analytical Framework*, Technical report no. 14, Resources and Relations series, University of Göteborg.

Kagan, R. 1978. *Regulatory Justice: Implementing a Wage-Price Freeze*, New York.

Kahn, A., H. Lamm and R.E. Nelson 1977. Preferences for an equal or equitable allocator. *Journal of Personality and Social Psychology* 35, 837–44.

Kahn, A., R.E. Nelson and W.P. Gaeddert 1980. Sex of subject and sex composition of the group as determinants of reward allocations. *Journal of Personality and Social Psychology* 38, 737–50.

Kahn, A. and T.E. Tice 1973. Returning a favor and retaliating harm: the effects of stated intentions and actual behavior. *Journal of Experimental Social Psychology* 9, 43–56.

Kahneman, D., J. Knetsch and R. Thaler 1986. Fairness as a constraint on profit seeking: entitlements in the market. *American Economic Review* 76, 728–41.

Kahneman, D. and A. Tversky 1982. The psychology of preferences. *Scientific American* 246, 160–73.

Kamenka, E. and A.E. Tay (eds.) 1979. *Justice*. London: Edward Arnold.

Karuza, J. and G.S. Leventhal 1976. Justice judgments: role demands and perception of fairness. Paper presented at the meeting of the American Psychological Association, Washington, DC, September.

Katz, M.G. and L.A. Messé 1973. A sex difference in the distribution of rewards. Paper presented at the meeting of the Midwestern Psychological Association, Chicago, May.

Katzmann, R.A. 1980. *Regulatory Bureaucracy: The Federal Trade Commission and Antitrust Policy*, Cambridge, MA.

Kaufmann, F.Z., G. Majone and V. Ostrom (eds.) 1986. *Guidance, Control and Evaluation in the Public Sector*, New York.

Kawashima, T. 1967. Dispute resolution in contemporary Japan. In A.T. von Mehren (ed.), *Law in Japan: The Legal Order in a Changing Society*, Cambridge, MA: Harvard University Press, pp. 41ff.

Kayser, E. 1983. *Laymen's Social Psychologies: The Inference from Social Behaviors to Group Type*. Bericht aus dem Sonderforschungsbereich 24: Universität Mannheim.

Kayser, E., M. Feeley and H. Lamm 1982. *Laienpsychologie sozialer Beziehungen: Vorstellungen über gerechtes und tatsächliches Verhalten*. Bericht aus dem Sonderforschungsbereich 24: Universität Mannheim.

Kayser, E. and H. Lamm 1980. Input integration and input weighting in decisions on allocations of gains and losses. *European Journal of Social Psychology* 10, 1–15.

1981. Causal explanation of performance differences and allocations among friends. *The Journal of Social Psychology* 115, 73–81.

Kayser, E. and T. Schwinger 1982. A theoretical analysis of the relationship among individual justice concepts, layman psychology and distribution decisions. *Journal for the Theory of Social Behavior* 12, 47–51.

Kayser, E., T. Schwinger and R.L. Cohen 1984. Laypersons' conceptions of social relationships: a test of contract theory. *Journal of Social and Personal Relationships* 1, 433–548.

Kayser, E., T. Schwinger and V. Kramer 1981. *Distributive Gerechtigkeit, Attribution und moralische Reife: Die moralische Bewertung der persönlichen Verursachung von Leistung und Bedürftigkeit.* Bericht aus dem Sonderforschungsbereich 24: Universität Mannheim.

Keil, L.J. and C.G. McClintock 1983. A developmental perspective on distributive justice. In D.M. Messick and K.S. Cook (eds.), *Equity Theory: Psychological and Sociological Perspectives,* New York: Praeger.

Kellerhals, J., J. Coenen-Huther and M. Modak 1987. Stratification sociale, types d'interactions dans la famille et justice distributive. *Revue Française de Sociologie* 28, 217–40.

1988a. *Figures de l'équité. La construction des normes de justice dans les groupes,* Paris: Presses Universitaires de France.

1988b. Justice norms and group dynamics: the case of the family. *International Sociology* 3, 111–27.

Kelley, H.H. 1973. The process of causal attribution. *American Psychologist* 28, 107–28.

Kelsen, H. 1953–75. *Was ist Gerechtigkeit?* 2nd edn 1975. Vienna: Deuticke.

1957. *What is Justice? Justice, Law, and Politics in the Mirror of Science.* Berkeley, Los Angeles and London: University of California Press.

1967. *The Pure Theory of Law.* Berkeley, Los Angeles and London: University of California Press.

1973. What is Justice? In O.Weinberger (ed.), *Hans Kelsen: Essays in Legal and Moral Philosophy,* Dordrecht: Reidel. Original 1953.

Kemp, M. and Y.-K. Ng 1987. Arrow's independence condition and the Bergson-Samuelson tradition. In G. Feiwel (ed.), *Arrow and the Foundations of the Theory of Economic Policy,* London: Macmillan, pp. 223–41.

Kidder, L.H., G. Bellettirie and E. Cohn 1977. Secret ambitions and public performances. *Journal of Experimental Social Psychology,* 13, 70–80.

Kidder, L.H., M.A. Fagan and E.S. Cohn 1981. Giving and receiving. Social justice in close relationships. In Lerner and Lerner 1981.

Kleinig, J. 1971. The concept of desert. *American Philosophical Quarterly* 8, 71–8.

Kleist, H. von 1810/1979. *Michael Kohlhaas: Aus einer alten Chronik,* Stuttgart: Reclam.

Kluckhohn, C. 1951. Values and value-orientations in the theory of action: an exploration in definition and classification. In T. Parsons and E.A. Shils (eds.), *Toward a General Theory of Action. Theoretical Foundations for the Social Sciences,* New York: Harper and Row.

Kluckhohn, F.R. 1953. Dominant and variant value orientations. In C. Kluckhohn, H.A. Murray and D.M. Schneider (eds.), *Personality in Nature, Society and Culture,* New York: Knopf.

Kluegel, J.R. and E.R. Smith 1986. *Beliefs about Inequality. Americans' Views of What Is and What Ought to Be,* New York.

Kolm, S.-C. 1969. The optimal production of social justice. In *Public Economics,* London: Macmillan, pp. 145–200.

1972. *Justice et équité,* Paris: Editions du Centre National de la Recherche Scientifique.

1976. Unequal inequalities, I and II. *Journal of Economic Theory* 12, 416–42 and 13, 82–111.
1984. *La Bonne économie: la réciprocité générale*, Paris: Presses Universitaires de France.
1985. *Le Contrat social libéral: philosophie et pratique du libéralisme*, Paris: Presses Universitaires de France.
1987. The freedom and consensus normative theory of the state: the liberal social contract. In P. Koslowski (ed.), *Individual Liberty and Democratic Decision-Making*, Tübingen: Mohr (Paul Siebeck), pp. 98–126.
1988. Public economics. In *New Palgrave Dictionary of Economics*, Cambridge: Cambridge University Press, pp. 1047–55.
Komorita, S.S. and J.M. Chertkoff 1973. A bargaining theory of coalition formation. *Psychological Review* 80, 149–62.
Krebs, D. 1982. Prosocial behavior, equity, and justice. In Greenberg and Cohen 1982a.
Kreveld, D. van and E.K. van Beemen 1978. Distributing goods and benefits: a framework and review of research. *Gedrag: Tijdschrift voor Psychologie* 6, 361–401.
Kreveld, D. van, R. Vermunt and H. de Vries 1985. How much of what does a person deserve for what? Unpublished manuscript.
Kronman, A.T. 1980. Contract law and distributive justice. *Yale Law Journal* 89, 472–511.
Kumar, N. 1986. Inequity in job perception: a study of Indian managers. Unpublished doctoral dissertation. Delhi: Indian Institute of Technology.
Lagrou, L., B. Overlaet and E. Schokkaert 1981. Beoordeling van inkomensverdeling. *Psychologica Belgica*, 123–47.
Lamm, H. and E. Kayser 1978a. The allocation of monetary gain and loss following dyadic performance: the weight given to effort and ability under conditions of low and high intra-dyadic attraction. *European Journal of Social Psychology* 8, 275–8.
1978b. An analysis of negotiation concerning the allocation of jointly produced profit or loss: the roles of justice norms, politeness, profit maximization, and tactics. *International Journal of Group Tensions* 8, 64–80.
Lamm, H., E. Kayser and V. Schanz 1983. An attributional analysis of interpersonal justice: ability and effort as inputs in the allocation of gain and loss. *The Journal of Social Psychology* 119, 269–81.
Lamm, H., E. Kayser and T. Schwinger 1981. Justice norms and other determinants of allocation and negotiation behavior. In M. Irle (ed.), *Decision Making: Social-Psychological and Socio-Economic Analyses*, Berlin and New York: de Gruyter.
Landman, J. 1987. Regret and elation following action and inaction: affective responses to positive versus negative outcomes. *Personality and Social Psychology Bulletin* 13, 524-36.
Lane, I.M. and R.C. Coon 1972. Reward allocation in preschool children. *Child Development* 43, 1382–9.
Lane, I.M. and L.A. Messé 1971. Equity and the distribution of rewards. *Journal of Personality and Social Psychology* 20, 1–17.
1972. Distribution of insufficient, sufficient, and oversufficient rewards: a clarification of equity theory. *Journal of Personality and Social Psychology* 21, 228–33.
Lansberg, I. 1981. Distributive justice: a theoretical overview of fairness in organizations. Unpublished manuscript, Columbia University.
1984. Hierarchy as a mediator of fairness: a contingency approach to distributive justice in organizations. *Journal of Applied Social Psychology* 14, 124–35.

Larenz, K. 1979. *Richtiges Recht*, Munich: Springer.
Larrain, J. 1983. *Marxism and Ideology*, London.
Lawler, E.E., III 1968a. Equity theory as a predictor of productivity and work quality. *Psychological Bulletin* 70, 596–610.
  1968b. Effects of hourly overpayment on productivity and work quality. *Journal of Personality and Social Psychology* 10, 306–13.
  1971. *Pay and Organizational Effectiveness: A Psychological View*, New York: McGraw-Hill.
Lee, M.T. and R. Ofshe 1981. The impact of behavioral style and status characteristics on social influence: a test of two competing theories. *Social Psychology Quarterly* 44, 73–82.
Lehning, P.B. 1986. *Politieke Orde en Rawlsiaanse Rechtvaardigheid*, Delft: Eburon.
Lenski, G. 1966. *Power and Privilege: A Theory of Social Stratification*, New York: McGraw-Hill.
Lerner, M.J. 1974a. Social psychology of justice and interpersonal attraction. In T.L. Huston (ed.), *Foundations of Interpersonal Attraction*, New York: Academic Press.
  1974b. The justice motive: 'Equity' and 'parity' among children. *Journal of Personality and Social Psychology*, 29, 538–50.
  1975. The justice motive in social behavior: introduction. *Journal of Social Issues* 31, 1–20.
  1977. The justice motive: some hypotheses as to its origins and forms. *Journal of Personality* 45, 1–52.
  1980. *The belief in a Just World: A Fundamental Delusion*. New York: Plenum Press.
  1981. The justice motive in human relations. Some thoughts on what we know and need to know about justice. In Lerner and Lerner 1981.
  1986. Integrating societal and psychological rules of entitlement. Paper delivered at the International Conference on Justice in Human Relations, Leiden.
Lerner, M.J. and S.C. Lerner (eds.) 1981. *The Justice Motive in Social Behavior. Adapting to Times of Scarcity and Change*, New York: Plenum Press.
Lerner, M.J., D.T. Miller and J.G. Holmes 1976. Deserving and the emergence of forms of justice. In Berkowitz and Walster 1976.
Lerner, M.J. and L.A. Whitehead 1980. Procedural justice viewed in the context of justice motive theory. In Mikula 1980a.
Leventhal, G.S. 1973. Reward allocation by males and females. In L. Messé (Chair), Individual differences in equity behavior. Symposium presented at the meeting of the American Psychological Association, Montreal, August.
  1976a. The distribution of rewards and resources in groups and organizations. In Berkowitz and Walster 1976.
  1976b. Fairness in social relationships. In Thibaut, Spence and Carson 1976.
Leventhal, G.S. and D. Anderson 1970. Self-interest and the maintenance of equity. *Journal of Personality and Social Psychology* 15, 57–62.
Leventhal, G.S. and D.W. Lane 1970. Sex, age, and equity behavior. *Journal of Personality and Social Psychology* 15, 312–16.
Leventhal, G.S. and J.W. Michaels 1969. Extending the equity model: perceptions of inputs and allocations of reward as a function of duration and quantity of performance. *Journal of Personality and Social Psychology* 12, 303–9.
  1971. Locus of cause and equity motivation as determinants of reward allocation. *Journal of Personality and Social Psychology* 17, 229–35.
Leventhal, G.S., J.W. Michaels and C. Sanford 1972. Inequity and interpersonal conflict: reward allocation and secrecy about reward as methods of preventing conflict. *Journal of Personality and Social Psychology* 23, 88–102.

Leventhal, G.S., A.L. Popp and L. Sawyer 1973. Equity or equality in children's allocation of reward to other persons. *Child Development* 44, 753–63.

Leventhal, G.S., T. Weiss and R. Buttrick 1973. Attribution of value, equity, and the prevention of waste in reward allocation. *Journal of Personality and Social Psychology* 27, 276–86.

Leventhal, G.S., T. Weiss and G. Long 1969. Equity, reciprocity, and reallocating rewards in the dyad. *Journal of Personality and Social Psychology* 13, 300–5.

Levine, J.M. and R.L. Moreland 1987. Social comparison and outcome evaluation in group contexts. In J.C. Masters and W.P. Smith (eds.), *Social Comparison, Social Justice, and Relative Deprivation. Theoretical, Empirical, and Policy Perspectives*, Hillsdale, NJ: Erlbaum.

Levinger, G. and L.R. Huesmann 1980. An 'incremental exchange' perspective on the pair relationship: interpersonal reward and level of involvement. In K.J. Gergen, M.S. Greenberg and R.H. Willis (eds.), *Social Exchange. Advances in Theory and Research*, New York: Plenum Press.

Liebermann, J.K. 1981. *The Litigious Society*, New York: Prentice-Hall.

Lind, E.A. and T.R. Tyler 1988. *The Social Psychology of Procedural Justice*, New York: Plenum Press.

Lipsky, M. 1980. *Street-Level Bureaucracy: Dilemmas of the Individual in Public Services*, New York.

Llompart, J. 1981. Gerechtigkeit als geschichtliches Rechtsprinzip. *ARSP* 67, 39–60.

Luban, D. 1985. Bargaining and compromise: recent work on negotiation and informal justice. *Philosophy and Public Affairs* 14, 397–416.

Lucas, J.R. 1980. *On Justice: ΠΕΡΙ ΔΙΚΑΙΟΥ*. Oxford: Clarendon Press.

Luhmann, N. 1973. Gerechtigkeit in den Rechtssystem der modernen Gesellschaft. *Rechtstheorie* 4, 131ff.

1974. Reply to Dreier. *Rechtstheorie* 5, 201ff.

Lukes, S. 1982. Marxism, morality and justice. In Parkinson 1982, pp. 177–205.

1985. *Marxism and Morality*, Oxford: Oxford University Press.

L'Utile et le juste 1981. Collection of essays in *Archives de Philosophie du Droit* 26.

Lyons, D. 1978. Mill's theory of justice. In Goldman and Kim 1978, pp. 1–19.

1984. *Ethics and the Rule of Law*, Cambridge: Cambridge University Press.

Macaulay, S. 1973. In D. Black and M. Mileski, *The Social Organization of Law*, Chicago: Chicago University Press, chapter 3.

Macaulay, S. and E. Walster 1971. Legal structures and restoring equity. *Journal of Social Issues* 27, 173ff.

McClintock, C.G. and E. van Avermaet 1982. Social values and rules of fairness: a theoretical perspective. In V.J. Derlega and J. Grzelak (eds.), *Cooperation and Helping Behavior*, New York: Academic Press.

MacCormick, D.N. 1981. Natural law reconsidered. *Oxford Journal of Legal Studies* 1, 99–109. A review of Finnis 1980.

1982a. *Legal Right and Social Democracy*, Oxford: Oxford University Press.

1982b. Justice: an un-original position. In MacCormick 1982, pp. 84–102.

1984. On reasonableness. In C. Perelman and R. Vander Elst (eds.), *Les Notions à contenu variable en droit*, Brussels: Bruylant, pp. 131–56.

MacIntyre, A. 1984. *After Virtue*, 2nd edn, London: Duckworth.

1988. *Whose Justice? Which Rationality?* London: Duckworth.

McKinney, J.P. 1971. The development of values: prescriptive or proscriptive? *Human Development* 14, 71–80.

McMahon, A.M. 1984. The two social psychologies: postcrises directions. *Annual Review of Sociology* 10, 121–40.

MacPherson, C.B. 1985. The rise and fall of economic justice. In *The Rise and Fall of Economic Justice and Other Papers*, Oxford and New York: Oxford University Press, pp. 1–20.

Major, B. and J.B. Adams 1983. Role of gender, interpersonal orientation, and self-presentation in distributive-justice behavior. *Journal of Personality and Social Psychology* 45, 598–608.

Major, B. and K. Deaux 1982. Individual differences in justice behavior. In Greenberg and Cohen 1982a.

Malewski, A. 1959. Der empirische Gehalt der Theorie des historischen Materialismus. *Kölner Zeitschrift für Soziologie und Sozialpsychologie*, 281–305.

Mann, M. 1970. The social cohesion of liberal democracy. *American Sociological Review*, 423–39.

1973. *Consciousness and Action among the Western Working Class*, London.

Marcic, R. 1969. *Rechtsphilosophie*, Freiburg im Breisgau: Rombach.

Margolis, H. 1981. *Selfishness, Altruism and Rationality*, Cambridge: Cambridge University Press.

Mark, M.M. 1980. Justice in the aggregate: the perceived fairness of the distribution of income. Unpublished doctoral dissertation, Northwestern University.

Markovsky, B. 1985. Toward a multilevel distributive justice theory. *American Sociological Review* 50, 822–39.

1986. Prospects for a cognitive-structural justice theory. Paper presented at the International Conference of Social Justice in Human Relations, Leiden, The Netherlands.

Martin, J., P. Brickman and A. Murray 1984. Moral outrage and pragmatism: explanations for collective action. *Journal of Experimental and Social Psychology* 20, 484–96.

Martin, J. and J. Harder 1988. *Bread and Roses: Justice and the Distribution of Financial and Socio-emotional Rewards in Organizations*. Research paper No. 1010, Stanford: Graduate School of Business, Stanford University.

Martin, J. and A. Murray 1983. Distributive injustice and unfair exchange. In Messick and Cook. 1983.

1984. Catalysts for collective violence: the importance of a psychological approach. In Folger 1984.

Martin, J., M. Scully and B. Levitt 1988. *Injustice and the Legitimation of Revolution: Damning the Past, Excusing the Present, and Neglecting the Future*. Research paper No. 1011, Stanford: Graduate School of Business, Stanford University.

Marx, W. 1983. *Gibt es auf Erden ein Mass?* Hamburg: Meiner.Translated by T.J. Nenon and R. Lilly as *Is There a Measure on Earth? Foundations for a Nonmetaphysical Ethics*, Chicago and London: University of Chicago Press.

1986. *Ethos und Lebenswelt: Zum Mass des Mit-Leiden-Könnens*, Hamburg: Meiner.

Mashaw, J.L. 1983. *Bureaucratic Justice*, New Haven, CT.

Masters, J.C. and L.J. Keil 1987. Generic comparison processes in human judgment and behavior. In Masters and Smith 1987.

Masters, J.C. and W.P. Smith (eds.) 1987. *Social Comparison, Social Justice, and Relative Deprivation. Theoretical, Empirical and Policy Perspectives*, Hillsdale, NJ: Erlbaum.

Mauss, M. 1965. *Sociologie et anthropologie*. Paris.

Mayer, K.U. 1975. *Ungleichheit und Mobilität im sozialen Bewusstsein*, Opladen.

Mayer-Maly, T. 1984. Gerechtigkeit und gesetztes Recht. In P. Gordan (ed.) *Gerechtigkeit, Freiheit, Friede*, Graz: Styria.

Meeker, B.F. and G.C. Elliot 1987. Counting the costs: equality and the allocation of negative group products. *Social Psychology Quarterly* 50, 7–15.

Meier, C. 1985. Zur Diskussion über das Rechtsgefühl: Themenvielfalt Ergebnistrends – neue Forschungsperspektiven. Thesis, University of Zürich.

Merton, R.K. 1968. *Social Theory and Social Structure*, New York.

Messick, D.M. and K.S. Cook (eds.) 1983. *Equity Theory: Psychological and Sociological Perspectives*, New York: Praeger.

Messick, D.M. and K. Sentis 1979. Fairness and preference. *Journal of Experimental Social Psychology* 15, 418–34.

1983. Fairness, preference, and fairness biases. In Messick and Cook 1983.

Miaille, M. 1978. *Une Introduction Critique au Droit*, Paris: Maspero.

Michotte, A.E. 1946. *La Perception de la Causalité*, Paris: Vrin. (English trans. 1963. *The Perception of Causality*, New York: Basic Books.)

Mikula, G. 1972. Die Entwicklung des Gewinnaufteilungsverhaltens bei Kindern und Jugendlichen. *Zeitschrift für Entwicklungspsychologie und Pädagogische Psychologie* 4, 151-64.

1973. *'Gerechtigkeit' und 'Zufriedenheit beider partner' als zielstetzungen der aufteilung eines von zwei personen gemeinsam erzielten gewinns*, Graz, Berichte aus dem Institut für Psychologie der Universität Graz.

1974a. Nationality, performance, and sex as determinants of reward allocation. *Journal of Personality and Social Psychology* 29, 435–40.

1974b. Individuelle Entscheidungen und Gruppenentscheidungen über die Aufteilung gemeinsam erzielter Gewinne: Eine Untersuchung zum Einfluss der sozialen Verantwortung. *Psychologische Beiträge* 16, 338–64.

1975. *Studies on Reward Allocation in Dyadic Groups*, Graz: Berichte aus dem Institut für Psychologie der Universität Graz.

1977. *Consideration of Justice in Allocation Situations*. Graz: Berichte aus dem Institut für Psychologie der Universität Graz.

1980a. Introduction: Main issues in the psychological research on justice. In Mikula (ed.) 1980.

1980b. On the role of justice in allocation decisions. In Mikula (ed.) 1980.

1984. Justice and fairness in interpersonal relations: thoughts and suggestions. In H. Tajfel (ed.), *The Social Dimension: European Developments in Social Psychology*, Cambridge: Cambridge University Press.

1986. The experience of injustice: toward a better understanding of its phenomenology. In Bierhoff, Cohen and Greenberg 1986.

1987. Exploring the experience of injustice. In G.R. Semin and B. Krahe (eds.), *Perspectives on Contemporary German Social Psychology*, London: Sage.

1988. *Topics in Recent Research on Justice and Injustice*, Graz, Berichte aus dem Institut für Psychologie der Universität Graz.

Mikula, G. (ed.) 1980. *Justice and Social Interaction: Experimental and Theoretical Contributions from Psychological Research*, New York: Springer-Verlag.

Mikula, G. and E. Korytko 1989. *Just As You Like It: How Allocators Decide in Cases of Conflict Between Own and Recipients' Views of Justice*, Graz: Berichte aus dem Institut für Psychologie der Universität Graz.

Mikula, G. and G.F. Müller 1983. Procedural preferences in the allocation of jointly produced gains and losses. *The Journal of Social Psychology* 121, 117–24.

Mikula, G., B. Petri and N. Tanzer 1988. Antecedent conditions of experiences of injustice. Paper presented at the International Conference on Social Justice and Societal Problems, Leiden, Holland.

1990. What people regard as unjust: types and structures of everyday experiences of injustice. *European Journal of Social Psychology* 20, 133–49.

Mikula, G. and K. Schlamberger 1985. What people think about an unjust event: toward a better understanding of the phenomenology of experiences of injustice. *European Journal of Social Psychology* 15, 37–49.

Mikula, G. and T. Schwinger 1973. Sympathie zum Partner und Bedürfnis nach sozialer Anerkennung als Determinanten der Aufteilung Gemeinsam Erzielter Gewinns. *Psychologische Beiträge* 15, 396–407.

1978. Intermember relations and reward allocation: theoretical considerations of affects. In H. Brandstätter, J.H. Davis and H. Schuler (eds.), *Dynamics of Group Decisions*, Beverly Hills, CA: Sage.

Miller, D. 1976. *Social Justice*, Oxford: Clarendon Press.

Miller, D.T. and N. Vidmar 1981. The social psychology of punishment reactions. In Lerner and Lerner 1981.

Miller, R. 1974. Rawls and Marxism. *Philosophy and Public Affairs* 3, 167–91. Reprinted in Daniels 1975b, pp. 206–30.

Mills, J. and M.S. Clark 1982. Exchange and communal relationships. In L. Wheeler (ed.), *Review of Personality and Social Psychology* vol. 3, Beverly Hills, CA: Sage.

Mirrlees, J. 1982. The economic uses of utilitarianism. In A. Sen and B. Williams 1982, pp. 63–84.

Montada, L. 1980. Developmental changes in concepts of justice. In Mikula (ed.) 1980.

Montada, L., M. Schmitt and C. Dalbert 1986. Thinking about justice and dealing with one's own privileges: a study of existential guilt. In Bierhoff, Cohen and Greenberg 1986.

Montada, L. and A. Schneider 1988. *Justice and Emotional Reactions to Victims*. Existentielle Schuld-Bericht 7. Trier, Germany: Fachbereich I – Psychologie, Universität Trier.

Moore, B. Jr. 1978. *Injustice. The Social Bases of Obedience and Revolt*, London: Macmillan.

Moore, S.F. 1978. *Law as Process: An Anthropological Approach*, London.

Morgan, W.R. and J. Sawyer 1967. Bargaining, expectations, and the preference for equality over equity. *Journal of Personality and Social Psychology* 6, 139–49.

Morgenthau, H.J. 1974. Justice and power. *Social Research* 41, 163–75.

Morse, S.J., J. Gruzen and H.T. Reis 1976. The nature of equity-restoration: some approval-seeking considerations. *Journal of Experimental Social Psychology* 12, 1–8.

Moschetti, G.J. 1979. Calculating equity: ordinal and ratio criteria. *Social Psychology* 42, 172–5.

Moscovici, S. 1976. *Social Influence and Social Change*, New York: Academic Press.

Moulin, H. 1987. Equal or proportional division of a surplus, and other methods. *International Journal of Game Theory* 16, 161–86.

Moulin, H. and J. Roemer 1986. Public ownership of the external world vs. private ownership of self. Working Paper, Department of Economics, Virginia Polytechnic Institute and State University.

Mueller, D.C. 1989. *Public Choice*, Cambridge: Cambridge University Press.

Murphy, C.F. 1972. Distributive justice, its modern significance. *The American Journal of Jurisprudence* 17, 153–65.

Murphy-Berman, V., J.J. Berman, P. Singh, A. Pachauri and P. Kumar 1984. Factors affecting allocation to needy and meritorious recipients: a cross-cultural comparison. *Journal of Personality and Social Psychology* 46, 1267–72.

Narveson, J. 1983. On Dworkinian equality. *Social Philosophy and Policy* 1, 1–23.

Nelson, S.A. and C.S. Dweck 1977. Motivation, competence and reward allocation. *Developmental Psychology* 13, 192–7.
Newbery, D. and N. Stern 1987. *The Theory of Taxation for Developing Countries*, Oxford: Oxford University Press.
Newman, R.A. (ed.) 1973. *Equity in the World's Legal Systems*, Brussels: Bruylant.
Ng, S.H. 1981b. Equity theory and the allocation of rewards between groups. *European Journal of Social Psychology* 11, 439–43.
   1984. Equity and social categorization effects of intergroup allocation of rewards. *British Journal of Social Psychology* 23, 165–72.
   1986. Equity, intergroup bias and interpersonal bias in reward allocation. *European Journal of Social Psychology* 16, 239–55.
Ng, Y.-K. 1975. Bentham or Bergson? Finite sensibility, utility functions and social welfare functions. *Review of Economic Studies* 42, 545–69.
   1981a. Welfarism: a defence against Sen's attack. *Economic Journal* 91, 527–30.
Ng, Y.-K. and F. Cram 1987. Fairness and biases in intergroup relations: a study on reward allocation and intergroup differentiation. Final Report submitted to the SSFRC, Psychology Department, University of Otago, Dunedin, New Zealand.
Nielsen, K. 1979. Radical egalitarian justice: justice as equality. *Social Theory and Practice* 5, 209–26.
   1982. Capitalism, socialism and justice. In Regan and van de Veer 1982, pp. 264–86.
   1985. *Equality and Liberty: A Defense of Radical Egalitarianism*, Totowa, NJ: Rowman and Allanheld.
Nino, C.S. 1980. *Introduccion al analisis del derecho*, Buenos Aires: Depalma.
   1984. *Etica y Derechos Humanos*, Buenos Aires: Paidos.
Nonet, P. and P. Selznick 1978. *Law and Society in Transition: Towards Responsive Law*, New York.
Nozick, R. 1975. *Anarchy, State and Utopia*, New York: Basic Books.
Ott, W. 1986. Die Equity-Theorie aus Sicht der Juristen. *Rechtstheorie* 17, 359ff.
O'Brien, D.M. 1979. *Privacy, Law and Public Policy*, New York.
O'Neill, O. 1976. Nozick's entitlements. *Inquiry* 19, 468–81.
Overlaet, B. 1989. The use of merit criteria as a justification of professional income differences. Paper presented at the 1st European Congress of Psychology, Amsterdam, Holland, 2–7 July.
Overlaet, B. and L. Lagrou 1981. Attitudes towards a redistribution of income. *Journal of Economic Psychology*, 197–215.
Overlaet, B. and E. Schokkaert 1986. Criteria for distributive justice in a productive context. Paper presented at the International Conference on Social Justice in Human Relations, Leiden, Holland.
Parkin, F. 1972. *Class Inequality and Political Order*, London.
Parkinson, G.H.R. (ed.) 1982. *Marx and Marxisms*, Cambridge: Cambridge University Press.
Parsons, T. 1940. An analytical approach to the theory of social stratification. *American Journal of Sociology* 45, 841–62.
   1951. *The Social System*, New York: The Free Press.
   1953. A revised analytical approach to the theory of social stratification. In R. Bendix and S.M. Lipset (eds.), *Class, Status, and Power*, New York.
   1970. Equality and inequality in modern society, or social stratification revisited. *Sociological Inquiry* 40, 13–27.
Patchen, M. 1961. *The Choice of Wage Comparisons*, Englewood Cliffs, NJ: Prentice Hall.

Paul, J. (ed.) 1981. *Reading Nozick: Essays on Anarchy, State, and Utopia*, Totowa, NJ: Rowman and Littlefield; reprint Oxford: Blackwell, 1982. Contains an extensive bibliography of articles on Nozick 1974.

Pazner, E. and D. Schmeidler 1978. Egalitarian equivalent allocations: a new concept of economic equity. *Quarterly Journal of Economics* 92, 1–45.

Perelman, C. 1971. In Buch 1971, pp. 319ff.

1972. *Justice et raison*, 2nd edn, Brussels: Bruylant.

1977. In H. Ingber (ed.), *Egalité*, Brussels: Bruylant, vol. 5, pp. 324ff.

1978. La motivation des décisions de justice. In C. Perelman and P. Foriers (eds.), *La Motivation des décisions de justice*, Brussels: Bruylant, pp. 415–26.

Pettit, P. 1980. *Judging Justice*, London, Boston and Henley: Routledge.

1982. Habermas on truth and justice. In Parkinson 1982, pp. 207–28.

Piaget, J. 1927. *La Causalité physique chez l'enfant*, Paris: Alcan.

Posner, R.A. 1977. *Economic Analysis of Law*, 2nd edn, Boston: Little Brown and Co.

1981. *The Economics of Justice*, Cambridge, MA: Harvard University Press.

Pospisil, L. 1974. *Anthropology of Law: A Comparative Theory*, New Haven, CT: HRAF Press.

Pound, R. 1951. *Justice According to Law*, New Haven, CT: Yale University Press.

Prentice, D.A. and F. Crosby 1987. The importance of context for assessing deservingness. In J.C. Masters and W.P. Smith (eds.), *Social Comparison, Social Justice, and Relative Deprivation. Theoretical, Empirical, and Policy Perspectives*, Hillsdale, NJ: Erlbaum.

Price-Williams, D.R. 1985. Cultural psychology. In G. Lindzey and E. Aronson (eds.), *Handbook of Social Psychology*, vol. 2, New York: Random House.

Pritchard, R.A. 1969. Equity theory: a review and critique. *Organizational Behavior and Human Performance* 4, 176–211.

Pynoos, J. 1987. *Breaking the Rules*, New York.

Rabbie, J.M. 1982. The effects of intergroup competition and cooperation and intragroup and intergroup relationships. In V.J. Derlega and J. Grzelak (eds.), *Cooperation and Helping Behavior*, New York: Academic Press.

Rabbie, J.M. and M. Horwitz 1969. The arousal of ingroup-outgroup bias by a chance win or loss. *Journal of Personality and Social Psychology* 69, 223–8.

Radbruch, G. 1950. *Rechtsphilosophie*, 4th edn, Stuttgart: Koehler.

Raphael, D.D. 1970. *Problems of Political Philosophy*, New York: Praeger Publishers.

1980. *Justice and Liberty*, London: The Athlone Press.

1987. Political thought and its history: the concept of justice. Howard Warrender Memorial Lecture, 1986. Sheffield: The University of Sheffield.

1990. Justice. In *Problems of Political Philosophy*, 2nd edn, London: Macmillan, pp. 113–52.

Rawls, J. 1971. *A Theory of Justice*. Cambridge, MA: Belknap Press of the Harvard University Press; reprint Oxford: Clarendon Press, 1972.

1974. Some reasons for the maximin criterion. *American Economic Review* 64, 141–6.

1978. The basic structure as subject. In Goldman and Kim 1978, pp. 47–71.

1980. Kantian constructivism in moral theory (The Dewey Lectures). *The Journal of Philosophy* 77, 515–72.

1982a. Social unity and primary goods. In Sen and Williams 1982, pp. 159–86.

1982b. The basic liberties and their priority. In S.M. McMurrin (ed.), *The Tanner Lectures on Human Values III*, Salt Lake City: University of Utah Press; Cambridge: Cambridge University Press, pp. 3–87. A reply to Hart 1973.

1985. Justice as fairness: political not metaphysical. *Philosophy and Public Affairs* 14, 219–51.

1987. The idea of an overlapping consensus. *Oxford Journal of Legal Studies* 7, 1–25.

Raz, J. 1980. *The Authority of Law*, Oxford: Oxford University Press.

1982. The claims of reflective equilibrium. *Inquiry* 25, 307–30.

1986. *The Morality of Freedom*, Oxford: Oxford University Press.

Rechtsbedürfnis und Rechtshilfe 1978. *Jahrbuch für Rechtssoziologie und Rechtstheorie* 5.

Rechtsgefühl 1985. Das sogenannte Rechtsgefühl. *Jahrbuch für Rechtssoziologie und Rechtstheorie* 10, ed. E.-J. Lampe.

Regan, T. and D. van de Veer (eds.) 1982. *And Justice for All: New Introductory Essays in Ethics and Public Policy*, Totowa, NJ: Rowman and Littlefield.

Rehbinder, M. 1983. Questions of the legal scholar concerning the so-called sense of justice. In M. Gruter and P. Bohannan (eds.), *Law, Biology, and Culture: The Evolution of Law*, Santa Barbara, CA: Ross-Erikson, pp. 34–45.

Reis, H.T. 1981. Self-presentation and distributive justice. In J.T. Tedeschi (ed.), *Impression Management Theory and Social Psychological Research*, New York: Academic Press.

1984. The multidimensionality of justice. In Folger 1984.

1986. Levels of interest in the study of interpersonal justice. In Bierhoff, Cohen and Greenberg 1986.

Reis, H.T. and L.A. Jackson 1981. Sex differences in reward allocation: subjects, partners and tasks. *Journal of Personality and Social Psychology* 40, 465–78.

Reiter, B. 1981. The control of contract power. *Oxford Journal of Legal Studies* 1, 347–74.

Rescher, N. 1966. *Distributive Justice. A Constructive Critique of the Utilitarian Theory of Distribution*, New York: The Bobbs-Merrill Co., Inc.

1987. Rationality and moral obligation. *Synthese* 72, 29–43.

Richards, D.A.J. 1982. Justice and equality. In Regan and van de Veer 1982, pp. 241–63.

Richey, M., L. McClelland and A. Shimkunas 1967. Relative influence of positive and negative information in impression formation and persistence. *Journal of Personality and Social Psychology* 6, 322–7.

Riezler, E. 1969. *Das Rechtsgefühl, rechtspsychologische Betrachtungen*, 3rd edn, Munich: Biederstein.

Ripert, G. 1953. *La Règle morale dans les obligations civiles*, Paris: Sirey.

Robbers, G. 1980. *Gerechtigkeit als Rechtsprinzip: über den Begriff der Gerechtigkeit in der Rechtssprechung des Bundesverfassungsgerichtshofs*, Baden Baden.

Robbins, L. 1938. Interpersonal comparisons of utility. *Economic Journal* 48, 635–41.

Robiliant, E. di 1987. *Libertà e Società tecnologia avanzata*, Turin: CIDAS.

Robinson, R.V. and W. Bell 1978. Equality, success and social justice in England and the United States. *American Sociological Review* 43, 125–43.

Rodota, S. 1974. Quale equità? *Politica del Diritto* 5, 31ff.

Roemer, J. 1985. Equality of talent. *Economics and Philosophy* 1, 151–87.

1986a. Equality of resources implies equality of welfare. *Quarterly Journal of Economics* 100, 751–84.

1986b. The mismarriage of bargaining theory and distributive justice. *Ethics* 73, 88–110.

Röhl, K.F. 1987. *Rechtssoziologie*, Cologne: Heymanns, chapter 19.

Rokeach, M. 1973. *The Nature of Human Values*, New York: The Free Press.

Romer, D. 1977. Limitations in the equity theory approach: toward a resolution of the 'negative-inputs' controversy. *Personality and Social Psychology Bulletin* 3, 228–31.

Rook, K.S. 1984. The negative side of social interaction: impact on psychological well-being. *Journal of Personality and Social Psychology* 46, 1097–108.

Ross, A. 1958. *On Law and Justice*, London: Routledge. 2nd edn, London: Stevens, 1974.

Rowley, C.K. and A. Peacock 1975. *Welfare Economics: A Liberal Restatement*, London: Martin Robertson.

Runciman, W.G. 1966. *Relative Deprivation and Social Justice*, London.

    1967. Justice, congruence and professor Homans. *Archives Européennes de Sociologie*, 115–28.

Rytina, J.H., H.W. Form and J. Pease 1970. Income and stratification ideology: beliefs about the American opportunity structure. *American Journal of Sociology*, 703–16.

Rytina, S. 1986. Sociology and justice. In Cohen 1986c, pp. 117–51.

Sadurski, W. 1983. Social justice and legal justice. *Law and Philosophy* 3, 329ff.

    1985a. *Giving Desert its Due: Social Justice and Legal Theory*, Dordrecht, Boston and London: Reidel.

    1985b. Justice: 'partial' or 'complete' virtue? A critique of Rawls on relations between justice, liberty and utility. *ARSP* 71, 488–98.

Samek, R.A. 1981. Justice as ideology: another look at Rawls. *Canadian Bar Review* 59, 787–811.

Sampson, E.E. 1969. Studies of status congruence. In L. Berkowitz (ed.), *Advances in Experimental Social Psychology* vol. 4. New York: Academic Press.

    1975. On justice as equality. *Journal of Social Issues* 31, 45–64.

    1976. *Social Psychology and Contemporary Society*, New York: John Wiley and Sons.

    1980. Justice and social character. In G. Mikula 1980.

    1981. New perspectives on the social dimension of justice. In Lerner and Lerner 1981, pp. 97–124.

    1983. *Justice and the Critique of Pure Psychology*, New York: Plenum Press.

Samuel, W. 1976a. Suggested amendments to 'New directions in equity research'. *Personality and Social Psychology Bulletin* 2, 36–9.

    1976b. In further support of the Adams ratio: a reply to Dr. G. William Walster. *Personality and Social Psychology Bulletin* 2, 45–7.

    1978. Toward a simple but useful equity theory: a comment on the Romer article. *Personality and Social Psychology Bulletin* 4, 135–8.

Samuelson, P. 1947. *Foundations of Economic Analysis*, Cambridge, MA: Harvard University Press.

    1977. Reaffirming the existence of 'reasonable' Bergson-Samuelson social welfare functions. *Economica* 44, 81–8.

Sandel, M. 1982. *Liberalism and the Limits of Justice*, Cambridge. Cambridge University Press.

Sarbin, T. S. and V.L. Allen 1968. Role theory. In G. Lindzey and E. Aronson (eds.), *The Handbook of Social Psychology*, vol. 1. Reading, MA: Addison-Wesley.

Sayles, L.R. 1958. *Behavior of Industrial Work Groups: Prediction and Control*, New York: Wiley.

Schmitt, M. and L. Montada 1982. Determinanten erlebter Gerechtigkeit. *Zeitschrift für Sozialpsychologie* 13, 32–44.

Schnoor, C. 1989. *Kants Kategorischer Imperativ als Kriterium der Richtigkeit des Handelns*, Tübingen: Mohr (Paul Siebeck).

Schoeninger, D.W. and D.W. Wood 1969. Comparison of married and ad hoc mixed-sex diads negotiating the division of a reward. *Journal of Experimental Social Psychology* 5, 483–99.

Schokkaert, E. and L. Lagrou 1983. An empirical approach to distributive justice. *Journal of Public Economics* 21, 33–52.

Schokkaert, E., L. Lagrou and B. Overlaet 1982. De houding tegenover inkomensverdeling en crisispolitiek, *Tijdschrift voor Economie en Management*, 197–223.

Schokkaert, E. and B. Overlaet 1989. Moral intuitions and economic models of distributive justice. *Social Choice and Welfare* 6, 19–31.

Schramm, A. 1983. Anmerkungen zu Ilmar Tamellos *Theorie der Gerechtigkeit*. *ARSP* 69, 234ff.

Schuyt, C.J.M. 1985. Sturing en het recht. In M.A.P. Bovens and W.J. Witteveen (eds.), *Het Schip van Staat: Beschouwingen over Recht, Staat en Sturing*, Zwolle.

    1989. Rise of lawyers in the Dutch welfare state. In R. Abel and P.S.C. Lewis (eds.), *Lawyers in Society* vol. 2, Los Angeles, chapter 5.

Schwinger, T. 1980. Just allocation of goods: decisions among three principles. In Mikula (ed) 1980, pp. 95–125.

Schwinger, T. and W. Nährer 1982. *Prinzipien der gerechten Vergabe von interpersonalen Ressourcen in verschiedenen Sozialbeziehungen*. Berichte aus dem Sonderforschungsbereich 24, 1982: Universität Mannheim.

Schwinger, T., W. Nährer and E. Kayser 1982. *Prinzipien der gerechten Vergabe von Zuneigung und Geld in verschiedenen Sozialbeziehungen*. Bericht aus dem Sonderforschungsbereich 24: Universität Mannheim.

Seidler, V.J. 1986. *Kant, Respect and Injustice: The Limits of Liberal Moral Theory*. London, Boston and Henley: Routledge.

Sen, A. 1970a. The impossibility of a Paretian liberal. *Journal of Political Economy* 78, 152–7.

    1970b. *Collective Choice and Social Welfare*, San Francisco: Holden-Day.

    1973. *On Economic Inequality*, Oxford: Clarendon Press.

    1976. Liberty, unanimity and rights. *Economica* 43, 387–403.

    1979a. Personal utilities and public judgements: or what's wrong with welfare economics? *Economic Journal* 89, 537–58.

    1979b. Equality of what? Reprinted in Sen 1982a, pp. 353–69.

    1981. A reply to 'Welfarism: A Defence against Sen's Attack'. *Economic Journal* 91, 531–5.

    1982a. *Choice, Welfare and Measurement*, Oxford: Basil Blackwell.

    1982b. Introduction. In Sen 1982a, pp. 1–38.

    1983. Liberty and social choice. *Journal of Philosophy* 80, 5–28.

    1984a. Rights and capabilities. In Sen 1984c, pp. 307–24.

    1984b. Rights as goals (xerox, Text of the Austin Lecture given on 6 April 1984).

    1984c. *Resources, Values and Development*, Oxford: Basil Blackwell.

    1985a. *Commodities and Capabilities*, Amsterdam: North-Holland.

    1985b. The moral standing of the market. *Social Philosophy and Policy* 2, 1–19.

    1985c. Social choice and justice: a review article. *Journal of Economic Literature* 23, 1764–6.

    1985d. Rights as goals. *ARSP* Beiheft 21, 11ff.

    1987. *The Standard of Living*, Cambridge: Cambridge University Press.

Sen, A. and B. Williams (eds.). 1982. *Utilitarianism and Beyond*, Cambridge: Cambridge University Press.

Shapiro, E.G. 1975. The effect of expectations of future interaction on reward allocations in dyads: equity or equality. *Journal of Personality and Social Psychology* 31, 873–80.

Shaw, M.E. and P.R. Costanzo 1982. *Theories of Social Psychology*, New York: McGraw-Hill.

Shepelak, N.J. 1987. The role of self-explanations and self-evaluations in legitimating inequality. *American Sociological Review* 52, 774–84.

Shepelak, N.J. and D.F. Alwin 1986. Beliefs about inequality and perceptions of distributive justice. *American Sociological Review* 51, 30–46.

Sher, G. 1979. Effort, ability, and personal desert. *Philosophy and Public Affairs* 8, 361–76.

Sherif, M. 1966. *Group Conflict and Co-operation: Their Social Psychology*, London: Routledge.

Sherif, M., O.J. Harvey, B.J. White, W.R. Hood and C. Sherif 1961. *Intergroup Conflict and Cooperation: The Robbers Cave Experiment*, Norman, OK: University of Oklahoma Book Exchange.

Simmonds, N.E. 1986. *Central Issues in Jurisprudence*, London: Sweet and Maxwell.

Simons, R. and M. Klaassen 1979. Children's conceptions and use of rules of distributive justice. *International Journal of Behavioral Development* 2, 253–67.

Skarzynska, K. 1985. *Psychospoleczne aspekty decyzji alokacyjnych* (Psychosocial Aspects of Allocation Decisions), Warsaw: Ossolineum.

In press. Evaluative perspective and distributive justice. In N. Eisenberg, E. Staub and J. Reykowski (eds.), *Social and Moral Values: Individual and Societal Perspectives*, New York: Erlbaum.

Slote, M.A. 1973. Desert, consent, and justice. *Philosophy and Public Affairs* 2, 323–47.

Slovic, P. and S. Lichtenstein 1968. Relative importance of probabilities and payoffs in risk taking. *Journal of Experimental Psychology* 78, Part 2.

Smith, A. 1776. *An Inquiry into the Nature and the Causes of the Wealth of Nations*, London: Methuen.

Starck, B. 1985. *Droit civil: les obligations*, 2nd edn by H. Roland and L. Boyer, Paris: Sirey.

Steensma, H., J. von Grumbkow and H. Wilke 1977. Boete, beloning en billijkheid. *Nederlands Tijdschrift voor de Psychologie* 32, 519–26.

Steensma, H., F. Roes, R. Wippler and F. Zoete 1981. Billijkheidsherstel door mannen en vrouwen na inductie van on billijkheid door bijdrage- en opbrengstmanipulatie. *Gedrag – Tijdschrift voor Psychologie* 9, 143–59.

Stein, P. and J. Shand 1974. *Legal Values in Western Society*, Edinburgh: Edinburgh University Press.

Steiner, H. 1985. Relativizing Justice. *ARSP Beiheft* 21, 33–8.

Steiner, I.D. 1972. *Group Process and Productivity*, New York: Academic Press.

Sterba, J.P. 1976. Justice and the concept of desert. *The Personalist* 57, 188–97.

1986. Recent work on alternative conceptions of justice. *American Philosophical Quarterly* 23, 1–22.

Stolte, J.F. 1983. The legitimation of structural inequality: reformulation and a test of the self-evaluation argument. *American Sociological Review* 48, 331–42.

1987. The formation of justice norms. *American Sociological Review* 52, 774–84.

Stone, J. 1965. *Human Law and Human Justice*, London: Stevens.

1979. Justice not equality. In Kamenka and Tay 1979, pp. 97–115.

1984. *Visions of World Order: Between State Power and Justice*, Baltimore: Johns Hopkins Press.

Storme, M. and H. Casman (eds.) 1978. *Towards Justice with a Human Face*, Antwerp.

Strasnick, S. 1976. Social choice theory and the derivation of Rawls' difference principle. *Journal of Philosophy* 73, 85–99.
Sugden, R. 1981. *The Political Economy of Public Choice*, Oxford: Martin Robertson.
Syroit, J.E.M.M. In press. Interpersonal and intergroup injustice: some theoretical considerations. In Vermunt and Steensma.
Szirmai, E. 1986. *Inequality Observed*, Groningen.
Tajfel, H. 1982. Psychological conceptions of equity: the present and the future. In P. Fraisse (ed.), *Psychologie de demain*, Paris: Presses Universitaires de France.
Tajfel, H. (ed.) 1978. *Differentiation Between Social Groups*, New York: Academic Press.
Tajfel, H., C. Flament, M. Billig and R.P. Bundy 1971. Social categorization and intergroup behavior. *European Journal of Social Psychology* 1, 149–78.
Tallman, I. and M. Ihinger-Tallman 1979. Values, distributive justice and social change. *American Sociological Review* 44, 216–35.
Tammelo, I. 1971. *Rechtslogik und materielle Gerechtigkeit*, Frankfurt: Luchterhand.
  1977. *Theorie der Gerechtigkeit*, Munich.
  1982. *Zur Philosophie der Gerechtigkeit*, Frankfurt: Athanäum.
Tanner, J. and R. Cockerill 1986. In search of working-class ideology: a test of two perspectives. *The Sociological Quarterly* 389–402.
Taylor, C. 1985. The nature and scope of distributive justice. In *Philosophy and the Human Sciences: Philosophical Papers* 2, Cambridge: Cambridge University Press, pp. 289–317.
Taylor, D.M. and F.M. Moghaddam 1987. *Theories of Intergroup Relations: International Social Psychological Perspectives*, New York: Praeger.
Taylor, D.M., F.M. Moghaddam, I. Gamble and E. Zellerer 1987. Disadvantaged group responses to perceived inequality: from passive acceptance to collective action. *Journal of Social Psychology* 127, 259–72.
Tebaldeschi, I. 1979. *La vocazione filosofica del diritto*, Milan: Giuffrè.
Teichman, M. 1971. Satisfaction from interpersonal relations following resource exchange. Unpublished doctoral dissertation, University of Missouri, Columbia, Missouri.
Ten, C.L. 1987. *Crime, Guilt and Punishment*, Oxford: Oxford University Press.
Theriault, R.D. 1978. Equity theory: an examination of inputs and outcomes in an organizational setting. *Dissertation Abstract International* 38 (7-B), 3476.
Thibaut, J. and L. Walker 1975. *Procedural Justice: A Psychological Analysis*, Hillsdale, NJ: LEA.
Thibaut, J., T. Spence and R.C. Carson (eds.) 1976. *Contemporary Topics in Social Psychology*, Morristown, NJ: General Learning Press.
Thibaut, J.W. and H.H. Kelley 1959. *The Social Psychology of Groups*, New York.
Thomas, K. 1973. Situational determinants of equitable behavior. *Human Relations* 26, 551–66.
Thompson, V.A. 1975. *Without Sympathy or Enthusiasm: The Problem of Administrative Compassion*, Alabama.
Thomson, W. and H. Varian 1985. Theories of justice based on symmetry. In L. Hurwicz, D. Schmeidler and H. Sonnenschein (eds.), *Social Goals and Social Organization. Essays in Memory of Elisha Pazner*, Cambridge: Cambridge University Press.
Tinbergen, J. 1975. *Income Distribution*, Amsterdam: North-Holland.
  1978. Equitable distribution: definition, measurement, feasibility. In W. Krelle and A.F. Shorrocks (eds.), *Personal Income Distribution*, Amsterdam: North-Holland, pp. 35–50.

Tomasic, R. 1986. *The Sociology of Law*, London.

Törnblom, K.Y. 1971. Own expectations and behavior: theory and experiments. Doctoral dissertation, University of Missouri-Columbia.

1977a. Distributive justice: typology and propositions. *Human Relations* 30, 1–24.

1977b. Magnitude and source of compensation in two situations of distributive injustice. *Acta Sociologica* 20, 75–95.

1977c. *The Psycho-Sociological and Behavioral Definitions of Equity and their Extension to Social Dimensions*. Reports/Studies EQU.2. Paris: Unesco.

1982. Reversal in preference responses to two types of injustice situations: a methodological contribution to equity theory. *Human Relations* 35, 991–1014.

1988. Positive and negative allocations: a typology and a model for conflicting justice principles. In E. Lawler and B. Markovsky (eds.), *Advances in Group Processes* vol. 5, Greenwich, CT: Jai Press.

In preparation a. The attribution of friendship: modes of giving and receiving resources.

In preparation b. Positive and negative outcome allocation: age strata differences in justice evaluations.

Törnblom, K.Y. and U.G. Foa. Choice of a distribution principle: crosscultural evidence on the effects of resources. *Acta Sociologica* 26, 161–73.

Törnblom, K.Y. and E.M. Fredholm 1984. Attribution of friendship: the influence of the nature and comparability of resources given and received. *Social Psychology Quarterly* 47, 50–61.

Törnblom, K.Y., E.M. Fredholm and D.R. Jonsson 1987. New and old friendships: attributed effects of type and similarity of transacted resources. *Human Relations* 40, 337–60.

Törnblom, K.Y. and W.L. Griffith. In preparation. *Beyond Equity Theory: Emerging Approaches to the Social Psychological Study of Justice in Resource Allocation*, New York: Plenum Press.

Törnblom, K.Y. and D.R. Jonsson 1985. Subrules of the equality and contribution principles: their perceived fairness in distribution and retribution. *Social Psychology Quarterly* 48, 249–61.

1987. Distribution vs. retribution: the perceived justice of the contribution and equality principles for cooperative and competitive relationships. *Acta Sociologica* 30, 25–52.

Törnblom, K.Y., D.R. Jonsson and U.G. Foa 1985. Nationality, resource class, and preferences among three allocation rules: Sweden vs. USA. *International Journal of Intercultural Relations* 9, 51–77.

Törnblom, K.Y., S.M. Mühlhausen and D.R. Jonsson. In press. The allocation of positive and negative outcomes: when is the equality principle fair for both? In Vermunt and Steensma.

Tunc, A. 1972. Tort law and the moral law, *Cambridge Law Journal*, 247–59.

1981. *La Responsabilité civile*, Paris: Dalloz.

Turner, J. 1980. Fairness or discrimination in intergroup behavior? A reply to Branthwaite, Doyle and Lightbown. *European Journal of Social Psychology* 10, 131–47.

Tyler, T. 1987. Procedural justice research. *Social Justice Research* 1, 41–65.

Uray, H. 1976. Leistungsverursachung, Verantwortungszuschreibung und Gewinnauteilung. *Zeitschrift für Sozialpsychologie* 7, 69–80.

Utne, M.K. and R.F. Kidd 1980. Equity and attribution. In Mikula (ed) 1980.

van Avermaet, E. and C.G. McClintock 1988. Intergroup fairness and bias in children. *European Journal of Social Psychology* 18, 407–27.

van der Veen, R. 1988. *Social Policy and Social Justice*, Leiden.

van der Veen, R.J. and P. Van Parijs 1985. Entitlement theories of justice: from Nozick to Roemer and beyond. *Economics and Philosophy* 1, 69–81.

Van Parijs, P. 1987. De l'efficience à la liberté. Xerox, text of lecture for the VIIe Congrès des Economistes Belges de Langue Française, Charleroi.

    Forthcoming. Liberté formelle et liberté réelle – la critique de Rawls par les libertariens. *Revue Philosophique de Louvain.*

Varian, H. 1974. Equity, envy and efficiency. *Journal of Economic Theory* 9, 63–91.

    1975. Distributive justice, welfare economics and the theory of fairness. *Philosophy and Public Affairs* 4, 223–47.

    1980. Redistributive taxation as social insurance. *Journal of Public Economics* 14, 49–68.

Vecchio, R.P. 1982. Predicting workers' performance in inequitable settings. *Academy of Management* Review 7, 103–10.

Vermunt, R. and M.J. Lerner 1987. Conflict between allocation motives: the Netherlands vs. Canada. *British Psychological Bulletin,* December.

Vermunt, R. and H.O. Steensma (eds.) 1991. *Social Justice in Human Relations* Vol. 1. New York: Plenum Press.

Vickrey, W. 1960. Utility, strategy and social decision rules. *Quarterly Journal of Economics* 74, 507–35.

Villey, M. 1975. *Philosophie du droit,* Paris: LGDJ.

Vogelaar, A.L.W. and R. Vermunt 1991. Allocation standards: equity, equality and asymmetry. In Vermunt and Steensma.

Voigt, L. and W.E. Thornton 1984. *The Limits of Justice: A Sociological Analysis,* New York: University Press of America.

Wahner, U. 1986. Bewertungen der Gerechtigkeit in unterschiedlichen Kontexten: Personale Determinanten erlebter Verteilungs- und Verfahrensgerechtigkeit. Unpublished Diplomarbeit im Fachbereich I – Psychologie der Universität Trier.

Walker, N. 1980. *Punishment, Danger and Stigma,* Oxford: Blackwell.

Walster, E., E. Berscheid and G.W. Walster 1973. New directions in equity research. *Journal of Personality and Social Psychology* 25, 151–76.

    1976. New directions in equity research. In Berkowitz and Walster 1976.

Walster, E. and G.W. Walster 1975. Equity and social justice. *Journal of Social Issues* 31, 21–43.

Walster, E., G.W. Walster and E. Berscheid 1978. *Equity: Theory and Research,* Boston: Allyn and Bacon.

Walster, G.W. 1975. The Walster, *et al.* 1973. Equity Formula: a correction. *Representative Research in Social Psychology* 6, 63–4.

    1976. Reply to Dr William Samuel: suggested amendments to new directions in equity research. *Personality and Social Psychology Bulletin* 2, 40–4.

Walzer, M. 1983. *Spheres of Justice: A Defence of Pluralism and Equality.* New York: Basic Books; Oxford: Martin Robertson. See critiques in Dworkin 1985b and Steiner 1985.

Weaver, S. 1977. *Decision to Prosecute: Organization and Public Policy in the Antitrust Division,* Cambridge, MA.

Webster, M. Jr and L.R.F. Smith 1978. Justice and revolutionary coalitions: a test of two theories. *American Journal of Sociology* 84, 267–92.

Wegener, B. 1987. The illusion of distributive justice. *European Sociological Review* 3, 1–13.

Weick, K.E. 1966. The concept of equity in the perception of pay. *Administrative Science Quarterly* 11, 414–39.

Weick, K.E. and B. Nesset 1968. Preferences among forms of equity. *Organizational Behavior and Human Performance* 3, 400–16.

Weinberger, O. 1981. Analytisch-dialektische Gerechtigkeitstheorie: Skizze einer Handlungstheoretischen und non-kognitivistischen Gerechtigkeitstheorie. *Rechtstheorie* Beiheft 3, 307–30.

1985. Die *Conditio Humana* und das Ideal der Gerechtigkeit. *ARSP* Beiheft 29, 58–70. This is translated and reprinted as: The *Conditio humana* and the ideal of justice. In N. MacCormick and O. Weinberger (eds.) 1986, *An Institutional Theory of Law: New Approaches to Legal Positivism*, Dordrect: Reidel, pp. 207–22.

1986. In D.N. MacCormick and O. Weinberger, *An Institutional Theory of Law*, Dordrecht: Reidel, chapter 10.

Weiner, B. 1980. A cognitive (attribution)-emotion-action model of motivated behavior: an analysis of judgments of help-giving. *Journal of Personality and Social Psychology* 39, 186–200.

Weinreb, L.L. 1987. *Natural Law and Justice*, Cambridge, MA and London: Harvard University Press.

Weinstein, A.G. and R.L. Holzbach 1973. Impact of individual differences, reward distribution, and task structure on productivity in a simulated work environment. *Journal of Applied Psychology* 58, 296–301.

Wellbank, J.H., D. Snook and D.T. Mason (eds.) 1982. *John Rawls and his Critics: An Annotated Bibliography*, New York and London: Garland.

Wender, I. 1986. Children's use of justice principles in allocation situations. Focus on the need principle. In Bierhoff, Cohen and Greenberg 1986.

1987a. Analyse der Aufteilungsgerechtigkeit von deutschen und türkischen Jungen und Mädchen. *Zeitschrift für Entwicklungspsychologie und Pädagogische Psychologie* 182–93.

1987b. *Entwicklung der Aufteilungsgerechtigkeit von minderbegabten Kindern.* *Braunschweiger Arbeiten* 1987/1, Forschungsbereich 9, Technische Universität Braunschweig.

Wettstein, H. 1979. *Uber die Ausbaufähigkeit von Rawls' Theorie der Gerechtigkeit*, Basle: Social Strategies Publishers Co-operative Society.

Wicker, A.W. and G. Bushweiler 1970. Perceived fairness and pleasantness of social exchange situations: Two factorial studies of inequity. *Journal of Personality and Social Psychology* 15, 63–75.

Wicksell, K. 1896. A new principle of just taxation. Reprinted in R. Musgrave and A. Peacock (eds.) 1962, *Classics in the Theory of Public Finance*, London: Macmillan, pp. 72–118.

Wilding, P. 1982. *Professional Power and Social Welfare*, London.

Wilke, H. and T. Steur 1972. Overpayment: perceived qualifications and financial compensation. *European Journal of Social Psychology* 2, 273–84.

Williams, B. 1985. Theories of social justice – where next? In Guest and Milne 1985, pp. 27–31

Williams, R.M. Jr. 1970. *American Society*, New York: Knopf.

Willman, P. 1982. *Fairness, Collective Bargaining and Income Policy*, Oxford.

Wish, M.M., M. Deutsch and S.J. Kaplan 1976. Perceived dimensions of interpersonal relations. *Journal of Personality and Social Psychology* 33, 409–20.

Wish, M.M. and S.J. Kaplan 1977. Toward an implicit theory of interpersonal communication. *Sociometry* 40, 234–46.

Wittig, M.A., G. Marks and G.A. Jones 1981. Luck vs. effort attributions: effect on reward allocations to self and other. *Personality and Social Psychology Bulletin* 7, 71–8.

Wolff, R.P. 1977. *Understanding Rawls: A Reconstruction and Critique of* A Theory of Justice, Princeton, NJ: Princeton University Press.

Wood, A. 1972. The Marxian critique of justice. In Cohen *et al.* 1980, pp. 3–41.
　1979. Marx on right and justice: a reply to Husami. In Cohen *et al.* 1980, pp. 106–34.
Wosinska, W. 1983. Psychologiczne prawidlowosci dotyczace poczucia spolecznej niesprawiedliwosci doznawanej przez pracownikow (Psychological regulatives describing injustice perceived by employees). *Organizacja i Kierowanie* 33, 101–17.
　In press. *Psychologi niesprawiedliwosci w stosunkach interpersonalnych* (Psychology of injustice in interpersonal relationships), Katowice, Poland: University of Katowice Press.
Wosinska, W. and Z. Ratajczak (eds.) In press. *Sprawwiedliwosc i zaufanie interpersonalne w swietle wspolczesnych teorii i badan* (Injustice and interpersonal trust in light of contemporary theories and research). Katowice, Poland: University of Katowice Press.
Würtenberger, T. 1988. *Zeitgeist und Recht,* Tübingen: Mohr.
Yaari, M.E. and M. Bar-Hillel 1984. On dividing justly. *Social Choice and Welfare* 1, 1–24.
Yamagishi, T. 1984. Development of distribution rules in small groups. *Journal of Personality and Social Psychology* 46, 1069–78.
Zaborowski, Z. 1986. *Psychospoleczne problemy sprawiedliwosci i rownosci* (Psychosocial problems of justice and parity). Warsaw: PWN.
Zanfarino, A. 1967. *Pluralismo sociale e idea di giustizia,* Milan: Giuffrè.
Zelditch, M. Jr, J. Berger, B. Anderson and B.P. Cohen. *Equitable comparisons.* Pacific Sociological Review, 1970, 13, 19–26.
Zuckerman, H.A. 1975. A comment on the equity formula by Walster, Berscheid, and Walster (1973). *Representative Research in Social Psychology* 6, 63–4.
Zweigert, K. and H. Kötz 1987. *Introduction to Comparative Law.* 2nd edn, trans. Weir, Oxford: Oxford University Press.

Index